Transformations of Patriarchy in the West, 1500–1900

Interdisciplinary Studies in History

Harvey J. Graff, General Editor

Transformations of Patriarchy in the West, 1500–1900

PAVLA MILLER

Indiana University Press

BLOOMINGTON AND INDIANAPOLIS

Indiana University Press acknowledges the
kind support of the School of Social Science
and Planning of the Royal Melbourne
Institute of Technology in the publication
of this volume.

The paper used in this publication meets
the minimum requirements of American
National Standard for Information
Sciences—Permanence of Paper for Printed
Library Materials, ANSI Z39.48-1984.

Manufactured in the United States
of America

Miller, Pavla, date
Transformations of patriarchy in the west :
    1500–1900 / Pavla Miller.
        p.   cm. — (Interdisciplinary
    studies in history)
    Includes bibliographical references and
    index. ISBN 0-253-33469-1 (cl : alk
    paper)
    1. Historical sociology.   2. Patriar-
    chy.   3. Social institutions.   4. Social
    control—History.   I. Title.   II. Series.
    HM104.M55   1998
    306.83—dc21   98-35746
    1 2 3 4 5 03 02 01 00 99 98

CONTENTS

Acknowledgments

Some ten years ago, this book began as a joint project with Ian Davey, now of the University of South Australia in Adelaide. It grew out of many conversations and shared writings on the history of schooling. During the early years, Ian contributed great ideas, infectious enthusiasm, and extensive knowledge of history. Later, as Ian's administrative duties became more onerous, leaving him less and less time for research, the project curiously became more and more ambitious. In the end, Ian provided moral support while I did the research and wrote the book. In these circumstances, we decided that the book should be published under my name. But if his contribution does not make him a joint author, Ian's robust friendship made the writing of this book a far more confident and pleasant experience than would otherwise have been the case. For all this, I am sincerely grateful.

There are many other friends and colleagues whose support over the years has been very important to me. Some generously read and commented on drafts; others shared exciting ideas stemming from their own research. I am particularly grateful to Bruce Curtis, David Levine, Alison MacKinnon, Alison Prentice, Wally Seccombe, Mary Jo Maynes, Craig Campbell, and Kevin McDonald for their constructive criticism and firm support. Jenny Laurence and Fiona Mackenzie carried out small amounts of extremely useful research assistance. Harvey Graff was generous with advice, support, and encouragement regarding publication and editing of the final manuscript. Finally, Jock and Bruce McCulloch made their delightful presence felt as only they know how.

INTRODUCTION

Reading a book is like taking a journey. Situating it on a map of history and social theory makes travel easier and the landscape more familiar.

In 1821, a judgment of the Indiana Supreme Court proclaimed that "the minor is considered as having no legal will. He has neither the power nor the right of choosing, whether he will obey or disobey the commands of his master. The law, therefore, on account of the immaturity of his will, can not presume that any of his services are involuntarily performed." Apprentices, the court went on to observe, "are minors, and for want of discretion, are necessarily under the control of parents, guardians or masters; and obedience is exacted from them, whether considered as children, wards or apprentices. They are incapable of regulating their own conduct, and are subjected by nature and by law to the government of others; and that government, instead of humbling and debasing the mind, has a tendency to give it a regular direction, and a suitable energy for future usefulness."[1] Two centuries earlier, a similar passage, concerning a prince's government of his subjects, could have been found in a treatise on statecraft. As a description of a father's judicious mastery of his servants, wife, and children, it could have belonged equally well in a popular almanac. Today, women, wage workers, even children appear to be endowed with more robust wills; natural subjection to the government of others has gone out of legislative fashion.

This is a glimpse of the territory my book explores. Best described as an essay in historical sociology, it charts some aspects of the changing familial, economic, and political modes of governance in the West between the sixteenth and the nineteenth centuries, and examines how these were linked to new forms of solidarity and identity. There are many precedents for tackling this enormous task. My own approach is distinctive in that it focuses on changing forms of patriarchy—in particular, the rise and fall of a patriarchalist social order and its replacement by fraternal forms of governance. A key theme of the book concerns attempts by various reformers to instill self-mastery, originally expected of monks and masters, into subject populations.

Feminists have long pointed out that much existing scholarship deals with men while appearing to speak of humanity. Women and girls—their concerns, their interests, their products and activities—tend to remain invisible, as does the actual masculinity of the men who populate the pages of history and theory. Over the last three decades, a vast amount of work has been accomplished chronicling the lives of famous women, the social history of humble families, the relations between laboring men, women, and children, the history of sexualities, and the place of women and the feminine in politics, philosophy, and the arts. While some feminist writers continue to stress the patriarchal continuities underpinning these varied accounts, many others have begun to emphasize differences and discontinuities in the lives of different social groups, and the disadvantages of employing global concepts such as patriarchy. Inspired and instructed by these different approaches, I focus on long-term changes in what could be called the key institutional embodiments of the gender order.

This guiding curiosity has made the writing of this book at once exciting and extremely difficult. As a child, I was fascinated by the strange objects, creatures, and plants that turned up behind the cushions of an armchair, in between rocks, under stones. Now I find myself researching the odd spaces between great bodies of history and social theory. Demography, military history, political and feminist theory, geography, studies of colonialism, Foucauldian accounts of power and governmentality, social history of families, of mass schooling, of nationalism, and of national states, frequently exist side by side; some of the most useful and innovative scholarship can be found in the spaces which separate them.

To give a few examples, accounts of the defeat of patriarchalism by liberalism in political theory, as Pateman and others pointed out, ignored the patriarchal continuities in the new order, more accurately described as a fraternal social contract. Pateman herself, however, has little to say about the age dimension of patriarchal governance, or the uneven development of families, economies, and states which is the stuff of social history. Foucauldian work on governmentality typically ignores both patriarchalism and fraternalism; work on the civilizing process largely neglects gendered aspects of the monopoly on violence, and pays insufficient attention to the gendering of subjectivities. On their part, feminist historians, understandably keen to rectify the neglect of women (and of ordinary women in particular), have so far paid relatively little attention to traditionally "masculine" fields of study such as state formation, military history, and the rise of bureaucracies. It was silences and omissions such as these that inspired my search for fragments of the story of changing forms of patriarchal governance around which this book is organized.

Exploring uncharted spaces is not only exciting but risky. Too busy examining the gaps that separated one corpus of learning from another, I did not become an expert in any one field. The bulk of my argument is based not on original research, but on a reconfiguring of some major contributions to social history and theory. Most of the literature I use is limited to texts published in English, and reflects the biases that this implies. The geographical focus of the study moves from Germany and England in the first half of the text to Britain, Canada, Australia, and the United States in the second half. In part, this shift is justified by my attempt to locate the European sources of Anglo-American and Australian institutions. But it also reflects my familiarity with particular literatures, and the attempt to keep the argument to a manageable size. Since the book is emphatically not a coherent, chronological history of the West but rather an attempt to elaborate and illustrate particular theoretical points, I opted for innovative case studies rather than even coverage. In spite of obsessive attention to detail and much good advice, the text will necessarily contain oversimplifications, omissions, and errors. Mindful of the limitations of a single author undertaking work of this kind (and without any aesthetic leanings to postmodern pastiche), I often ask questions rather than supply the answers, lay out some pieces of a patchwork rather than complete the pattern.

Although much of this pattern is tentative, I lay strong claims to a particular style of analysis. Recently there has been much emphasis on texts and discourse in history and social theory alike. While acknowledging many debts to such work, my account is unashamedly and emphatically materialist. By this I mean that weather, crop failures, the balance between births and deaths, hunger, physical violence, the way production was organized and houses built, cannot be left out of accounts of how people were governed and governed themselves.[2] But to claim that explanations which ignore the material circumstances of people's lives are seriously flawed in no way commits me to some form of economic determinism.

Indeed, the second major objective of my work is to question forms of social theory built around some overwhelming power impervious to human agency. Throughout, the book balances accounts of material constraint and individual and collective agency, chance, intentionality, and the ironies of history, of the powerful range of institutions and discourses that drive citizens into an administrative grid and the enormous countervailing forces that disrupt the process of normalization and at times subvert it altogether. Impressive schemes of social control rarely worked as their promoters imagined they should; different aspects of patriarchy were transformed at different paces at different times; uneven development and regional variations make nonsense of any attempts to organize history into orderly and exclusive stages.

My account of governance, patriarchal forms, and age relations of necessity involves an examination of educational theories and practices. But the book also represents a more ambitious and self-conscious contribution to arguments about the origins, timing, and nature of school systems. Such debates were particularly vigorous in North America and Europe in the 1960s and 1970s, when a new generation of "revisionist" historians challenged the traditional Whig interpretation of the progressive and democratic nature of state schooling. The initial revisionist accounts contended that state school systems were forced into existence as a means of social class control in a period of rapid urbanization and industrialization. In the mid-1970s these accounts were reworked by Marxist social historians to emphasize the role of schooling in the reproduction of capitalist social relations. Since then, the earlier texts have been criticized for their fixation on metropolitan industrial capitalism and class relations, and for their neglect of pre-industrial regions and of the dynamics of state and patriarchy. Feminist scholars began to chart the role of schools in the reproduction of gender inequalities, poststructuralist and other critics attacked the adequacy of reproduction theories, and historians became much more tentative about their generalizations. By linking schooling, state-building, and transformations of patriarchal forms of [self-]governance, this book reopens the debate about the social forces that produced state school systems in western societies, and about the ways schools altered society.

Throughout the text, I emphasize the changing and historically specific nature of social categories concerning age, gender, and class relations and state formation, and at times I refer to contemporary theoretical debates about these concepts. Rather than relatively fixed building blocks of historical analysis, I argue, these social categories were (and still are today) defined and redefined, contested, made and remade; their articulation—the way they related to each other—changed over time.[3] My use of the word "patriarchy" is a case in point.

In the 1970s, feminist writers took up the term "patriarchy" to designate systems of male dominance. Since then, many authors have questioned the precision with which this concept can describe varied forms of male-dominated social organization in a range of different societies, social groups, and spheres of life. The responses can be roughly grouped into three different categories. First, there are those theoreticians who insist that the similarities outweigh the differences, and that it *is* possible to identify some common underlying transcultural and transhistorical continuities in the forms of male oppression of women.[4] In contrast, an increasing number of authors, impressed by the sheer diversity of gender relations and forms of subordination, argue that global concepts such as patriarchy confuse rather than elucidate feminist analyses.

Finally, some theoreticians argue that the word "patriarchy" is too closely linked with its specific meaning as a rule of fathers, and prefer to use some more abstract term, such as "andarchy," "androcracy," or "viriarchy," as a collective designation for male-dominated gender orders. Here, most writers have gone on to draw a distinction between a gender order characterized by the rule of fathers (patriarchy, patriarchalism, patrist social order) and a more recent western one characterized by the rule of adult men (fraternalism, fratriarchy, fraternal social contract, etc.); yet others have identified a move from a private to a public patriarchy.[5] My own approach falls within a related camp. Impressed by diversity and uneven development, I nevertheless believe that historically specific mid-range concepts are invaluable in gaining a clearer grasp of the dynamics of historical change. I use "patriarchy" as a collective term for different forms of male-dominated gender orders, but discuss in detail the dynamics of patriarchalism and the various forms of fraternalism that replaced it.

Patriarchalism, the topic of chapter 1, is characterized by a series of interlocking pyramids of household rule. From humble peasant patriarchs governing their dependents to territorial rulers managing their domains, masters were expected to control the everyday behavior of those under their authority and in turn render obedient service to those above. Fraternalism is a much less precise and more descriptive concept, designating various forms of governance characterized by the theoretical equality of men and their categorical superiority over women. The institutions and forms of governance that can be described by this term are discussed in chapters 3, 6, and 8.

Like patriarchy, the state cannot be seen as a fixed, unchanging entity, however sophisticated the analysis of that entity might be. As Curtis put it, "The 'state' can best be understood as a *process of rule* in and through which the activities of classes and groups lead to the creation, solidification and normalisation of political forms and practices in the largest sense."[6] In this process of rule, contingency and historical specificity play an important role. Michael Ignatieff expressed well the widely shared concern about functional analyses when he noted that there was no *a priori* reason to assume that just because an institution exists, it is "functional" to capital (or to patriarchy). It might be just as useful to think that institutions such as prisons—and schools—fail their constituencies but limp along because no alternative can be found or because conflict over alternatives is too great to be mediated into compromise.[7]

In describing the uneven development of state power, I make use of the term "governmentality." Coined by Foucault, it refers both to a process of change in the forms of governance and to the results of that process. Governmentality is a complex and diffuse form of contemporary state power directed at populations, informed predominantly by political econo-

my, and underpinned by a range of security apparatuses. It is also the twin
process through which this form of state power comes into being, both by
gradual increases in state capacity and through transformations of earlier
forms of territorial governance.[8] Since my analysis of the process of change
differs in some crucial aspects from that of Foucault, I make no attempt to
use the concept in its original form.

Indeed, it can be argued that the concept is not used accurately in the
writing of many Foucauldian scholars either. Over the last twenty years,
these writers have analyzed the flowering of disciplines, the surge in governmentality, the augmented power of surveillance, the increasing effectiveness of control over populations, and the growing capacity of discourses to constitute and reshape subjectivities. Although occasional links
between the weakening of one and the strengthening of the other form of
governance are made, the overwhelming impression is of populations ever
more intensively controlled. In his later work, Foucault himself provides
brilliant insights into forms of governance both before and after the great
divide of modernity, but typically pays little attention to how the earlier
patriarchal forms survive and are re-created in the modern era. I use the
term "governmentality," in contrast, as part of an effort to chart the erosion
of patriarchalist powers by new state capacities, and the emergence of
differently gendered knowledges and institutions.

The patriarchal transformations that are the subject of this book were at
many points linked to the development of capitalism. But this does not
mean that they were determined by the industrial revolution and attendant
urbanization. Pockets of capitalist production existed in late medieval Italy;
much of early industrialization and capitalist development occurred in the
countryside; some large manufactories were staffed by serfs; key sectors of
modern capitalist industry were supplied from slave plantations in the
Americas. Even at the height of the first industrial revolution, only a minority of laboring people worked in factories. At the same time, any causality worked both ways. Encroaching capitalism changed families, but
capitalism expanded in part because of particular familial and demographic
regimes.

Although it focuses on the lives of laboring people, this book often looks
at class through the prism of gender and age relations. Indeed, it suggests
that in some respects, at least, class relations developed out of forms of
household subordination. Taking a lead from E. P. Thompson, I character-
ize class as a "happening" rather than as a preexisting structure. During the
long process of capitalist development, the relations between wage workers and employers varied between trades and regions, and were subject

to continuous contest and negotiation. Households represented by their heads, married couples, male subcontractors, and individual men, women, and children could work for wages in a myriad different ways. As capitalism developed, the interests of workers on many issues became antagonistic to those of capital. But contradictory interests did not necessarily lead to a unified working class confronting capital. Some groups of laboring people hardly organized at all. More often than not, those who did articulate common interests organized on the basis of exclusive trades or skills. They were divided by gender, ethnic, or religious issues; only rarely were they able to forge common causes and forms of organization that bridged the many divisions among them.

The discussion of age relations involves the frequent use of notoriously imprecise categories such as "child" and "infant." In my own reading, the age of majority alone was defined by different legal systems for different purposes and different constituencies at seven, nine, twelve, thirteen, fourteen, fifteen, sixteen, eighteen, twenty, twenty-one, twenty-five, or even thirty years of age. At one extreme, as an Italian commentator put it in 1564, "a male who is a child is not always a child but becomes a man with time: but the lady is a child all her life."[9] At the other extreme, under British law, the sovereign alone attained full majority at eighteen, three years before other property owners, but for legislative purposes was never an infant.[10] I resolve the issue by calling those (perhaps over five years of age) who were physically capable of sustained work, but were under the appropriate age of majority, "young people." The term "child" is used predominantly for the most problematic age group, from about five to thirteen, who were most often expected to attend school, and whose full-time employment was subject to the most regulation. The word "infant" is used in its legal sense to refer to people under the age of majority, and by extension to those carrying parallel legal disabilities.

While the relations of gender, age, and class pervade the whole account, the spatial aspects of social change are not systematically integrated into the text. More important, the relations of race and ethnicity make only a sporadic appearance. This is a serious shortcoming, and to remedy it will require another round of research. I believe that such research can best be carried out in the healthy winds of scholarly controversy.

*****

The first part of the book deals with the rise and fall of a patriarchalist system of social relations. The consolidation of patriarchalism in early modern Europe, chapter 1 argues, was perceived to constitute the most effective way of safeguarding economic resources in a precarious balance between land and population. It was also inseparably linked with the efforts of territorial rulers to extend and consolidate their power. Linked by the Reformation revaluation of family and marriage, the early process of state formation and attempts to balance land and population both drew on the resources of peasant and craft households. Such households were the basic units of production in their societies and provided the foundation of legal codes governing master-and-servant relations. They also served as the basic units of social discipline, and furnished both a practical and a theoretical model of state power. In this form of analysis, patriarchalism provides a powerful conceptual link between two dominant perspectives guiding the study of western societies: one centering on populations, agrarian cycles, and economies, the other concerned with war and the process of state formation.

Chapter 2 disrupts the image of a powerful patriarchalist social order by focusing on some aspects of its unstable foundations. The supposed absolute power of household heads need not necessarily lead, in theory or in practice, to their subjection to the absolute authority of the crown. Conversely, whatever the complexion of the household, a growing number of political thinkers began to argue that it no longer provided an adequate model of state power. Patriarchalist rule affirmed the superiority of men over women, yet it relegated increasing numbers of increasingly rebellious adult men to class-based, childlike dependence on masters and mistresses of households. In the long term, the same factors that helped strengthen patriarchalism contributed to its demise. Changing technologies of war, confessionalization, systematic taxation, closer supervision of families by church and state, all increased governmentality, and with it the capacity of state bureaucracies to expand the realm of direct rule. Finally, a number of developments began eroding the dominance of the peasant household in the European countryside. But while centralizing states, princes, administrators, and merchants in seventeenth- and eighteenth-century Europe disrupted, constrained, and reorganized household-based patriarchal power, in practice they were unable to relinquish their reliance on patriarchalist forms of governance.

Chapter 3 deals with an age of revolutions in the late eighteenth and the first half of the nineteenth century. During these decades, the various processes undermining a patriarchalist system of power came to a head; in the same period, some of the material constraints on the expansion of governmentality were eased. The American, French, and industrial revolutions, the emergence of fully proletarian families, and the consolidation of public spheres can all be seen as part of a diverse process of destroying patriarchalist rule. Invariably, the discourses and institutions that emerged from the ruins of the old order contained reinvented forms of gender, class, and age superiority.

The guiding theme of the next section of the book is an elegant hypothesis regarding governance. In the early modern world, only masters were expected to possess thorough self-mastery. This attribute was considered necessary for detailed personal government of servants, children, and wives, who lacked self-mastery themselves. As the patriarchalist social order began to falter, a number of thinkers speculated that peace, order, and prosperity could be secured if subjects as well as masters internalized a rigorous government of the self. Concentrating on the rulers rather than the ruled, chapter 4 traces several themes within the complex history of western subjectivities. Transformations of families, states, churches, and economies, it argues, not only affected the way people understood themselves and were seen by others, but also formed the basis for reconceived notions of femininity and manliness. Informed by contemporary debates, the chapter looks at the civilizing process theorized by Elias, Weber's Protestant ethic, the engendering of the middle class described by feminist historians, the discovery of childhood, and the invention of nations and national traditions.

The common denominator in various forms of the civilizing process among the privileged was rigorous self-command; one of the distinguishing features of plebeian (and "native") mentalities was considered to be a lack of it. Chapter 5 outlines several educational projects designed to moralize and to instill self-mastery into the "masterless poor," and contrasts them with less grandiose methods of exacting obedience and docility. Pietist schools conducted by judicious fatherly masters, machine-like monitorial institutions, and kindergartens designed around the powers of a "mother made conscious"—the three most influential precursors of the "rational schooling" that triumphed as the most desirable form of mass tuition in all western societies by the third quarter of the nineteenth century—are placed alongside violence, hunger, deference, the dull compulsion of the market, and family reform.

Chapter 6 examines some aspects of the actual building of education systems against a background of state formation and uneven development. It addresses the fact that modern school systems were first established in relatively backward absolutist states, and examines the one area where this paradox was most apparent: the link between industrialization, transport, and mass schooling. It then looks at the interplay between local communities and the development of school regulations, the role of inspection and statistics in the accumulation of state knowledge, and the consolidation of gendered bureaucracies. Here again, I suggest, patriarchal dynamics played a crucial, but far from predictable, role in the nineteenth-century expansion of governmentality.

Chapter 7 undermines some aspects of the elegant hypothesis. It surveys various forms of self-presentation among working women and men, and concludes that the educators' attempts to produce a subjectivity built around introspection, self-scrutiny, and self-problematization among the poor largely failed. During this period, laboring men and women did appear to change the way they thought and saw themselves. Many exercised iron self-control; others embarked on a particular form of an enlightenment project. But schools were rarely implicated in these projects, and in any case their end results were often the very opposite of what the educators wished for. I then return to the debates about public spheres introduced in chapter 3, and argue that education, literacy, and schools were a key stake in many social movements. The educational strategies of radical groups were impractical for many of the laboring people or women they claimed to represent, and the technologies of power pursued by "efficient" schools clearly discriminated against the poor. But the same curriculum could be used in many different ways, and radical forms of self-mastery cannot be equated with social control.

But this does not mean that the schools had no effect at all. Over time, the new institutions transformed the geography of everyday life; they invested the bodies of working-class children with new disciplines and contributed to fundamental redefinitions of age, gender, and class categories. At a further remove, compulsory schooling became associated with a historically unprecedented form of self-mastery. In early modern Europe, a balance between population and resources was maintained above all through the tightening of patriarchal restrictions on the possibility of marriage. For the first time in history, women stopped having children long before they reached the end of their reproductive life.

Focusing on demographies, families, and age relations, the final chapter discusses the emergence of a new patriarchal equilibrium in nineteenth-century western societies. It surveys theoretical debates about the demographic transition and the rise of male breadwinner families, and concludes with a discussion of new forms of age and gender relations.

TRANSFORMATIONS OF PATRIARCHY IN THE WEST, 1500–1900

CHAPTER ONE

The Consolidation of Patriarchalism in Early Modern Europe

The complexities of early modern European history, with its regional differences and uneven development, cannot be covered in a few pages. Nevertheless, according to many historians, it is possible to discern (for a time, at least) some common threads across the vast diversity of western and central Europe. In the sixteenth century, they tied together regions that supported the Reformation and territories that maintained or reverted to an allegiance to Rome. They linked countryside and cities, large and powerful kingdoms and petty princedoms. Some of the most significant of these common threads concerned efforts to bolster the authority and social significance of patriarchal family households and to tighten legislative and other controls over marriage, while simultaneously restricting the sway of an older form of patriarchal governance.[1]

Where these reforms were successful, they often became part of a patriarchalist combination of familial and political power, typically exercised by married men but occasionally delegated to women. In such regimes, economic, political, and judicial power over wife, children, servants, and apprentices living in households was held by the paterfamilias, who represented the family to the wider community. In the case of the master's extended absence, exile, or death, this power was delegated to his surrogate, often his wife or widow. In many regions, political power in larger administrative units was said to be organized in an analogous way to the governance of households: the lord, the priest, and the magistrate held paternal power over his subjects; much more controversially, the monarch exercised similar natural fatherly power over the nobility—and was himself answerable to God the Father. By definition, each level of patriarchal authority was limited by the one above it. All this was usually strengthened (but sometimes undermined) by what could be termed viriarchy: the categorical superiority of men over women, inscribed in scriptural and "natural law" prescriptions that posited man as the head of the woman.[2] Even though some contemporary political thinkers attempted to theorize more impersonal forms of political authority, their royal patrons continued to practice and rely on patriarchalist powers.

One of the key arguments of this book is that the dynamics of patriarchal governance provide a powerful conceptual link between two dominant perspectives guiding the study of western societies. One perspective centers on populations, agrarian cycles, and economies; the other concentrates on war and the process of state formation. Both forms of explanation contain a persuasive depiction of the motive forces of historical change. The consolidation of patriarchalism in early modern Europe, particularly as played out in the religious conflicts associated with the Reformation, was arguably fueled by both of these processes. On the one hand, it was perceived to constitute the most effective way of safeguarding economic resources in a precarious balance between land and population. On the other, it was inseparably linked with the efforts of territorial rulers to extend and consolidate their power.[3]

WAR, PATRIARCHY, AND THE STATE

Many influential scholars claim that war constituted the major driving force of modern western history. Charles Tilly, for example, comes close to arguing that state structure appeared chiefly as a by-product of rulers' efforts to acquire the means of war, and that relations between states, especially through war and preparation for war, strongly affected the entire process of state formation.

National states began to emerge as the dominant form of territorial governance in Europe from the sixteenth century. Eventually they would become territorially coherent and unbroken areas with sharply defined frontiers, governed by a single sovereign authority according to a single system of administration and law, and with a monopoly of violence within their frontiers.[4] Most medieval European kingdoms, city-states, empires, and federations of cities were far removed from this model. Medieval society was crisscrossed with fragmented and overlapping jurisdictions and conflicting loyalties to a great number of belligerent rulers. Up to about the fifteenth century, under a widespread system of governance often called patrimonialism, tribes, feudal levies, urban militias, and similar customary forces played the major part in warfare, and monarchs generally extracted the capital they needed as tribute or rent from lands and populations that lay under their immediate control.[5] Major powerholders were themselves active military men, more rarely women. Kingship was typically based on a form of contractual relationship between a sovereign and his or her vassals, who each held, as their patrimony, powers we now associate with the state. The heads of noble families owed the sovereign allegiance and military service. In turn, just as the peasant patriarch had personal jurisdiction over those in his household, it was the nobles and their personal servants, not the monarch or the state, who exercised military, legal, and economic jurisdiction over great households, their lands, and the people who tilled them. Great nobles had the power to make and administer laws, impose taxation, and raise and keep an army in their domains; they extracted labor services, payments in kind, or cash rents from the peasants in return for a measure of economic and military protection.[6]

The emphasis on military capacity, service, and protection was born out of necessity in an age of continued and widespread conflict. According to Tilly, in a period of fragmented sovereignty, the differences among soldiers, bandits, pirates, rebels, and lords doing their duty was blurred. Between great battles, local campaigns multiplied; the devastation caused by pillaging armies was supplemented by violent exactions on the part of local overlords. Before 1500 in the region now called Europe, the more meaningful questions were not *when* states warred, since most states were warring most of the time, but who fought whom, how often, and how vigorously.[7]

One of the decisive factors that finally broke this cycle of feuding and warfare was changes in military organization and financing, coupled with new military technology. Military enterprise became commercialized, the cost of weapons and fortification escalated, and private armies were replaced by hired mercenary troops and conscripts. According to McNeill, these changes began with the rise of infantry forces capable of challenging the supremacy of armed knights on the battlefield in twelfth-century Italy, and were consolidated with the replacement of armed city militias by paid professional soldiers in the fourteenth century, and later the political management of standing armies. In these armies, civilians controlled supply, soldiers were paid regularly with money derived from tax revenues, and infantry, cavalry, and artillery were differentiated and coordinated. By the mid-seventeenth century, a somewhat similar development—this time augmented by regular drill, strict regulations, and clear hierarchical lines of command—began on a far larger scale on the other side of the Alps, in countries such as the United Provinces, France, the Germanys, Sweden, and England.[8] These organizational and technological developments were accompanied by dramatic increases in army size. Victorious fifteenth-century armies would number some 20,000 fighters; by the 1630s, the armed forces maintained by the leading European states totaled perhaps 150,000 soldiers each.[9] Over time, these developments contributed to fundamental changes in the disposition of power.

As the new means of waging war spread, the territories of nobility who were, for one reason or another, unable to train, finance, equip, and supply a large, efficient, modern army almost invariably fell prey to those who mastered the new technologies of defense and attack. Only rulers capable of raising large sums of cash—typically through extensive taxation and loans, sometimes supplemented by exploitation of overseas territories— proved capable of long-term survival, and of accomplishing the internal pacification of their domains. The first national taxes in early modern Europe were levied to finance the first armies. By degrees, tax collection for the support of armed forces began to conform to bureaucratic regularity over wider and wider areas of the European continent.[10] From the sixteenth to the eighteenth century, up to four-fifths of state expenditure was typically allocated to the army. As the armies were augmented, modernized, and professionalized, expenditures rose; taxes to cover them multiplied and became more systematic, and state administration was further centralized. According to one influential theoretician of this change, "the territorial property of one warrior family, its control over certain lands and its claim to tithes or services of various kinds from people living on this land, is [gradually] transformed . . . into a centralised control of military power and of regular duties or taxes over a far larger area."[11]

Yet for a long time, the existing state of military technology made it practically impossible for any one ruler to conquer his rivals securely or for any length of time.[12] In his history of European politics and war, Kaiser argues that in the period 1559 to 1659, the almost continuous wars that plagued Europe revolved around unsuccessful attempts on the part of European monarchs to impose their authority upon great aristocrats and to secure religious uniformity throughout their domains—tasks which they lacked the necessary resources to accomplish. Central authority was generally fragile, state machinery weak, and political violence commonplace. Monarchs laid claims to power, but great aristocrats with their autonomous armies challenged this power, repeatedly and bloodily.[13] According to Kaiser, it was only in the period 1661 to 1715 that monarchs brought European violence largely under control, and changed the pattern of international conflict in ways that strengthened their own authority. Royal power, underpinned by conceptions of the divine right of kings, began to override the limited and reciprocal relationship between medieval patrimonial kings and nobles.[14] State power was consolidated, and civil wars mostly disappeared; unruly nobles were subdued, and their class as a whole was disciplined and domesticated. The interior of many kingdoms was systematically demilitarized, and fortresses and city fortifications were destroyed or intentionally left in disrepair.[15]

In medieval Europe, Elias notes, the nobles alone were warriors, and all warriors were nobles. Now the monopoly control of weapons and military power passed to the prince or king who could support the largest standing army, preferably on tax income, and without devastating the local economy.[16] In the process, men of the nobility were changed from relatively free warriors or knights into officers, in the service of the central lord, of plebeian troops who had to be paid.[17] During this period of active state-building, many rulers created substantial permanent bureaucracies, built massive standing professional armies and navies drawn increasingly from their own national populations, and absorbed the increasingly bureaucratized armed forces directly into the state's administrative structure.[18] By the eighteenth century, such nationalization of warmaking was commonly associated with the transition from indirect to direct rule, from patriarchalism to bureaucracy.

The changing balance of power brought previously unattainable levels of public peace and private wealth to Europe. Even though their troops still moved astonishingly slowly by our standards, the overwhelming force of well-drilled armies was able to subdue both the protests of the poor and aristocratic challenges to royal power with new speed and decisiveness. In turn, the consolidation of the state system, the segregation of military from civilian life, and the disarmament of the civilian population sharpened the distinction between war and peace. War became more intense and destructive, more continuous once it started, but a much rarer event. From the late seventeenth century, most European rulers outlawed private armies, made it criminal, unpopular, and impractical for most of their citizens to bear arms, and made it seem normal for armed agents of the state to confront unarmed civilians.[19]

The process of centralization and unification, however, still left the territories of even the mightiest European monarchies patterned much more on the "estate" than on the notions of territorial integrity with which we are familiar today. The state was conceived as the patrimony of the monarch, and therefore the title deeds could be inherited, gained by marriage, or lost in war. Foreign enclaves found themselves deep in another state's territory. Territories within one state could also be dependent on another lord who now happened to be part of another state and therefore, in modern terms, under dual sovereignty. "Frontiers," in the form of customs barriers, often ran between different provinces of the same state. Territories ranging in size from great empires to "free imperial knights," whose estates, often no bigger than a few acres, happened to have no superior lord, showed the same lack of territorial unity and standardization, depending on the vagaries of a long history of piecemeal acquisition and the divisions and reunifications of family heritage.[20]

It was the French Revolution which, it is commonly argued, formed a watershed in the consolidation of national states in Europe. Followed by Napoleon's conquests and the unifications of Germany and Italy in the nineteenth century, it accelerated the process of dividing Europe into mutually exclusive states having permanent, professional armed forces and exercising substantial control over people in areas of 100,000 square kilometers or more.[21] After the French Revolution, it also began to be assumed that the state should represent a single "nation" or linguistic group, although states that actually contained only one nationality were (and are) rare. These two contradictory ideals—of military and economic viability alongside cultural and ethnic unity—would prove a constant source of tension and conflict, not least in schools.

POPULATIONS, AGRARIAN CYCLES, ECONOMIES

While some historians focus on organized violence and state formation, others pay more attention to subsistence cycles, populations, and family forms. Taking an extended view of the economies of late medieval and early modern Europe, some scholars have discerned several long waves of agrarian and demographic development. Between the tenth and the thirteenth centuries, the population of Europe probably doubled. Huge expanses of previously unpopulated and marginal land were colonized. The average size of holdings in fertile regions shrank, often to an acreage which could not support a family in lean years. Pastures were plowed for wheat, and the number of farm animals was reduced. There was less manure, and the cattle and horses available to harness to the plow were weaker. Gradually the productivity of land fell; a failed harvest brought many families to the brink of starvation. Many peasants lost their livelihoods; the demand for labor shrank even as the ranks of the landless poor swelled. Confronted with stagnating and falling incomes, their hand strengthened by a shortage of land and an abundance of labor, the landed aristocracy tightened their exploitation of the peasantry. Attempting to make ends meet, the impoverished peasants further exhausted the land; their lords launched into wave after wave of predatory warfare. Weakened by hunger and disease, the population of Europe was on the verge of an ecological catastrophe when the plague struck in 1347. In the following four years, about a quarter of the inhabitants of western Europe perished; by the end of the century, a series of subsequent epidemics had increased the carnage to an estimated two-fifths. While some communities escaped relatively lightly, others disappeared from the map. In England, the population declined by more than half between 1348 and 1450; in some regions of France and Italy, the loss was between 60 and 70 percent.[22]

The catastrophic population losses reversed the previous imbalance between land and people. Now land was plentiful, labor was scarce, and noble incomes were reduced to a fraction of their previous levels—and peasants, realizing their new bargaining power, were increasingly rebellious. In the later decades of the fourteenth century, a wave of peasant insurgency swept across Europe, culminating in a number of regional revolts against feudal dues and state taxes. Peasants who previously had clung to their few acres now abandoned their villages in search of better land and more accommodating landlords. Young people, confident that they could buy good land with savings from their wages, deserted family farms to escape the oppressive authority of lords and peasant fathers alike. In the face of unprecedented peasant mobility, the class discipline of the lords crumbled; fathers lost the power to dictate their sons' future course. The young people themselves did not seem to be rushing into marriage: men saved to buy a modest holding, women to build up their dowries. Indeed, it is likely that this period saw the emergence of the restrictive western European marriage pattern, in which both men and women typically married in their late twenties, and up to a fifth of the population remained single throughout their lives.[23]

By the late fifteenth century, sustained population growth was renewed; between 1450 and 1600, the population of western Europe almost doubled. Land became scarce and expensive, and demand for wage labor fell. Gradually, the ratio of land to people deteriorated again; the ranks of the nearly landless swelled, and real wages were driven down at the very moment when the village poor were becoming increasingly dependent on wage income to survive. In the absence of alternative sources of livelihood, propertied fathers began to regain their authority. Designated heirs again became obliged to make a substantial commitment to their parents' upkeep in order to retain their favor; the prospects of secondary sons worsened. But while those better-off waited longer to marry, there is some evidence that in the early sixteenth century the proportion of married people among the poor grew, their age of marriage fell, and as a result the size of their families increased.[24]

On many occasions, demographic trends visible to statisticians went unnoticed by contemporaries. In this case they became the focus of public attention. When, in the late sixteenth century, all the familiar symptoms of overextended feudal agriculture reappeared, the upper classes became obsessed with the multiplication and behavior of those without property. Patriarchs at all levels of authority attempted to tighten control over family formation. Peasant householders, village and town communities, landlords, and religious authorities all agreed that one way of averting or at least alleviating the looming crisis was to consolidate landholding, discipline the younger generation, and make sure that the very poor did not marry.

Sixteenth-century expansion, overpopulation, and stagnation was once more followed by population losses. In a large part of the continent, the Thirty Years' War (1618–1648) and the epidemics and economic crises associated with it decimated whole regions. The population of Germany dropped by about 40 percent; the whole territory of the Holy Roman Empire lost more than a quarter of its people, while the populations of Brandenburg, Saxony, and Bavaria were cut in half; and the population of Spain was reduced by a third between 1590 and 1650.[25]

The cyclical development of the agrarian economy and its gradual conversion into capitalist agriculture occurred alongside slow changes in the production of goods for sale. In the Middle Ages, most industrial production for the market took place in towns and was regulated by guilds. In many urban areas, increased opportunities for local and long-distance trade led to the flowering of craft output, often accompanied by innovative changes in the gender division of labor. By the eighteenth century and sometimes earlier, many of these towns began to stagnate, fettered by guild regulations and impoverished by cheap competition from the countryside. The many goods that peasants traditionally made for their own use did not enter the market in any significant quantities before the sixteenth century. Over time, however, a variety of factors combined to promote the growth of specialist "proto-industrial" regions in the countryside, which still relied on household production but now supplied long-distance trade.

Economic differentiation occurred hand in hand with uneven development of social relations. In most of western Europe, feudal ties had been irreversibly loosened, with feudal dues giving way to money and produce rents.[26] Sixteenth-century England saw the beginnings of commercialized agriculture, with its attendant polarization between large and small landholders, enclosures of common land, and the growth of formally free labor. At the other end of the scale, in eastern and east-central Europe, above all in the fertile agricultural plains and valleys, feudal bonds were strengthened and a "second serfdom" was reimposed. From the early fifteenth century, the old system based on feudal payments and obligations was transformed into one relying on serf labor, this time no longer simply for the feudal estate, but for a world market.[27] What began as different, equally successful strategies of surplus extraction became over time part of an asymmetrically arranged world market. The industrial centers in western Europe, employing "free" labor, reserved the manufacture of finished goods for themselves. By the late eighteenth century, up to three-quarters of the output of some industrial regions was destined for foreign, often overseas, markets. In contrast, the peripheral regions, which extended from east-central Europe to America, employed servile or slave labor, and were restricted to the production of foodstuffs and raw materials.[28]

In eastern Europe, market pressures from the West contributed to the atrophy of nascent capitalist centers and to the resurgence of feudalism based on profitable grain sales to the West. It was to achieve this grain surplus that the nobility set out to deprive the peasants of their freedom and of all their land other than that needed for their bare subsistence, and imposed ever-growing labor services for the lords' own quasi-commercial large-scale farming enterprise. Serfdom bound peasants to a lifetime of servitude, restricted their mobility, and gave their lord the right to rule on their disputes, punish their transgressions, and control their marriage choices, the disposition of their property, and the future of their children. In the mid-seventeenth century, after the devastation caused by the Thirty Years' War, servile conditions were further extended and made harsher. All over eastern and northern Europe, from Bohemia to Prussia and Denmark, laws to deprive the peasants of their land and their freedom were passed or tightened. By the eighteenth century, serfdom was associated in parts of peripheral Europe both with developing modern industry elsewhere and with its absence at home.[29]

Against the background of economic polarization and demographic crises, Europe slowly filled with people. In the two centuries between 1550 and 1750, the total number of inhabitants nearly doubled.[30] In the following one and a half centuries, from 1750 to 1900, the peoples of *western* Europe almost trebled their numbers again. Moreover, they did so despite the emigration of some 45 million people to overseas colonies and settlements between 1800 and 1914.[31] Another way to represent these changes is to note that Europe (without Russia) grew 7 percent in the seventeenth century, 54 percent in the eighteenth, and, despite massive emigration, 102 percent in the nineteenth.[32] In the colonial outposts themselves, the white population registered spectacular increases, even as the numbers of the original inhabitants were further decimated. In what is now the United States, the population increased from 6 million in 1800 to 23.5 million in 1850 and 76 million in 1900; in Canada, it grew from 0.5 million to 5.25 million during the same period. In Australia, the white population grew from 48,000 in 1824 to 3.75 million in 1900.[33]

By themselves, figures describing population growth in Europe and its outposts tell only part of the story. Equally significant is that most of the additional people were proletarians, people who had nothing to their name except their capacity to work. According to estimates made by Charles Tilly, the population increase in Europe between 1550 and 1843 was almost entirely accounted for by the expansion of the proletarian population, with the numbers of non-proletarians hardly growing at all. In 1500, Europe had about 56 million people, 17 million (about 30 percent) of whom were proletarians of one kind or another. By the mid-eighteenth century, nearly 60 percent of the 131 million inhabitants of Europe could be considered proletarian. Between 1750 and 1843, the proletariat doubled, and came to account for more than 70 percent of the total.[34] In England itself, according to Levine, the proletarian population grew from 2.5 million in 1700 to 16.5 million in 1871.[35]

Historians and social theorists have long been interested in the new forms of social control invented to deal with this mass of impoverished people during a period when, as one historian put it, "the accelerated growth of the lower class threatened to crush as with a steam roller the traditional social structures."[36] Some, taking their inspiration from Malthus, explicitly linked demography to family and the economy, while others, such as Marx, focused mainly on economic developments. In the past ten years, there has been an upsurge in Foucauldian analyses of social institutions. Biopower, normalization, controlling bodies, and disciplinary techniques and strategies have been some of the concepts used, often to great effect, in analyses of nineteenth-century societies. Such analyses assume a new significance against the background of exponential population growth: "strategies of discipline—'bio-power'—and 'normalisation' were created in the context of a labour force that seemed to be out of control."[37] By the same token, the sheer weight of numbers frequently diluted the effectiveness of disciplining techniques.

Since most accounts of social control focus on cities and industrialization, it is sobering to note that demographers and historians locate the initial period of population growth in the countryside, where the overwhelming majority (some 85 percent) of people lived. This population growth is indeed often linked to industrialization, but one based on rural domestic production rather than urban factories. According to Tilly, from the sixteenth to the mid-nineteenth century, most of Europe's proletarianization took place in village and country; most migrants from the countryside to the nineteenth-century city were already proletarianized. It was only in the nineteenth century that cities became increasingly important as sites of proletarianization, the countryside, with about 150 million people, having come close to its population limit.[38]

* * * * *

Different cultural traditions, and different ways of making a living within one region, tended to foster distinct relations between the generations, and between men and women. To many historians, these differences were significant and systematic enough to warrant making a distinction between peasant, proto-industrial, and proletarian households. Indeed, some argue that changing dynamics of family formation were at the heart of some of the most fundamental developments in modern history. This discontinuity thesis, which has recently been reiterated by Wally Seccombe in *A Millennium of Family Change* and *Weathering the Storm,* differs considerably from the influential conclusions of the Cambridge Group for the History of Population and Social Structure. In the early 1970s, studies by Laslett and his associates documented the relatively low *average* size of households in Europe since at least the sixteenth century. Since then, these scholars have argued that nuclear families existed in Europe as far back as the historian can see, changed little over several centuries, and underwent no basic structural change during the industrial revolution. Their opponents claim that one average can conceal substantial qualitative differences. If families are studied over their life cycle, if questions are asked about the structural relations of family members, and if relations between households and local communities are taken into consideration, the appearance of stability cannot be sustained. This does not mean, these historians hasten to add, that households modernized, at a steady pace, from traditional to more recent family forms. Rather, some changes occurred at a glacial pace, while others were accelerated. Whole regions sometimes defied general trends, and different family forms coexisted.[39] At the same time, as feminist scholars have repeatedly pointed out, many forms of historical discontinuity and innovation affected men far more than women, or even had opposite effects on the two sexes. While the types of work and the social status of men were greatly diversified during the early modern era, caring for the physical and emotional needs of others and bearing and raising children formed the persistent core of most women's lives.

PEASANT HOUSEHOLDS

The foundation of European society throughout the early modern period was a productive peasant household; it was around this household that a patriarchalist social order was built. While their contours varied from region to region, peasant households had several common features. There were a certain number of productive "niches" in a relatively stable economy; securing one of these was a prerequisite to marriage. Most "surplus" and "masterless" people were redistributed among households to ensure that wealthy farmers and masters had enough labor, that children of poorer families would not "eat their parents out," and that everybody was subject to a master. In the countryside, (overlapping) entitlements to subsistence parcels of land formed the minimum prerequisite for the formation of new families. In towns, where a small minority of the population lived, a similar system operated: guild regulations attempted to ensure that journeymen would marry only when they finished their lengthy apprenticeship and a productive niche became available to them. Until then, they resided in their master's household and were subject to his paternal authority. Their future wives were much less likely to be formally apprenticed, but they too went into service or learned production skills at home while saving for their dowry. Local epidemics, cyclical subsistence crises, and other unforeseen calamities would expand or contract the conditions for "proper" marriage in the most unpredictable manner. Particularly in periods when land was tight and subsistence precarious, the village community (or guild), parents, and local notables put a lot of effort into ensuring that new households were formed only when land (or a master's position) became available to support them.

Since the founding of a family was normally tied to the ownership or inheritance of a full peasant holding, peasant marriage was above all a property transaction between families. While attraction between the young people was important, it must not undermine the family's economic viability and reputation. Only the most foolhardy young people would risk disinheritance by contracting an inappropriate or clandestine match. This family regime, which in parts of Europe congealed into a unique western

European marriage pattern, had important demographic consequences. Waiting to inherit (or saving up to purchase) a livelihood usually meant late marriage, and excluded many in the lower classes from family formation and reproduction altogether. These two forms of bodily discipline and birth control, all else being equal, produced fewer children, and relatively stable population numbers in the society as a whole.[40] By 1650, when village reconstitution studies by historians become sufficiently numerous and reliable, the western European marriage pattern was firmly in place. Most men married in their late twenties; women at first marriage tended to be twenty-four or older; 7 to 20 percent of women never married; and the incidence of childbirth out of wedlock was below 3 percent. The resulting fertility was less than half the rate that would have obtained if all women between fifteen and fifty were married.[41]

In both peasant and artisan households, men, women, and children were all directly and visibly engaged in productive labor. In the countryside in particular, however, rigorous customary separation of the labor performed by males and females, coupled with the fact that most people left home by their mid-teens (and often much earlier) to work in other households, meant that most people lived for most of the time in a homosocial system. They became integrated into a powerful same-sex peer group, sometimes organized into more formal fraternities, from which not all left to get married—and those who did leave did so only in their mid-to late twenties. In a society such as this, weddings were big and significant affairs, marking the transition of a couple to a status that many of their peers would never attain.[42] A married man could become part of the governing body of his village or town, a role from which single men were excluded.[43] As head of the family, he was expected to manage, police, judge, punish, catechize, educate, and represent not only his wife and children, but also the servants, laborers, and apprentices residing in his household. The master's wife, who organized and performed the myriad of women's special tasks, likewise assumed a measure of authority over dependent members of the household. But while she was acknowledged as an indispensable and valued partner in the household productive enterprise, she was, or at least was supposed to be, under the firm patriarchal control of her husband at home, and excluded from most formal positions of community power by law and custom alike.

In feudal and refeudalized regions, most entitlements to land were simultaneously relations of personal subjection to its feudal owner. Since all family members of the household shared the servile status of the tenant head and were burdened by the same set of obligations, peasant dependency entailed the rigorous subjection of the family as well as the individual—obligations which the peasants were not free to quit or evade with impunity. In northwestern Europe, the decline of serfdom did not leave peasants free from seigniorial discipline and constraint. It did, however, weaken the sinews of oppression, enabling country people to forge more autonomous village communities.[44]

In both regions, the inheritance system provided the bedrock of patriarchal authority between the generations. Only those with land or property found it easy to establish independent households. Young men without land or money and women without dowries were forced to emigrate or stay on as servants on the home farm or in the households of wealthier neighbors, under the patriarchal control of their head. If fathers or their widows decided to pass down the farm or workshop during their own lifetime, they were in a position to draw up legally binding contracts for their own subsistence. More frequently, drawn-out handovers of productive property gave them considerable power to encourage obedient and industrious heirs and punish others. According to Sabean, "Land and other goods were part of a wider set of exchanges and reciprocities through which people were disciplined. . . . Land and its exploitation provided a focus for socialisation, character formation, emotional commitment, and the long apprenticeship which instilled obligation."[45] In northwestern Europe, a relatively flexible system of impartible inheritance made children compete, in an atmosphere of explosive uncertainty, for their father's favor in what was to be the key determination of their futures. As Sabean put it, step by fateful step, a father's intentions and biases were revealed: the naming of the primary heir; the arrangement of sibling marriages; the determination of dotal portions; the disposal of supplementary lands among secondary sons; the drafting of a will. This was a deadly serious game of family politics, translating heritable property into different forms of patriarchal power and obligation.[46]

For the minority of town dwellers, gender, generation, and class were combined into a similar form of household economy. Roper, writing about early modern Augsburg, notes that "only adult married masters could elect their guild representatives or vote for civic office-holders. . . . The master's wife was . . . guarantor of her husband's achieved adult masculinity: she proved his masterhood, while at the same time being responsible for the food, light, bedding, heat, water, and other domestic needs of the shop's small labour force. With his own self-contained business, the master incorporated within himself financial independence, public honour, sexual maturity, and political adulthood." The master was supposed to control the journeymen; any disputes between them tended to be conceptualized in terms not of class conflict but of youthful insubordination, a result of faulty upbringing within the family.[47]

Gillis, looking at regional variation in England, paints a similar picture. In early-sixteenth-century Coventry, all single persons, regardless of age or rank, were referred to as "lads" or "maids" and were expected to show proper deference to the married "masters" and "dames" who were simultaneously their guardians, employers, and governors. In Sheffield in 1615, only 12 percent of the population were classified as householders, mainly married men to whom the rest of the city was supposed to defer. Indeed, in the seventeenth century, the word "husband" was still the same as that for the small property owner (husbandman), a privileged, enfranchised position that only a part of the population would ever attain.[48] Since for most purposes servants, apprentices, and other dependents remained infants, full adulthood was in effect impossible to attain without substantial savings or parentally sanctioned entitlements to land or trade—and among women, only widows formed a significant group of property owners. This division between masters and subordinates had significant implications for contemporary notions of subjectivity and citizenship: in order to discipline and command women, children, and servants, masters should internalize godly authority and exercise self-control; only such men could be trusted with the responsibilities of citizenship.

MASTERS AND SERVANTS, WOMEN AND INFANTS, THE HIGH AND THE LOW

Since most forms of productive work in sixteenth- and seventeenth-century Europe centered on the peasant or craft household, the legal codes governing employment tended to overlap with those designed to guide family conduct. In early modern England, for example, it is possible to draw a line between two basic forms of relations between workers and employers. One constituted a diverse range of less personal contracts for the supply of goods and services; the other, accounting for the largest category of laboring people, resembled household dependence. Servants in the narrow meaning of the term were hired by the year and lived in their master's household. Some worked around the house, while others labored on the farm or in the workshop. The master-and-servant legal codes which governed their status developed in the fourteenth and fifteenth centuries as feudal obligations of villeins (tied peasants) were commuted to money rents, and the relations between masters and those who worked for them were put on new legal footing. The legal position of servants substantially overlapped with that of other household dependents: apprentices, children, and wives.[49] In Britain's colonial outposts, most of the legal conditions of service were applied (in the letter of the law, at least) also to "covenant servants," debt servants, African Americans, and Indians (and later Australian Aborigines), all of whom were subject to exemplary punishment and restricted freedom of movement, and faced harsh criminal penalties for absconding or refusing to work.[50]

The master–servant relation itself was conceptualized in two different ways: as a form of property lease by which the master gained total ownership of the servant's physical capacities for a specified period, and as a form of "status contract" through which the master and servant assumed a legal relationship resembling that of father and child. Under the first principle, everything the servant produced during the term of service belonged to the master. In a similar way, the fruits of a wife's domestic labor were regarded as her husband's property. Servants who ran away were treated like thieves who stole any other form of property: imprisoned for a criminal offense and compelled to serve the rest of their contract. A lesser penalty was meted out to those found to be "enticing" away a master's servant, child, or wife. Servants could be—and often were—sublet to others, with the master retaining the right to any rewards for such work; in early modern England, masters occasionally sold some years of an apprentice's labor to another freeman. Injury to a servant, wife, or working child by a third party, like damage to buildings or other property, was recoverable by the master. In each case, compensation was calculated according to the total amount of labor (formal or informal) that a master lost, minus the cost of the dependent's subsistence.

Under the second principle, residence in the employer's household resulted in the partial juridical merger of a servant into the legal persona of the master. Just as a wife, being part of the juridical body of her husband, could not sue him for rape, so children, servants, and apprentices, unlike other people, were not able to sue the master for workplace injuries. As governor of the household, the master was entitled to reverence, honor, and obedience in return for duty of care. Servants, like children and wives, could be moderately beaten or restrained by the master; it was widely believed that such dependents, not being endowed with self-mastery, would neither work nor behave in an orderly manner without physical coercion. Like a limited-term marriage, the master–servant relationship could be dissolved mid-term only under strictly limited circumstances, and generally only with the permission of justices of the peace or other local officials.

Masters were obliged to care for sick or injured servants and were prevented by law from turning them out; servants who were brutally treated had to seek official authorization before they could leave. Similar provisions applied to apprentices, whose agreements usually spanned five or more years, and stipulated the master's duty to initiate the apprentice into the secrets of the trade.

Upon marriage, typically in their mid-to late twenties, servants usually established their own household, and their status changed. Women exchanged legal infancy for coverture, a higher form of dependence that carried some of the same legal disabilities. They were now subject to the mastery of their own husband. All their labor now belonged to him, and could be sublet to others, as it were, only with his permission. Men generally ceased to serve for a term and began working in a wide range of contracts reckoned, in custom as in law, outside master–servant relations. Artificers, handicraftsmen, and workmen were employed by the day, the week, or the task. They were their own masters in the evenings and on Sundays, but by the same token had no legal call on the care of those they worked for when ill or injured. Particularly in times when labor was scarce, strenuous attempts were made to compel such workers to complete the work they agreed to undertake. In England, the 1562 Statute of Artificers and related legislation extended criminal penalties for leaving a job or stopping work before the contract was up to those employed by the day or the task. However, there are grounds for doubting the scope, effectiveness, and persistence of these sanctions, particularly with regard to artisans and those working in cottage industries.[51] The only recourse most employers of "free labor" had, it seems, was to sue recalcitrant workers for breach of contract at common law.

Apart from master-and-servant statutes, there was little in common law specifically relating to infants. English law *did* contain a substantial body of specific provisions for those under twenty-one, the legal age of majority, but the bulk of these came under equity law, and applied to those with property.[52] Until their scope and function were extended in the late nineteenth century, they protected wealthy young people and adjudicated on disputes regarding the administration of their property. Precise and detailed rules governed everything from the appointment and duties of guardians and trustees, annuities, and shareholdings to the leasing of land, insurance of factories, marriage settlements, and provisions for the education and maintenance of infants according to their rank and station. The general impression one gets from reading Simpson's *Treatise on the Law and Practice Relating to Infants* is that of a collective paternal provision by the

propertied classes for their under-age members: making sure they were
not swindled out of their inheritance, did not take on disadvantageous
obligations, and were given the sort of treatment and care a wise father
would provide. Importantly, under equity law a contract between an adult
and an infant was binding on the adult but not on the infant, and had to be
rescinded if it was prejudicial to the infant.[53] If more modest families
wanted to avail themselves of the court's assistance, they were first advised
to settle a sum of money, however small, on the infant, in order that the
court have something to act on. At a time when laboring men were lucky to
earn a pound a week, the court's idea of a small endowment was one
hundred pounds.[54]

From the sixteenth century, the protection of equity courts began to be
extended to limited numbers of married women. Through the medium of
trustees, they could hold property separate from their husbands, and free
from their common-law rights of possession or control. Here again, the use
of such provisions was restricted to those wealthy enough to hire lawyers to
draw up marriage settlements, set up trusts, and conduct expensive proceedings in equity courts; the majority of women were outside their jurisdiction.[55] Even more than in the case of propertied infants, the main bene-
ficiary of these legal provisions was not the woman herself but her family of
origin: "The essence of the arrangement which equity upheld was the
preservation of wealth within the [paternal] kinship group which provided
it. . . . It also protected the capital against incursions of the husband, his
family, and the recipient herself."[56]

Although in some European regions Roman law precedents were used to
give all married women similar limited rights over their property, England
for the most part followed Germanic customary laws, under which all
matrimonial property was placed under the husband's control.[57] Under
English common law, which became the basis of legislation throughout the
English-speaking world, the status of servants and of married women
overlapped. The fruits of a wife's labor—including her children—belonged
to a husband whom she was expected to obey and in whose legal personality she was subsumed. "Whatever she earns," Theophilus Parsons wrote in
1873, "she earns as his servant, and for him; for in law, her time and her
labour, as well as her money, are his property. . . . He is the stronger, she is
the weaker; whatever she has is his."[58] All of a woman's earnings and
personal property such as furniture or money were transferred to the husband on marriage, and could be used or given away by the wife only with
his consent. Any income from her land was his to use or sell, although he
could not actually sell the land itself. A woman's ability to engage in

business was hampered by her inability to enter into binding contracts: "The dumb, the deaf, the insane, and the female cannot draw up a contract, neither alone nor through a representative, since they are subservient to the authority of others."[59]

Just as villeins in feudal society did not have access to the public courts in matters affecting relations with their lord, women in Britain could not sue their husbands (who were classified in law as their barons), or indeed sue or be sued at common law in their own name at all. If a woman was raped or otherwise injured or had her possessions stolen, her husband or father, not the woman herself, would have to sue for damages. Until recently, the rape of a wife by a husband was considered to be a legal impossibility, since the marriage contract formally gave the husband access to her body, which she could not retract.[60] On the other hand, women, villeins, and servants were fully responsible for their own crimes.

Under common law, husbands were empowered to beat their wives but had no right to kill them. Exactly how far their violence could legitimately go was frequently debated in conduct literature and explored in ecclesiastical courts, particularly when members of the community feared that excessive beating threatened the wife's life and the peace of the neighborhood. When husbands overstepped the legal boundary and *did* kill their wife or a servant, they were charged with murder. In contrast, the statutes provided that "if any servant kill his Master, any woman kill her husband, or any secular or religious person kill his Prelate to whom he owes Obedience, this is [petty] treason," similar in kind to threat or assault on royal government, which was defined as high treason. One justice of the peace succinctly explained in 1618 that a wife or servant who "maliciously killeth" a husband or master was accused of treason, while a husband or master who "maliciously killeth" a wife or servant was accused of murder, "for that one is in subjection and oweth obedience, and not the other." Until 1790, the punishments for petty treason were more spectacular and severe than those for murder. For men, punishment for high treason was more elaborate still; for women, both high and petty treason were punished by burning at the stake. In England, petty treason was abolished, and the offense converted to murder, in 1858.[61]

*****

In late-sixteenth-century England, William Harrison distinguished four "degrees of people": gentlemen, the citizens and burgesses of the cities, yeomen in the countryside, and those who had "neither voice nor authority in the commonwealth but are to be ruled and not to rule other"; it was in this last group that women and servants were included. As the typology suggests, however, even household heads were not equally masterful; a gulf wider than that separating men and women, or infants and adults, differentiated the highborn from the rest. While many in early modern Europe believed in a fundamental equality of all souls before Christ, others were reluctant to believe that the poor were fully human. "The numerous rabble that seem to have the signatures of man in their faces are but brutes in their understanding," wrote Sir Thomas Pope Blunt in 1693. "'Tis by the favour of a metaphor we call them men, for at best they are but Descartes' automata, moving frames and figures of men, and have nothing but their outsides to justify their titles to rationality."[62]

Throughout western Europe, the aristocracy constituted a small but immensely powerful section of society, perhaps only 4 or 5 percent of the population. The social distinctions and noble titles of their men were seen as prerequisites to public office "that the people may know and distinguish such as are set over them, in order to yield them their due respect and obedience."[63] Unlike common people, gentlemen wore wigs or powdered their hair; they wore lace ruffles, silk stockings, and other finery, which commoners were by law prevented from owning. Similarly, their wives and daughters, from their elaborately coiffed headdresses to their decorative feet, constantly demonstrated to the fashionable world—and to the lower classes—that they were distinct from ordinary people, not least because they could not possibly do the slightest amount of coarse work.[64] Gentlemen and commoners not only differed markedly in stature and in costume, they were frequently thought to have different souls, be moved by different emotions, and possess different natures. Most important, gentlemen were free—free from want, from the necessity to make a living, from ignorance, from the caprice of others. They were distinctive by being independent in a world of dependencies, learned in a world only partially literate, leisured in a world of laborers. They were those "whose Minds seemed to be of a greater Make than the Minds of others and who are replenished with Heroic virtues and a Majesty of Soul above the ordinary Part of our Species."[65]

THE REFORMATION OF HOUSEHOLDS

The relations of mastery and service, concerns with balancing land and population, and matters of territorial governance all found expression in the Reformation and Counter-Reformation. One of the most important aspects of this process concerned the development of new links between Christian churches and conjugal households. In medieval Europe, many aspects of the church's teachings impeded the full development of a patriarchalist social order. Many clerics lived with women; some were infamous as womanizers, but all believed that homosociality rather than heterosexuality pleased God. Celibacy and the corporate life of religious communities for both men and women were exalted as superior to conjugal households and heterosexual marriage, which was seen as an honorable second best for those too weak to subdue the lustful impulses of the flesh. Reflecting a lingering ambivalence about marriage as a wholly honorable Christian vocation, the western Christian church began seeking full jurisdiction over its solemnization only in the eleventh century. The innovations in canon law introduced over the next three centuries included insistence on the full consent of both bride and groom to the marriage, the publication of banns, and the celebration of a special mass and a blessing of the marriage in church. In spite of persistent demands for the elimination of clandestine unions, however, popes, academic lawyers, and church courts alike continued to recognize them as true marriages. Under fifteenth-century canon law, two people were seen as legally married if they showed "marital affection" for one another, exchanged private vows, and then engaged in sexual intercourse, without necessarily securing the consent of their parents or having a priest perform the marriage. While the church condemned familial disobedience, it remained committed to the principle that individuals could choose their marriage partners freely, whether their parents consented or not. The penalty routinely imposed on the offending couple was an order to regularize their union with a formal wedding. As a result, canon lawyers often sanctioned privately contracted marriages which the peasant patriarchs, local notables, and village communities saw as illegitimate, and which many municipalities punished with heavy fines.[66]

During the Reformation, pressures both inside and outside the church to tighten control over marriages intensified and became more successful. By the middle of the sixteenth century (a period of increasing pressure on land), the model of Christian virtue and governance became the household of the craft master or the substantial peasant, who both demanded closer control over family formation, and in whose eyes "the old papist monks were targets of ridicule and symbols of godlessness because they did not head households but, like the sexually immature and licensed journeymen, banded together in brotherhoods."[67] In many regions, the Catholic cleric became a repository of a set of fears about manhood, particularly for the first generation of Protestant clergy leaving the all-male environment of the monastery and having to prove their manliness in companionship with their wife.[68] Heterosexuality, marriage, and fatherhood, rather than celibacy, homosociality, and brotherhood, would open the heavenly gates and ensure earthly authority.

In their various attempts to challenge the authority of the medieval Catholic church, many humanist and Renaissance thinkers had already put a new emphasis on marriage and the family household, often assigning them a political significance far greater than they were accorded in feudal, monastic, or courtly society.[69] Reformation theologians throughout sixteenth- and seventeenth-century Europe followed suit, attempting simultaneously to reduce the authority of the priest and to elevate that of the patriarchal head of the household. The task of reformation was to begin at home: "Let the master reform his servant, the father his child, the husband his wife."[70] Luther, one of the most influential of these reformers, believed that strong, godly patriarchal families had a key role to play in reforming the church and educating the mass of people in the right Christian faith. His new marriage codes, which were successfully enforced in many Lutheran cities and principalities in the first half of the sixteenth century, explicitly prohibited marriages without the permission of both sets of parents. The first article of the marriage code would typically state, "No one, male or female, still under the authority of their parents shall secretly promise marriage; rather every child, girl or boy, should marry honourably with the advice, previous knowledge and consent of his parents or, in their absence, the next of kin and guardian."[71] Christian authorities, Luther believed, should not merely forbid marriages contracted without parental consent, but should hold them invalid. Calvin's legislation in Geneva similarly included a provision that rescinded marriages contracted by young people without the blessing of their parents, while the marriage court that Zwingli established in Zürich also held such marriages invalid.[72]

Numberless contemporary catechisms and household manuals decreed the "housefather" to be king inside the household, representing his servants and dependents to the authorities and ruling them with a firm but kind and just hand, just as God the Father ruled the universe. A typical publication on household government insisted that "the husband without any exception, is master over all the house, and hath more to do in his house with his own domestical affairs, than the magistrate."[73] But this power carried its own responsibility: "To have children and servants is thy blessing, O Lord," ran a 1553 English prayer for householders, "but not to order them according to thy word deserveth thy dreadful curse."[74]

While theologians such as Luther put strong emphasis on familial Christianity and obedience to worldly rulers, events associated with the early stages of the Reformation undermined rather than strengthened patriarchal authority, whether in the household, noble estate, church, or kingdom. Initially a revolt within the clerical hierarchy against what the reformers saw as abuses in church practices and doctrines, the Reformation soon turned into a profoundly radical movement, preaching the spiritual equality of all Christians, male and female, young and old, rich and poor, valuing the prophetic talents of daughters as well as sons, and even denying the need for a priesthood. Such ideas, which held a particular appeal for the poor and dispossessed, were used as rallying points in the series of peasant wars and uprisings which erupted throughout Europe between the fourteenth and the sixteenth centuries. Again and again, peasants demanded the elimination of noble privileges and an end to compulsory labor services and taxation. In some localities, they experimented with communities of believers in which property was held in common; in others, they burned and ransacked castles and murdered landlords; at times they challenged the notion that fathers had natural authority over their sons.[75] There is much evidence that similar radicalism affected gender relations as well. Women took an active part in leading and prophesying. In a few localities, a general emphasis on the positive valuation of wives and companionate marriage was consolidated into experiments with sexually egalitarian communities (the best-known of which were the Anabaptists and Diggers). All this had the potential of leading to an affirmation of specifically female forms of piety and public presence; many historians have indeed claimed that the Reformation improved the status of women in early modern Europe.

It is now generally acknowledged that the Reformation soon lost most of its radical potential with regard to the relations between the rich and the poor. In his 1525 tract *Against the Murderous and Thieving Hordes of Peasants,* Luther himself condemned what he saw as the misuse of his doctrines by unruly mobs, and appealed to the princes to destroy armed bands of militant peasants in order to preserve the divinely appointed worldly authority to which all owed obedience. Soon, reformed church hierarchies joined in repressing their more radical brethren. According to historians such as Roper, the legacy of the Reformation was no better with regard to the relations between women and men. In spite of its radical origins, a process of domestication gradually transformed radical evangelism into consoling, socially conservative pieties of Protestant guildsfolk, with women denied even their own distinctive forms of piety and defined as wives, daughters, and servants in submission to the male head of the family.[76] Indeed, in some localities, the contemporary drive against women preachers extended into edicts prohibiting any gatherings of women to discuss religion at all.[77] Keith Thomas similarly argues that although radical sects during the English Civil War laid great emphasis on the spiritual equality of all believers and made considerable concessions to women in the sphere of church government, "as soon as they took on institutional form even the most radical sects became conservative as regards the organisation and discipline of the family." For the most part, they assumed that wives should remain subservient to their husbands, that franchise should be restricted to male householders, and that women's participation in public speech and action should be limited.[78]

In an influential study of one German town, Roper argues that the resurgence of class- and gender-based forms of patriarchal governance was closely linked; the politics of marriage were central to the long-recognized domestication of the Reformation. By promising a religion of wedded life and a politics of the control of marriage, the evangelical message recruited masters of the innumerable small craft workshops for a Reformation which favored them, and which gave powerful articulation to the craft values of order, discipline, and the authority of the master. In turn, the craft work-shops became the nurturing soil of populist Protestantism, and their work patterns and civic moralism became the touchstone for the whole society.[79] In the long run, the masters played a key role in redefining Protestantism, so evangelical moralism was harnessed to an older conservative tradition that defined women as wives in submission to their husbands: "As the Reformation was domesticated—as it closed convents and encouraged nuns to marry, as it lauded the married state exemplified by the craft couple, and as it execrated the prostitute—so it was accomplished through a politics of reinscribing women within the 'family.'"[80]

While they might differ about the causes, a number of historians agree that Lutheranism was formulated around the needs and aspirations of the craft masters who provided its most solid base of support, and that as a result its appeal to the majority of the population, the peasants, was likely to be diminished.[81] In his work on a small German principality, Robisheaux found that peasants had indeed paid little attention to the religious tenets of the Reformation. However, he argues that peasant elders, largely propertied males and widows controlling households, valued and made full use of those aspects of Luther's teaching and legal reforms that allowed them to bolster their own patriarchal authority vis-à-vis the younger generation, even though they overwhelmingly utilized these to manage pressures on limited land and resources rather than to indoctrinate youth in the Lutheran faith.[82] The householders benefited especially from the new Lutheran marriage codes which forbade marriages without parental consent. In the sixteenth and seventeenth centuries, these laws bolstered peasant elders' independent efforts to control when and whom their children would marry. With the help of Lutheran marriage courts and watchful pastors, many family elders successfully opposed the pressures of their children to disperse the family resources, a trend that peasants in many other parts of Europe were unable to resist. Village young people, on the other hand, ironically the group that Luther hoped would pass on the new doctrine, were alienated from pastors who served only to subordinate them to parents and authority.[83] Similarly, in rural Württemberg, the state bureaucracy, the church, local corporations, and parents all worked together to rear children to religious and work discipline and active participation in the process of self-regulation on which the rural market relations in this society depended. The greatest, if not the only, sufferers were outsiders— foreigners, the mobile, the illegitimate, the marginal—and the young.[84] In the country and the city, such tensions often fed into new forms of "fraternal" associations established by disenfranchised groups of young men.

Often arguing that the Reformation was a major causal factor, a number of historians note that an appreciable tightening of household patriarchal relations did in fact occur in both Protestant and Catholic regions of Europe during the first half of the sixteenth century. Not only did marriage and household governance in general come under closer control, but there is some evidence that childhood was redefined and young people were subjected to stricter discipline. Protestant cities typically led the way in this process, with rural areas and Catholic lands following suit. Every Protestant territory passed a marriage ordinance stressing wifely obedience and proper Christian values, and set up a new tribunal to deal with marriage and moral cases that had previously been handled by church courts.[85]

The Catholic church indirectly bolstered parental authority over children by reforming the canon law articles on marriage at the Council of Trent (1545–63). Although the Council stopped short of agreeing to demands to include parental consent as a necessary stipulation for a valid marriage, after the Tridentine reforms only those marriages performed publicly before a priest and two or three reliable witnesses were recognized as legally binding. As soon as the relevant regulations had been published and explained to the faithful (and in some regions this could take decades), clandestine marriages were legally considered to be invalid and of no effect.[86]

During the sixteenth century, it became much harder to get married in defiance of patriarchal familial authority in Protestant parts of Germany.[87]

Many communities, such as those in rural Württemberg, used both church and temporal courts to maintain a strict form of family discipline, and to deal with children who refused to obey fathers, mothers, or masters, who were idle or immoral, or who were overheard by neighbors to speak evil words against their superiors. Sons might be put in the stocks or locked in a house of correction on bread and water; girls or boys might be ordered to be put to a master.[88] In sixteenth- and seventeenth-century England, an age when notions of sin and crime were not clearly differentiated, church courts ruled on disputes over marriage contracts, punished those who bore and fathered bastards, committed adultery, or seduced their servants, and adjudicated on willful absences from church, failure to receive the communion, drunkenness, talebearing, scolding, defamation, usury, witchcraft, and sorcery.[89] In Geneva in the mid-sixteenth century, Calvin had decreed the death penalty as the punishment for disobedience to parents. A century later, two American colonies used this decree as the basis of their own legislation. In Connecticut, a 1642 law allowed the magistrates to commit a child to the house of correction on complaint from the parents about "any stubborn or rebellious carriage," while Massachusetts in 1646 imposed the death penalty for any son over sixteen who "shall curse or smite their natural father or mother," or even refuse to obey their orders.[90]

In Catholic France, where family formation came under one of the strictest systems of control in Europe, a series of royal decrees proclaimed between 1556 and 1639 extended patriarchal control over marriage far beyond the principles agreed at the Council of Trent, and brought it under the jurisdiction of secular courts. In the process, the discretionary power of the younger generation and of women was sharply curtailed. The age of majority was raised from twenty to thirty for men and from seventeen to twenty-five for women, and was finally made irrelevant when a statute made parental consent to marriage (on pain of disinheritance) necessary regardless of age or previous marriage, for both men and women. Those who married without the consent of both sets of parents risked being sued for a capital offense and banished or imprisoned, sometimes for years.[91] In addition, women's pregnancy and childbirth were brought under public supervision, inheritance rules were changed and tightened so that only blood children of an original legal marriage could inherit, husbands were given power to regulate the conditions of marital separation arrangements, civil procedures were set up to register vital statistics, and legal procedures were established to appeal contested cases to the Parlement of Paris. While the decrees were initiated by the some of the most powerful men in French society—legally trained officeholders in the Parlement of Paris and kings and royal councilors who gradually began to focus on state-building—they were welcomed by peasant elders who similarly used them to reinforce parental control over their children's marriages, and to develop stronger patriarchal control over youths.[92] According to Foucault, the celebrated *lettres de cachet,* or orders under the king's private seal, "were in fact demanded by families, masters, local notables, neighbours, parish priests; and their function was to punish by confinement . . . disorder, agitation, disobedience, bad conduct."[93] They were frequently used by parents to incarcerate their children, without a hearing, for the sake of familial order and reputation.

The new forms of familial discipline were much easier to enforce in cities than in the countryside, and in large states than in smaller principalities, whose administrative structures were poorly suited to achieve more ambitious aims, and which had neither the old corporate institutions of cities nor the substantial funds required to set up centralized policing agencies. In Protestant imperial cities in the German lands, for example, the consistories and special tribunals became permanent institutions, with the sole purpose of policing the moral life of the state's subjects in a way that courts in small principalities could never do.[94] In addition, there were other political, historical, and ecological factors, such as the quality of soils, the density of settlement, or the relative power of local nobility, which helped account for the uneven force of patriarchalist social relations in different regions. What remains clear, however, is that familial patriarchalist authority was generally strongest where state and church authorities had the most power to police its functioning.

THE FAMILY HOUSEHOLD AS THE BASIC UNIT OF SOCIAL DISCIPLINE

For many reformers, the social significance of strengthened patriarchal families went beyond the Christian government and education of those already resident within them. Ideally, the alarmingly increasing numbers of "masterless" persons—servants between positions, "sturdy beggars," wandering journeymen, mercenary soldiers, and their camp followers—would be integrated, one way or another, into reinvigorated patriarchal households. These would redouble their service as basic units of order and discipline in a society in which class and familial relations overlapped, family government was considered one of the foundations of political order, and the household was almost a part of the constitution of the state.[95]

Once under firm patriarchal control, the poor and the destitute would be prevented from undesirable coupling. Among other benefits, this would alleviate pressure on land—even as it accelerated the polarization between the rich and the poor.

In some regions, this ideal remained at the level of unproclaimed edicts; in others, it closely structured the lives of the majority of the population. Orphans typically were allocated as servants to householders who were made their guardians; poor children were sent into service or assigned as apprentices.[96] In many parts of Europe, the adult poor were not allowed to marry or find independent accommodation, but were expected to remain as servants in the households of others. Outsiders who managed to find work were moved on as soon as they finished their contracts. In England, all those between the ages of fifteen and forty-five who were unmarried and without estates of their own were required by law to be in service.[97] In the Plymouth Colony in North America, a 1669 act proclaimed that "henceforth, no single person be suffered to live of himselfe," that is, away from household government.[98] Often, even economically self-sufficient but "masterless" women were pressured to join male-headed households so that they, too, could have a rightful master. In France and Germany, laws were passed that forbade unmarried women to move into the cities, made it an offense for innkeepers to take in any woman traveling alone, required widows to move in with one of their male children, and obliged unmarried women to lodge with a male relative or employer.[99] It was in this same period that poor unattached women experienced an unprecedented wave of trials and executions for witchcraft and infanticide. In Protestant areas, as religious communities were disbanded, nuns were likewise considered to be masterless women and were encouraged to marry or go live in the households of their male relatives. In Catholic regions, it had become papal policy by 1566 to suppress all female religious congregations that did not practice strict enclosure.[100]

In extreme cases, such as in Upper Austria, the authorities standardized peasant holdings, deliberately blocked the creation of a class of smallholders, and forced all masterless people to reside, as servants or lodgers, in the households of hereditary tenants. Whereas in Bavaria, for example, the creation of a large class of smallholders and cottagers was tolerated, Austrian magnates enforced a two-class division which collapsed class and patriarchal relations. On the one hand there were the owners of hereditary tenant holdings (which could not be divided among their heirs); on the other hand there was a growing class of non-housed, dispossessed, and propertyless laborers who were supposed to rent their lodgings from one of the tenants or to labor as their servants, and who often spent their lives in a desperate cycle of escape from their masters, starvation, reintegration, exploitation, brutalization, and escape. As late as 1727, when a royal investigation revealed that there were 25,000 masterless persons in Upper Austria, the estate authorities were forbidden to increase the number of cottages to these people, who were supposed to be integrated into regular peasant houses, and the unemployed were again forbidden to marry.[101] Only in the 1770s did the state stop blocking the expansion of the cottager class and allow them some expanded economic functions, such as keeping and dealing with livestock.

＊＊＊＊＊

Effective as they were, patriarchalist forms of discipline were not a perfect instrument of social control. On the most basic level, the various courts charged with overseeing and enforcing familial order could also strengthen and make more visible the resistance of household dependents. Sabean, for example, writing about Neckarhausen in early seventeenth century, notes that Pietist consistories were designed explicitly to discipline and control popular culture and to create a set of hard-working, well-ordered family groups. Ironically, the church consistory was used primarily by women, in their alliance with the pastor, to try to discipline the many men whose behavior fell far short of Christian ideals. As in many other places, the independent husband, with his legal power of chastisement, was arrayed against the wife-pastor alliance with the powerful backup institution of the consistory.[102] Similarly, in sixteenth-century Augsburg, the city council knew full well that town patriarchs were not the wise governors they ought to be. They drank and gambled; they were lazy good-for-nothings who did not exercise their disciplining duties with paternal mildness but punched, beat, kicked, and bit their wives.[103] As the council "adjudicated the endless stream of marital disputes where husbands attacked wives, wives insulted their husbands, or men would not 'share their earnings,' its daily experience contradicted—and worse[,] the punishments it meted out actually undermined—the vision of natural patriarchal authority and female subservience which it held so dear." The more the council tried to uphold "proper" marriage, the more it exposed the fragility of the patriarchal order it wished to reinforce.[104]

Several historians have identified a similar dynamic in England. In the early seventeenth century, one list of articles given to high constables for presentment contained a clause requiring "all unlawful games, drunkenness, whoredom and incontinency in private families to be reported, as on their good government the commonwealth depends."[105] The various courts were active in enforcing wifely subjection, and the legal system was heavily weighted against women. Yet the very vehemence and frequency of attempts to discipline them suggests that in many localities, women were felt to be resisting and overstepping the boundaries of their proper—that is, subordinate—place in the household. Evidence of women scolding and brawling with their neighbors, single women refusing to enter service, and wives dominating or even beating their husbands indicates that women in this disorderly period posed a much more tangible threat to the patriarchal system than moralistic writings and patriarchal legal codes lead one to expect.[106] As the author of one influential early-seventeenth-century household manual, the Puritan rector William Gouge, complained, "Among all other parties of whom the Holy Ghost requireth subjection, wives for the most part are most backward in yielding subjection to their husbands."[107] Everywhere, indeed, even as women's real authority was restricted, they were imagined to remain in possession of dangerous forces: "the other side of Reformation morality was a sexual prurience convinced of the awesome power of female desire."[108]

And yet, if we take current demographic estimates as an indicator, both the measures aimed at limiting family formation and the government of the poor in early modern Europe were remarkably successful. Regional variations aside, the overall numbers of rural and urban tenants and property holders in European populations increased only slightly over three centuries. At the close of the long sixteenth-century boom, all classes of people, including proletarians, began to get married later in life, and an increasing proportion never married. By 1650, the average age at first marriage for women was twenty-four, 7 to 20 percent of women never married, and the incidence of childbirth out of wedlock was below 3 percent. In England, the crude birth rate dropped from 38.5 in the mid-sixteenth century to 27.5 a century later, and the proportion of women who never married leapt from 4 to 23 percent. At the same time, the proportion of extramarital births fell from around 4.5 percent of all births in 1605 to less than 1 percent sixty years later. In France, women's mean age at first marriage rose by about two and half years during the same period. In rural regions, births out of wedlock hovered around the remarkably low rate of 1 percent, while the rates of bridal pregnancy fell.[109]

In the course of the sixteenth century, village communities across western Europe began to polarize, a process that continued right up to the nineteenth century. Reflecting and aiding this process were determined efforts by the minority of well-to-do peasants to prevent their children from marrying poorer neighbors. While the numbers of property-holding households remained relatively stable, land-poor and landless households proliferated. Roughly 88 percent of the total growth of the European population between 1500 and 1800 was due to the expansion of those dependent, in whole or in part, on wage income for their subsistence.[110] Importantly, on current evidence it appears that between 1500 and 1750, the growth of the landless poor was a product more of the downward mobility of peasants and their children than of demographic self-expansion of those without property. Because of the obstacles to establishing independent households, proletarian women and men tended to marry even later than their peasant counterparts, and to have fewer surviving children because of higher infant and child mortality rates. It was only by the mid-eighteenth century that the consolidation of alternative means of livelihood radically undermined patriarchal controls over marriage and family formation among the laboring poor, and helped unleash a population explosion. For the first time in recorded European history, the households of the land-poor and propertyless became larger on average than those of their class superiors.[111] From then on, some decades before they began constructing their own consciousness as a distinct social class, the European proletariat made themselves through natural increase.

FAMILIAL POWER ANALOGOUS TO STATE POWER

So far, patriarchal power has been discussed with regard to the strengthening of controls over the marriage choices of the younger generation, the disciplining of servants and family members, and the integration of masterless men and women into orderly households. But contemporary political thought and practice extended the same principles of patriarchal governance far beyond the family household. It was here that philosophers and their royal patrons attempted to resolve the seemingly incompatible principles of absolute power at several different levels of authority. Perhaps the best example is the French political theorist Jean Bodin, who in the 1570s began formulating what later became the basis of absolutist theory of the state. His systematic theory of absolute and indivisible royal sovereignty, and a concept of the state as an embodiment of that sovereignty, represented a conscious effort to find means of joining in harmony a disorderly welter of baronial powers and corporate jurisdictions.[112] In his scheme, the family was not only the true source and origin of the commonwealth, but also its principal constituent. "The well-ordered family is a true image of the commonwealth, and domestic comparable with sovereign authority." As the monistic God ruled the universe, so the earthly states were to be viewed as ruled by single fatherly rulers. The king was the head of the body, and the shepherd of the flock. Just as God does not ask the advice or seek the consent of the lower orders of creation, so genuine monarchs should not seek the consent of their subjects.[113]

According to Jordan, the parallel between the state and the family was the rediscovery of the Humanists; Erasmus was the first of them to link a wife's obedience to the more general injunction against disobedience to all governing authorities, which applied to all Christians.[114] Ordinary sermons and sophisticated treatises regarding the nature of political power all came to share a basic fundamental premise regarding the similarity between familial and wider political and religious authority. Paternal authority was invoked by princes, magistrates, pastors, and schoolmasters to justify their power; the image of paternity suffused the self-image of the ruling elite. Lutheran and Calvinist princes, Catholic monarchs, and Protestant kings all called themselves father to their people.[115]

In England, the patriarchal theory of obligation constituted the official doctrine of the Anglican church and was accepted by the dissenting clergy. During the reign of James I (who also called himself *parens patriae*), it was further elaborated and linked to absolutist political theory.[116] "In a family, the master or paterfamilias, who is a kind of petty monarch there, hath authority to prescribe to his children and servants," a seventeenth-century sermon by Robert Sanderson pointed out. It followed that "what power the master hath over his servants for the ordering of his family, no doubt the same at least, if not much more, hath the supreme magistrate over his subjects, for the peaceable ordering of the commonwealth: the magistrate being *pater patriae* as the master is *paterfamilias*."[117] Conversely, according to a 1612 English publication on household government, "It is impossible for a man to understand how to govern the common-wealth, that doth not know to rule his own house, or order his own person; so that he that knoweth not to govern, deserveth not to reign."[118] Perhaps the most famous exposition of patriarchalism was written on the eve of its demise in the mid-seventeenth century by the Englishman Sir Robert Filmer. According to Schochet, Filmer broke with the traditional patriarchal argument by claiming that patriarchal and political power were not merely analogous but identical.[119] Political hierarchy, obedience, and authority were natural; just as children were born naturally subject to their father, all people were born naturally subject to their king.[120]

Contemporary catechisms, whether in Stuart England or in Lutheran Germany, reiterated the same principles. The commandment regarding children's obedience to their parents was invariably interpreted to include what were considered to be essentially identical relations of servants and apprentices to their masters, and subjects to their magistrates, priests, lords, and kings. According to Luther's *Larger Catechism* of 1529,

> All other forms of authority flow from and are extension of parental authority. . . . Thus all those who are called "lords" stand in the parent's stead and necessarily take their power and authority from [the parental office]. Therefore the Bible calls them all "fathers," because they exercise in their rule the office of a father and ought to regard their folk with a fatherly heart.[121]

A 1689 English catechism spelled out the link between parental and political authority even more explicitly:

> These words, Father and Mother, include all superiours, as well as a Civil Parent (the king and his Magistrates, a Master, a Mistress, or an Husband) and an Ecclesiastical Parent (the Bishop and Ministers) as the natural parent that begat and bore thee: To all these I owe Reverance and Obedience, Service and Maintenance, Love and Honour.[122]

It followed that God himself had a firm opinion on the appropriate political system among His earthly subjects: democracy, it was frequently asserted, would be "a manifest breach of the Fifth Commandment."[123]

The links between familial and political power went far beyond useful analogies. One striking example is provided in Sarah Hanley's pioneering work on the gendering of the actual process of state formation in early modern France. The state, according to Hanley, was "engendered" as the series of edicts tightening familial authority

> provided a formidable family model of socioeconomic authority which influenced the state model of [absolutist] political power in the making at the same time. French political theorists and legists complemented abstract medieval organological and corporate analogies for the body politic with marriage and family metaphors that explained the king's limited constitutional relationship to the kingdom. . . . Not in the least abstract, the family model of authority that infused such metaphors already required "patrimonic" behaviour, or loyalty to family and patrimony, by law.[124]

And yet, on closer inspection, the practical achievement and maintenance of absolute political power, the science of ruling, might require the elaboration of separate principles and procedures—such as Neostoicism or Cameralism—which could not be deduced from those useful in governing families and households.[125] It is the Cameralists who are credited with transforming knowledge about "all the contrivances of the great house-keeping of the state" into a systematic academic discipline. In eighteenth-century German lands, their new science was favorably received by the rulers themselves. Although Cameralism never replaced law as the preparation for government office, its study was at times made compulsory for all candidates for administrative posts, and its assumptions and preoccupations became standard wisdom for a broader Enlightenment public. Lacking an independent mechanism for generating order, the theory held, society had to be constituted by the state. The ruler needed to establish a balance between the productive classes, and the equilibrium that made social hierarchy productive had to be maintained by "police"—that is, detailed and judicious government regulation.[126]

This gradual conceptual separation of different forms of patriarchalist rule in European political thought is addressed in a particularly interesting way in Foucault's lecture on governmentality. Early modern discourses on the art of government, Foucault notes, constantly recall that one speaks also of governing a household, souls, children, a province, a convent, a religious order, a family. While some authors attempted to distinguish between different categories of power, they invariably stressed the interde-pendence of those categories in the actual practice of government. La Mothe Le Vayer, writing in seventeenth-century France, for example, ar-gued that there were three fundamental types of government, each of which related to a particular science or discipline: the art of self-government, connected with morality; the art of governing a family, which belonged to economy; and the science of ruling the state, which concerned politics. The art of government, however, consisted in establishing a continuity between these three spheres. On the one hand, the prince must first learn to govern himself, his goods, and his patrimony before he could successfully govern the state. On the other hand, when a state was well run, the heads of families looked after their households and patrimony properly, and so individual people behaved as they should. Even mercantilist and Cameral-ist doctrines, which went furthest in developing autonomous notions of bureaucratic forms of governmentality, never completely broke with the familial model underpinning their explorations of the economy of a state. A successful science of government would extend the principles of house-hold economy to the rule of a state—and by the same token might need to encroach on the autonomy of individual masters: "To govern a state will therefore mean . . . exercising towards its inhabitants, and the wealth and behaviour of each and all, a form of surveillance and control as attentive as that of the head of the family over his household and his goods."[127] Just as the post-Reformation prince owed to God the securing of confessional uniformity throughout his domain, and the housefather was bound by his reformed faith to work ceaselessly for the prosperity of his household, so the eighteenth-century absolutist ruler, informed by both Pietism and Cameralism, should so combine and order the individual and corporate components of society that they would promote the collective happiness of the whole state.[128]

CONFESSIONALIZATION AND STATE-BUILDING

To heads of households, I argued earlier, the Reformation promised prosperous families and more power to discipline their children, servants, and apprentices. To many territorial rulers (without whose support the Reformation would arguably not have taken place), the movement promised new domains and powers gained by the secularization and confiscation of church lands and a takeover of some episcopal functions, closer supervision and visibility of their subjects through orderly household rule and compulsory adherence to state religion, and an increased dignity for themselves as first servants of the church.[129] This is an important point: domesticated and shorn of its early radical promise, the Reformation provided a tangible bridge between the ambitions of many territorial rulers and the survival strategies of propertied householders. Frequently it was the new marriage, birth, and death registers, as well as records of catechism instruction and examination, which provided the most useful "statistical" bases for taxation and conscription: the means of regulating families and educating the faithful were of immediate practical benefit to state formation. In the long term, Neostoic doctrines that provided practical guidance in the construction of strong states with disciplined armies helped standardize the nature of competing faiths. Conversely, a parallel process of "confessionalization" in Lutheran, Calvinist, and Catholic regions made a powerful contribution to state-building. This process of state-building would eventually undermine household patriarchal powers. Until the late eighteenth century, however, rulers were forced to rely on domestic patriarchalism.

In medieval times, the *Respublica Christiana*, or Christendom, was perhaps the only plausible basis for seeing the region as a distinct entity.[130]

Even though the popes failed to unify Europe under their rule, the church had by far the most complex and extensive administrative apparatus. By the eleventh century, it owned about a quarter of all the wealth in western Europe. In many regions, the greatest "spiritual lords" held the largest feudal estates;[131] frequently it was they who pioneered modern methods of what would later become capitalist farming. Religion constituted the language of community, the language of politics and social organization, of power in all its complex forms.[132] In some parts of fifteenth-century Europe, an early process of political centralization became discernible with the adoption of Roman law, the rise of an academic jurist class, the growth of bureaucracies, and the reduction of local, particularist privileges. Inescapably, this process was contested by, drew on, disrupted, and reorganized religious modes of governance.

State formation and religion became particularly closely intertwined in the century after 1550, as new forms of uniform faith were imposed on different territories under the provision *cuius regio, eius religio*. Many rulers who had previously been in conflict with the church now integrated it into civil authority and looked to it to condemn tyrannicide and disobedience.[133] The widespread social turmoil of the 1520s showed clearly that religious ideas could have revolutionary consequences. As a matter of practical politics, it seemed no longer possible to segregate faith from worldly affairs. Anxiety over unorthodox beliefs replaced the initial Reformation zeal for spreading the Word as a liberating message. An unambiguous form of religion was needed to prevent popular unrest and strengthen the power of worldly authorities.[134]

Religion was gradually transformed from a vague but intense piety mingled freely with magic to a solemn duty of subjects to the state. As the ruler of one German principality put it, legitimate governments had been commanded by God not merely to guard the social order, but also to see to it that God's saving word was being preached free of error, and uncontaminated by false teachings.[135] Religion in medieval Europe, according to Obelkevich,

> bridged elite and populace, its symbols and rituals expressing the ethos of an entire society or culture. . . . This relatively open situation passed, however, in the sixteenth and seventeenth centuries as the Reformation and Counter-Reformation gathered force. The militant clergy of both faiths sought to impose on the masses what was essentially an elite pattern of religion. . . . When the reformers dismantled medieval Christianity, they transformed the definition of religion itself. Protestant and Catholic alike attacked the popu-

lar folklorized Christianity inherited from the Middle Ages; magic in particular, previously tolerated as an inferior form of religion, was condemned as not religious at all, but as antithetical to true religion. At the same time, they shifted the accent from religion as an attitude—as "faith," or "piety," or "religiousness"—to religion as belief. Christianity in their hands hardened and materialized into articles of belief, its defining act becoming intellectual assent to a creed.[136]

Protestant leaders, often convinced that their religion could—and should—be comprehended only through words, made this transformation if anything more difficult for the mass of the people than Catholics, who were more willing to simplify the creed for common folk and to communicate or at least to accommodate correct faith with images, statues, processions, pilgrimages, and venerations of relics.[137]

A recent Foucauldian interpretation of the emergence of state school systems in eighteenth-century Prussia emphasizes the separate development of religion and bureaucracy. According to Hunter, Prussian schools were the first to integrate two departments of existence that until then had been radically autonomous. In an unprecedented historical compromise or a purely contingent *modus vivendi,* the bureaucratically based government of the nation-state, "characterised by 'mundane' ends and supported by a technically-based expertise which construed political difficulties as technical problems open to 'objective' (administrative) solution," was deployed together with the religiously based cultivation of moral personality. The end result of this remarkable process of historical improvisation, the argument continues, was "the fashioning of a hitherto unknown institution capable of serving simultaneously as an instrument for the social disciplining of the population and for the pastoral supervision of the individual soul . . . the elementary school."[138] Hunter's argument that bureaucracy and Protestant evangelicalism were "radically autonomous departments of existence" in absolutist monarchies with state churches becomes particularly difficult to sustain given recent historical work on the Reformation. This indicates, on the contrary, that church and state formed an inextricable matrix of power in a process in which the consolidation of the early modern territorial state, the imposition of social discipline, tightened control over family formation, and the consolidation of professional churches transformed society.[139] The same literature can be used to modify Foucault's own claim that the sixteenth century lies at the crossroads of two processes, "the one which, shattering the structures of feudalism, leads to the establishment of the great territorial, administrative and colonial states; and that *totally different movement* which, with the Reformation and the counter-Reformation, raises the issue of how one must be spiritually ruled and led on this earth in order to achieve eternal salvation."[140]

Rather than focus on the splintering of the Christian church, the differences between Catholics and Protestants, or the conflicts between church and state, some historians have introduced the concept of "formation of confessions" or "confessionalism" to emphasize the similarities in the development of Lutheran, Calvinist, and Catholic reformations. According to writers such as Schilling, Blaschke, and Oestreich, the three major confessions—Lutheranism, Calvinism, and Tridentine Catholicism—came to share many fundamental features. Motivated in part by an intense competition for souls, all developed coherent systems of doctrines, rituals, personnel, administration, and institutions. Catholic and Protestant churches alike were often in conflict with state authorities, but set aside their differences in matters of social disciplining. As one French preacher put it in the early 1500s, "Ecclesiastical discipline does not diminish the authority of the Magistrate at all, but, on the contrary, is the Magistrate's organ in disposing man's heart and will with the aim to make him more obedient."[141] In the severe ordinances laid down in Geneva in 1582, which served as a pattern for Calvinists everywhere, it was expressly stated that there was no conflict between spiritual and temporal discipline.[142] Indeed, Protestant disciplinary ordinances held that failure to observe God's (and the prince's) laws would lead to dearth, hunger, crop failure, war, plague, pestilence, and other punishments which God would visit on earth and its people—disasters commensurate with Catholic visions of divine retribution.[143]

According to Oestreich, it was Neostoicism, particularly as reconstructed by the late-sixteenth-century Dutch scholar Lipsius, which supplied some of the common features of contemporary Calvinism, Puritanism, Pietism, and Catholicism: self-control, moderation, pious yet active faith, genuine reverence for God, and submission to worldly rulers. Coupled with its emphasis on the central role of force and of the army, Neostoicism also provided a coherent set of precepts which rulers of all confessions used in their projects of modernizing their armies, strengthening their hold on state power, and disciplining themselves and their subjects.[144]

Next to extensive efforts to bolster and reconstitute "proper" patriarchal households, church and civil authorities alike attempted to secure regular habits of religious observance, ecclesiastical discipline, and catechism instruction by better-educated and -supervised clergy. As Roper noted, as familiar as the sentiments of the Discipline Ordinances may have sounded to the ears of contemporaries, this time they meant business. In place of the confessional or the spasmodic punishment, the miscreant now confronted the much more powerful combined forces of church and secular authority, which usually managed to bury their differences sufficiently to produce a much more effective system of moral policing.[145] Church and civil authorities cooperated in tightening control over festivals, fairs, mystery plays, and other popular amusements. In cities throughout Europe, new sumptuary laws attempted to limit expenditure on dress, restrict public dances and carnivals, and prohibit gambling and prostitution.

Pastors and priests would read out proclamations and orders from the central government. In Sweden, clergymen conducted and recorded annual catechism examinations of every parishioner, young and old. Most important, the clergy became responsible for one of the key instruments for regularizing family formation: marriage, birth, and death registers. In German lands, thorough and closely documented "visitations" by teams of lay and ecclesiastical officials from the central government questioned the locals about details of their religious life, noted the state of church buildings, the conduct of the clergy, church attendance, marriages, baptisms, communions, and burials, and the presence of heretics and of unorthodox religious beliefs.[146]

Each of these pieces of local ecclesiastical intelligence led to increased "governmentality": it had the potential to make not only local households but their individual members more visible to state authorities, and consequently more open to interventions such as systematic taxation or conscription. In England, for example, Cromwell's 1538 Injunctions for the Clergy, which made it mandatory for the clergy to register all births, deaths, and marriages in the parish, provoked widespread popular resentment, not least because people feared their use for taxation purposes.[147] In Sweden, arguably the first larger European state to attempt direct rule, large sectors of public administration were placed in the hands of Lutheran pastors, and the Lutheran catechism examination and other registers were used extensively as bases for increasing bureaucratic control of the population.[148]

According to Heinz Schilling and Wolfgang Reinhard, from about 1560 to 1650, this process of confessionalization constituted an inseparable part of the making of German territorial states. Confessionalization strengthened political centralization as the early modern state used religion to consolidate its territorial boundary, to incorporate the church into the state bureaucracy, to widen the field of state activities, and to impose social control on its subjects.[149] In turn, the parallel development of religious doctrines, systems of policing, and religious personnel devoted to enforcing and inspecting religious observance and uniformity helped to alter

popular mentalities and prepared the ground for the emergence of absolutist states by making people more visible, obedient, and disciplined. It was
confessional uniformity, rather than national bonds of some kind or national consciousness, which supplied the basis of social integration in these
early modern states. Indeed, according to Oestreich, disciplining inspired
by Neostoicism played a more important role in the expansion of absolutist
state power in the late seventeenth and eighteenth centuries than centralization, institutionalization, and rationalization. The spiritual, moral, and
psychological changes that social discipline produced in the (male) individual, whether he was engaged in politics, army life, or trade, Oestreich
argues, were far more fundamental, far more enduring, than institutional
changes in politics and administration.[150]

CHAPTER TWO

Patriarchalism Challenged

Chapter 1 described the consolidation of patriarchalism in early modern Europe. Powerful as it was, this social order rested on inherently unstable foundations; the articulation between different levels of patriarchal authority was far more complex than smooth analogies suggested. For one thing, the relative power of husbands and wives within the patriarchal household was the subject of continuous and heated debates, frequent amendments of myriad local and regional regulations and codes of law, and constantly shifting and contested domestic relations. The late medieval *querelle des femmes,* feminist texts of the Renaissance and their misogynist refutations, all shared a pervasive concern with questions of authority and subordination, in particular with the origin of the control of man over woman and with the rights of a woman who was subject to a male superior. Most often at stake was the autonomy with which the mistress of a substantial household could make moral, political, or economic judgments, particularly in light of the more or less absolute power and authority of her husband over her.[1] These debates accentuated the ambiguity of the political implications of marital relations. In most places, wives, unlike servants and children, were supposed to be subordinates to but also partners of their husbands; in some ways they shared authority as "joint governors" in managing the household, and they would frequently exercise patriarchal authority in the case of the husband's absence or death. Was the monarch (or magistrate) then to have authority analogous to a father, a husband, or simply the head of a household? And could the monarch be a woman, particularly a married woman?

In this chapter, I will look in more detail at four other issues. The first is the fact that the dominance of the household head was repeatedly undermined by increasingly powerful state institutions, even as they enforced injunctions to honor and obey fathers. The same was true of the intermediate strata of regional nobility, whose finely balanced local rule could be irreparably damaged by forceful intervention of central authorities. Second, the supposed absolute power of household heads did not necessarily lead, in theory or practice, to their subjection to the absolute authority of the crown (it certainly had not done so in medieval Europe). English Puritans, for example, anticipating arguments later systematized in liberal democratic theory, agreed that fathers had absolute authority in the family; ergo, authority in the state was that of *all* heads of households.[2] Conversely, whatever the complexion of the household, a growing number of political thinkers began to argue that it no longer provided an adequate model of state power.

Third, there was the problem of the subordination of adult males to the authority of masters and mistresses of households. At stake here were two complementary but increasingly incompatible principles of patriarchal governance—one giving precedence to adult men, simply by virtue of their maleness, over women and children; the other revolving around the power of the master and mistress to rule all others in the household, whatever their age, gender, or possible merit. Finally, whatever philosophers wrote and rulers commanded, the peasant household, the very foundation of a patriarchalist social order, began to lose its key position in the European countryside.

FAMILIAL PATRIARCHAL AUTHORITY UNDERMINED BY CHURCH AND STATE

In chapter 1, I argued that the Reformation and confessionalization helped put in place a patriarchalist social order. In the long run, however, the effects of these historical movements were more complex. As the example of education will show, they also contributed to reducing the power of household heads and increasing the capacities of centralizing governmental agencies.

The priesthood of all believers proclaimed by early Reformation movements implied that one did not need an official church, and that different believers might not necessarily have the same understanding of God's teachings. As Reformation theologians lost their original enthusiasm for changing the world and assumed common cause with territorial rulers, such views soon came close to heresy. In any case, as measured by the reformers' increasingly rigorous criteria, most household heads proved to be either too ignorant or too lazy to carry out their religious duties, or, alternately, so zealous that they spread dangerous heresies or even initiated the rise of independent congregations. In German lands, systematic visitations almost invariably found patriarchal power and discipline wanting: pastors poorly prepared to carry out their duties, popular immorality and disorder, ignorance of the catechism, and "disobedient children who do not treat their parents with the usual honour, but who treat them rather disgracefully and unscrupulously."[3] As faith was standardized and the faithful were inspected, the reformers began to see with awful clarity what was in a sense an artifact of their own making: the huge extent of un-Christian behavior and ignorance of the masters. The reformed churches, desiring both to foster and to control household worship, vacillated between stricter supervision of parishioners and edicts forbidding householders to venture beyond the repetition of approved texts. In the end, it was only in regions such as Sweden, where the church and the state were able to exercise close control over household heads, that the masters' educational duties remained integrated into state policy. Elsewhere, whenever resources permitted, authorities set up schools to accomplish what delinquent masters were manifestly unable to do: catechize and discipline the younger generation.

These issues are explored with particular clarity in *Luther's House of Learning* and a series of later articles by Gerald Strauss. In his pioneering work, Strauss placed the educational project of the German Reformation firmly within the problematic of confessionalization, social disciplining, and family formation.[4] The small Lutheran principalities of sixteenth-century Europe, he notes, saw some of the earliest experiments with mass state schooling in the West. In German lands, more than a hundred educational ordinances were laid down before 1600; of these, about forty explicitly called for the establishment of girls' schools alongside those for boys.[5] The first ordinances, directed at individual towns and cities, later provided a model for the reorganization of schools in the larger German provinces, and beyond them in Denmark and Norway. Each locality, they typically decreed, was to have at least one school and to cover most of its costs; each school was to conform to the methods and course of instruction laid down; and all boys and girls, usually between the ages of five and twelve, were to attend.[6]

The Lutheran states initially based their model of education on the household head, whose duty was to read the Bible and teach his dependents the appropriate Christian lessons. The beginnings of state schooling are to be found in the realization by Luther and his followers that not all heads of household were capable of doing or willing to do their Christian duty, that the Bible in the wrong hands might be subversive, and that the church alone was unable to produce the desired social change. "The common man can do nothing," wrote Luther in 1524. "He doesn't have the means for it, he doesn't want to do it, and he doesn't know how."[7] Reluctantly at first, and only dimly aware of the far-reaching consequences of their actions, the reformers turned to schools. At first they hoped that local communities would organize and tax themselves to provide formal schooling, but they soon concluded that voluntary, participatory procedures were inadequate to the gigantic task of reform. Only under worldly justice, they reasoned, was there some prospect of making an impression on the great body of non-believers, the young, the simple, the "wild crowd" that made up the over-whelming mass of fallen humanity. "If they themselves will not do it in the interests of their own salvation," wrote Luther to the Elector Johann of Saxony in 1526, "Your Grace has ample power to compel them." Surely a government that could send its subjects to war "can use even greater force to compel them to send their children to school." Most rulers, for their part, became convinced that the conscience of their subjects was the legitimate business of the Christian state; that, indeed, was one of the reasons they were called *patres patriae,* and why the government was in effect a "common father."[8]

Schools would train children, according to their respective station in life, "to become responsible men and women who can govern churches, countries, people, households, children, and servants."[9] More advanced and expensive schools for boys would educate, in Latin with a smattering of Greek and Hebrew, a new generation of godly preachers, governors, administrators, and householders who would carry out their God-given duties properly, while vernacular schools would catechize the rest of the boys and girls and teach them obedience to worldly and ecclesiastical authority. After initial enthusiasm about putting the Bible into the hands of all believers, Luther and his followers grew adamant about the need for expert interpretation of the Lord's word. "Nowadays everyone thinks he is a master of the Scripture," Luther complained in the 1520s, "and every Tom, Dick and Harry imagines he understands the Bible and knows it inside out." This was quite wrong, he went on:

> All the other arts and skills have their preceptors and masters from whom one must learn, and they have rules and laws to be obeyed and adhered to. Only Holy Scripture and the Word of God seems to be open to everybody's vanity, pride, whim and arrogance, and is twisted and warped according to everybody's own head. That is why we have so much trouble now with factions and sects.[10]

Since ignorant reading of the Bible could give people so many wrong ideas, the majority of men and all women should stick to memorizing the unambiguous questions and answers of the catechism. The Bible itself should be introduced only to those boys who had been properly prepared for it by six or seven years of systematic instruction, and even then in Latin rather than in German.[11]

I noted earlier that the Reformation of the early sixteenth century was associated with a downswing in a long agrarian cycle, when the pressure on land increased and patriarchal elders, local communities, and landlords were anxious to tighten controls over family formation. Strauss, without recourse to scholarly literature on family history, similarly believes that during this period, the head of household's authority in the family was put in question, at least as judged by the fact that reformers preached sermon after sermon deploring "this abominable form of disobedience" in which children chose their own marriage partners in opposition to their parents' wishes. "Every catechism made acquiescence in an arranged marriage a proof of loyalty to parents, the social order, and God" in a world that seemed to be going awry. As Strauss suggests, reformers believed that the "bonds of society were coming loose," and "that the repairing of these ties must be accomplished where they had their origin: in the family"—even if it required state intervention through schooling to do so.[12]

However, as Strauss comments, in those Lutheran principalities that set aside the family's traditional role in education in favor of administrative action directed by the state,

> even as they seemed to be mobilising all available resources of law and exhortation to strengthen the power of husband over wife, father over children, master over servants, [they] were engaged in draining the household association of essential responsibilities. Sermons and proclamations, religious tracts and law books extolled the authority of the paterfamilias. But the real object of these rhetorical acclaims of the fourth commandment was to inculcate in the population habits of submission and obedience leading beyond parents to the higher authorities governing state and church.

Gradually, the notion that reform could proceed from within the household and congregation was abandoned as a matter of practical policy. In principle, parents remained responsible for educating their offspring to the minimum standards of Christian citizenship. In practice, many states and state churches possessed, or developed during the sixteenth century, instruments for usurping parental responsibilities for the instruction of children.[13]

The "godly houses of learning" achieved mixed results. In terms of state-building and increased governmentality, the whole educational effort seems to have been a remarkable success. It is true that the progress of confessionalization was impeded by territorial nobility clinging to their feudal prerogatives and unwilling to concede jurisdiction over their subjects to central powers, and that many major cities, jealous of their traditions of self-government, refused to let themselves be inspected. Central authorities, they reasoned, had no business monitoring the contents of their inhabitants' minds. But in the German countryside, according to Strauss, the "visitations" were a bureaucrat's dream. Control was centralized, and lines of authority and jurisdiction were clearly designated. A network of officials fanned out over the country, reaching every village and hamlet. Everything was put in writing and filed away. The long questionnaires, probing questioning, and verbatim records of the answers that constituted the heart of the visitation procedure were equally useful to short-term administrative needs and to long-term planning. They were sufficiently alike from year to year to allow meaningful comparisons. Perhaps most important, they brought church and state into practical and intimate association while reinforcing the supremacy of the latter.[14] The inspection and policing of the faithful were not a monopoly of the Protestants. Trying to cope with identical difficulties in advancing their own reformation, Catholic rulers often adopted similar measures, including regular visitations.[15]

By the religious standards of Reformation leaders, however, confessionalization in general, and schools in particular, failed to reform the world. According to Strauss, the harder the visitors inquired, the more disheartening was the information brought to light. Certainly there were a few exemplary regions and a sprinkling of godly households elsewhere, and some Lutheran teachings, such as the ones on the housefather's authority, were eagerly taken up by those who stood to benefit from them. By all accounts, Lutheranism was more widely accepted and understood in urban areas than in the countryside, but most city communes refused to conduct visitations. Nevertheless, after three-quarters of a century or more of Christian instruction, the majority of parishioners in localities where Lutheranism became state religion were shockingly ignorant of even the rudiments of Evangelical religion and displayed a disheartening apathy toward it.

Even worse, people tenaciously clung to their old beliefs.

> People said the Lord's Prayer while casting lead to tell fortunes. They gathered occult substances on Christian holidays and invoked the names of the Father, the Son, and the Holy Ghost to protect chickens from hawks and humans from the evil eye. They rang church bells against storms and hail, addressed Christian prayers to the devil [and] used altar vessels to locate

missing objects. . . . Village healers cured cattle of worms by spitting three
times in appeal to the Trinity. Wise women called on God to bless the crystal
in which they saw the face of a thief. They concocted infusions of baptismal
water against bed-wetting and chanted gospel verses while curing or inflicting injury.[16]

Faced with popular demand for blessings and sacred objects, many Protestant pastors bent the rules and improvised rituals close to those of the
Catholics. Elsewhere, when confronted with the new religious doctrines,
laboring people kept their "superstitions," but grew increasingly uninter-
ested in religion as such. As religion became less useful in explaining and
managing the events of everyday life—a sick child, a dry well, missing
sheep, a hazardous journey to the market—a way was left open to explanations based on Enlightenment rationality.[17]

Visitation and other records have been used to suggest that the standards
of the new literal religiosity were little better in some Calvinist areas of
Germany and in the Dutch Republic, as well as in much of rural England,
Scotland, and Ireland. In all, the surviving evidence indicates a widespread
inability on the part of the reformers—in not just one, but several different
countries—to create an acceptably pious laity within the first century of the
Reformation.[18]

Popular indifference and resistance was made worse by theological dissension among the religious leaders themselves, particularly in the second
half of the sixteenth century. As a result of frequent doctrinal changes,
many ministers were removed from their pulpits, and those allowed to
remain were forced to make public recantations of their former beliefs.
Incessant disputes on the fine points of theology were forcing "lay people
and common folk to doubt the very articles of the faith and to hold the
preachers, indeed the entire religion, in contempt."[19] Certainly there were
regions where people clung to their reformed faith and were well-informed
about its teachings, but these often constituted minority, oppositional, or
even underground forms of religion. It is true that the efforts of sixteenth-
century Protestant and Catholic nobles, princes, prelates, and magistrates
to make religious education compulsory for their subjects did establish
extensive networks of parish schools throughout central and western Europe.[20] Educational provision became more centralized and systematic,
both in Protestant and in Catholic territories. In principle, all children able
to walk to school, church, or a sexton's house were expected to present
themselves for instruction. In practice, parental prerogatives over their
sons and daughters were too firmly entrenched to enable reformers and

teachers to do more than plead. Even if 70 percent of parishes in a district such as Saxony had schools before the outbreak of the Thirty Years' War in 1618, most had only a handful of boys and fewer or no girls, and even then for only a few weeks of the year.[21]

Half a century after Luther became disillusioned with housefathers' capacity to reform religion, a similar dynamic was played out in England with the Puritan challenge to the Anglican church. There, emphasis on the religious duties of heads of households had been part of the Protestant tradition since the early days of Protestant governments. But toward the close of the sixteenth century, household religion was given renewed significance by the Puritans as a remedy for what they saw as the shortcomings of the state church. At first the Puritans advocated a different, more democratic, form of church government. But with the suppression of this movement in the early 1590s, they put renewed emphasis on preaching, household discussion, and education. The household, ruled by godly fathers of families, became at least a supplement, and almost an alternative, to the parish ruled by "dumb dogs and hirelings." During this brief period, according to Hill, men could envisage bringing about fundamental reform in the state through reform in the household.[22]

But even as they pressed for reforms, many Puritans shared with the church hierarchy an uneasiness about family prayers and discussions. They tended to agree that not all men had assumed the perfection necessary to lead worship in their own families; many were not capable of repeating a sermon or catechizing their dependents. The church leaders often glimpsed an even more serious challenge in household worship: congregational independence and sectarian separatism. To guard against this, in 1583 the Anglican church proclaimed the first of many prohibitions of "all preaching, reading, catechism and other such-like exercises in private places and families whereunto others do resort, being not of the same family." This sentiment was expressed well in a treatise dedicated to Bishop Laud: Household worship should be extended to the whole family only if "the master . . . be well fitted and qualified thereunto, and presume not beyond his measure." He must "keep himself within the compass of his own charge, not admitting any [worshippers] of other places; for then he becomes offensive to the state, who hath, and that justly, a jealousy over all such assemblies." These fears were confirmed once the old ecclesiastical regime had broken down after 1640. Householders, particularly those of the "industrious sort," educated for more than two centuries by governments, priests, and volume upon volume of improving literature regarding their religious duties, had stepped in in place of the ministers. Many a master strove, as he had been exhorted to do, "to make his house a little church, to instruct every one of his family in the fear of God, to contain every one of them under holy discipline, to pray with them and for them." It was as extensions of such household prayers that many independent congregations broke from the established church.[23]

BUILDING THE EDUCATIONAL STATE IN ABSOLUTIST SWEDEN

In German lands, as we have seen, sixteenth-century educational projects made a significant contribution to state-building, even though contemporaries concluded that they failed to bring the literacy and doctrinal knowledge of the population to a satisfactory level. But there was one European region where *both* aspects of the process were remarkably successful: rural Sweden (of which Finland was a dependency), and to a lesser extent Denmark (which also controlled Norway and Iceland). A century after the first Lutheran experiments, and to some extent influenced by the Second Reformation associated with Pietism, literacy campaigns in Scandinavian countries taught virtually everyone how to read while building up detailed and precise state knowledge of local populations. In towns and cities, where about a tenth of the population lived, schools were set up much as in other parts of Europe. In the countryside, however, satisfactory knowledge of catechism and almost universal reading literacy was achieved in the late seventeenth and eighteenth centuries by using the family as the agency of instruction in accordance with Luther's original conception, albeit backed up by severe and effectively policed penalties against illiteracy and ignorance of basic religious knowledge.[24]

For historians of education, the case of Scandinavia illustrates several important points. First, in the right social conditions, the Reformation project of catechizing the society through godly families could work successfully. Second, as Johansson's pioneering work showed, nearly universal literacy could be achieved with only minimal intervention from schools.[25] Finally, as in central Europe, systematic education played a significant part in state-building. Bengt Sandin, who has reworked some of Johansson's evidence, placed the Scandinavian education campaigns squarely in the context of absolutist state formation and (even though he does not use the term) increasing governmentality.[26]

In the second half of the seventeenth century, the Swedish king and the church initiated a political and religious campaign that aimed at the universal diffusion of religious knowledge. In the countryside, this campaign focused not on schooling, but on the householder's duties to instruct all others under his authority in "reading, praying, and singing the word of God": the Catechism, excerpts from the Bible, psalms, prayers for home and the church. The Church Law of 1686, for example, said that children, farmhands, and maidservants should learn to read and "to see with their own eyes what God bids and commands them in His Holy Word," while a royal decree in 1723 ordered parents and guardians to "diligently see that their children applied themselves to book reading and the study of the lessons in Catechism." Although in many parishes clergymen, parish clerks, and other assistants contributed to the educational effort, the main responsibility, according to Johansson, rested with parents and godfathers.

To ascertain whether the king's subjects were doing their duty, parishes began keeping elaborate and detailed annual examination registers on all inhabitants between six years and old age. (The oldest extant ones date back to the 1620s.) In the registers, "parishioners are arranged according to district, village and household. The social position is stated for every individual within the household: husband, wife, son, daughter, maidservant, farmhand, lodger, and so on. Age, reading marks, and catechism knowledge are, together with names, noted in special columns." Ten of these were reserved for evaluating various types of knowledge.[27] The sanctions against dereliction of duty were simple and effective. Negligent householders were fined, with the money used for the instruction of poor children in the parish. At the same time, to be admitted to communion and to be confirmed, people had to be able to demonstrate, at annual examinations conducted by the church, an adequate level of reading and religious knowledge. Without confirmation, a person was not allowed to be married; indeed, "one who cannot read is nobody in the eye of the law." Fines and other punishments, such as the pillory, were imposed on those who did not turn up for interrogation. On the whole, the laws seemed to be diligently enforced. In any case, studies of church examination registers in Sweden suggest that by 1800, virtually the whole population was able to read familiar religious texts. Universal ability to write, however, was not achieved until the beginning of the twentieth century.

In his work, Sandin illuminates the many links between Swedish absolutism and the literacy campaigns. Certainly, many laboring people themselves wanted to learn to read (and write) for a variety of religious and secular purposes. But the Swedish absolutist state, engaged in an ambitious campaign of military conquest and consolidation, needed increased taxes and a continuous supply of new soldiers. To assemble these, the recording not only of wealth and taxes but of potential soldiers had to become more effective. The church registers were cross-checked with fiscal and other records, and aided in the compilation of lists of able-bodied men. The local minister knew the population better than most state bailiffs, and he could also testify that no farmhands were hiding away in the forests.[28] As Sweden became a great power in European politics in the seventeenth century, its central administration was reorganized and became more efficient. Both state and church officials argued that a close tie existed between the secular law and the law of God. A crime against one was a crime against the other, regardless of local customs or practicalities. Women might well have a tradition of independent authority in the countryside in an age when large numbers of men—often up to half of all the males in a parish—were drafted into the army and perished in distant lands.[29] The Catechism taught that obedience to God and King began with submission to one's father or husband. In this light, Sandin argues, the teaching of reading and of the Catechism should be seen less as an internal reformation within the Lutheran church than as "a consequence of the close cooperation between State and Church in a process of attempted state control over each and every aspect of rural life. . . . The Church Law [of 1686] made the Church into an integrated part of . . . absolutist state power, curbing the relative independence of local parish and diocese consistories in legal and religious matters." In this process, "the individual became visible not only as a taxpaying unit but also as an individual with a mind—a political mind, as religious attitudes were political—the control of which was seen as essential for the reproduction of social and political order."[30]

But many of these considerations applied to other absolutist states as well. What was different about Sweden? According to Sandin, the great majority of the rural population were not subject to the control of any local gentry. The manorial system was developed only in some parts of the country; elsewhere the centralizing state had to rely on the cooperation of the church and autonomous peasant village administration. Perry Anderson similarly argues that the Swedish form of absolutism was unique in a way that greatly contributed to its stability. In western Europe, an aristocratic absolutism typically ruled over non-servile peasantry and ascendant towns; in the east, it governed a servile peasantry and subjugated towns. In Sweden, by contrast, the peasantry was free, and the towns had little power and significance (this meant that they could not mount a challenge to aristocratic monopoly on political power); at the same time, the aristocracy was so small that it could neither subjugate the peasantry nor resist its own integration into a centralized monarchy. All this made for an unusually stable social order.[31] In these conditions, literacy campaigns helped build the local state.

At the height of its success, the Scandinavian educational system, based on household instruction and examination, began to be undermined by an accelerating process of proletarianization. From the mid-eighteenth century, the emergence of a large rural proletariat, enclosures, new villages, a modernized and commercial agriculture, all increased the numbers and mobility of the poor, and gave rise to demands for a school-based system of popular instruction. Here the numerous schools set up in seventeenth- and eighteenth-century Swedish towns provided a curious legacy. These schools were attended by the poorest boys, whom we would most expect to work, and shunned by those we would expect to attend. The reason was simple: schoolboys held an official monopoly on singing in churches, processions, weddings, and funerals, as well as on begging in the streets. For poor lads, to go to school was to gain a license to work at two of the most profitable of the modest options open to them. By the same token, seeing schools as mendicant institutions, wealthier citizens of the town shunned them and preferred to educate their sons and daughters at home. As begging and street processions were restricted by the state, school attendance ceased to be profitable to the poor. Faced with empty classrooms, many urban schools in Sweden tried to attract children with clothes, free meals, and sometimes even money.[32] In this case as in many others, social control could be exchanged only for institutional provisions deemed useful by the poor.

GOVERNMENTALITY AND ITS LIMITS

Debates about household worship and religious instruction were just one indication of a larger social dynamic: the political and administrative processes explicitly designed to strengthen the authority of family heads in early modern Europe paradoxically weakened their jurisdiction vis-à-vis increasingly powerful state authorities. Most of these new processes and institutions were welcomed and supported by influential sections of local communities. Invariably, villagers, both male and female, learned to use them for their own purposes, as a prominent part of their domestic strategies. Yet in many ways the same institutions also accelerated the current they were attempting to reverse, and undercut the very familial authority they were intended to uphold.[33] Several authors conclude detailed studies of particular regions in the sixteenth and seventeenth centuries by arguing that the net result was a bolstering of the centralization of bureaucratic authority at the expense of household heads and local nobility alike. According to Sabean, for example, while the early decades were marked by an ideology of patriarchal authority, in the later period competing institutions intervened directly in internal family affairs.[34] Similarly, Rebel, writing about early Hapsburg absolutism, argues that what were originally positions of patriarchal and feudal authority became, in the period around 1600, bureaucratic functions. A non-feudal legal-rational state order was grafted on to the feudal estates, making them administrative units of the state, and their owners and managers administrators and executors of state regulations. The heads of the peasant households were required to maintain, as before, the sacred peace and tranquillity of the house, but now were responsible for all who lived in the house not only to the lord but to bureaucratic state authorities.[35]

Robisheaux agrees that in sixteenth-century Germany, church and state embraced the ideal of the patriarchal family, and imposed, with the cooperation of village elders, as strict a marital discipline as the society would bear. Sixty years later, the old bonds of community and the patterns of domination rooted in the princes' *Herrschaft* were supplemented by hardening horizontal ties based on class and obedience to the territorial state. Absolute monarchs, aided by increasingly effective confessional, bureaucratic, and military resources, began making successful attempts to reach down all the way into individual households, with ordinances regarding matters such as the taxation, conscription, religion, or even education of their subjects. Where they were successful, they altered the day-to-day practices of domination, replacing personal ties of deference and protection, and the subtle give-and-take of power associated with these, with impersonal extortion and dictate.[36]

And yet the advances in governmentality had strict limits. With the exception of Sweden, the strictly educational campaigns of the Reformation and its aftermath were a sad failure. But more than that, confessionalization could mobilize resistance to the consolidation of princely power. The struggles between princes and cities, central government and estates, "foreign" nobility and local peasantry, were often played out in confessional confrontations.[37] Indeed, the link between Reformation and state formation could take many forms. In many regions, radical strands of Reformation theology survived in more or less systematic forms of oppositional Christianity. In the city-state belt in southern and central Germany, the Reformation offered an important base of resistance to centralizing monarchs. In England and the Nordic countries, rulers promoted and co-opted their own versions of the Reformation, which established extensive state control over the religious apparatus and close cooperation between clergy and lay officials in local administration. Elsewhere, as in the Netherlands, Protestantism provided an attractive doctrinal basis for resistance to imperial authority, especially authority buttressed by claims of divinely sanctioned royal privilege.[38]

But there were also what could be called technical limits to the possibilities of governmentality. Military historians, as I noted in chapter 1, consistently claim that until the second half of the seventeenth century, at least, no one ruler had the military capacity to enforce his power over the nobility. The resulting fragmentation of power made nonsense of any neat pyramid of paternalist authority, where the monarch would hold comparable everyday power over the nobility that the lords themselves held over their households and peasants. By the same token, it made unthinkable any form of detailed centralized rule over individual subjects. In a later period, a monopoly on violence and taxation would become one of the bases of competing bureaucratic-based forms of direct governance. In early modern Europe, territorial rulers found it difficult enough to strengthen and maintain a patriarchalist system of indirect rule.

Centralizing states, feudal lords, princes, administrators, parliaments, and monarchies in seventeenth- and eighteenth-century Europe disrupted, constrained, and reorganized household-based patriarchal power. Yet they were unable to relinquish their reliance on patriarchalist forms of governance. Certainly they greatly expanded the bureaucratic capacities that would eventually become the mainstay of state power. But bureaucratic authority, with its surveillance, uniform rules and procedures, collection of statistics, and flow of information to the center and of directives to the periphery, was impossible without substantial sums of money and reasonably speedy means of transport and communication. It is true that most seventeenth- and eighteenth-century European states achieved a far larger tax base than their predecessors. Yet their program of territorial integration and administrative centralism, and even their attempts to create national markets, were limited by their meager (by modern standards) financial resources—particularly when the bulk of this money was spent in fighting costly wars. As long as the means of transport and communication remained slow, costly, and cumbersome, the center had no means of exercising detailed supervision of its regional officers, and in any case had an extremely patchy and imprecise idea of local conditions. Hobsbawm notes that even though the late eighteenth century was, by medieval or sixteenth-century standards, an age of abundant and speedy communication, for most people the world was incalculably vast. Those who conducted government business or commerce were by no means cut off from one another. Yet it was easier to link seaports and distant capitals than country and city. In the 1760s, the journey from London to Glasgow still took ten or twelve days; the news of the fall of the Bastille reached the populace of Madrid within thirteen days, one day before it was received in Peronne, a bare 133 kilometers from the capital.[39]

In a passage that could have come from a text on historical materialism, Foucault similarly notes that until the eighteenth century, massive and elementary historical factors blocked advances in governmentality. "The art of government could only spread and develop in subtlety in an age of expansion, free from the great military, political and economic tensions which afflicted the seventeenth century from beginning to end." It was only the centralization of political power, the consolidation of territorial states, a changing balance of military powers, and economic transformations, coupled with the beginnings of exponential population growth, that finally made possible the de-restriction of the art of government, and the recentering of the theme of economy on a different plane from that of the family.[40]

Even in absolutist France, monarchic authority had only a partial influence on what came to be known as the provincial level, and hardly any, or none at all, in local government. Virtually complete local autonomy prevailed in the fields of justice, religion, schools, administration, and police. There were still 360 local legal codes, as well as a division between customary and Roman law, on the eve of the Revolution of 1789.[41] Individual or corporate authorities had control of the land and of those who worked it, of the rights of patronage, and of police activity, without any interference from the new administration of the sovereign state.[42] What counted as centralization of the state in the seventeenth and even the eighteenth century was to a large extent the success of central administration in securing the cooperation of local officeholders. Indeed, most public offices depended on the capacity of men of substance to mobilize authority—and deference—by drawing on the social standing, power, and resources of themselves and their families.

In eighteenth-century England, much of public business was likewise an extension into government of private social relationships. Most office-holding was seen as a burden that men of quality owed to the community—a service for which they were eminently qualified because of their virtue, talents, independence, and prominence. Before dense institutional networks were established in Europe's colonial outposts, local officeholders relied to an even greater extent on their own social respectability, influence, connections, and power to command public allegiance, deference, and obedience. Here, even the law courts were collections of prominent amateurs, whose limited knowledge of legal matters was offset by the social respect they commanded in the local community. Those who had the property and power to exert influence in any way—whether by lending money, doing favors, or supplying employment—created obligations and dependencies that could be turned into political authority. Not surprisingly, they were not always willing to use this authority in supporting central administration.[43]

Finally, scholars who have studied in detail the actual exercise of power at the village level stress that the process of state-building and social control did not simply flow from the top down. Not only have peasant revolts repeatedly upset the balance of noble power, but their resistance helped shape the transition to agrarian capitalism and give it its final form. The "Byzantine complexity" of social life in the village, according to Robisheaux, reflected not simply the growth of state power as it shaped the social order, but also the real limits to state domination, the tentative and conditional use of state power, and the subtle uses and often ironic consequences of paternalism and deference. "The villagers themselves knew where the power lay in their communities, and they understood how to lay their hands on a share of it."[44] As E. P. Thompson noted with regard to eighteenth-century England "The poor might be willing to award their deference to the gentry, but only for a price. . . . Seen in this way, the poor imposed upon the rich some of the duties and functions of paternalism just as much as deference was in turn imposed upon them."[45]

PATRIARCHS AGAINST MEN

The intricacies of governmentality, confessionalization, and state formation provide an important and necessary perspective on the consolidation and subsequent decline of a patriarchalist social order. But patriarchalism was also challenged—and rebuilt—on other fronts. The following two sections will look at the way it came under increasing practical and theoretical pressure from disenfranchised men. Their "fraternalism"—new modes of association, political theories, and ideals—proclaimed at one and the same time the equality of (most white) men and their categorical superiority over all women. The final part of the chapter will return to the dynamics of populations, families, and economies, and consider some of the effects of increasing proletarianization.

Throughout early modern Europe, restrictions on marriage, coupled with an accelerating process of social polarization, prolonged the period of semi-dependency between childhood and mastery. Increasing numbers of men found it difficult to "grow out of" class-based dependency on masters and mistresses of households, a status resembling in some respects the subordinate position of women. Lyndal Roper teases out some of the complexities of this issue in her study of the historical meanings attached to the familiar Reformation figure, the "common man," in early modern Augsburg. She argues that the common man was imagined, in the early sixteenth-century urban commune, as the craftsman capable of bearing weapons; "common woman," in contrast, meant a prostitute: "While the common woman stood for all that was papist and ungodly, the common man embodied what was decent, upright and populist in the early Reformation movement." For many key ceremonial purposes, community was an assembly of such men, with women required to stay indoors. There was, however, another current vision of the common man as the head of a house, a social father figure under whose governorship servants, wife, children, apprentices, and journeymen lived. He could thus be seen as the representative of his house in the wider household of the commune. This was a role that was to be increasingly theorized in the literature of the Reformation and post-Reformation era. Yet in the early-sixteenth-century town, this was an obviously contradictory political principle: widows, who headed households, were not politically common men; and sons, servants, and apprentices, who swore the communal oath, were not governors of households. Roper speculates that in early modern German towns, "perhaps what the sixteenth century witnessed was a shift from a sense of political inclusion based on military capacity towards one centred on the notion of fatherhood, both biological and social."[46]

Although standard histories of youth pay little attention to such issues, there is some evidence that many men, disenfranchised by their subordination to household heads, began redefining traditional associations of youths and inventing new fraternal cultural practices and institutions that affirmed and celebrated their masculinity while opposing both women and many aspects of patriarchalist power.[47] In *A History of Youth*, Mitterauer stresses the key function of fraternities in traditional rural societies of western, central, and northern Europe, but has little to say about their potential as alternative forms of patriarchal power and association. Fraternities played a key role in regulating sexual relations and courtship practices among unmarried people, and often also in policing unwritten rules of community morality and behavior. In some areas they engaged in displays of military prowess; in many cities they were integrated into the militia. Urban fraternities, providing economic assistance to their members and serving as centers of conviviality, can also be seen as the precursors of union organization.[48]

Gillis, in his influential *Youth and History,* similarly regards fraternities as forms of homosocial organization that complemented, rather than challenged, a patriarchalist social order. According to him, in the seventeenth and eighteenth centuries, the concept of brotherhood, and to a lesser extent sisterhood, gave form and meaning to most of the institutions, apart from the household, with which a (male?) youth came in contact. Urban and rural fraternities policed the morality of their members and sometimes of whole communities, not least as initiators of charivaris. They provided a surrogate family for apprentices and journeymen, and gave positive meaning to the long years of celibacy before most men were able to marry. On occasion, journeymen's fraternities could serve as places of agitation and organization against abusive masters, from which strikes and boycotts could be carried forth and class-based organizations could develop. On the whole, however, they provided powerful controls over youths, supporting rather than disrupting the order of a patriarchalist society. Gillis also notes that "eighteenth-century traditions of fraternity, particularly the Masonic and the academic, were to take on an increasingly political meaning *after* the French Revolution." However, he attributes this above all to the secretive nature of the brotherhoods and, beyond noting that some student reformers retained the same distrust of female companionship that was evidenced in earlier Pietist and Masonic movements, has little to say about the gender implications of their political involvement.[49]

In a 1980 article, Mary Ann Clawson prefigured a different emphasis when she argued that fraternal organizations both supported and undermined patriarchal authority. Like other writers, Clawson noted that fraternalism had long and complex historical roots in various late medieval and early modern organizations (such as fraternities, guilds, and youth abbeys), which over centuries elaborated and practiced modes of relations, address, behavior, and organization based on the categorical exclusion of women and the idea that men could participate and hold power in gradations according to age and merit, regardless of their status as householders. These organizations, which often set up surrogate kin groups under the rule of fictive fathers, both upheld patriarchal social order and morality, and protected the members' distinct, often class-based interests: "Fraternal institutions were critically linked to the authority structures of the patriarchal household in a relationship that was sometimes antagonistic, often supportive, but always close."[50] Importantly, Clawson notes that fraternal youth organizations developed only among those groups who could either anticipate an eventual succession to patriarchal authority or assert their moral right to it. They were not found among servants, casual laborers, or young women, only among journeymen and peasants.[51] A similar line of thought has subsequently inspired important research into fraternal forms of organzation in early modern Europe.

Merry Wiesner, in her work on guilds and male bonding in early modern Germany, has argued convincingly that the gradual exclusion of women (whether craftswomen in their own right or servants, wives, daughters, or widows of male craft masters) from guilds was closely linked to increasing emphasis on "male honor" by the journeymen. The earliest guild ordinances in Germany, from the late thirteenth to the early fifteenth century, did not regard craft work as a male preserve. Craftsmen almost certainly outnumbered craftswomen, but guild regulations routinely referred to male and female apprentices and masters, and even to a few all-female guilds. From the late fifteenth century, however, there is increasing evidence of attempts to exclude women from craft work. Two centuries later, some craftsmen were in a position to boycott all masters who allowed women into the workshop, and to refuse to work alongside any journeyman who was known to have worked in such "dishonorable" shops, or who had parents who practiced a "dishonorable" domestic-based trade, such as milling or linen-weaving, in which women continued to participate.[52] Boycotts and strikes, in other words, were organized not only to get better wages and conditions, but also to achieve and preserve new forms of homosociality: the exclusive masculinity of the most valued craft work.

Elaborating on this theme, Jean Quataert argues that the proto-industrial challenge to craft work from the sixteenth century onward was redefined by the craftsmen in gender terms. According to the new codes of honor they developed and increasingly managed to enforce (frequently against their own immediate economic interests), girls could work as servants but not as apprentices, married women must be maintained by their husbands and not engage in any "regular manufacture," and the household must cease producing goods for sale. In the end, only work that could be clearly dissociated from the household economy came to be designated as honorable. In a world obsessed with status, breaking any of these strictures could cause the household members and their work to be shunned as dishonorable by respectable folk. These fiercely defended ideals anticipated, by a good century, Evangelical and Romantic ideals of the separate spheres appropriate to men and women.[53] Arguably, they made a significant contribution to the changing status of women in various regions and social groups, and indeed to the consolidation of polar and exclusive gender categories as such. Paradoxically, by attempting to exclude the female members of the master's household from craft production, they depreciated the economic value of marriage and families—one of the original grounds for the industrious classes' support for the Reformation.

Indeed, many journeymen's associations were not only anti-women but against marriage and family itself, and this again could not be explained on economic grounds alone. The prohibition on marriage was originally seen as part of the life cycle when a journeyman resided in his master's household, before establishing a family on becoming a master in his turn. The craft masters themselves, as we have seen, formed the bulwark of Reformation revaluation of marriage and the patriarchal household. In contrast, as their own opportunities to establish independent workshops began diminishing in the sixteenth century, many journeymen turned restrictions imposed upon them into virtues. Rather than push for the right to marry, they expected each other to remain single, and fervently opposed allowing any married journeyman the right to work. Instead of setting up their own households, they often asserted the right to live in all-male journeymen's hostels, and in some cases they pressured guilds that originally had accepted married journeymen to forbid them. In addition, journeymen's associations also banned, sometimes effectively, any member known to frequent prostitutes.

Indeed, in many Protestant cities, the closure of brothels, formerly the pleasure ground of unmarried men, resulted in an even sharper alignment of heterosexual experience with masterhood.[54] The new forms of male bonding among journeymen, elaborated in complex rituals, indelibly marked a particular form of masculinity, separate from that of the masters and increasingly distinct from that proposed by religious and political authorities. "Transience, prodigality, physical bravery and comradliness made one a true man among journeymen, in sharp contrast to the masters' virtues of thrift, reliability and stability." To the master craftsmen, honor involved being the husband and father at the head of a patriarchal household; to the journeymen, it was linked with an increasingly class-specific fraternity and exclusion of women.[55] The masculinity of the masters helped to define and was strengthened by the Protestant ethic; that of the apprentices and journeymen tended to undermine it. Journeymen in Protestant areas might well have taken part in ridiculing single-sex communities of monks and nuns and advocating the closure of convents and monasteries, but they passionately defended their own forms of homosocial organization.

Issues such as these were markers of an increasing polarization within guild and craft organizations. Many large masters found that their interests no longer coincided with those of the majority of workers in their craft; the increasingly militant demands of poor journeymen were often directed at the new production methods and work organization favored by their wealthy employers. In England, for example, by 1500 most fraternal guilds reestablished themselves as chartered craft companies under the aegis of municipal civil authority. In the process, they formalized significant distinctions of status, function, and wealth by creating "liveries" of merchant traders and larger craft masters distinct from "yeomanries" of smaller masters, journeymen, and covenant servants, who made up the major part of the craft's workforce. While the livery concentrated on devices that limited entry to mastership, the yeomanry pursued, with increasing militancy, traditional rights to search out illegal products and illegally employed strangers and apprentices. By the late seventeenth century, most large merchants and masters had no more use for such limitations on production and employment. In the following decades, many craft organizations split into antagonistic combinations of masters and merchants on one side and journeymen on the other.[56]

This process of polarization coincided with attempts to reassert and strengthen central powers. As part of this process, already established group entities such as boroughs and guilds were reinvented as creations of the crown through royal charters or franchises affirming their rules and legitimating their existence. Thenceforth, associations acting without leave, or engaging in unsanctioned activities, were deemed to constitute a challenge to royal prerogative, and could be tried and prosecuted for conspiracy against the crown. By the eighteenth century, conspiracy was routinely invoked against journeymen's associations simply because their bare existence was unsanctioned by the crown and therefore illegal. The journeymen's efforts to continue unilaterally the corporate traditions that had earlier structured social and economic relations within crafts increasingly came up against the joint opposition of employers and the state. The laws of conspiracy developed during this period were to play a crucial role in nineteenth-century labor struggles in Britain and the United States.[57]

While craft workers gradually redefined their interests and masculinity through journeymen's associations, more privileged men were finding a parallel site of fraternal association in student fraternities, literary salons, and Masonic lodges. According to Gillis, from the seventeenth century, middle- and even upper-class men began to join masons' lodges, which had their origins in the craft organizations of traveling builders. Attracted by both the exotic character and the forms of sociability the lodges offered, these men began to elaborate what would become highly influential forms of fraternal organization. By the early eighteenth century, some of the "operative" lodges of practicing craftsmen were transformed into "speculative" lodges offering their middle-class members "refreshment, smoking and conversation, in circumstances of ease rather than elegance, [rational pleasure] undisturbed by the society of women." In 1717 the first Grand Lodge of this new freemasonry was founded in England, the beginning of a movement that spread quickly to the rest of Europe and to other parts of the world. For men affected by the Enlightenment suspicion of organized Christianity, Freemasonry offered a surrogate religion. Disaffected by the exorbitant social and economic demands of the court and the salon, unhappy about prevailing forms of patriarchalism and deference, men found a republican society that prided itself on brotherly affection and sincerity, "real Worth and personal Merit." According to Gordon Wood, "It would be difficult to exaggerate the importance of Masonry for the American Revolution": many of the revolutionary leaders were members of the fraternity, which had since produced more than a dozen American presidents.[58] Similarly, "the runaway popularity of Freemasonry" in France has been seen by some historians as an integral part of the "democratic sociability" whose principles and practices they identify as *the* motor of the French Revolution. According to these writers, in eighteenth-century French philosophical societies, rank and birth were second to abstract oratorical ability: "the highest social circles, the academies, the masonic lodges, the cafes and theatres, . . . gradually fused into an Enlightened society, very largely aristocratic yet also open to non-noble talent and money"[59]—but predominantly, if not always totally, closed to women. The "Republic of Letters" as a whole may have served, as Habermas and others have argued, as a prototype for the (manly) politics of the republican public sphere, and this regardless of the exact message delivered by any individual or group.[60] When a theoretical challenge to the patriarchalist social order became influential in the late seventeenth century, it intersected at many points with the traditions of fraternal organizations.

*****

Many of the regions where patriarchal authority was strengthened during the Reformation, then, also witnessed the growth of masculinist but anti-patriarchalist institutions. Over time, many fraternal associations transformed notions of age-based subordination into new principles of manly association polarized along class lines. Even though guilds gradually lost their control over most aspects of the production process, they left a lasting legacy to the gendering of personal identities, work, and political life. In addition to being one of the sources of the ideology and practice of separate spheres, the fraternal journeymen's organizations, stressing the dignity of male labor and the exclusively masculine nature of the "mysteries of craft," helped engender the civic organization of many European towns, with perhaps their strongest impact in Germany.[61] They also strongly influenced the gendering of work, technology, and workers' organizations during the industrial revolution, and more generally acted as "seedbeds of fraternity as a popular belief."[62] These forms of fraternity were complemented by institutions that catered to men from higher social strata, such as Freemasons, societies of university students, even the Republic of Letters. In turn, early attempts to suppress journeymen's associations built up a legacy of conspiracy laws which played a crucial part in debates about the legitimacy of nineteenth-century working-class organizations, and in the prosecutions mounted against early unions.

BROTHERS AND CITIZENS

In early modern Europe, the concepts of adulthood and legal personality overlapped with that of (active) citizenship: some boys would grow up to be masters and citizens; only a handful of women would do so, provisionally, for brief periods of time. Masters of independent means, moreover, were reckoned much more masterful than others; for most intents and purposes, men of the increasingly numerous "industrious classes" were excluded from government and politics. Patriarchalist political theory explained and justified this social order by reference to the natural government of households: political rule was ideally built up of ascending pyramids of patriarchal power, with higher authorities commanding the same natural and irrevocable respect and obedience from their subjects that children owed to their fathers, and wives to their husbands.[63]

The English Civil War of 1642–46 and the Glorious Revolution of 1688 are often identified as turning points in the articulation of radically different visions of politics. On the Continent, similar developments are usually dated from the Peace of Westphalia, which ended the Thirty Years' War in 1648. In England, Germany, and France, an increasingly influential group of social contract theorists gradually came to reject most (though not all) of the axioms of patriarchalist political theory. Monarchs and their advisers tried to build up bureaucracies and formulate the principles of administrative political rule while maintaining a firm personal hold on power. Social contract theorists moved in a different direction. Their arguments typically started by claiming that the family itself was not, should not be, or need not be characterized by the despotic and absolute rule of the father and husband, and therefore did not provide a clear model of natural and lifelong patriarchal subordination for the rest of society. In their support, enlightened educational writers typically argued that "parental tyranny" had dire social consequences. To prevent strife and disappointment, children should be brought up firmly but lovingly and without violence to internalize the appropriate moral virtues. Similarly, the authority of husbands and the subordination of wives should be based on love and respect rather than force. In what was almost invariably seen as the more powerful, serious, and influential part of the argument, social contract theorists went on to assert that in any case familial and political rule were distinct and did not and should not obey the same principles, not least because the family stood outside politics. Political authority and obligation, they concluded, were conventional rather than natural, and political subjects were civil equals. Whatever was thought appropriate for daughters and wives, sons were born free and equal and, as adults, were free like their fathers before them. Government was possible and necessary as a result of a social contract entered into by these men. What they lost in giving up their natural liberty, Rousseau added in his *Social Contract* (1762), they more than compensated for by gaining in civil and moral liberty. The individualist premises of social contract theories were considerably different from Cameralist doctrines, which held that the individual's private pursuit of happiness was legitimate only to the extent that it coincided with the needs of the state.

Generations of radical critics, increasingly joined by feminist commentators, have drawn attention to the fact that even in theory the demise of patriarchalism as the organizing principle of political life did not mean that all children would grow up to be equal under the law. The relationship between sons and fathers might have become more democratic, but women remained subordinate to men and workers to employers in patriarchally governed private spheres of the home and "private enterprise" respectively. "Natives" were likewise assumed to require life-long tutelage.

Seen in this way, the educational writings of social contract theorists assume new political significance. It is here that the psychological preconditions of new forms of democratic relations are explored, the boundaries of the private and the public are experimentally redrawn, and the exclusion of some types of people from the political nation is justified. Indeed, Jay Fliegelman and Gordon Wood go so far as to argue that Locke's educational treatise, with its compelling arguments against absolute domestic power of the paterfamilias, was more influential in transforming the ideology and practice of American society in the late eighteenth century than were his explicitly political writings. A domestic republicanism prepared the ground for political republicanism in an age when debates about the relationship of colonies to Britain between Whigs and Tories frequently resembled a quarrel over the proper method of child-rearing.[64] Where Wood and Fliegelman emphasize the political implications of new forms of relations between the generations, feminist scholars point to the radically different educations that writers such as Rousseau envisaged for boys and for girls.

As recapitulated over two centuries by thousands of philosophers, liberal politicians, and political scientists, the logic of social contract arguments applied to all people, male or female. Yet a closer reading of the texts shows that the fathers of liberal democratic theory invariably ended up agreeing with their patriarchalist opponents that women, as future wives, remained naturally subject to men and husbands.[65] In *Some Thoughts Concerning Education*, Locke discusses the best ways of bringing up gentlemen's sons. As Neostoic authors had done before him, he put great emphasis on acquiring rational mastery over one's desires as the foundation of virtue: "the great Principle and Foundation of all Vertue and Worth, is placed in this, That a Man is able to *deny himself* his own Desires, cross his own Inclinations, and purely follow what Reason directs as best, tho' the appetite lean the other way."

Children must be made obedient, and parents must establish, as soon as possible, entire and absolute authority over them. But this should be done through affection, reason, benevolence, and understanding rather than force, love rather than fear and violence, guided freedom rather than constraint, in behavior as in dress. While *Some Thoughts Concerning Education* is specifically about boys, Locke's several brief mentions of girls reflect nothing of Rousseau's fear and contempt of women: the same principles, it seems, should be applied to the early upbringing of both sons and daughters.[66] In his *Second Treatise on Civil Government*, Locke even spends several paragraphs toying with the theoretical possibility of different forms of limited marriage contracts, and the wife's "liberty to separate from [the husband] where natural right or their contract allows it,"[67] before acknowledging that in the last instance familial rule "naturally falls to the man as the abler and the stronger."[68] Such musings are left behind in central discussions of citizenship, which assume that once women are married in current social and political conditions, they will inevitably be subordinated to their husbands and subsumed in their status as citizens.[69]

Locke's treatises on government are undoubtedly addressed to men. When he argues eloquently that man being born . . . with a title to perfect freedom and an uncontrolled enjoyment of all the rights and privileges of the law of nature, equally with any other man . . . in the world, hath by nature a power not only to preserve his property, that is, his life, liberty, and estate, against the injuries and attempts of other men, but to judge and punish breaches of that law in others[70]

"man" does not include woman, whatever individual women and men might have read into his words.

Like Locke, the Frenchman Jean Jacques Rousseau stressed that self-mastery alone allows one an independence of all other masters and enables one eventually to live within society yet uncorrupted by the servile dependencies it encourages. Rousseau, however, rejected Locke's claim that the best way to educate children was to reason with them, and instead argued for a "natural education," skillfully contrived by Providence and guided by a tutor's hidden hand.[71] Self-mastery, however, had completely different connotations for men and for women. "When a man renounces liberty he renounces his essential manhood, his rights, and even his duty as a human being," Rousseau wrote in *The Social Contract*.[72] Yet women, according to Book 5 of *Emile*, "must be trained to bear the yoke from the first so that they may not feel it: to master their own caprices and submit themselves to the will of others." Throughout their lives, women "will have to submit to the strictest and most enduring restraints, those of propriety." They need above all to be taught self-control: "the life of a good woman is a perpetual struggle against self." Her self-control, however, is in no way a preparation for mastery:

> This habitual constraint produces a docility which woman requires all her life long, for she will always be in subjection to a man . . . and she will never be free to set her own opinion above his. . . . She should learn early to submit to injustice and to suffer the wrongs inflicted on her by her husband without complaint.[73]

Men should be educated to be true to themselves, uncontaminated by fashion and culture; women should be educated to please men:

> A woman's education must . . . be planned in relation to a man. To be pleasing in his sight, to win his respect and love, to train him in childhood, to tend him in manhood, to counsel and console, to make his life pleasant and happy, these are the duties of woman for all time, and this is what she should be taught when she is young.[74]

To paraphrase Donzelot, Rousseau imagined internalized coercion for young women, protected freedom for young men.[75] One suspects that while the first four books of Rousseau's educational treatise won him lasting fame, it was the fifth, on educating Sophy, which came uncomfortably close to actual enlightened educational practice for the masses.

Accordingly, in commenting on the debates between patriarchalists and social contract theorists, feminist scholars argue that what in fact took place was a contest between champions of two different forms of patriarchy, rather than one between patriarchalists and the proponents of civil equality of all people. According to Pateman, equality, liberty, and fraternity should be understood literally; in the realm of political theory, at least, a contract between free and equal brothers replaced the "law of the father" with public rules that bound all men equally as brothers. Women remained subject to men, but under a different set of rules.[76]

As radical commentators have repeatedly pointed out, nor did Locke and most other detractors of patriarchalism intend their principles to apply to all men. Undoubtedly influenced by contemporary laws and practices relating to masters and servants, seventeenth-century English Levellers saw the suffrage as the birthright of all English men (not women), but considered that servants (including wage laborers) and beggars, through their dependence on others, had forfeited their birthright to a voice in elections.[77] Politically, servants, apprentices, women, and children were simply "included in their masters."[78] Locke insisted on the contractual nature and limitations of the relation between master and servant, yet assumed that while in his employ, the servant would be placed "into the Family of his Master and under the ordinary Discipline thereof."[79] Indeed, Locke assumed that while the laboring class was a necessary part of the nation, its members were not in fact full members of the body politic and had no claims to be so, not least because, not having property, they could not live a fully rational life.[80] In turn, the man who had not shown the ability to accumulate property was not a full man, and could therefore hardly be expected to govern his family. Similarly, the German philosopher Immanuel Kant confidently asserted that "women in general . . . have no civil personality, and their existence is, so to speak, purely inherent." A like fate befell those men whom social circumstances required to be another's servant or to enter into the employment contract. As such, they lacked the criterion for possession of "civil personality" and so were excluded from citizenship.[81]

* * * * *

Citizenship, in summary, required the capacity for self-mastery and rational thought, and was held to be incompatible with personal dependence. Children, married women, the insane, servants, and wage workers were by definition dependent on others. Like the poor, even noble ladies were thought to lack the capacity for fine reasoning; neither did their bourgeois sisters have the daily experience of rational calculation of gain that the active control of wealth gave male owners of capital; besides, all females naturally lacked self-control, except for its gentler forms such as chastity, frugality, and industry.[82] For all disenfranchised groups, the apparent promise of liberalism, coupled with the restrictions on their own rights, proved a continuing spur to action for change.

PROTO-INDUSTRIAL HOUSEHOLDS

The challenge to patriarchalism represented by fraternalism and liberal political theory occurred in the context of profound social change. As we saw earlier, it is estimated that about a third of the population of Europe in 1500 were proletarians of one kind or another. Over the following three centuries, the emergence and consolidation of national and international markets in grain and manufactured products, the abolition of multiple entitlements to land, the spread of capitalist farming, the emergence of a vigorous market in land, the enclosure of the commons, and the concentration of land ownership all contributed to the gradual proletarianization of the European population. By the mid-eighteenth century, only a minority of people were born to property-holding peasant or artisan households. In Britain, where this process was occurring most rapidly, by 1600 at least a third of the population no longer had any access to land or craft; of those who did, only a minority actually owned the land they farmed. By 1790, some 85 percent of English land was farmed by tenant farmers.[83] Elsewhere in Europe—and North America—the peasant economy survived into the nineteenth century, but arguably lost many of its erstwhile political, religious, and educational functions. The social foundation of the patriarchalist social order was eroded, and with it many of the effective checks on increased population growth.

In early modern Europe, as I argued in chapter 1, householders, aided by church and civic authorities, were remarkably successful in confining, disciplining, or at least moving on the masterless poor. Over time, however, increasing numbers of those without property managed to form new families. Some subsisted on a combination of waged work, cultivation of a scrap of garden or field, and the keeping of a cow, a goat, or a few chickens or rabbits. Those even poorer found it difficult to live together in any semblance of a settled household; some invented forms of temporary marriage to suit their predicament. In England, horrified mid-seventeenth-century observers thought that "vagabonds be generally given to horrible uncleanness, they have not particular wives, neither do they range themselves into families, but consort together as beasts."[84] A substantial proportion of land-poor and landless country people nevertheless managed to eke out a living in a new form of viable family economy, one based on proto-industrial production. It is this family form that assumes a key role in many demographers' accounts of European population growth.

As peasants lost their land and the numbers of smallholders multiplied, many households attempted to increase their income by producing handicraft goods for sale. What was initially a means of supplementary income for women and children in the off season sometimes developed into the major or even the sole source of subsistence.[85] The first regions of relatively dense rural industry had developed in England, the southern Low Countries, and southern Germany in the late Middle Ages.[86] By the eighteenth century, "dense rural manufacturing industries which produced for supra-regional markets covered Europe like a veil."[87] In their fully developed form, proto-industrial households were organized around domestic production of commodities such as cloth, nails, lace, gloves, straw hats, buckles, or cutlery for regional and often international markets. As in the peasant economy, the household remained a unit of production, but one that contained different internal dynamics and related differently to the rest of society. Historians originally believed that most of these households approximated to a single model; more recently they have acknowledged that it is impossible to establish one behavioral pattern for all proto-industrial populations. The branch of industry in question, the concrete shape of the work process, the availability of raw materials, the strength and form of local corporate and class relations, the underlying agrarian system, and the extent and nature of the combination of agrarian and industrial activities, all gave rise to quite different proto-industrial household forms.[88] Nevertheless, several tendencies did distinguish such households from those of the peasants.

Patriarchal relations, so prominent in the peasant economy (and urban guilds), were frequently altered and weakened both within and outside the proto-industrial household. Even though it could function as a subsidiary form of employment for a lower class in a society dominated by wealthy peasants, cottage industry typically flourished in regions where patriarchalist authority was already weak and guild control did not reach—in forest settlements, freehold villages, urban suburbs, mountainous regions, and on poor land—and it further contributed to the weakening and transformation of this authority.[89] Many historians argue that proto-industrial regions tended to be more independent-minded and rebellious than agricultural ones. Writing about England, Levine argues that "the opportunity for intellectual independence afforded by . . . proto-industrial mode of production was crucial to the emergence of a world-view that was not interpreted according to the patriarchal organisation of knowledge."[90] Similarly, Gillis argues that early industrial regions often produced strong local communities with their own powerful sense of morality, a morality which the local gentry tended to see as heresy and insubordination:

> Close kin ties, something virtually unobtainable among the rural proletariat . . . became a prominent feature of the proto-industrial areas. Community took on a new stability and identity, reinforced by either religious nonconformity or some more secular form of plebeian culture, which contrasted sharply with that imposed by the church or the gentry in arable regions. A village of miners, weavers or framework knitters was much more likely to show an independent spirit, yet to be no less strict in its own distinctive forms of social and moral discipline.[91]

Patriarchal relations *within* most forms of proto-industrial households were rearranged and weakened as well, with regard to both gender and age; the discipline and economy of people's bodies changed accordingly. In general, peasants could marry only after many years of saving were supplemented by land or other wealth passed to them from the older generation. The children of proto-industrial workers, in contrast, could frequently marry and set up viable households without their parents' help or consent as soon as they reached "adulthood," and could subsist with a minimum of land or on wage labor alone. In German lands, according to a contemporary observer, "what happens is that the son of a small-holder or a cottager, once a mere 17 or 18 years of age, will be poorly trained by a Pfuscher and will learn to weave in the shortest time; he will then find himself a woman and will produce more Pfuscher who will all sit in their cottage like swallows in the rafters."[92] Parents not only lost much of their leverage with regard to the marriage-making of the younger generation, but the new arrangements also undermined their ability to make binding agreements about subsistence in infirmity and old age with their children, and thus loosened the structural connection between the generations.[93]

Before marriage, however, the children's links with their parents often grew tighter. In many cases, to function properly, the proto-industrial family had to rely on the full powers of both spouses *and* several children to make ends meet. An often-quoted remark by a Northampton shoemaker expresses this well: "No single-handed man can live; he must have a whole family at work, because a single-handed man is so badly paid he can scarcely provide the necessaries of life. . . . As soon as [the children] are big enough to handle an awl, they are obliged to come downstairs and work."[94] Indeed, children were so crucial to most forms of proto-industrial production that a couple would often marry only *after* the young woman "proved" (to be pregnant).[95] The evidence also indicates that children in proto-industrial households tended to start work younger than their peasant counterparts, and remained with their families, rather than going out to service, until their own early marriage. Indeed, it was in regions of domestic industry (and early factories) that the greatest opportunities for utilizing child labor were identified by contemporaries.[96]

By the time children were eight or ten, they covered the cost of their living expenses; as sons and daughters grew older, their combined contribution to the household income became increasingly important, typically exceeding that of the father. This economic power was often said to give young people strong leverage in their dealings with the older generation. As one English parson reported, "It makes parents afraid of offending their children, who thus become hardened and intractable."[97] Even when they lived at home, young people frequently had money of their own and a voice in family affairs. The realignment of patriarchal power suggested by such evidence is important, since the interests of parents and children tended to diverge on several crucial issues. Parents tried to keep their sons and daughters at home as long as possible to enhance the combined product of the family. From the children's standpoint, the logic worked the other way around: for them, it often made sense to marry young and get over the strain of supporting unproductive toddlers (several of whom were likely to die in infancy), while their own productivity was still at its peak. As a contemporary proverb put it, "With the birth of children, the parents become poor; with their maturation, they become rich; and with their marriage, they fall back into poverty."[98]

Compared to most nineteenth-century factories, cottage industry appeared to offer youngsters idyllic working conditions. Their lot was often worse than in a peasant economy, however, particularly in periods when proto-industry declined. In the later half of the eighteenth century, competition sharpened and the prices of industrial products fell. To make the same income, cottagers had to double or treble their output. The working day lengthened and intensified, and younger and younger children were pressed into service as assistants.[99] The mortality of adults frequently declined during periods of emerging proto-industrialization, and the mortality of infants and children surpassed that in predominantly agrarian regions. According to Medick, the causes were to be found primarily in the deterioration of the living conditions of industrial producers—insufficient food and unhealthy housing—and to a lesser extent in the physical deprivation of children and young people through the work process.[100]

The fabric of life in proto-industrial regions diverged from that of peasant households in yet other ways: in most, contemporaries observed marked changes in the relations between men and women, including a reorganization of the sexual division of labor. Significantly, it was above all the blurring of gender boundaries in rural industries that made their work dishonorable in the eyes of urban craftsmen. At times, men continued to work as miners, agricultural laborers, or ironworkers, but their wives and children engaged in silk weaving or nailmaking. In areas with relatively high wages and work opportunities, women's industrial production often raised their families from destitution to getting by. In some expanding industries, indeed, women's wage rates were at least equal to those received by male agricultural laborers, and sometimes much higher.[101] Frequently, however, the redivisions of labor went further. In many textile regions, men returned to the household to do women's work such as spinning, weaving, and lacemaking. Elsewhere, women worked alongside men as cutlers and nailmakers. Since both spouses now labored under the same roof, the traditional gender division of labor was often relaxed still further: while a wife was out hawking the family's wares, the husband might take care of the home and mind the children.[102] Middle-class observers were troubled that men in weaving villages "cook, sweep and milk the cows in order never to disturb the good diligent wife in her work."[103] Even though this might be a short-lived experience, scholars such as Quataert argue that the redrawing of a gender hierarchy in the cottage industry system put women in a more powerful position than the one they held in the peasant economy. Both men and women engaged in "status consumption" and "plebeian sociability" such as drinking and smoking, and both took part in food riots and actions against excessive price rises. Indeed, women were said to be "more disposed to be mutinous . . . in all public tumults they are the foremost in violence and ferocity."[104]

At the same time, women began to take more initiative in sexual encounters and in marriage matters. Since the proto-industrial household depended to an unprecedented degree on the labor of all within it, it was a woman's demonstrated capacity as an artisan (as well as her traditionally prized ability to bear healthy children), even more than her father's occupation, property, or social status, which made her a desirable marriage partner, and gave her new bargaining power vis-à-vis men. In some areas, indeed, a significant minority of women chose to dispense with formal marriage altogether, "maintaining themselves and their children under their parents' roof without a murmur."[105] Gillis notes that in England, the growth of female independence evident in the late eighteenth century gave rise to heightened anxiety and violence among young men. During the same period, E. P. Thompson identified an increase in "rough music," a form of noisy, ritualized community action against violent husbands.[106]

In the long run, the altered patriarchal dynamics of many proto-industrial regions had a further significant effect on contemporary society. According to many demographers, they were the key to unleashing the exponential population growth of eighteenth-century Europe. As one influential account put it, "Proto-industrialisation broke through the demographic-economic system which regulated the feudal agrarian societies of Europe."[107] For the first time in European history, land-based constraints on marriage and family formation had been decisively broken; a powerful engine of social discipline all but disintegrated. Paradoxically, because of the location of most proto-industrial settlements away from fertile agricultural lowlands, the fastest growth tended to occur in regions least able to feed the expanding population. Subsequent historical research has tended to modify the initial strong causality attributed to proto-industrialization, not least because many agricultural regions registered large rates of population increase as well. In east-central Europe, for example, it is argued that the commercialization of large estates, and their gradual replacement, from the mid-eighteenth century, of serf labor with wage labor, unleashed a population boom.[108]

In surveying this debate, Seccombe has pointed out that both those who saw proto-industrialization as the source of population growth and their critics tended to generalize from distinct regional patterns. Combined, their evidence shows that proletarianization by itself did not lead to population growth; only certain forms of it did. The original formulators of the theory were wrong to imagine a wave of rampant sexuality that flooded the countryside as the dam of traditional constraints on marriage broke. Diminished barriers to marriage were crucial, but so were increased incentives to marry. Both of these tended to vary regionally and depended a lot upon the "uneven dismantling of the traditional patriarchal controls on mate selection, courtship and marriage."[109] In many regions, the availability of alternative means of livelihood in the countryside meant that young people could marry younger and form new households without the assistance or sanction of their parents. Neither did they have to migrate to the cities, where filth and overcrowding killed poor immigrants with relentless ferocity—and this in turn was an important factor in the simultaneous fall in contemporary mortality rates (or failure of the mortality rates to rise in response to epidemics and increased pressure on finite resources). At the same time, there were often strong inducements for young people to start their own families as soon as possible. Where the whole household contributed directly to production and children began to pay for themselves before they were ten, more children meant greater income. If the couple married young, the greatest strain (before the first children were old enough to work) would occur during those years when the productivity of the parents was at its peak, and the children would begin to contribute to the family economy as the parents began to grow old and weaker.

Even early marriage, however, did not necessarily lead to population growth. Detailed demographic studies of Germany and Switzerland have identified two contrasting demographic patterns—a "regime of wastefulness" and a "regime of conservation."[110] In southern Germany, higher fertility and mortality rates and shorter intervals between births prevailed. Mothers were particularly exhausted, babies were rarely breastfed (and this in turn shortened intervals between births), and the indifferent nurture of infants and young children amounted to what could be described as a disguised form of infanticide. Similarly, in one proto-industrial region of eighteenth-century Switzerland, extraordinarily high age-specific marital fertility combined with enormous infant and child mortality. Such a wasteful demographic regime, combined with considerable out-migration, resulted in a stagnating population. In northern Germany, in contrast, lower rates of birth and death, longer intervals between births, and the breastfeeding of infants were more common. Both regimes produced roughly stable populations, but arguably had different sources in and implications for mentalities, not least with regard to the meaning and preservation of life, patterns of investment in child care, and the impacts on personality of early childhood experiences.

＊＊＊＊＊

Proto-industrialization did not invariably signal the undermining of patriarchalist powers; neither was it automatically accompanied by increased population growth. Nevertheless, the rapid increase in the proportion of such households in many regions represented as powerful a challenge to the patriarchalist social order as all the societies of disaffected brothers and the liberal theories penned by learned men.

CHAPTER THREE

Revolutions

In early modern Europe, patriarchalism was challenged on many fronts, but remained a viable and powerful system of rule. By the end of the eighteenth century, all this began to change. Spreading from England, the forces conjured up by the industrial revolution helped redraw international relations, trade and industry, the governance of states, and the fabric of everyday life. It was during this period that new democratic doctrines, which in effect secularized the Christian belief in the equality of all souls before God, became the fervent conviction of influential social groups and, on occasion, revolutionary masses. The political revolutions that erupted in America, France, Belgium, and the Netherlands in the late eighteenth and the early nineteenth century were the most visible arena in which new forms of social governance and solidarity were tested and forged in practice. In what has subsequently been called the age of democratic revolutions, the fraternal social contract became a central focus of political struggle and social transformation.

While Britain managed to ride out the political storms relatively unscathed, as in the rest of Europe the contours of familial, political, and economic life there were redrawn in radically new ways. Many of the remaining structures of patriarchalism began to give way; reformers from all walks of life started imagining and experimenting with new forms of solidarity and governance. Corrigan and Sayer speak of a revolution in government which occurred against a backdrop of apparently unchanging institutional forms. E. P. Thompson and other historians have charted the making of the working class during a period of rapid industrialization; Levine and Seccombe are among those who chronicle dramatic changes in proletarian family forms; Dorothy Thompson, Barbara Taylor, and other feminists document the gendering of working-class movements; Davidoff and Hall trace the re-invention of separate spheres and the engendering of public institutions which underpinned the making of the middle class; and Tomlins reminds us how "private enterprise" became sheltered behind a novel distinction between the public and the private. In the account that follows, I focus on four of these radical changes: the industrial revolution, the crisis-ridden transformation of laboring households, and the American and French political revolutions.

Characteristically, there is—and was—little agreement about the content and meaning of these events and their interconnections. Changes in family forms, for all their importance, are often too uneven, spread out, and "private" to be described as revolutionary. An important group of economic historians stress continuity over change in the eighteenth-and nineteenth-century British economy and argue that the transformations were too gradual to warrant the title "revolution"; others (whose argument I find more persuasive) assert that a qualitative break in the economic sphere did occur.[1] Marxist scholars used to claim that eighteenth-and nineteenth-century political revolutions were class struggles ignited by major changes in productive forces; their opponents argue that conflict *between* classes had little to do with French or American political upheavals. The French Revolution has been depicted, in both scholarly and popular writing, as the precursor of grassroots democracy or of totalitarian dictatorship. Its causes have been seen as axiomatic of crisis tendencies in social, economic, and class forces, or alternatively of the power of discursive practices and political contingency against a background of social continuity.[2] Indeed, seizing control of interpretations of the revolution is widely seen as a major aspect of seizing control of the definition of the present and future political identity of France.[3] Similarly, the American Revolution has been appropriated in different ways to form the bases of self-understanding of the most diverse range of groups and interests in American society. It has been condemned for betraying the interests of women and blacks and embraced as the beginning of their struggle for equality. It has been depicted as a war of independence coupled with a political and legal modernization which preserved existing social structures much as they were, or as "one of the greatest revolutions the world has known, a momentous upheaval that not only fundamentally altered the character of American society but decisively affected the course of subsequent history."[4]

Neither of the two major interpretations of the French Revolution—one as a fiscal-political crisis that got out of hand, the other as a class struggle between the rising bourgeoisie and the aristocracy of the *ancien régime*—pays systematic attention to contemporary transformations of patriarchal relations. It was only recently that women's part in the democratic revolutions has been addressed directly; more recent still are attempts to chart comprehensive overviews of the multiple gendered and patriarchal dimensions of these events.[5]

My own position will be clear from the account that follows. Briefly, I find more compelling those arguments which say that the industrial revolution did indeed take place, and that the political revolutions and profound changes in family forms were inseparably linked to contemporary economic developments. However, the fact that I have chosen to discuss the industrial revolution before the political ones does not imply that I believe in economic determinism. I am not convinced that economics caused political and familial change (or vice versa, for that matter), and in any case I am neither qualified to attempt nor interested in trying to prove strong causality. Rather, as in the rest of the book, my argument revolves around the proposition that attention to transformations in patriarchal forms of governance provides a crucial conceptual link between analyses of phenomena in apparently distinct spheres of life.

INDUSTRIAL REVOLUTION AND A CENTURY OF BRITISH DOMINANCE

By the mid-eighteenth century, as I noted in chapter 2, several European regions developed extensive and relatively sophisticated centers of proto-industrial production. Then, within several decades, England pushed this development past a qualitative threshold. With the advantage of hindsight, many historians have come to identify a range of technical innovations in a group of key industries and economic sectors, together with a change in their organization and a rapid increase in their output, as the beginnings of the industrial revolution. The cotton industry is invariably seen as the prime example of such change. Gathering producers under one roof reduced the pilfering of materials and made it possible to lengthen the working day, speed up production, and make people work steadily throughout the week. The assembling of large numbers of laborers in one place facilitated a reorganization of the work process; breaking down the task to be done into a number of simple operations that could be performed by untrained operatives lowered production costs. Most important, the invention of spinning and other machines, used in factories powered by a single motive power, allowed for a further drastic increase in output and reduction in costs. It has been estimated that an eighteenth-century Indian hand spinner took more than 50,000 hours to get through a hundred pounds of cotton; a power-assisted mule, introduced toward the end of that century, reduced the time to 300 hours, and an automatic mule, introduced around 1825, cut it to 135 hours. In the space of a hundred years, the cost of yarn was reduced to between 2 and 3 percent of its original price.[6] Flooded by cheap imports, markets both at home and abroad grew and grew. For the world as a whole, Pollard notes, production per head of population increased by about two and a quarter times between 1800 and 1913; foreign trade per head grew by more than twenty-five times.[7] This in turn provided an impetus to innovations in marketing, in finance, and in machine-building, and indirectly to developments such as labor migration and improvements in transport.

Importantly, the earliest stages of the industrial revolution were strongly dependent on female and child labor. The textile industries accounted for almost half of the value added in British industry, both in 1770 and in 1831. At the end of the eighteenth century, about half of the workers in most textile mills were children; in 1789, only 14 percent of the people who worked in Arkwright's factories at Cromford were men.[8] The linen industry contributed more to value added in 1770 than did the iron industry, and only about 2 percent less in 1831. Silk, where the proportion of women and children to men could be as high as fourteen to one, contributed more than 4 percent of value added in 1770, the same proportion as for coal. By 1831, the position of coal was more important, at 7 percent, but silk's had equally grown, after a dip, to 5 percent. According to Berg, "When we talk of industry in eighteenth and early nineteenth century [Britain], we are talking of a largely female workforce."[9]

There is no one answer to why Britain—or even Europe—was the place where the industrial revolution began. Most historians agree that such a major change was most likely to occur where non-industrial forms of capitalism were fully developed, and where feudalism had lost much of its impact. And indeed in Britain, after two centuries of slow preparation, there was no real shortage of any factors of production, and no really crippling national obstacles to full capitalist development. The political and legal system discreetly upheld the power of the wealthy, did not interfere in the accumulation of capital, and on occasion mobilized the full force of the state to defend and expand the scope of market operations. The country had a long tradition of industrial employment and commercial enterprise, an extensive network of transport and communication, a relatively high level of accumulated wealth, and markets that were expanding and capable of further expansion both beyond and inside national frontiers. While England itself had been free from foreign invasions for many centuries, Britain had colonies that it could plunder, and to which it could export as much as it wanted. Apart from some marginal regions, there were no peasants in Britain and virtually no feudal privileges; instead, the country's capitalist agriculture was capable of rapid expansion to feed a growing population, and there was a large and growing class of laboring people used to working for money wages.[10] Finally, Britain was favored by the fortuitous presence, in one geographical region, of all the factors of production that were needed in the succession of phases that made up the first industrial revolution.[11]

This raises the larger question of why capitalism and the industrial revolution originated in western Europe rather than in one of the other great civilizations of the world, which had in earlier times achieved similar or greater levels of technological capacity. Here the debate is even less conclusive,[12] although two reasons deserve to be singled out. The first, long stressed by left-wing writers, is the decisive contribution of unequal exchange between Europe and the rest of the world, as well as of outright plunder, to the primitive accumulation of capital. Ernest Mandel, for example, estimated that in the three centuries from 1500, the total amount plundered by European colonial empires from the rest of the world amounted to over a billion pounds sterling, about eight times the British national income for one year, or more than the capital of all the industrial enterprises operated by steam that existed in Europe around 1800.[13]

The second set of reasons, linking the onset of industrialization to a particular form of age and gender relations, has recently been outlined by Seccombe.[14] According to him, the western European marriage system made a decisive contribution to the breakthrough of industrial capitalism. While all the other causal factors occurred at other times in other places, late and non-universal marriage was unique to northwestern Europe. This system, which seems to have developed earliest in England, had several marked advantages in terms of local accumulation of wealth. First, delayed and less frequent marriage improved the life expectancy of the poor, and this in turn meant that less of women's (and society's) child-rearing labor was "wasted" on children who never reached, let alone completed, productive life. At the same time, restrictive and non-universal marriage improved women's lifetime productivity in terms of material goods, since they were able to devote all their energies to such work until their mid-twenties and often later, without the exhaustion and injuries associated with childbirth. Second, the high property-based hurdles to marriage encouraged—and made possible—saving among the poor, and thus enhanced capital formation. Since age differences between spouses tended to be relatively low, men were less likely to die when their children were still in infancy. Both of these factors tended to improve children's life expectancy, and made it more likely that families would survive crisis periods intact. But the western European marriage system also proved more conducive to supplying prospective employers with workers. Life-cycle domestic service provided a steady supply of labor to those who needed it, as well as opportunities to save for young people eager to marry and establish their own families. This incentive, in fact, led many of them to migrate in search of wage labor. Crucially, as the demand for workers escalated in some regions with the beginnings of industrialization, the lowering of the age of marriage and the increasing proportion of people marrying led to a rapid rise in the birthrate, providing employers with a seemingly inexhaustible stream of cheap, mobile labor.

*****

Britain's early lead in the industrial revolution turned into a century of world domination. Indeed, this was the first time in world history that a single power had exercised such world hegemony; all of the great empires of the past had been regional powers.[15] Most commentators agree on the main reasons for this development. The first country to develop new technology acquired an advantage that nobody else could have. In Britain, in contrast to everywhere else, the leading economic sectors and regions were not faced with the rapid emergence of rivals that had to be met quickly on the pain of de-industrialization. Instead, they developed slowly, organically, the speed dictated by the availability of labor, supplies, and market opportunities, and undisturbed by the emergence of more powerful rivals abroad. No matter how slow and clumsy the way forward, everyone else was much further behind. By 1790, Britain achieved an output of 15 kilograms of iron per head, a level not reached by Europe until 1870; it used 2 kilograms of raw cotton, a level that was reached by Europe only in 1885; and around 40 percent of the population was left in agriculture—the level reached by the Continent only in the middle of the twentieth century. Even in 1870, when its dominance was coming to an end, Britain was still making half of the world's pig iron.[16] This helps explain why European industrialization occurred on the British model, built around coal and steel. Britain had, for a crucial period, almost total hegemony over crucial innovations in energy substitution, and over the transforming of this energy into motion. Regions with alternative sources of energy, such as timber, water, or oil, did not develop these to rival the coal and steel of Britain, and instead remained economically underdeveloped and backward.[17]

From the end of the eighteenth century, the rapidly increasing productivity of key sectors of British industry, coupled with the miraculously low prices of their products, seemed to leave the rest of the world only two options. If they themselves were involved in the world market, they had to follow suit and industrialize in a hurry, or find themselves at the mercy of British capital, exploited, and with indigenous domestic industries destroyed by cheap competition. Even regions that had, until then, remained relatively insulated from the full force of a world economy began to feel the impact of an international commodity and labor market. By 1850, those European nations which did not maintain high tariffs were swamped by English manufactured exports. The wealthy and powerful in many parts of the world saw the economic bases of their power melt in front of their eyes; the future of their subjects and their own political fortunes seemed to be influenced, more and more, by British statesmen and investors. In all corners of Europe, new nations were formed, fortified, regrouped—and schooled—partly in order to resist the encroachments of British power.

It did not matter that few factories were built in Ireland; English industrialization and government policy were quite sufficient to wreak havoc in the Irish economy. The removal of Ireland's cotton tariff in 1826 wiped out the country's flourishing cottage-based textile industry within a couple of years. Using British yarns, Prussian and Swiss weavers and Saxon knitters and lacemakers began to swamp markets in Russia, Italy, and the rest of Germany. As other industrial centers in Europe strengthened, English manufactured goods began to be pushed out of European markets. Britain responded by gradually reorienting the export of capital and manufactured goods to colonies such as India and to white settlements such as Australia and Canada.[18] Here again, the immense flow of goods and capital gouged deep marks in the social landscape. In one country after another, local agriculture was reorganized to produce staple crops for Britain rather than mixed crops for local people to use. India, for centuries an exporter of cotton cloth, was systematically de-industrialized, and by the mid-nineteenth century became a huge impoverished market for Lancashire cottons.[19] The more marked the British lead was, the less the putters-out and merchant capitalists in the rest of Europe—and soon the rest of the world—could avoid taking over the new technologies and entering the process of capitalist industrialization aided by them. Any procrastination would lead to domestic and foreign markets' being lost to their British competitors and to the indigenous industries being obliterated.

The industrialization process, it is important to stress, fostered not only uniformity but regional unevenness. Thus for many decades, early industrialization not only coexisted with but also provided the impetus for the further development of earlier modes of production; merchant capitalism, agricultural capitalism, proto-industrial and industrial capitalism, and do-mestic-based outwork existed side by side. Even in mid-nineteenth-cen-tury Britain, the impact of the new industrialism was still very limited. Only in some textile trades were a majority of the workers employed in factories; that was exceptional, rather than normal, elsewhere. Thus em-ployment in the manufacturing and mining sectors, let alone in the services or agriculture, was typically still in the kind of workshops or working conditions that had been familiar a hundred years earlier.[20] Around 1850, factory workers constituted barely 5 percent of the total population in England, 3 percent in France, and they were a minuscule component of the laboring classes in Germany. According to Samuel, in metalwork and engi-neering, the small workshop rather than the factory dominated until the 1880s; in boot- and shoemaking, cottage industry prevailed. It has been estimated that even in the 1840s, more than three-quarters of industrial production was derived from these "diverse, dispersed and unspectacular industries."[21] Sometimes appropriate machinery existed, but manufactur-ers preferred cheaper, familiar, more reliable hand labor, even in the sec-ond, more technology-intensive stage of industrialization. Haulage was often done by people rather than machines or even horses; men, women, and children were used as runners, as the motive force of machinery, instead of balances or lifts. Only in regions of relatively high wages and a shortage of labor, or less effective union opposition, as in the United States, was available technology used more extensively.[22]

Not only did different modes of production, authority relations, and levels of technology exist side by side, but frequently they were directly dependent on each other. The most advanced sectors of the economy were often responsible for much of the massive growth of contemporary "pre-industrial" production, for which they often provided cheaper and more plentiful raw materials, just as, at a later stage of industrial development, they could lead to its wholesale destruction. Indeed, around 1800, the most advanced sector of British industry was tightly linked to the most primi-tive form of exploitation: nearly 90 percent of the raw cotton used in Britain's cotton factories originated on the slave plantations of Brazil, the Caribbean, and the American South.[23] Samuel, writing about a later period, makes the same point: mechanization in one department of production was often complemented by an increase in sweating in others; the growth of large firms by a proliferation of small producing units; the concentration of work in factories by the spread of outwork in the home.[24] Over time, many flourishing proto-industrial regions were de-industrialized in the next phase of economic development, and their workforce had to move elsewhere to find work or starve—the plight of the Irish and the starvation of some half-million English handloom weavers who were unable to compete with the prices of machine-made cloth are just two examples familiar to students of British history.[25] Technical factors, such as accessibility of raw materials and proximity of markets, explained part of this uneven development. In addition, then as now, capital often abandoned localities where workers were well organized and commanded relatively high wages, to move to areas where new technology could be introduced with less resistance, workers could be paid less, or male tradesmen could be replaced by badly remunerated and supposedly unskilled women and children.[26]

* * * * *

In this age of revolution, the dynamics of everyday life were radically transformed. The serf system, which in many of the re-feudalized regions of Europe survived into the nineteenth century, both on the land and in some early manufactories, now began to be seen as an obstacle to economic progress. In 1802, a Prussian minister wrote, "Serfdom and true industry are clear contradictions. Serfdom does not exist in any country or province in which agriculture and manufacturing prosper." Such observations were brought home forcefully, especially from the 1840s, by the increasing rebelliousness of the peasants themselves.[27] In the century from the 1780s, in a process spurred on by the French Revolution and the revolutions of 1848, feudalism was abolished, usually on terms extremely disadvantageous to the peasants.[28] Authority and productive relations, however, were transformed within the households of industrial workers as well. A protracted domestic revolution occurred alongside the industrial and political upheavals of the late eighteenth and early nineteenth centuries.

INDUSTRIALIZATION AND THE PROLETARIAN FAMILY

In proto-industrial regions, as I argued in chapter 2, patriarchal relations both inside and outside the household were likely to be less clearly demarcated than those in regions where peasant and artisan families remained the norm. This was in spite of the fact that the average size of the household hardly changed, and men, women, and children continued to work from morning to night for their subsistence. Expansion of the wage economy and factory industrialization brought further dramatic changes to proletarian domestic relations. In the first instance, some families continued to labor as a unit under the general direction of the husband and father, but now no longer on the estate or in cottage industry but in workshops, mines, or factories, where a form of family subcontracting might exist well into the nineteenth century. In this system, the employer paid the head of the family team, rather than individual workers. If some of these workers came from other households, the subcontractor would pay them (or their parents) himself. Although a substantial proportion of married women worked in such family teams, there is evidence that the separation of home and workplace made it increasingly difficult for them to take part in wage labor. Indeed, many working men complained bitterly that the spread of the factory system took remunerative work away from their wives.[29] For this type of family economy, early marriage and many children remained both possible and desirable.

The decline of family hiring and the expansion of industrial employment for individual women and children seemed to push existing tensions in domestic patriarchal relations beyond a qualitative threshold. Not only were women and children often employed in ways that were widely per-ceived to be immoral, but their employment could in various ways under-cut some of the remaining material sources of patriarchal power among laboring men. Far too often, women and children seemed to gain public presence, power, and independence relative to that of men and heads of families. In cottage industry, working under the authority of their fathers and husbands, women and children were expected, as a matter of course, to do much the same range of tasks as men. Such division of labor had long been proscribed in the minority of "honorable" guild-controlled trades. Now, as production moved outside the confines of the household and family team, new uses of wage labor seemed to precipitate a crisis. Cer-tainly, much of the critique of laboring families was formulated by middle- and upper-class observers, and fueled their own schemes of intervention. But there is ample evidence that the painful process of redrawing and reinventing authority relations at work and at home, between men, women, and children in their roles as workers and family partners, became the focus of domestic and industrial politics of the working class as a whole.

Many of the objections against female workers were couched in moral terms. Women and children were now doing dirty and dangerous work in hot and sweaty environments (which they had always done, in one way or another), but now not only out of their own homes and in the company of men, but away from the supervision of family and kin and in close proxim-ity to strangers. In English cotton districts, there was much debate about the morality of females working, scantily dressed, in the hot and humid rooms, and next to men who also were not "properly" clothed.[30] In brickworks, visitors were scandalized by girls and women "sparsely clad, up to the bare knees in clay splashes, and evidently without a vestige of womanly delicacy," learning to "treat with contempt all feelings of modesty and decency."[31] In the mines, similarly, the problem was seen not so much as the physical exertion and indignity of much work done by women and girls, but as the fact that their tattered work clothes provided a "disgustingly indecent" view of their bodies, and that they washed in public after work.[32] All of this, it was feared, would lead to an epidemic of sex and illegitimate children. Even rigorous sex segregation at work would not have resolved all the problems: children and young women were picking up foul language and independent, defiant, and "knowing" habits from each other. Critics alleged that, to make matters worse, overworked factory women often had neither the time nor the energy (nor the help of their children who might be working in the factory as well) to perform any but the most essential household tasks. Indeed, they might never have learned to cook, clean, sew, or mend because waged work disrupted the long informal apprenticeship that women traditionally received in their own homes or during their employment as domestic servants.[33] Even where work had not moved outside the home, as in the sweated trades, women might not have been able to manage their home duties, simply because there was too much to do. Many observers feared that in the long run, women's double burden "would undermine the reproductive capacity of the working class and produce a generation of weak, feeble, and disabled men and women."[34]

The perceived crisis of familial relations, however, was fueled by even more alarming trends. The lower wages paid to women and juveniles, combined with the shift of authority and supervision over the immediate work process from the heads of producer families to employers and supervisors, were at the heart of the problem. As competition from cheap, mass-produced goods slowly strangled the cottage economy, and family subcontracting was abandoned in one industry after another, men, women, and children began to compete, as individuals, in an overcrowded labor market. Women were paid around half the rate of men even for identical work; children were employed for a few pence a week. Frequently they tended machines or performed newly deskilled tasks in direct competition with male craftsmen attempting to defend their traditional privileges and work organization. In the early stages of factory industrialization, adult men, used to being their own bosses, would rather starve than work in the factories; in any case, manufacturers themselves preferred to use what they saw as more docile female and child labor in defeating trades organizations and undercutting male rates of pay.[35] Andrew Ure, an enthusiastic (and often unreliable) admirer of the new system, identified its benefits to the employers in precisely this way:

> It is, in fact, the constant aim and tendency of every improvement in machinery to supersede human labour altogether or to diminish its cost, by substituting the industry of women and children for that of men; or that of ordinary labourers for trained artisans. In most of the water-twist . . . cotton mills, the spinning is entirely managed by females of sixteen years and upwards. The effect of substituting the self-acting mule for the common mule, is to discharge the greater part of the men spinners, and to retain adolescents and children. The proprietor of a factory near Stockport states . . . that, by such substitution, he would save 50 a week in wages, in consequence of dispensing with nearly forty male spinners, at about 25s. of wages each.[36]

In a few regions which contemporaries believed were the precursors of a general trend, adult men, the nominal heads of families, could be unemployed for years, depending for their subsistence on the wages of their wives and children. Frederick Engels discussed at length what he regarded (erroneously) as the typical tale of poor Jack, who was discovered by his friend Joe in a damp cellar minding the children and mending his wife's stockings while she earned the family subsistence. Deeply ashamed, Jack confessed,

> "No, I know this is not my work, but my poor missus is i' th' factory; she has to leave by half-past five and works till eight at night, and then she is so knocked up that she cannot do aught when she gets home, so I have to do everything for her what I can, for I have no work, nor had any for more than three years and I shall never have any more work while I live"; and then he wept a big tear.

In this part of Lancashire, things used to be different; Jack earned enough for two, they had a good furnished cottage, and his wife did not have to go out to work. But now, things were upside down: "she had been the man in the house and [Jack] the woman." Indignant, Engels asked whether anyone could imagine a more insane state of things than this condition, which "unsexes the man and takes from the woman all womanliness without being able to bestow upon man true womanliness, or the woman true manliness." Even worse, "this condition which degrades, in the most

shameful way, both sexes, and through them, Humanity," was the last result and final achievement of "our much-praised civilisation."[37]

By the 1840s, commentators from all sides of the political spectrum
agreed that throughout Britain, France, and Germany, the working-class
family was falling apart under the impact of rapid and anarchic industrialization; a sense of sexual crisis was heard very clearly in all the popular
movements of the time, including Owenism and Chartism.[38] According to
Lord Ashley, the evil of the gradual displacement of male by female labor in
a large proportion of industrial occupations in England was "spreading
rapidly and extensively . . . desolating like a torrent, the peace, the economy
and the virtue of the mighty masses of the manufacturing districts. Domestic life and domestic discipline must soon be at an end; society will consist
of individuals no longer grouped in families; so early is the separation of
husband and wife, of parents and children."[39] In England, among the poor
of Manchester, according to Frederick Engels,

> the employment of women at once breaks up the family; for when the wife
> spends 12 or 13 hours everyday in the mill, and the husband works the same
> length of time there or elsewhere, what becomes of the children? They grow
> up like wild weeds; they are put to nurse for a shilling or eightpence a week,
> and how they are treated may be imagined.[40]

Chartist women themselves justified their political involvement through
their concerns about family disintegration. They worked as hard as was
humanly possible to feed and nurture their children, only to see them cry
from hunger and die of preventable injuries and malnutrition. This inhuman system forced them into the public arena of political strife; they joined
their voices to demands for conditions that would again allow them to
properly discharge their duties as wives and mothers.[41]

On their part, anxious middle- and upper-class observers were alarmed
not only about the maintenance of what were considered to be proper
gender relations between men and women, but also about what was perceived as the breakdown of patriarchal relations between the generations,
between the young and the old. It was routinely argued that men who were
political radicals could expect only rudeness and insubordination from
their own children. What was more, not only married women but even
young people might regard their individual wage packets as their own to
spend (just as the men were learning to do). Instead of handing over their
whole pay to their parents, they made a contribution for board and kept the
rest. Indeed, individual wages made it possible for some young people to

find independent lodgings at a time when parents still desperately needed their economic contribution.[42] Boys and girls receiving their own wages, it was feared, would not obey their parents anymore—and once respect for fathers and family discipline was gone, the younger generation would lose respect for *all* authority. Disobedient girls would never become virtuous wives and mothers; boys would grow up to be thieves and radicals.[43] Of English female textile workers it was said, "They had their father to keep, and would not be dictated by him."[44] Even worse, Lord Ashley warned that working girls were "forming clubs and associations, and are gradually acquiring all those privileges which are the proper portion of the male sex."[45] The economic leverage of the young was contrasted with the parents' lack of any inheritable property: a family without inheritance, many bourgeois reformers thought, was a logical impossibility.

We cannot take alarmist accounts of breakdowns of patriarchal authority, disintegrating families, abandoned morality, insubordinate youth, cheeky factory women, and rising illegitimacy at face value.[46] In the first place, the biggest proportion of employed women, both before and after the industrial revolution, were domestic servants. In England, 40 percent of all women workers were servants in 1851, while only 22 percent were textile factory operatives; in France, the comparable figures in 1866 were 22 percent in domestic service and 10 percent in textiles; in Prussia, servants accounted for 18 percent of the female labor force in 1882, while factory workers were about 12 percent.[47] At the same time, workshop and factory organization, whether in England or on the Continent, made full use of traditional forms of patriarchal authority and subordination.[48] This was particularly significant where a large proportion of early factory workers were women and children. Even when male workers were not actually needed for any technical reasons to operate new machinery, some men were usually kept on because of their perceived capacity to discipline female or juvenile helpers, whom they sometimes still employed and paid themselves. Women typically tried to keep children working with promises of food or other rewards. To make ten- and twelve-year-olds labor consistently through thirteen-hour days, however, the prospect of a beating from an adult man was probably more effective.[49]

Finally, the full-time waged employment of married women was a minority experience. In the English textile districts, on which public attention was riveted, the rate of married women's extra-domestic employment remained at 20 to 30 percent throughout the nineteenth century. Elsewhere, however, it seldom exceeded 10 percent. Most factory women were single, and most of the rest were widowed, deserted, or childless.[50] And although married women did receive their own wages, under British law their earnings legally belonged to their husbands. At the same time, the average size of a co-resident proletarian family *increased,* and laboring households became more complex during this period, rather than contracted as we would expect if the family were disintegrating. On average, young people did not desert their families but seemed to reside with their parents longer than their rural counterparts. Families desperately needed their children's earnings, and most working-class girls and boys had a fierce loyalty and attachment to their mothers. In any case, independent accommodation was difficult to find on their pitiful wages, the unpaid labor of their mothers proved difficult to replace, and landladies were reluctant to take them in without parental approval.[51] Finally, there was indeed little property that working-class parents could leave their children, but their willingness and ability to pay an apprenticeship premium was necessary if a son was to secure an apprenticeship, their support essential if a daughter was kept in school long enough to get a job as a pupil teacher, and their local knowledge invaluable in getting a good unskilled job. On their part, most employers preferred to hire children and teenagers through their parents.

But the widespread feeling of crisis was real enough. In the first place, the same developments that troubled outside observers resulted in a dramatic escalation of sexual antagonism and violence. Artisan families in which women replaced men as the major breadwinners were ripe for violent confrontation, as men attempted to assert authority that had lost its material basis. Everywhere, tensions about the distribution of inadequate incomes, the misery that attended men's unemployment, men's dependence on the earnings of their wives and children, women's inability to integrate waged work with domestic tasks, and the subsequent disintegration of older patterns of authority and shared expectations could at any moment flare up into violence.[52]

Whether they endured their misery peacefully or not, there is abundant evidence that factory workers soon became sickly, stunted, and undernourished. If it had not been for the influx of fresh blood from the countryside into the factories, the employers might well have wiped out their labor supply within two or three generations. In many urban areas, fourteen-hour working days, inadequate nutrition, cramped, unsanitary housing, and bad water combined to create the beginnings of an ecological catastrophe. Whatever the relative merits of the case for increased or decreased standards of living—and of housework—in working-class households during industrialization, the bodies of laboring people were indelibly marked by grinding poverty. Factory workers, contemporaries noted, were "almost all weakly, of angular but not powerful build, lean, pale and of relaxed fibre, with the exception of the muscles especially employed in their work." Workers in domestic industries were thought to be useless for military recruitment and common laboring alike; handloom weavers were said to be "decayed in their bodies; the whole race of them is rapidly descending to the size of Lilliputians."[53]

Children in particular were affected by the voracious appetite for labor in early factories. Certainly, very young people had always worked, in one way or another, to support the household economy of their parents or masters; a few of their occupations were extremely hazardous, and some of their masters brutal. In the early nineteenth century, the worst conditions of previous decades were multiplied, and the pace of work in domestic sweated industries intensified. But there was no precedent for keeping tens of thousands of children eight, nine, and ten years old working at repetitive tasks with only minimum breaks for twelve and more hours per day, six days per week. As E. P. Thompson put it with regard to England, "The crime of the factory system was to inherit the worst features of the domestic system in a context which had none of the domestic compensations. . . . The exploitation of little children, on this scale and with this intensity, was one of the most shameful events in our history."[54]

Graphic contemporary accounts of proletarian ill health are amply supported by statistics on class and urban-rural differentials in height and life expectancy. The children of poor city workers typically died at half the age of their country counterparts or well-off city dwellers; one in two did not survive past the age of five, and those who did were around twenty centimeters shorter than the sons and daughters of the upper class. In all, the life expectancy of workers in many large industrial cities was half that of their employers. When cholera and typhus reappeared in Europe in the 1820s, the poor in their overcrowded slums were struck down at several times the rate of wealthy residents. At the height of the cholera epidemic in 1832, for example, the disease claimed one person in three in the poorest quarters of Paris, but only one in nineteen in the richest. By the turn of the century, up to 40 percent of the men from large industrial towns who volunteered for the Boer War were deemed by the British army to be physically unfit to fight.[55]

To many observers, an equally alarming indicator of a crisis among laboring families was an increase in cohabitation and the number of illegitimate children. Historians agree that the rate of childbirth outside marriage rose all across western Europe after 1750. In England, less than 2 percent of births were illegitimate in 1700, compared to more than 5 percent a century later. In France, the rate almost quadrupled: from 1.2 percent in 1740–49 to 4.7 percent by 1800–1809. Swedish rates nearly trebled from 1750 to 1820, while in Norway and Finland they more than doubled in the sixty years after 1750. The rise in Germany was even more dramatic, from 2.5 percent before 1750 to 11.9 percent in 1780–1820.[56] It is likely that there was some increase in premarital sexual activity among the young as the supervision of kin and parents was eroded; it is certain that with greater mobility of labor and weakened community sanctions, young women who got pregnant after a solemn promise of marriage were abandoned by their lovers much more frequently than in the past.

A number of the "illegitimate" babies, however, must have been born to the increasing number of couples who lived together without formal marriage. Social historians as well as contemporaries have noted a sharp rise in cohabitation among the laboring poor at the beginning of the nineteenth century in many industrializing regions in northwestern Europe. Gillis estimated that possibly a fifth of the population of England and Wales lived at one time or another in common-law marriages; among some groups of itinerant workers, only about 10 percent of couples were legally married. According to Donzelot, concubinage was practiced by one-third to one-half of French working-class couples. Some working people avoided formal marriage because of the high cost of a license or because they did not have good enough clothes, others because of hostility to the Established Church, or the existence of alternative customary forms of common-law marriage.[57] Some working-class women in England, fully aware of the legal disabilities of wives, refused to marry the man with whom they lived on the grounds that it would reduce their power within the family; in France, men were unwilling to commit themselves to a woman without a dowry.[58]

Industrialization, proletarianization, and mass migration to the cities undercut the many patriarchal controls that regulated the marriages of the younger generation. For young men, the move can be seen as a partial emancipation from the rule of the father backed by community elders. For young women, the new freedoms carried greater risks, not least by increasing their vulnerability to men of their own generation.[59] As Gillis put it, "Marriage no longer held the privileged status it had among the smallholders, nor did it have the support it had enjoyed among the proto-industrial community. Proletarian couples no longer had to contend with possessive parents and jealous siblings; their marriages were no longer a class issue. But although they were free to marry when and whom they wished, they were wholly on their own and subject to new strains for which there was little relief, especially for women." Even in courtship, as the advantages that women had in the proto-industrial community receded, their role became more passive and defensive as time passed.[60]

*****

Early industrial capitalism, as Seccombe put it, offered no support to the nuclear family. Proletarianization had cut the patriarchal order from its traditional property roots and shaken both the gender and the generational axes of family hierarchy. It would take some time—and far more than a crusade by church and state—before domestic patriarchy could be regrafted onto the bones of the private wage system by means of the hardening cast of the male breadwinner norm.[61]

THE AMERICAN REVOLUTION

The effects of rapid industrialization caused upheavals in the household economies of laboring populations; exported, they jeopardized the wealth and prosperity of many of the world's regions and put in question the power of their rulers. The increasing British dominance of the world economy went hand in hand with disruptions of colonial enterprise. In the 1760s, Britain tightened restrictions on North American trade and industry, increased taxation, and enacted a range of prohibitions on colonial assemblies.[62] Within a decade, this policy helped ignite a successful war of independence against America's colonial master. The English settlements in North America were already in turmoil. Factors such as accelerated local proto-industrialization, rising living standards, and rapid development of internal markets made for increased confidence and ambition on the part of local elites. In contrast, population growth and mobility, shortages of land, increasing numbers of poor whites, weakness of the social hierarchy, fragmented churches, and disrupted networks of local paternalism led to the increasing restlessness and rebelliousness of the population at large. Out of all these factors, historians have woven a multiplicity of narratives explaining the origins, outcomes, and meanings of the American Revolution.

From my perspective, one form of interpretation is particularly compelling. In a recent book, Gordon Wood argues that the enormous radicalism of the American Revolution consisted of the defeat of patriarchalism in all its forms and its relatively rapid replacement by a new system of governance built around the civil equality of (white) men pursuing their private interests.[63] The gendered dimensions of the new order, which have recently been analyzed in the rapidly growing feminist literature on this period of American history, can be glimpsed between the lines of Wood's book, but receive little systematic attention. Put together, the two forms of historical narrative can be used to argue that the American Revolution against patriarchalist authority eventually resulted in the establishment of novel forms of patriarchal association.

In the 1770s, according to Wood, the existing republican tendencies of American life were brought to the surface. Republicanism

> challenged the primary assumptions and practices of monarchy—its hierarchy, its inequality, its devotion to kinship, its patriarchy, its patronage, and its dependency. It offered new conceptions of the individual, the family, the state, and the individual's relationship to the family, the state and other individuals. Indeed, republicanism offered nothing less than new ways of organizing society.

Even though divisions between rich and poor remained, the extent of the patriot assault on courtiers eventually made it impossible to re-create pre-war chains of family and patronage.[64] Contemporaries soon realized that the old patriarchalist social order was, for good or ill, irretrievably lost; many, alarmed at the unprecedented radicalism of their communities, would have agreed with John Adams that "to contrive some Method for the Colonies to glide insensibly from under the old Government, into a peaceable and contented submission to new ones" was "the most difficult and dangerous Part of the Business Americans have to do in this mighty contest."[65]

Historians such as Wood, Countryman, and Coontz claim that this transition, which with the advantage of hindsight may seem to have been orderly and predictable, was in fact characterized by prolonged and complex debates and conflicts, over at least a decade, about the forms of governance that were to replace the ancient pattern of institutions, beliefs, habits, and usages that made up the British constitution in the United States. Even though the final result upheld individual rather than collective rights and enshrined economic, gender, and racial inequalities, in the 1770s many women developed a consciousness of themselves as female patriots,[66] slaves sued for their own freedom, and a radical millennial movement coexisted with practical moves to set up an egalitarian, corporatist society. Mobs took action to control profiteering and hoarding of scarce foodstuffs; crowds closed courts; militiamen debated with their officers; women discussed political tracts and penned their own; and towns elected powerful revolutionary committees. In some of the democratized state legislatures, artisans, small traders, and farmers passed tax, currency, debt, and other laws that worked against the social, political, and material interests of the old colonial upper class and the new entrepreneurs alike.[67] The first draft of the Pennsylvania constitution of 1776 held that the government should be able to regulate property in the interest of equality; most states did not specifically prohibit black suffrage or officeholding in their initial voting laws; and New Jersey admitted women to the vote two days after the Declaration of Independence, and confirmed this in 1796 by specifically referring to voters as "he" and "she." (The same piece of legislation disenfranchised all blacks.) In this state, at least, independent women retained the right to vote until 1807.[68]

The egalitarian and corporatist proposals of some sections of the population were matched by the attempts of others to preserve social privilege. One state constitution after another had tried, unsuccessfully, to find a way of giving special representation to wealth. In the end, influential property holders, recognizing the "wisdom of sacrifice," forged a compromise between populist corporatist demands and the new liberal defense of private property and the free market. Many state constitutions placed more tax and other burdens on the rich than they had ever borne before, but managed to preserve their decisive ability to influence events: with the adoption of radical policies, the rights of property were protected and conservative institutions were able to take hold.[69] The potential radicalism of state-level democracy was further restrained by the national constitution. Embodying principles congenial to the most "progressive" economic forces in the world, it was not democratic even by the standards of the day, aiming to limit rather than encourage involvement in politics.[70] By incorporating the laws of master and servant, the constitution also retained important aspects of feudal relations, cutting off the sphere of workplace relations from political intervention.[71]

In the period of social conservatism after 1790, racial lines began to be drawn more sharply: abolitionism, like feminism and "leveling" fell into disfavor. Having emancipated themselves from "enslavement" to British colonial rule, American legislators hesitated to abolish slavery. Most states adopted the first explicit denials of women's right to vote during the 1790s.[72] Wealthy single women were again disenfranchised. Only one truly radical measure remained. By 1825, whether or not they had any property or were seen as dependent on others, adult white males could vote in all states except Rhode Island, Virginia, and Louisiana.[73] As Coontz put it, "The revolution proclaimed the brotherhood of man, yet the constitution legalised slavery. Republican theorists celebrated the death of dependence and the responsibility of individuals to make their own moral decisions, yet politically and economically they subsumed the woman and children of the household in the person of the man."[74] Slavery and domestic and workplace relations were reckoned outside the (public) sphere of politics, contained in redefined, overlapping, but distinct private spheres of the home and private enterprise.

In the case of workplace relations, at least, such conservatism involved a significant amount of legal innovation. The laws of master and servant, as noted in chapter 1, had since the late medieval period governed the relations between household heads and those who resided under their roof. While the legal status of servants resembled that of children, married workers were, as a rule, employed on terms that acknowledged their (relative) independence. From the 1750s in England and the 1820s in America, a series of legal innovations gradually obliterated this long-standing distinction between employment and service. In eighteenth-century England, a flurry of legislative activity recast older property and employment relations and enacted new measures for protecting every conceivable form of property.[75] In the process, long-standing distinctions between employment and service—between nominally free and unfree labor—were gradually obliterated. Not only were criminal penalties against day laborers' failure to perform reaffirmed and more rigorously enforced, but many of the principles previously restricted to governing master–servant relations in the narrow sense of the term were extended to cover *all* wage workers. The magisterial authority of the master over those in his household was transferred into the person of the employer, who also was now given a right to the exclusive use and enjoyment of the worker's energies for the period or purposes specified in the agreement. Blackstone's famous 1763 *Commentaries on the Laws of England* confirmed the emergence of a single category of "Master and Servant" as the operative legal description for all relations of manual employment, whether by those resident in the employer's household or by those living elsewhere. In the post-revolutionary United States, the previous clear distinction between free and unfree labor was likewise eroded, this time through legal (rather than legislative) innovations and reinterpretations of common law. By the 1820s, American legal treatises commonly asserted that day laborers were servants, along with covenant and debt servants, apprentices, menials, and slaves.[76]

Under the new comprehensive definition of service, the legal position of the increasing numbers of (non-domestic) wage workers changed. Once a person entered a wage contract, he or she became subject to the master's private magisterial authority, and no longer faced him as a member of "the public." Like marriage, but unlike most other contracts, the agreement to perform work for pay was held to automatically put one party in a superior and the other in a subordinate position: it entailed the employee's assent to "serve" and the employer's right to mastery. In England, until organized labor succeeded in its campaign to eliminate criminal sanctions for premature departure in 1875, increasing numbers of workers were jailed for breach of contract when they left one employer to work for another.[77] In the United States, similar provisions applied until the mobility of the population made the practice unworkable. In the early nineteenth century, American courts began to affirm that, for white adults, at least, the state would not countenance the enforcement of work contracts by detaining employees and forcing them to work against their will. But even as they acclaimed the freedom of employees to quit work, courts denied outstanding wages to those who did not serve out their full term or whose conduct failed to exhibit due fidelity, respect, and obedience. They conceded to employers the capacity to exercise the power of detailed regulation over workplace relations without holding them responsible for industrial accidents caused by the negligence of managers, supervisors, or fellow workers, injuries for which the company would have assumed liability had they been inflicted on an ordinary member of the public. The employer was able to sue a third party for injury to a worker that resulted in a loss of value from the worker's services. Workers, in contrast, did not have any legal redress for injuries to the master, having no property in "the company, care, or assistance" of the superior. They could no longer be arrested for deserting their master, but by the same token they could be sacked the moment they became ill. Finally, employers retained the ability to sue third parties for enticement, a right many used to prosecute unions that advised their members to avoid working for particular firms.[78]

As Orren and others noted, these legal precepts governing workplace relations were largely immune to political intervention. Since the master's authority was lodged in the judiciary, it was also removed from the electorate and resistant to legislation. The few American antebellum labor statutes enacted by state legislatures, such as those limiting the hours of work, were generally ignored by the courts; most of the laws passed since the 1880s, including ones affecting the employment of adult males and legalizing the activities of labor unions, were invalidated as violating common-law rights of both workers and their employers. Other statutes, such as child labor laws, had little practical effect.[79]

In sum, while the dominant image of employment in the nineteenth-century United States was that of a mutually beneficent relationship between free and equal parties and secured by the courts, in legal practice the magisterial authority of the master over those in his household was transferred into the person of the employer.[80] This change was particularly significant in an era in which the workplace less and less resembled the small domestic workshop or farm, which was the site of most production until the early 1800s. By the mid-nineteenth century, large industrial enterprises employed a substantial proportion of working people. Their numbers grew even more as the United States entered into full-scale industrialization after the Civil War of the 1860s.

During the same period in which white adult workers in the United States, Australia, Canada, and England were reinscribed into a sphere of private enterprise governed by modified master-and-servant laws, the word "servant," with its connotations of servility, became increasingly repugnant to them. As an American woman domestic worker pointed out to an English visitor, "Why, I am Mr. x's help. I'd have you know, *man,* that I am no *sarvant;* none but *negers* are *sarvants.*" In 1812, a justice of the Pennsylvania Supreme Court observed, "We do not call even apprentices servants. Speaking of hired persons, we may call them servants; but not speaking to them, but at the risque of losing their service." In the United States, from the time of the revolution, the word "servant" was in common speech increasingly restricted to black workers. From about 1850, with the influx of immigrants from Europe, the term was reintroduced for whites as well, this time for immigrant women performing menial domestic service. The making of the American working class was also the making of notions of white supremacy and black exclusion and subordination.[81]

* * * * *

During the American Revolution and its aftermath, conceptions of citizenship, politics, and leadership underwent a profound change. A powerful image of selfless public service, civic heroism, and noble virtue modeled on classical Greek and Roman precedents gradually gave way to an understanding of politics as the legally arbitrated collision of private interests. Depictions of virtue ceased to be preoccupied with manliness, government service, and heroic death in battle, and gradually came to be associated with voluntary organizations, the family, and the private accomplishments of women. A homosocial vision of masculine virtue began to give way to heterosexual, familial, even feminine notions of civic conduct: "women and emotions became increasingly associated with moral activity while men and reason became more exclusively associated with the utilitarian pursuit of self-interest."[82]

"The only principles of public conduct that are worthy of a gentleman or a man," proclaimed James Otis Jr. in 1761, "are to sacrifice estate, ease, health, applause, and even life, to the sacred calls of his country. These manly sentiments, in private life, make the good citizen; in public life, the patriot and the hero."[83] As feminist scholars such as Kerber noted, this language of patriotism and nationhood excluded women, suffused as it was with an image of Britain as an unnatural mother, its leaders as effeminate fops, and Americans as vigorous youths ready to assume the responsibilities of manhood, not least by a vigorous rejection of domesticity and family ties. The men who remodeled the American polity after the war emphasized at one and the same time its reasonableness, its solidity, its link to classical models, and its manliness and freedom from effeminacy. The construction of the autonomous, patriotic, male citizen required that the traditional association of women with unreliability, unpredictability, and lust be emphasized. Women's weakness became a foil for republican manliness.[84]

But already in the 1760s, a new vision of virtue began to emerge. Over time, the ideal of manly sacrifice on the altar of the republic began to give way to a more homely willingness to get along with others for the sake of decency and prosperity. This new form of virtue could be expressed by women as well as men; some, in fact, thought that it came more naturally to women. Gordon Wood agrees with many feminist writers when he says that "the importance of this domestication of virtue for American culture can scarcely be exaggerated."[85] The public good, political leaders were coming to agree, was likewise "best promoted by the exertion of each individual seeking his own good in his own way."[86] Not disinterested public virtue but private interest appeared to be the cement that would hold this new society together. To many contemporary observers, the government appeared weak, the churches divided, social institutions fragmented. They were astonished that in spite of this, order seemed to grow out of chaos, and people guided themselves without the check of any controlling power, other than that administered by the collision of their own interests balanced against each other. Americans eventually came to see the republic as a sum of small households whose independence was the basis of the liberty that prevailed in the larger polity and economy.[87] The competitive individual turned out to be a harmonious household represented by its male citizen head.

It was not the hidden hand of the market alone that accomplished this miracle; it was in the newly independent household of the small farmer, manufacturer, or artisan, and his reconstructed family, that the link between the pursuit of profit and the establishment of social order and harmony could be reconciled. The older view of women as more closely tied than men to base physical nature began to be gradually displaced by an image of women as particularly receptive to moral education. Virtue, if still regarded as essential to the public good in a republican state, became ever more difficult to distinguish from private benevolence, personal manners, and female sexual propriety.[88] "In the present state of society," declared Joseph Hopkinson in 1810, "woman is inseparably connected with everything that civilises, refines, and sublimates a man." Consequently, wives and mothers, as guardians of a moral domestic sphere, were now urged to use their special talents to cultivate in their husbands and children the proper moral feelings—the virtue, benevolence, and social affections— necessary to hold a sprawling and competitive republican society together.[89] To prepare young women for the duties of such republican motherhood, increasing numbers of commentators agreed that girls as well as boys should be sent to school; virtuous women, in turn, made good teachers.

As American households in the early nineteenth century faltered under economic and other pressures, men and women, often coming together in myriad new forms of "association" or "society," experimented with novel social and familial values, practices, and functions that would allow them to ride out the storm: "there was nothing in the Western world quite like these hundreds of thousands of people assembling annually in their different voluntary associations and debating about everything." A few commentators, as we will see later, began to see in some of these organizations a great "normal school of democracy" capable of making people more orderly and governable; more prosaically, a number of the associations themselves were directly concerned with the setting up and running of schools.[90] In many of the societies, women took the lead, this time not through claims to classical virtue but through the homely values of evangelical religion. As Mary Ryan shows in her work on Oneida County, New York, in the 1830s and 1840s it was in various forms of association that local women and men worked out the serious problems confronting their families. Almost half of these associations took novel forms, dispensing with fathers and enrolling women or youth exclusively. Yet the new ideals that these public associations developed—such as the pure, loving mother, the sober, cautious breadwinner, the docile, passionless child—would end up being superintended in the private home by the mother. In other words, the association itself helped to usher in the ultimate triumph of the privatized home.[91]

Although in the United States the extent of this process seems to have been exceptional, voluntary associations mushroomed throughout the West. Not all of them were approved by those in power. "Good men to associate, bad men to conspire," as one English society for the prosecution of felons put it succinctly.[92] Institutions that helped construct middle-class identity tended to be perceived as virtuous; those that took part in the making of the working class, illegal. Of the organizations actively pro- scribed as illegitimate "self-created societies" encroaching upon republican institutions and "warring from the outside against the total structure of American society," trade unions were the most prominent and numerous.[93] Extrapolating from laws of conspiracy, notions guaranteeing the sanctity of private property, and redefined master-and-servant laws, a series of highly politicized trials declared virtually all forms of union activity illegal. The journeymen themselves saw their associations as fitting representa- tions of revolutionary republicanism, and condemned the attempt to elimi- nate them as an affront to the democratic principle of popular sovereignty.[94] But it was only from the 1870s that, according to Orren, the labor move- ment finally managed to extend liberalism into the workplace. During some six decades of conflict spanning the end of the nineteenth century, the unions brought about fundamental changes in the American state by drag- ging workplace relations, at least to some extent, under the rule of the legislature.[95]

* * * * *

In many cases, the law is ineffective, disorganized; it reflects rather than helps shape social conditions. This situation was arguably different. A series of court cases relating to issues such as the legality of union action and to workplace injuries helped redraw the boundaries of social life. The cases failed to prevent the rise of unions, even though they constricted forms of union action. More important, they helped establish the dividing line between the employer's private sphere of magisterial authority and the public sphere of legitimate political intervention. A new private sphere was born, structured by reinvented relations of subordination and authority but emptied of the mutuality of obligation and care that had previously charac- terized master–servant relations.

FRENCH REVOLUTION

Thirteen years after the Declaration of Independence was signed in July 1776, and six years after Americans won their war against the British, the workers of the Faubourg St. Antoine stormed the Bastille. The fourteenth of July, symbolizing the beginning of the French Revolution, is still celebrated as the National Day of republican France. The Declaration of the Rights of Man, debated throughout August 1789 and published as a preface to the constitution of September 1791, became the basic charter of European liberals for the next half-century. Though all were soon to return, the monarchy, the nobility, and the Roman Catholic church were briefly eclipsed. The abolition of the monarchy in this most populous state in Europe in 1792, the execution of the king a year later, and the nine months of Jacobin government in 1793–94 profoundly frightened the ruling classes in the whole of Europe; their repercussions were felt throughout the world. According to Hobsbawm,

> If the economy of the nineteenth-century world was formed mainly under the influence of the British Industrial Revolution, its politics and ideology were formed mainly by the French. . . . France provided the vocabulary and the issues of liberal and radical-liberal politics for most of the world. . . . France provided the first great example, the concept and the vocabulary of nationalism. France provided the codes of law, the model of scientific and technical organisation, the metric system of measurement for most countries.

The armies of revolutionary France set out to transform the world; it could be argued that many of its ideas actually did so.[96]

But what precisely were these ideas and events? And to what extent did they affect the lives of women as well as men? To this day, the French Revolution continues to be the focus of political and scholarly disagreement regarding its causes, content, meaning, and consequences. Some recent contributions to these debates allow us to return to the main topic of this chapter and ask whether the French Revolution, like the American one, can be seen as a catalyst in the destruction of old and the invention of new forms of patriarchal governance. This is precisely the argument of Lynn Hunt's book *The Family Romance of the French Revolution*. Supplementing more orthodox historical accounts by evidence drawn from sources such as novels, engravings, paintings, pamphlets, and pornographic literature, she argues that the revolutionary period witnessed a wide-ranging and profound reconfiguring of the forms and meanings of authority relations. While philosophical works on these subjects had considerable impact among a minority of the population, a far more accessible way of thinking about these issues was through imagining and representing different permutations and meanings of familial relations. And here, like

Fliegelman and Wood, Hunt detects a dethroning of patriarchalist authority and a desacralization of monarchy long before the king's head was
actually cut off. The practice of the revolution confirmed these changes by
gradually destroying the key legal foundations of patriarchalism and insti-
tuting a new, fraternal social order.

Yet Hunt stresses that the passage from patriarchalism to a fraternal
social contract was fraught with difficulties. Not only was the process
contested at every step by different groups of women and men, but the
brothers themselves had little idea what a fraternal social order might look
like in practice. Would the restriction of paternal authority make everyone
equal, brother with brother, brother with sister, and children with parents?
Would the model of the family be thrown out altogether in favor of political
association based on isolated, independent, self-possessing, contracting
individuals? And what exactly would replace deference and paternal authority as a basis of political consent? "As revolutionary leaders groped for
models of the family that would keep women out of politics," Hunt notes,
"they also tried to retain the main elements of the liberal notion of the
individual and restrain the power of fathers. This turned out to be quite
difficult and certainly not logically consistent."[97]

In political practice, royal authority was gradually restricted, until
the monarchy was abolished and in 1792 replaced by a republic. Several
months later, the king himself was tried and then executed. The male
subjects of an absolute monarch became the citizens of France. At first,
only independent white men over twenty-five years of age with some
property or regular wages were designated as "active citizens"; the rest of
their brothers and sisters remained "passive citizens." But within a couple
of years, serfdom, slavery, and the legal distinction between active and
passive male citizenship was abolished, the age of political majority was
reduced to twenty-one years, and male servants, mulattoes, and blacks
were admitted to the brotherhood. Since absolutism and paternal power
had been ideologically intertwined under the Old Regime, an attack on
absolutism seemed to entail an assault on excessive paternal authority as
well.[98] The notorious *lettres de cachet de famille* were abolished, the age of
majority was reduced to twenty-one years for both men and women, and
fathers lost legal control over their adult children. Fathers' discretionary
power over inheritance was whittled away until all children, male and
female, legitimate *and* illegitimate, had equal claims to the property of their
parents. In family disputes, a father's sole right of action was replaced by a
family council, and some of his prerogatives were taken over by the state. In
principle, at least, state education was made compulsory for all children in

1793. The legal reforms of 1791 gave women the status of civil individuals; as the Jacobins won power in national politics, a number of women's other demands were enshrined into law as well. By 1792, marriage was decreed to be a civil contract, with both partners being able to sue for divorce on the same grounds. Although husbands retained greater powers in marriage, fathers and mothers had equal rights over the children after divorce. All of these provisions not only revolutionized relations between the generations, they also considerably loosened patriarchal controls over women. For several short years, as an older form of patriarchy remained under siege, the revolution opened a sizable window to feminist claims and activism.

Although they never won formal citizenship rights and were therefore not able to assume many public roles, women became centrally involved in the revolutionary—and counterrevolutionary—process.[99] Starting with quasi-religious processions of supplicants, women of the popular classes provided a significant and essential component of the crowds that fueled the French Revolution. The huge march on Versailles in October of 1789 by the market women of Paris is widely seen as one of the crucial events of the revolution. From 1790 to August 1792, significant numbers of women were involved in the progressive radicalization of politics in Paris. They were among the editors and printers of journals, among the activists maneuvering both within and outside local and national institutions in Paris, and above all among the armed demonstrators and marchers, sometimes numbering in the tens of thousands, who paraded before the national assembly and even the king. These efforts helped undermine the supports of constitutional monarchy and establish a republic. In revolutionary practice, if not in law, thousands of Parisian women assumed a formidable presence as active revolutionary citizens: independent, free, vigilant, and armed. "Active citizens," one deputy reminded his colleagues in 1791, "are those who took the Bastille."[100] Between 1791 and 1793, women established their own political clubs in Paris and at least fifty provincial towns and cities. At first they were often supported by local men's clubs.[101] A significant minority of women and men used the revolutionary principles of liberty, equality, and justice to make repeated claims for women's rights and citizenship, for ending their legal subordination in marriage and customary subservience to men.[102] "Either no individual of the human race has true rights, or all of them have the same ones; and he who votes against the right of another, whatever his religion, his colour, or his sex, has from that moment abjured his own rights," argued Condorcet in 1790.[103]

Yet women's visible presence in symbolic action—and the customary allegorical representation of revolutionary virtues and of the republic as young women—was not easily accommodated in revolutionary discourse. In the United States, classical Greek and Roman models of male virtue were employed by men in imagining their emancipation from the despotic father of British monarchy; in France, these same models were counterposed to an image of depraved absolutism that was at once licentious and impotent. A recurring theme in contemporary speeches and writings was the contrast between aristocratic decadence and republican virtue: the sacrilegious destruction of the monarchy was justifiable because of its notorious corruption. In turn, it was to a large extent the influence of women that was seen as the defining characteristic of corruption under the old regime (just as it had been in the disreputable trades). Absolutism came to equal a sort of emasculated paternal tyranny. In the aristocratic world, women had a public role; their influence at court and in the salons in some ways did not differ significantly from men's. The bourgeois critique of aristocratic decadence and artifice now associated the license formerly enjoyed by "public women"—whether prostitutes, influential aristocrats, or the queen herself—with the overall and undesirable effeminacy of the monarchy and of aristocratic political rule.[104] Quite apart from other damage they might cause, public women would emasculate political men. As a foil to the corruption of the old regime, the manly, virtuous republic would be built around the rational activism—and healthy virility—of the brotherhood of men, surpassing both the tyranny of fathers and the polluting influence of women. The only place for women in this homosocial world where chaste brothers gave birth to the body politic was in the family home—and even that appeared to rest on shaky foundations. Personifications of male virtue as Roman bellicose heroes who spurned love and domesticity and did not hesitate to kill or sacrifice sons, fathers, or brothers to the glory of the republic did not sit easily with a robust republican motherhood and the sanctity of the home.[105]

As in America, this immaculately virile configuration of symbolic and political power was relatively short-lived. After the mid-1790s, the word "fraternity" itself dropped out of revolutionary slogans, to be replaced by "liberty" and "equality" standing alone: the revolutionary leaders did not attempt to transform themselves into fathers of the republic.[106] By the turn of the century, as the directorate and Napoleon gradually reinvented and reintroduced patriarchal controls over women, children, and workers, the family was rehabilitated as a political metaphor, albeit one headed by a reasonable father and not a despot.[107] Nevertheless, many scholars argue that this period saw the discursive exclusion of women from the newly emerging (bourgeois) public sphere—or the "purging of the female from the body politic"—with the disembodied "universal" becoming male, and the "particular" the sexed female.[108]

Masculinist discourse was soon joined by legislative action. From the second year of the republic, women began to be systematically excluded from formal assemblies and tribunals. In October 1793, two weeks after the execution of the deposed queen, Marie Antoinette, women's political clubs were outlawed, and *citoyennes* were explicitly denied the right to exercise political rights and to take an active part in government affairs or in popular and political gatherings.[109] Even then, women continued to self-identify with the sovereign people; they found alternative gender-specific political practices, places to hear the news and to air their political views.[110] After the fall of the Jacobins in July 1794, many of women's other gains, such as the right to divorce, were rescinded. In May 1795, the legislature ordered women to remain in their homes and decreed that groups of more than five women in public would be dispersed, by force if necessary.[111] Women's dependent status was confirmed and deepened in the Napoleonic codes of 1804, which became the model for legislation throughout much of the non-British West, from Turkey, Romania, and Poland to Spain, Portugal, Argentina, Mexico, and parts of Canada. Women had no political rights, and their legal status was that of dependents. As such, they could not sign contracts, buy or sell, or have bank accounts in their own names. Paternal authority over children was strengthened (insubordinate children could again be imprisoned for limited terms), and male family members regained some of their superior inheritance rights. Divorce was restricted in 1803 and abolished altogether in 1816, not to be revived until 1884. By now, male hostility toward women's political participation had crystallized into a fully elaborated domestic ideology, in which women were scientifically proven to be suitable only for domestic work[112]—even as thousands of them began to work in factories.

Patriarchal rule was reinstated not only in gender but in class terms. In North America, most white working men retained the vote while becoming subject to more comprehensive master-and-servant statutes. In revolutionary France, all associations of workers were outlawed in 1791.[113] Employers of the growing number of large enterprises demanded in addition that the legislature grant them the ability to devise legally enforceable regulations in each of their factories, similar to the powers of household heads over domestic servants, and those of masters over journeymen and apprentices in small workshops. The employment contract by itself, the employers argued, was not enough to discipline large groups of workers. And since each enterprise was unique, it was impossible for the state itself to make rules that would apply to all. In 1795, the Directoire accepted these arguments. Within two decades, several pieces of paternalist legislation granted employers extensive semi-feudal powers—including the authority to have workers imprisoned for up to three days for insolence. In most cases, these regulations came to include a whole series of disciplinary and moral requirements, far exceeding the physical needs of production and stretching beyond the workshop to encompass the attitudes and the behavior of the working class.[114] Under the post-1815 constitutions, paternalist workplace legislation was complemented by considerable restrictions on male franchise.[115]

While Orren stressed the role of the labor movement in defeating the most anti-democratic aspects of master-and-servant statutes in the United States, Donzelot and Perrot highlight the significance of two impersonal and more efficacious instruments of workplace control. The explosive tutelary industrial order in France, they argue, was eventually replaced by Taylorism, with its subordination of the worker to the machine, and secondly by social insurance. Importantly, both could be introduced only on the condition that the particularity of each enterprise was denied, and *common* conditions were recognized across different workplaces. Both measures reduced the employers' direct rights of command, but instead promised higher productivity, less class conflict, and greater socialization of the risks of capital: personal forms of patriarchal rule could be supplanted by bureaucratic regulation.[116]

*****

The age of democratic revolutions, first ignited in North America and France, continued for another half a century. In the 1820s, a wave of uprisings in Mediterranean Europe spread to Latin America, creating a network of republics throughout the continent. Between 1829 and 1834, most parts of Europe erupted again. Uprisings broke out in Belgium, Poland, Spain, Portugal, Switzerland, and various parts of Italy and Germany. At the height of Chartist mobilization, even Britain came close to a revolutionary outbreak, which was averted in part by the Reform Act of 1832 with its modest extensions of male suffrage. According to Hobsbawm, this period marks several momentous transformations in social and political life. Some of the most important changes were the definitive defeat of aristocratic by bourgeois power in western Europe and the emergence of working-class movements as an independent and self-conscious force in politics, and of nationalist movements in a number of European countries.[117]

The third and largest wave of insurrection—arguably the closest the world has come to a global revolution—occurred in 1848, at the end of a period of economic decline. Uprisings in which the laboring poor played a prominent role engulfed France, Italy, the German states, Switzerland, and the Hapsburg Empire, and unrest affected Ireland, Spain, Denmark, and several other countries. Within months, most of the old rulers who had been toppled from power were restored, and the institutional and political changes were reversed. Only the abolition of serfdom in the Hapsburg Empire proved irreversible. Hobsbawm notes that 1848 appears as the one revolution in the modern history of Europe which combines the greatest promise, the widest scope, and the most immediate initial success with the most unqualified and rapid failure.[118] The process of political reform soon resumed, but bourgeois and proletarian movements had parted company; in the future, liberal reformers would take care not to revolutionize the masses.

PUBLIC SPHERES

In early modern Europe, politics overlapped with the household affairs of monarchs and of noble families. Now a patriarchalist social order began to be displaced by new configurations of social power. In the age of democratic revolutions, the informal, convivial culture of eighteenth-century merchants, traders, and farmers was gradually superseded by one dominated by bureaucracies, clubs, associations, professions, white-collar jobs, and institutions of formal training. Demanding the transformation of arbitrary into rational authority, subject to the scrutiny of a citizenry organized into a public body beneath the protection of the law, men of the increasingly self-confident bourgeoisie helped create what has been conceptualized as one of the most significant products of this age: a liberal democratic public sphere. In his famous formulation, Habermas defines the ideal public sphere as

> first of all a realm of our social life in which something approaching public opinion can be formed. Access is guaranteed to all citizens. A portion of the public sphere comes into being in every conversation in which private individuals assemble to form a public body. They then behave neither like business or professional people transacting private affairs, nor like members of a constitutional order subject to the legal constraints of a state bureaucracy. Citizens behave as a public body when they confer in an unrestricted

fashion—that is, with the guarantee of freedom of assembly and association and the freedom to express and publish their opinions—about matters of general interest.[119]

In his critique of Habermas, Geoff Eley argues that instead of concentrating exclusively, as Habermas does, on what is in effect a sphere of bourgeois political activity, it is more accurate to speak of several competing public spheres. In the late eighteenth century, "the liberal desideratum of reasoned exchange also became available for nonbourgeois, subaltern groups, whether the radical intelligentsia of Jacobinism and its successors or wide sections of social classes like the peasantry or the working class." Each of these popular movements arguably produced its own distinctive form of a public sphere. At the very moment of its appearance, the liberal public sphere was faced with not only "a 'plebeian' public that was disabled and easily suppressed but also a radical one that was combative *and* highly literate."[120] Rather than seeing the public sphere, as Habermas implies, as the spontaneous and class-specific achievement of the bourgeoisie, Eley argues that it can be more usefully characterized as "the structured setting where cultural and ideological contest or negotiation among a variety of publics takes place."[121]

In an argument that closely parallels the one made in this book, Eley then draws on recent scholarly work to show that both the dominant bourgeois *and* the oppositional proletarian public spheres were highly gendered, indeed constructed around the exclusion of all matters feminine. First, modern political thought is highly gendered in its basic structure. From the fraternal social contract of Locke and Rousseau to the virtuous citizens of the American and French revolutions; from abstract ideas about reason, law, and nature to specific proclamations, laws, and constitutions— all rested upon a newly articulated opposition between women and men. Certainly these oppositions made use of many ancient and well-worn images, but in new and often unprecedented ways. Since women's nature was routinely identified with particularity, dependence, silence, modesty, and domesticity, but also with eroticism, artifice, insincerity, and unreason, manliness and citizenship were, at least in part, constructed around transcending the feminine.[122]

Second, it was in the emerging middle-class, masculine world of reading and debating societies, fraternities, clubs, and associations that the fraternal, democratic ideals of the French and American revolutions took shape; it was the same world that helped constitute the English and German middle class itself as a self-conscious social and political force. Indeed, voluntary association, independent from patriarchalist dependencies and state control alike—the very heart of the public sphere—was in principle the logical form of bourgeois emancipation and bourgeois self-affirmation.[123] But most of these organizations derived their pride and integrity from the categorical exclusion of women and a celebration of what they saw as true manliness. Indeed, the myriad associations, clubs, companies, institutes, lodges, and societies congealed into settled rules and routines at precisely the time when women found it hardest to act and to be heard in public.

Finally, the oppositional public spheres themselves engendered patterns of exclusion and gender polarization. Women were actively involved in the American and French revolutions, as I noted earlier, only to be excluded from political life as new institutions took shape. Similarly, according to Dorothy Thompson, women played an important role in the early years of British Chartism. Contemporary observers noted the presence of large numbers of females (and children) in radical crowds, riots, disturbances, and political meetings, and often attributed to them a "violence and ferocity" surpassing that of the men. In the 1830s, the illegal unstamped papers were hawked around the country by women as well as men. Women took part in a wide range of radical activities together with their husbands and families; at times they formed their own organizations.[124] Importantly, while the bourgeoisie was constructing its sharply segregated public and private spheres, the strength of early Chartism lay in the robust and imaginative creation of new forms of collective sociability—from public breakfasts, festivals, and dramatic productions to banners, commemorations, rituals, and tableaux—which reintegrated the public and the private in a distinct *public* space of independent working-class activity, at the same time defensively closed against the culture of the dominant class and affirmatively committed to a new way of life.[125]

But while Chartist women understood and presented themselves mainly in a multifaceted family role—as carers and nurturers demanding proper conditions to carry out their sacred family role, as reluctant contributors to the family wage, and as auxiliaries who demanded the vote for their male kinfolk in a bid to help the family as a whole—Chartist men gradually developed a language of masculine working-class citizenship. Rejecting the "female-centered" schemes for social amelioration formulated by the Owenites and other Utopian and popular Christian movements and drawing on doctrines of natural rights, they began to argue that male (but not female) workers had the same individual rights to the franchise as other propertied citizens: the property in their labor gave them the same manly independence that underpinned the rights of those already represented in the body politic, and differentiated them from childlike, female, and servile dependence.[126] Catherine Hall notes that the emergence of the working man as a political subject in his own right, fighting for his own right to vote, for his own capacity to play a part in determining forms of government, was part of the process of the development of male working-class consciousness. Female working-class activists, on the other hand, positioned themselves, and were positioned by others, as wives, mothers, and sisters supporting the cause of working men.[127]

Around the middle of the nineteenth century, women—and unskilled workers—became marginalized not only in oppositional concepts of citizenship but in political action. As the Chartist movement became more organized, it developed formal rules of procedure and a hierarchy of leadership, and lessened its dependence on unplanned mass action. Already in 1820, a contemporary noted that "the poor, when suffering and dissatisfied, no longer make a riot, but hold a meeting—instead of attacking their neighbours, they arraign the Ministry."[128] These developments were part of a perceptible "modernization" and masculinization of working-class politics. In a period of relative prosperity, skilled men in particular developed increasingly sophisticated organizations such as trade unions, political pressure groups, cooperative societies, and educational institutions. The way of life of most women and the unskilled made participation in these more structured political forms extremely difficult; in any case, the organizations themselves took increasing pride in the manliness of their members.[129] The defeat of Chartism and its eventual replacement by other forms of working-class organization was also, according to Taylor, a move from a gender-inclusive, family-oriented movement to one defined increasingly around the demands and sociability of men. However subversive working-class politics might be, it too came to rest on the integrity of a household dependent on and represented by a male breadwinner, this time a skilled tradesman or artisan whose property was his labor: popular sovereignty became fundamentally a male preserve. As the century wore on, most working-class movements would add forms of racial and ethnic exclusion to their self-definition. In turn, in many of their struggles for political rights, women and other disenfranchised groups would use the gap between the promise and the reality of political organization as a lever of political change.

CHAPTER FOUR

State Formation, Personality Structure, and the Civilizing Process

Mankind are found in various stages of cultivation. Some live chiefly by hunting, and are called *savages;* some have partially emerged from the savage state, and are called *barbarous;* and some, having good houses, cities, written laws, and many good institutions, are called *refined, enlightened, or civilised.*[1]

It is to be noted that to him that is a governor of a public weal belongeth a double governance, that is to say, an interior or inward governance, and an exterior or outward governance. The first is of his affects and passions, which do inhabit within his soul, and be subjects to reason. The second is of his children, his servants, and other subjects to his authority. Sir Thomas Elyot, 1531.[2]

All their life long, [women] will have to submit to the strictest and most enduring restraints, those of propriety. They must be trained to bear the yoke from the first so that they may not feel it: to master their own caprices and submit themselves to the will of others. Rousseau, 1762.[3]

The male is only a male now and again, the female is always a female. Rousseau, 1762.[4]

I do not think it desirable to allow individuality in the case of children. Inspector Stanton, 1887.[5]

The mode of production of material life determines the general character of the social, political and spiritual processes of life. It is not the consciousness of men that determines their being, but, on the contrary, their social being determines their consciousness. Marx, 1859.[6]

Women are capable of education, but they are not made for the more ad-vanced sciences, philosophy, and certain forms of artistic production, all of which require a universal faculty. Women may have quick wit, taste, and elegance, but they cannot attain the ideal. . . . Women regulate their actions not by the demands of universality, but by arbitrary inclinations and opinions . . . they follow the dictates of subjectivity, not objectivity. Hegel, 1821.[7]

Let us now radically alter our field of vision. The previous three chapters dealt with the transformations of families, economies, armies, churches, and governments between the sixteenth and the nineteenth century. Did any of this make much difference to the way people actually understood themselves and were seen by others? And how could we tell? Conversely, is any of this relevant to modern conceptions of selfhood? Historians, with generous aid from sociologists, philosophers, anthropologists, and psychologists, have long been fascinated by these questions, and have often attempted to answer them with remarkable ingenuity.[8] According to many scholars, changing social conditions went beyond affecting the day-to-day lives of contemporaries. In a way similar to how they influenced the long-term development of other cultural forms, social forces also contributed to the shaping and reshaping of mentalities and subjectivities. On closer inspection, the taken-for-granted nature of today's individuality turns out to be socially constructed rather than, for example, given by biology.[9] Seeking intellectual and emotional coherence and throwing off the shackles that constrain the free expression of our individuality might well improve our sense of well-being. But this does not make the ends and means of processes such as "the search for authenticity" into natural human attributes. Rather, subjectivity and the means of achieving it have a history, as do discourses and practices constituting sanity, sexuality, or the soul.[10]

Drawing on several influential traditions of thinking about these issues, this chapter links the governance of states, the organization of production, the increasing significance of self-governance, and the constitution of particular forms of individual subjectivity. Useful as they are, however, these same intellectual traditions contain problematic assumptions and unresolved questions—questions that are difficult enough to formulate, let alone resolve.[11] In the first place, much of the work on the development of western individualism says little about the forms of subjectivity that the new ways of understanding the self coexisted with or displaced; indeed, it often implies that people in medieval Europe were a bundle of wild instincts kept in check by fear of external sanctions. One approach, taken up in some forms of poststructuralist theory, portrays the free, undisciplined culture of pre-Reformation carnival, a vision that owes much to the work of the Russian cultural theorist Bakhtin on the writings of Rabelais. Here, as

Roper puts it, the people of early modern Europe are often treated as "colourful psychic primitives from a carnival world."[12] Like poststructuralist writers, Elias is deeply ambiguous about the final products of the civilizing process. Nevertheless, his use of "recapitulation theory" (which holds that phylogenesis, or the putative linear historical development of a species, culture, or race, is replayed in ontogenesis, or the lifetime development of individuals) lends itself to comparing people in medieval Europe to children today, and depicting the rise of individualism as the coming of age of the human race.[13]

In more conventional social sciences, the visions of primitive mentality and a unilinear civilizing process are far less ambiguous. Many branches of contemporary philosophy, psychology, and literary and educational theory put those who lack the symptoms of a full-blown individualism on a lower rung of human perfection. It is a commonplace of literary criticism that in their writing, workers often appear to lack the "significant selfhood" that organizes traditional autobiography: they do not exhibit flair and "personality."[14] In his *Three Essays on Sexuality* (1903), Freud suggested that the African, in not going though a period of latent sexuality in childhood, fails to develop an authentic superego. Colonizers routinely asserted that natives, like children incapable of self-control and rational thought, respond best to firm paternal control and beatings; it is useless to argue with them. By the 1920s, this common sense was enshrined by French and English scholars in the science of ethnopsychiatry. For some decades, their findings helped support the view that those who remained psychic children did not possess the intellectual preconditions of citizenship—that blacks were congenitally incapable of governing their own communities.[15] Kohlberg's work on the psychology of moral development rates a "punishment and obedience orientation" as the lowest on a six-point scale of moral development, and a "universal ethical principle orientation" as the highest. When tested on this scale, women rarely get past stage three.[16] Children, European women, and non-Europeans of both sexes also tend to do badly in terms of Piaget's five stages of intellectual development, rarely reaching the highest stage, formal operations, which consists of reasoning by hypothesis.

As Stoler has recently reminded us, added to these problems is the fact that even critical work on western subjectivity is confined mostly to the metropolitan countries. In focusing on the West, it ignores the possibility that crucial attributes of civilized "whiteness" were constructed in the highly contested spaces of colonial settlements. Attempting to forge categorical notions of civilized selfhood out of heterogeneous and overlapping categories of poor and disreputable whites, mixed race men and women, whites "gone native," wealthy indigenous inhabitants, upright Britishers, or "echte Hollander," settlers and colonial officials influenced the contemporary reshaping of metropolitan cultures. This highly significant work of cultural production was only partly abstract and discursive, elaborated in government regulations, newspaper articles, novels, and political debates. Much of it was also accomplished ad hoc, pragmatically, in the practical process of imperial expansion and day-to-day life.[17]

In their different ways, historians, philosophers, anthropologists, and feminist scholars have attempted to chart alternative forms of subjectivity to the manly independence and self-possessed rationality celebrated by philosophy, psychology, and liberal democratic theory alike. In *Sources of the Self*, Charles Taylor presents a brilliant history of the bodies of thought that went into the making of modern identity. One of his guiding themes is how sources of morality moved from the "outside" to the "inside" of individuals. Wisdom, morality, and happiness used to be defined as a person's ability to perceive, and act according to, the commands of gods, universal ideas, the laws of nature, God's will. In the modern era, such ideals are all but incomprehensible. The sources of the self now appear to reside in the depths of the individual psyche, in the clarity and power of a person's rational thought, in self-possession, in individual creativity. Taylor makes clear that his account does not constitute an actual social history of the self, something that is far more difficult and for which there are much less coherent sources.[18]

Natalie Davis and other historians of early modern Europe agree that sixteenth-century men and women conceived of themselves as members of collectivities, especially households, and understood themselves in their connections to, rather than independence of, groups. Moreover, they thought of the groups as prior to their individual members. Personal identity constituted an articulation or special case of the whole.[19] Roper has noted that in early modern Germany, one such collectivity was represented by the term *Gemeinde*—something between a church congregation, a communal unit, and a group of subjects—which had a powerful mobilizing force in the Peasants' War. Like many other forms of collective identity, however, she shows that it excluded women: *Gemeinde Mann*, the common man, was the embodiment of communal worth and pride; *Gemeinde Frau*, the common woman, was a prostitute. At present, historical material on these issues is at best sketchy, evidence is notoriously difficult to find, and theoretical work is in its infancy. Indeed, the collective identities of the most powerful groups in society are likely to be most visible and most clearly documented; those of the powerless and marginal, shadowy and indistinct.

The difficulty of conceptualizing alternative forms of subjectivity is only one of the issues confronting us. The second, equally intractable, problem is the link between subjectivities and the structure of constraints within which they develop. Historical accounts of mentalities often assume that changing social circumstances imprint themselves in a straightforward, rationally coherent way on the consciousness of groups, which in turn satisfactorily represents the mental universe of its individual members. Certainly, historians often insist on the unpredictable nature of individual agency: there is no guarantee that people understand, agree with, follow, or do not subvert dominant social prescriptions; that women do not imagine themselves as scholars, warriors, or priests; that the pressure of circumstances is interpreted in a "rational" way; that the same words mean the same thing to different people at different times; that the peasant who respectfully tugs his forelock in the daytime does not torch his lordship's barn at night. However, with the possible exception of psychoanalysis, social theory has little purchase on the irrational, on fantasy, or on individual psychic creativity. In addition, history and theory do a far better job accounting for mentalities than for the sexed bodies of individual protagonists, a form of historical agency that is even further removed from words.

THE CIVILIZING PROCESS AND THE MANLINESS OF MASTERS

The central thesis in the work of Norbert Elias concerns the relationship between the growth and extension of state monopoly over the means of violence in late medieval and early modern Europe and a tightening (self-)control over the passions of what could be termed the ruling class. Warriors under constant threat of armed violence, whose survival depended on fierce hand-to-hand combat, Elias notes, showed few of the constraints we have come to associate with civilized manners. These developed and became necessary as the men of the nobility were gradually disarmed and came to rely on the intricate machinations of courtly society to maintain and further their fortunes.

In the early passages of *The Civilizing Process*, Elias describes the intensity of piety, the violence of the fear of hell, the guilt, the penitence, the immense outbursts of joy and gaiety, the sudden flaring and the uncontrollable force of the hatred and belligerence of fifteenth-century warriors. He argues that these feelings were not contradictory, but were all evidence of the less constrained personality structure of people at the time (although he speaks mainly of men). He goes on to relate this personality structure to contemporary social organization, and in particular to the fact that there was no central power strong enough to compel individuals to restraint.[20] The eventual rise of such powers had significant implications for people's psychology: "The peculiar stability of the apparatus of mental self-restraint which emerges as a decisive trait built into the habits of every 'civilised' human being, stands in the closest relationship to the monopolisation of physical force and the growing stability of the central organs of society." Importantly, as society is pacified and passions are controlled, people return to them in dreams, books, pictures. In the course of the civilizing process, the wall of forgetfulness separating libidinal drives and consciousness or reflection has become harder and more impermeable; the geography of the self is redrawn.[21]

A similar transformation of the rulers' psychology is noted by other historians. Anderson, for example, argues that in early modern Europe, men of the nobility had to shed the military exercise of private violence, social patterns of vassal loyalty, economic habits of hereditary insouciance, political rights of representative autonomy, and cultural attributes of unlettered ignorance. Instead they had to learn the new avocations of a disciplined officer, a literate functionary, a polished courtier, and a more or less prudent estate owner.[22] In England, wealthy rentiers and the nobility, neither of whom needed to be personally involved in the running of their estates, eventually merged in the new character of the leisured gentleman. In turn, elaborate, seemingly effortless mastery of the self acquired and served as a prestige value, distinguishing the nobility from other strata of society. Where this system was fully developed, as in France, there was no other place except at court where the nobility could live without loss of status; this, in turn, made them even more dependent on the king.[23] Conversely, during the French Revolution it was dissimulation, or the ability to conceal one's true emotions, which was repeatedly denounced as the chief characteristic of effeminate court life and aristocratic manners, and which was identified as one of the main threats to the republic.[24]

Focusing on the actual conduct of courtly nobility, Elias argues that it was above all the increasing complexity, differentiation, and interdependence of society that led to increased self-control on the part of individuals who had to negotiate it. Rationality, constant self-restraint, and intense drive control, rather than spontaneous violence, became a means of survival in courtly society: "A man who knows the court is master of his gestures, of his eyes and expression; he is deep, impenetrable. He dissimulates the bad turns he does, smiles at his enemies, suppresses his ill-temper, disguises his passions, disavows his heart, acts against his feelings."[25] To courtiers, dissimulation became a matter of survival. But why should the princes themselves become self-controlled? In a fine essay dealing with the history of ideas, Hirschman traces the development of arguments about passions and interests of the powerful.[26] In early modern Europe, torn by murderous wars, with treasuries bankrupted by ill-considered conflicts and trade and commerce decimated by chaotic taxation policy, appealing to the rulers' reason and virtue might have led to one of those situations where everyone agrees with moral precepts and nobody carries them out. Following Machiavelli, many philosophers began to speculate that only appeals to (self-)interest might bring a measure of rationality, prudence, and predictability into the conduct of princes and the nobility, particularly since these were more abundantly endowed with human passions than ordinary mortals. "Interest will not lie," a contemporary saying went—and it was transparently clear that territorial rulers could not satisfy their craving for honor, glory, power, and wealth without curbing their passions and paying careful attention to proper husbanding of the realm's resources. Soon it became evident that laying down precise rules for furthering this desirable goal was anything but easy. Over time, indeed, "interest" came to be collapsed into "economic interest." Long before the triumph of capitalism, trade and commerce continued to be held in contempt, but were considered innocuous and even beneficial in their effects, certainly when compared with the often disastrous results of pursuing greatness and glory on the battlefield.[27]

In chapter 1, I noted Oestreich's contention that Neostoicism, particularly as popularized by Lipsius, supplied an essential ingredient of confessionalization in early modern Europe. From the perspective adopted here, Neostoicism constituted a major set of precepts guiding the civilizing process, on both an individual and the national level. Lipsius's work was popular and remarkably influential because his reading of classical texts produced a set of practical, integrated precepts for mastering the self, creating a strong state, and drilling and disciplining the army. The pivot of the strong state, Lipsius believed, was an exceedingly severe, controlled manliness in the Stoic mold. This new man would go beyond the Christianity of the Middle Ages to embrace the old Roman values, and demonstrate the importance of rationality in character, action, and thought. In the fortunes and misfortunes of political life he must retain his constancy, follow reason, curb his natural instincts, and be ready to act and to fight. He must be actively involved in life but maintain an inner emotional and intellectual detachment. The man who reins in the blind passions and emotions that threaten reasoned thought will finally achieve spiritual and moral freedom and so be enabled to deal with life in a creative manner.

The masculinity of the Dutch scholar's vision was made more potent by his style. The terse, laconic language, with its abundance of military similes and metaphors, was written for and appealed particularly to a select circle of military officers educated in the classics. According to Oestreich, the new manly virtues that Lipsius advocated were not the pale phantoms they would become a century later in the age of Enlightenment, but full-blooded, powerful, essential values designed for the exuberant and undisciplined mercenaries of the time.[28] But while his works were dedicated to the princes whose rule they were designed to strengthen, the general tenor of Lipsius's teaching was bourgeois rather than aristocratic, and had little to do with the old world of European nobility. Thus the new officer corps, performing routine duties within the army organization, was to be a professional class with a paid job to do, which it was expected to perform with ambition, diligence, scrupulous exactitude, and a keen sense of responsibility—a far cry from gentlemanly indolence, benevolent indulgence, and leisurely casualness.[29] In following Lipsius's precepts in personal conduct, men of the aristocracy would be able to combine their new dependence on the prince with unambiguous manliness—but in a way that threatened to undercut their own cultural claims to nobility. One thing, however, seemed certain: Neostoic disciplining, combining as it did moral restraint and energetic conduct, asceticism, and action, could not be a prescription for feminine behavior. While it was considered desirable (if often difficult) for women to exercise moral self-control, virile activism and readiness to fight came to be seen as the very antithesis of ladylike manners.

The manliness that is always present but never addressed directly in Oestreich's writings is the central theme of Joan Kelly's pioneering work on gender relations in early modern Europe. In her view, the civilizing process can be seen as a strategy through which men of a weakened nobility sought to regain a sense of power. Castiglione's famous and influential early-sixteenth-century work, *The Book of the Courtier* (a key text in Elias's *Civilising Process*), can be read as an attempt to construct a mannered way of life that could give to a dependent nobility a sense of self-sufficiency, or inner power and control, which they had lost in a real economic and political sense. Castiglione described the courtiers' "soft and feminine [faces] as many attempt to have who not only curl their hair and pluck their eyebrows, but preen themselves . . . and appear so tender and languid . . . and utter their words so limply."[30] Cool detachment, self-control, and mastery of the arts of war might provide the sinews of manliness to courtiers whose personal everyday dependence on the prince in many respects resembled the inferior and dependent position of women, and rendered them visibly effeminate.

And indeed, as contemporary debates suggest, the correct balance between gentility and manliness was not easy to achieve. Before the French Revolution put gentility itself in question, French courtiers typically argued that the English were too busy with their interests to have politeness and refinement; the English considered the French to be overrefined, foppish, and effeminate: too much gentility and politeness, they believed, unmanned a gentleman. Even England, some commentators feared, might be ruined as a nation by the increasing effeminacy of its male citizens.[31] By the late eighteenth century, chastened by revolutionary upheavals, gentlemen hoped to be men of leisure, graceful without foppishness, polite without arrogance, tasteful without pretension, virtuous without affectation, independently wealthy without ostentation, and natural without vulgarity.[32] It was through these virtues, still clothed in the robes of classical antiquity, that they imagined the essence of citizenship and articulated their own qualifications for the holding of public office.

The American and French revolutions, I argued earlier, can be seen as a watershed in the destruction of one form of patriarchal governance and the rise of another. One of the most visible manifestations of this change was a marked transformation in men's costume. In revolutionary France, Hunt notes, clothing was invested with great political significance. Dressed in sober, modest clothes, revolutionary deputies claimed that the plumed hats, colorful fabrics, laces, and gold trims of the aristocrats were signs of effeminacy and debauchery. Soon, simplicity in dress became fashionable.[33] According to one historian of costume, noblemen's clothing during the 1600s and 1700s outshone women's in color, design, and elaborateness. By the 1780s, fashions for men suddenly became more sober. Upper-class men—mannered, artificial, dandified, occupied with their snuffboxes, handkerchiefs, wigs, canes, gloves, muffs, paint, patches, and perfume—now appeared effeminate and ridiculous rather than noble and regal. "Powder, gold lace, tricornes and bagwigs disappeared almost suddenly. . . . Men had become more conservative in dress both in the home and on the streets." By the 1790s, wigs and powdered hair had almost completely gone out of fashion.[34] For women too, a lack of artifice, a soap-and-water freshness, became fashionable for the first time since the late Middle Ages. A slender, languid body and large eyes in a pale face expressed a new taste for simplicity and elegance and conveyed the delicacy of feeling and sentiment which was increasingly associated with true femininity.[35]

While men of the nobility proved their manliness through easy mastery of themselves and others, until well into the nineteenth century most shunned anything that might suggest deliberate learning or direct involvement in trade, manufacture, or commerce, and they had only scorn for intellectual exertion for profit.[36] According to Locke, trade was "wholly inconsistent with a gentleman's calling";[37] in pre-revolutionary France, noble status was legally forfeited if one followed an "ignoble" occupation. Although the reconciliation of the astonishing growth of English commerce with traditional notions of (male) gentility was from the beginning of the eighteenth century explored on paper by a number of thinkers— Defoe, Mandeville, Steele, and Addison among them—it was not until the age of democratic revolutions that a new vision of ruling-class masculinity slowly began to take hold. On his visit to America in the early 1830s, the Frenchman de Tocqueville was still astonished that genteel Americans not only thought that work was honorable, but believed that work specifically to gain money was compatible with the status of a gentleman.[38] A similar point is made by Jan Cohn in an overview of portrayals of the hero in English-language romantic fiction. In today's fiction, she notes, the hero's work is itself virile: it signifies his male energy and power; it is challenging, difficult, a struggle against the odds, a battle against competition. In most Victorian fiction, in contrast, the hero looked back to an earlier world. He was not an active man of business and did not have aggressive sexuality, both of which were reserved for the villain. He was blond, with perfect features and a languid disposition, and his power was that of old money and aristocratic authority over many dependents.[39] The modern association of social standing, virility, and sexual potency with the active control of capital, which I will discuss at more length below, is of recent origin.

*****

In several places in his work, Elias suggests that the civilizing process led to an improvement in the relative position of noblewomen, who had little status in the warrior culture of armed nobility. Kelly and later feminist scholars, although focusing on somewhat different issues, draw the opposite conclusion. In medieval Europe, they claim, patrimonial powers over lands could be inherited and administered by women, particularly in the absence of a suitable male heir. Noblewomen held both ordinary fiefs and vast collections of counties, and exercised in their own right the seigneurial powers that went with them. Abbesses similarly wielded both spiritual and temporal jurisdiction over great territories: they received homage from their vassals and sent them to war, ruled the laboring population, and made and administered laws. According to Kelly and Wiesner, women were still governing and defending domains in the fifteenth and sixteenth centuries: a contemporary treatise on warfare by Christine de Pisan, for example, was specifically designed to teach ladies how to command in defense and attack.[40] In addition to the noblewomen who assumed positions of command, wives of soldiers, women traders, cooks, carters, laundresses, and prostitutes were a normal part of European armies and even navies until well into the nineteenth century.[41]

There is much evidence, however, that feminine displays of power became the particular target of early modern rulers' efforts to erode the nobility's military, juridical, and political authority. Where these efforts were successful, noblemen became courtiers, sometimes statesmen, officers, and bishops; their sisters were trained to become docile ornaments in the homes of their future husbands, disarmed but subject to many forms of gender-specific violence. Castiglione himself countered some of the virulently misogynist contemporary views on women, but reconstructed their character to complement that of the suave, intricately groomed and attired, pleasing but ultimately dependent courtier. The role he accorded to ladies in his ideal court rendered them cultured but mute, chaste, and passive; contrary even to contemporary practice, he removed them from training at arms and horsemanship. To poems, ballads, sermons, and pamphlets attempting to regulate the attire and behavior of noblewomen, some of whom were still wearing short hair, boots and spurs, practical riding clothes, and weapons in the early seventeenth century, was at times added the weight of royal decree. Thus in 1620 James I of England ordered the bishop of London to instruct all clergy "to inveigh vehemently against the insolencies of our women, and their wearing of broad brimmed hats, pointed doublets, their hair cut short or shorne, and some of them stilettoes or poniards." Even though many noblewomen retained formidable political and economic power until the eve of the French Revolution and beyond, by the second half of the seventeenth century Castiglione's image of the disarmed, powerless lady prevailed throughout Europe as ideology—and increasingly as reality.[42] Ironically, it was precisely in this period that classical notions of virtue and citizenship as a manly willingness to die in battle gained wide currency.[43] By the time the French Revolution broke out, the image of dissimulating, scheming, sumptuously attired and sensual ladies of the court came to symbolize all that was corrupt and despicable in the ancien régime.

THE PROTESTANT ETHIC AND CAPITALISM

While violence and warmaking play a key role in accounts of civilizing the nobility, classical sociology has paid the most attention to links between the rising bourgeoisie and the increased inwardness and rationalization expressed in various Protestant movements. The key argument in Weber's famous essay *The Protestant Ethic and the Spirit of Capitalism* concerns the everyday implications of the ethics of ascetic religious movements, particularly the part they played in engendering and strengthening habits of mind congenial to the development of capitalism. In the doctrine of movements such as Calvinism, Puritanism, Pietism, Methodism, and the various Baptist sects, good works could no longer guarantee individual salvation, since who would be saved and who damned was predetermined by God alone, a God whose reason was totally inaccessible to people's understanding. The extreme inhumanity of this doctrine left a generation with a feeling of unprecedented inner loneliness and despair. The fear of hell induced in people a pressing need to know that they were one of God's elect. The psychological burden of this anxiety could be lightened by following a calling. This meant adopting an ascetic lifestyle and abstaining from leisure, luxury consumption, and sensual pleasures. Unremitting and unsparing self-control, self-scrutiny, and devotion to duty still did not purchase salvation, but proved one's faith and assuaged the individual's fear of eternal damnation. In the economic field, such psychological sanctions gave direction to individuals' practical conduct and held them to it: one consequence of the Protestant ethic was to channel energies into making a success of enterprises.[44]

In his exposition of the link between Protestant ethic and capitalism, Weber draws attention to a complex of psychological techniques which are in many respects similar to those described by Elias and Oestreich, and which are particularly pertinent to any discussions of changing forms of governance. The ascetic Protestant sects, he notes, began applying to the everyday conduct of lay people precepts similar to those that had previously been employed by monks in cloistered contemplative life. These included an incentive for the deliberate weighing of courses of action and their careful justification in terms of individual conscience, a methodical and systematic ordering of one's total moral life and actions in accordance with God's will, and a rationalization of conduct within this world, but for the sake of the world beyond.

One particularly fruitful example through which some of these issues have been thought out concerns the changing practices of confession. Abercrombie, Hill, and Turner note that in medieval Europe, confession and the notion of conscience were used as an instrument for the control of heresy and political protest, especially in remote and inaccessible regions. The confessional also played a major role in the maintenance of patriarchal authority in the household and in the surveillance, self-policing, and control of women, particularly in terms of their sensuality. In the society of the courts, however, confessional practices might also have contributed to the flowering of a culture that favored the individual development of personality. In the fourteenth and fifteenth centuries, the clergy added a new element to this dynamic: they began using confessions to make money. In objecting to the trade in indulgences, Reformation theologians did not so much destroy the traditional Catholic confessional system as redeploy it in new forms of belief and practice. Rather than confess to a priest, pious individuals searched their own conscience, wrote diaries, and privately appealed to God for forgiveness.[45]

In the modern period, many scholars argue, confessional practices were secularized. Long before the triumph of capitalism, as I noted earlier, it was believed that assiduous attention to their own interests might make princes more rational and prudent, and less subject to destructive passions. By the late eighteenth century, a number of economists and philosophers accepted Adam Smith's related but different proposition that the study of each (male) individual's own advantage necessarily led him to prefer that employment which was most advantageous to society. The wealth of nations was achieved not so much through the careful attention of *rulers* to their own interests as through the general pursuit of self-interest by individual subjects. Today, rituals such as psychoanalysis, consciousness-raising, and even questionnaires complement and build upon these technologies of the self.

As Weber himself pointed out, in studying capitalism and mentalities it would be as wrong to overemphasize religion as to ignore its role. In a sense, religion breached the wall of traditionalism; once the hold of capitalist institutions such as the market was secure, they exerted an independent educational role. One insightful exploration of the role of the market in shaping subjectivities is T. H. Haskell's complex argument regarding humanitarian reforms in the century after 1750.[46] According to Haskell, a significant change in perception and cognitive style was formed in the crucible of market transactions, shaped by the gradual expansion of the market and the more intensive reach of its discipline into spheres of life previously untouched by it:

> Adam Smith's "invisible hand" was, after all, not merely an economic mechanism but also a sweeping new mode of social discipline that displaced older, more overt forms of control precisely because of its welcome impersonality and the efficiency with which it allocated goods and resources. The spread of competitive relationships not only channeled behavior directly, encouraging people through shifting wage and price levels to engage in some activities and disengage from others, but also provided an immensely powerful educa-

tional force, capable of reaching into the depths of personal psychology. The market altered character by heaping tangible rewards on people who displayed a certain calculating, moderately assertive style of conduct, while humbling others.[47]

Some writers argue that market-driven precepts were not confined to people's "economic" behavior but affected their most intimate sense of physical self. One instance of this process concerns the gradual development of a scarcity notion of bodily fluids. In his characteristically earthy language, Luther argued in favor of marriage on the grounds that the superabundant nature of male and female bodies must not be unduly restrained, since it was created by God to His design. Both men and women need sexual release at least once a day; for men, if it does not go into a woman, it goes into the shirt.[48] Expanding on this theme, Roper notes that in early modern Germany, the body was seen as an imperfect container of fluids and forces constantly threatening to overflow and burst out, leaving their mark on the world outside. Vomiting, defecating, urinating, and ejaculating were visualized as both pleasurable and transgressive, both sensual and threatening to the social order, in popular imagination as in elaborate Latinate literature.[49] It is a world of difference from this imagery to the preoccupations with husbanding scarce and precious bodily fluids in Victorian Europe. In both medical literature and underground sexual advice, men were at once informed of their natural sexual urges and provided with dire warnings, couched in the most gruesome imagery, should they not manage to bring these under control. Warts, impotence, consumption, convulsions, stunted intellect, insanity, and death of the man himself, as well as the corruption of his posterity, were the wages of self-pollution; wasting the seed would dilute the potency of the white race.[50] Conversely, too much thinking on the part of women would disrupt menstruation and stunt their reproductive powers. In attempting to bring sexuality under control, a particular, sexualized vision of the body was emphasized, at once providing a foil to the improvident, sensuous poor and natives, justifying the exclusion of women from public life, and constantly threatening to deplete and subvert the rational, self-controlled, calculating masculinity of capitalist society.

ENGENDERING THE MIDDLE CLASS

While the psychological effects of the Protestant ethic and the capitalist market have long been the subject of theoretical debate, it is only recently that historians have begun to look in more detail at the actual making of the middle class in particular localities. Their work, already mentioned in the sections on the American and French revolutions, brings to life the complex process of cultural creativity through which the emerging bourgeoisie forged its new gendered identity. In post-revolutionary America, women and youth were frequently the main players in the thousands of church-linked associations that helped redefine the familial roles of men and women. In *Family Fortunes* and subsequent work focusing on race, Davidoff and Hall similarly argue that in late-eighteenth and early-nineteenth-century England, Evangelical groups elaborated a novel form of social relations as they tried to resolve some of the pressing problems confronting men and women of the emerging middle class. Drawing on Puritan and other precedents, they pioneered a new and rigorous categorization of the proper spheres of the sexes and new forms of relations between the generations. As missionaries dealing with the black inhabitants of British colonies, Evangelicals also contributed to contemporary definitions of black and white identities. By the 1840s, many of these precepts had become the common sense of the English middle class.[51]

In eighteenth-century Europe, claims to represent the public (and to social distinction) rested on the ideal of the disinterested gentleman, a man removed from the base activity of making money and able to philosophize independently from the security of his property. Gentlemen were manly because of their patriarchal authority over many dependents; their virility was enhanced by their sporting prowess. Middle-class men had little opportunity to acquire or display the mastery of the sporting gentleman; nor did they base their claims to manliness on the fine coordination of strength and skill which were the emblems of peasant and craft manhood. Their accomplishments were primarily sedentary and literate, the manipulation of the pen and the ruler rather than the sword, the gun, or the hammer. Although no less effective in yielding economic rewards that could lead to wealth and power, they implied not a physical but a cerebral control of the world, and even here not inborn courtesy and gentility but a calculating involvement in making money. In addition, many of the values associated with Evangelical Christianity—the stress on moral earnestness, the belief in the power of love, and a sensitivity to the weak and the helpless— resembled characteristics traditionally attributed to women.[52]

As they attempted to reconcile their earnest Christianity and claims to social standing with what they agreed (Adam Smith and the Utilitarians notwithstanding) was the profoundly amoral and ignoble world of the capitalist market on which their livelihoods depended, members of Evangelical congregations began to redraw the coordinates of everyday life. The home, they insisted, must be the basis of a proper moral order in the new world of the market; the new world of political economy necessitated a new sphere of domestic economy; men could operate in that amoral world only if they were rescued by women's moral vigilance at home.[53] In the early nineteenth century, the houses of wealthy families were rebuilt and modified to eliminate the pollution of cultured lives by dirt and bodily wastes, and to minimize contact between family and servants, men and women, children and adults, public and private family lives. Eventually the middle-class family home was physically separated from the places of business and located in the suburbs.

Bourgeois men not only reorganized their lives, they helped engender a whole range of new "public" institutions. The network of banks, insurance companies, mechanics' institutes, libraries, horticultural associations, farmers' clubs, Masonic lodges, charitable organizations, and scientific societies established during this period redefined civil society, creating new arenas of social power and constructing a formidable base for their members' claims to distinction.[54] Their societies provided opportunities for the public demonstration of middle-class weight and responsibility; the newspaper reports of their events, the public rituals and ceremonials designed for their occasions, the new forms of architecture linked to their causes, all acted to create a massive social underpinning of middle-class masculinity. The experience of such associations increased the men's confidence and contributed to their claims for political power as heads of households, representing their wives, children, servants, and other dependents. This homosocial public world was consistently organized in gendered ways and had little space for women—so much so that middle-class feminists from the second half of the nineteenth century focused much of their activity on attempting to conquer the bastions of this public world, a world that had been created by their fathers and grandfathers.[55]

In this process, a new definition of dominant masculinity began to emerge. No longer considered to be incompatible with the vocation of a gentleman, most ways of making large sums of money became a sign of virile manhood.[56] In terms of body shape, the masculine ideal in nineteenth-century salons, boardrooms, novels, and the eyes of employers of common labor started to converge into a tall, muscular, handsome figure. Laboring men would wait for a long time to become civic brothers; most were sickly, stunted, and undernourished, but their costume began to suggest a certain commonality. Rather than different clothing for different estates, gentry, industrialists, bankers, traders, clerks, farmers, and laborers all began to wear baggy trousers, hopefully concealing a powerful and virile masculine frame in which dwelt, harmoniously, controlled aggression, penetrating reason, and Christian sensitivity. In the later part of the century, these ideals were systematized by a number of movements promoting "muscular Christianity" in order to remedy what they saw as the inadequate manliness of British men.[57]

While middle-class men accumulated money and political power, their wives and daughters were producing, circulating, and policing private respectability.[58] Middle-class men gradually earned the right to be heard in public, to speak for themselves and their families. Women, already disenfranchised by the newly coded linguistic practices of correct grammatical speech, were condemned to silence in public: the fragile respectability of European ladies could be shattered if they tried to occupy physically, in speech or in print, a public forum. Just as making money was becoming respectable for all men, a virtuous middle-class woman must not only refrain from economic and political activity, but look and behave in ways that demonstrated her thorough inability to do so.[59] As one influential commentator put it, "Gentlemen may employ their hours of business in almost any degrading occupation and, if they but have the means of supporting a respectable establishment at home, may be gentlemen still; while, if a lady but touch any article, no matter how delicate, in the way of trade, she loses caste, and ceases to be a lady."[60]

In this period, it was never the laws of property alone that prevented the thousands of women who owned capital from using it actively, but rather the ways in which the laws of inheritance, the forms of economic organization, and the wording of wills, marriage settlements, and other documents intersected with aesthetic and moral definitions of femininity.[61]

By the 1830s, it became unseemly for a lady (whether she had a business to run or not) to have any contact with a workforce of day laborers. She should neither walk long distances nor ride horseback, even were it practicable to do so in the newly fashionable trailing dresses and layers of heavy petticoats.[62] To prepare wealthy women for their new gentility, their education no longer revolved around practical domestic skills, but typically included "a sound English education" and "the usual accomplishments." While, at its best, such education could be rigorous and challenging, it was never to diverge from its mission of strengthening women's intellect in the service of their moral goodness.[63]

In the genteel imagination, the contrast between the unpleasant bluestocking and the truly accomplished lady was clear. The one, with hard and unpleasant features, enshrined in an affected boudoir, was unnaturally competing with men. "Her dress arranged with studied negligence; her head a Babel; her speech a jargon of hard terms, and words of Johnsonian length," she was a figure of ridicule and scorn. The other, lovely, "unconscious of her own charms, and indifferent to their effect," could imbue the private sphere with the requisite virtue. She was

> always eager to oblige,—perfectly self-possessed . . . and with the most entire command of her attention to whatever should engage it at the moment . . . her opinions open as the light of day, and her feelings alone shaded from the eye of common observation, but always ready to act on every kind and generous emotion; and known in all their intensity to the few whom she could confidently trust; her conversation abounding in good sense and information, but flowing on without the smallest effort, untainted by pedantry, unsullied by satire; a heart expanding to every benevolent feeling, and countenance beaming with intelligence.[64]

Some influential men, John Stuart Mill among them, believed that women, like browns, blacks, and workers, had a potential for equality which could be realized in the future. Appropriate education, experience, and opportunities could open the door of reason and independence to well-to-do women; a longer process of learning civilization would eventually transform working-class individuals and native peoples. By the mid-nineteenth century, opponents of such views were able to draw on increasingly powerful notions of biological incommensurability of the sexes.[65] In a patriarchalist universe, the duties and attributes of men and women were read off their position within the household. Thus a 1735 German encyclopedia stated that "the female or woman is a married person, who, subject to her husband's will and rule, runs the household, and in the latter is the servants superior." Women in general did not have a fixed character; rather, "their humour, spirit, character, inclination and nature seem to be different in every land and condition."[66] A century later, in contrast, the majority of learned men came to believe that the laws of nature, history, and morality combined to create the "character of the sexes": universal opposed but complementary natures of men and women. Doctor J. J. Sachs spoke for the majority of the medical fraternity when (generalizing from the imaginary attributes of men and women of his own class) he wrote in 1830,

> The male body expresses positive strength, sharpening male understanding and independence, and equipping men for life in the State, in the arts and sciences. The female body expresses womanly softness and feeling. The roomy pelvis determines women for motherhood. The weak, soft members and delicate skin are witness of woman's narrower sphere of activity, of home-bodiness, and peaceful family life.[67]

For centuries, since the classical era, women had been depicted as one step lower on the great chain of being. Their bodies did differ from those of men, but in degree rather than in kind: they were less perfect specimens of basically the same organism.[68] Now, new scientific theories began interpreting much of the same accumulated biological knowledge in new ways. What had previously been conceptualized as differences in degree of perfection were increasingly understood as differences in kind.[69] Long before the basic histology and causes of menstruation were established, it was represented with martial imagery in such gory detail that readers were left in no doubt that "even in the healthiest woman a worm however harmless and unperceived, gnaws periodically at the roots of life," making it positively dangerous for her to vote, think, or study.[70] In time, some anatomists came to believe that biological differences between the sexes were so vast that women's development, like that of "primitive" peoples, had been arrested at a lower stage of evolution.[71] Medical thinking, inspired by debates about contemporary social relations, soon made its way back into philosophy. According to one of the fathers of social science, the Frenchman Auguste Comte, for example, "The study of anatomy and physiology demonstrates that radical differences, at once physical and moral . . . profoundly separate the one [sex] from the other." In his view, biology "has established the hierarchy of the sexes."[72]

To make sure that the dictates of nature were obeyed, learned men usually thought it prudent to preclude females from higher education.[73] In turn, as long as women were excluded from learned societies and university studies of science and medicine, they found it difficult to take part in scholarly debates about their own nature. Commenting on similar issues, one perceptive historian recently asked, "What does it mean when [feminists] engage with a theory of the subject in which the reasoning speaker— that is the person who displays possession of natural rights and a place in the civic sphere *through* . . . speech—is actually constituted on the male side of the sexual axis? And where does it take us with egalitarianism?"[74]

Not surprisingly, many middle-class women found the demands of gentility hard to negotiate. As the wife of one industrialist wrote in the early nineteenth century, "Oh did we but all know our proper stations and could but be content with acting properly in them, what a world of pain it would save us."[75] Bourgeois women were supposed to be paragons of Christianity, yet were excluded from the ministry of even those dissenting churches that had previously accepted women preachers. If a woman ran the household efficiently and took firm control, she had to do so through force of personality combined with strict routine. She had to be firm and businesslike, yet these qualities were the opposite of that softness, gentleness and submission of self that constituted the claim to feminine influence. Davidoff and Hall note that even though most women managed by picking their way through the discrepancies, often saying one thing and doing another, their frustrations or sullen retreat could on rare occasions flare up with spectacular violence. On their part, many daughters engaged in a form of passive resistance manifested by illness or such intense religiosity that they could not take part in normal family life.[76]

Importantly, while many historians emphasize women's exclusion from public life, another tradition of feminist writing, exemplified by Smith-Rosenberg's "The Female World of Love and Ritual," has celebrated the distinct culture that women constructed in their own sphere.[77] Yet others, building on long-standing feminist distrust of masculine virtues, note that the first appearance of the assertive female individuality today sought by the women's movement was pioneered in the colonies, by memsahibs taking a firm role in keeping the larger household of the empire neat and orderly.[78]

CIVILIZING THE YOUNG AND REINVENTING AGE RELATIONS

While Elias had little to say about gender, he was keenly interested in relations between the generations. His thesis, with all its problems, is simple and powerful: the civilizing process, which took several centuries to accomplish among the adults of the nobility, has been foreshortened in what is now accepted as the normal course of bringing up children. In several short years, children have to learn to discreetly dispose of bodily wastes, conceal appropriate parts of their bodies, avoid eating with their hands or dipping their fingers into a communal bowl of food, use the knife sparingly during meals (and only in certain designated ways), and control their rage and affection alike. In the European past, in other words, everybody behaved at least in part as children tend to do today. As adults were civilized and their society increased in complexity, growing up became more problematic.

Elias's thesis overlaps with work on the history of childhood inspired by the French historian Philippe Ariès. Ariès contends that childhood, as opposed to infancy, has not been a constant in European history. In the medieval world, he claims, there were few emotional bonds between parents and children in the first few years of life, not least because of extremely high child mortality rates. Indeed, mortality itself might have been increased by the parents' reluctance to raise too many offspring. As soon as children could walk and eat unaided, they were seen and treated as miniature adults.[79] The first "childlike" images of people began to appear in fourteenth- and fifteenth-century paintings. Childhood as a distinct stage of life was discovered during much the same period that Elias associates with the quickening of the civilizing process, and other scholars linked to tightening control over family formation. Like Elias, Ariès argues that the new practices were first adopted in the most privileged strata of society, and only much later, and in a modified form, by the poor. In the late sixteenth and early seventeenth centuries, the children of the wealthy were gradually separated from the world of servants and nurses, and imbued with new characteristics. "Childhood" among the nobility began to require special love and protection from moral and physical hazards that had not seemed necessary before. Two centuries later, new forms of child-rearing were adopted by some middle-class groups as a form of conspicuous consumption, a sign of their cultural distinctiveness and refinement.[80] It was only in the late nineteenth century, however, that institutions such as the school brought a measure of childish dependence to the sons and daughters of laboring people. Finally, a number of historians have used material on changing social prescriptions and practices of child-rearing to attempt an even more controversial task: charting the resultant psychologies of adults.[81]

There is, in fact, some statistical evidence that shows, in conformity with the Ariès hypotheses, that the infant mortality rate among the most privileged strata of society in early modern Europe was the same as or even higher than that of ordinary people. The vastly superior standard of living of the nobility was translated into dramatically reduced child mortality rates only in the seventeenth and eighteenth centuries.[82] Nevertheless, a number of historians claim that a more adequate examination of the available evidence shows much more continuity in the parental care of children than the Ariès thesis would allow; in particular, they argue that parents in early modern Europe exhibited just as much affection for their child and grief at its death as parents do today; yet others place the "discovery of childhood" in different historical periods.[83]

A related and somewhat less contentious thesis holds that in early modern Europe, parents and masters in all ranks of society gradually began to take a more active part in civilizing the young. According to Stone, in the sixteenth and seventeenth centuries, a newfound concern with making children obedient and well-mannered led to an escalation of violent means of control. Whipping was widely seen as the best way of producing a Christian character, in the home as in the school, for the poor as for the wealthy (although most of the examples Stone uses refer to boys). According to a typical contemporary commentator, "Surely there is in all children . . . a stubbornness, and stoutness of mind arising from natural pride, which must in the first place be broken and beaten down."[84] On the basis of French evidence, Ariès similarly claims that during this period, "the whole of childhood, that of all classes of society, was subjected to the degrading discipline [originally] imposed on the villeins."[85] Stone believes that it took more than a century for the dominant prescriptions for bringing up children to change from open physical violence to more subtle means of control, including a graduated system of rewards.[86] By the late eighteenth century, government of the self, nurtured in children by more or less overt guidance, a "manipulated providence," was posited as far superior to violence and imperiousness. Later still, education through love rather than violence would become associated with women's unique role: "a mother's tender ministration" became "the substitute for patriarchal will-breaking"; a new form of fragile, protected childhood became the complement of a redefined virtuous motherhood.[87]

In the early nineteenth century, others note, "precocity"—the unusually early assumption of adult behavior and responsibilities among the well-to-do—ceased to be admired as a mark of talent and became identified with a whole range of pathologies and social disorders. Just as (white) men and women were now thought to possess universal characteristics given by their biology, so all (proper) children were increasingly believed to possess a childlike character. In the United States, according to historians such as Kett, Kaestle, and Vinovskis, animosity to precocity rose after 1830 and flourished for roughly a century. Those who proscribed precocity equated it with premature sophistication, premature independence, and intellectual overexertion. Precocity was not merely analogous to a disease, it *was* a disease, resulting at best in the draining of intellectual and physical vitality, and all too often in insanity and premature death.[88] Kett notes that early critics of precocity were painfully aware that at first, few middle-class parents heeded their invectives against the luxuries and unhealthy stimulation of urban life. By the late nineteenth century, however, the new assumptions regarding young people's economic and emotional dependency on adults were "woven into a tapestry of organizations that aimed at prolonging childhood and adolescence both economically and psychologically."[89] Schools, protective factory legislation, reformatories, playgrounds, kindergartens, and youth organizations taught childish dependence to the poor.

The increasing use of certification, the consolidation of bureaucracies, and the increasing scale of organizational life made precocity less possible for wealthier men.

Although the early history of age relations remains the subject of some debate, there is wide agreement that new definitions of fragile childhood and intense parenting were first taken up by the wealthy, and only gradually became relevant to the laboring poor. Moreover, the peculiarities of class and region resulted in a series of complex transitions rather than the linear development of new age relations. More recently, feminist scholars have similarly demonstrated that the intersection of class and gender made the creation of a universal category of child (and later adolescent) problematic. Tyler, for example, draws out the logical inconsistencies in the definition of female and of child. On the one hand, women in a sense remain children all their lives. On the other, properly brought-up girls should never show the lack of restraint increasingly associated with childhood. For them, the civilizing process needed to occur much faster than for their brothers. Unless they rigorously (yet innocently) controlled their appearance and behavior, girls could arouse the sexual urges of men, just as adult women could. The need to monitor not only their own (potential) sexuality but also that of any males present made it extremely difficult for girls to have the proper sort of innocence. The family and the school were expected to work together to accomplish the impossible task of keeping girls "innocent" yet circumspect and dressed in a way that could not be interpreted as provocative. Perhaps predictably, wealthy families and expensive ladies' colleges were seen to succeed in this task much more often than state schools and working-class mothers.[90]

* * * * *

In his work on the civilizing process, Elias links state formation with increased *individual* self-control of men and women of the nobility. Approaching state formation from a different perspective, a number of scholars have traced its relevance to the emergence of new *collective* notions of identity. Historians such as Fliegelman, Wood, and Hunt, as we saw in the previous two chapters, have equated changes in prescriptive and perhaps actual age relations with a revolution against patriarchalist authority, a transformation that prepared the ground for the American and French political revolutions. Conversely, some of the conceptual tools developed to deal with age relations were later employed in debates about the political status of women and working men, and about the proper relationship between colonizers and the colonized. Similar to other dimensions of contemporary political change, the birth of new nations was thought through in terms of different possible relations between the generations and the sexes.

INVENTING NATIONS, NATIONAL STATES, AND NATIONALISM

In the century following the first democratic revolutions, the map of Europe was redrawn once again. Multiple jurisdictions began to seem intolerable and were eliminated. Most small territorial units were amalgamated into larger states, their size influenced by new notions of economic, political, and military viability. With the exception of Britain, all the European powers were substantially—in most cases even territorially—changed between 1856 and 1871. In the process, two large new united countries emerged: Italy and Germany.[91] States began to be thought of in terms of nations rather than individual rulers; many peoples who considered themselves a nation but did not have a separate state began struggling to acquire their own territorial units; nationalism became one of the most powerful forces in the history of the Atlantic world.[92] In this process, the French Revolution was of particular importance. According to Tilly,

> Starting in 1793, France's revolutionaries set a model for national-interest nationalism by drawing the entire population into their political and military efforts, fighting internal resistance to their program, and conquering other states in the name of their revolutionary mission. They also incited defensive national-interest nationalism in the countries against which they made war. The French forwarded state-claiming nationalism by broadcasting the doctrine that previously subject peoples had the right to dispose of themselves and by creating new states [such as the Batavian Republic, Switzerland, and Italy] on conquered ground in the name . . . of that doctrine.[93]

Here, the creative process of imagining, rethinking, and mobilizing images of citizens and foreigners, whites and blacks, national traditions and heritage ranked alongside a myriad of political, economic, and military acts which together assembled, with more or less permanency, modern national states. Indeed, Ben Anderson defines the nation as an imagined political community—imagined because the members of even the smallest nations will never know most of their fellow members, meet them, or even hear of them, yet in the minds of each lives the image of their communion; community because, regardless of the actual inequality and exploitation that may prevail in each, the nation is always conceived as a deep, horizontal comradeship, a fraternity.[94]

Importantly, while nationalist texts, speeches, and ceremonies typically emphasized the ancient origin of the traditions they were upholding, defending, and celebrating, many of these institutions and traditions were only recently invented in a process in which the nationalists themselves played a prominent part.[95] Such imaginings were not confined to those in power; they were—and are—equally significant to their socialist, feminist, or nationalist opponents. Together, they have come to constitute important elements of people's identity.

Hobsbawm and Ranger define invented traditions as a "set of practices, normally governed by overtly or tacitly accepted rules and of a ritual or symbolic nature, which seek to inculcate certain values and norms of behaviour by repetition, which automatically implies continuity with the past." They are distinctive in that the continuity with a suitable historic past that they invoke is largely fictitious, sometimes even involving outright forgery. The authors note that institutions and practices associated with the national state are particularly rich in the use of invented traditions. Not only have histories been rewritten and reimagined to create an appropriate continuity with ancient precedents, but a whole battery of entirely new symbols and devices came into existence as part of national movements and states, such as the national anthem (of which the British in 1740 seems to be the earliest), the national flag (still largely a variation on the French revolutionary tricolor), or the personification of "the nation" in a symbol or image.[96] During the eighteenth and nineteenth centuries, even national languages were compiled, defined, standardized, purified, homogenized, and modernized (usually by male grammarians following characteristically sexist rules) out of the jigsaw puzzle of local and regional dialects that constituted non-literary languages as actually spoken.[97] In most new states, the question of new language became an object of much controversy; dictionaries and elementary primers were among the earliest and most important cultural artifacts of a national tradition.[98]

Importantly, what mattered was not so much whether a particular rendering of tradition and national heritage was more or less accurate, but the process whereby certain beliefs and understandings became part of common sense, of everyday culture, of an orientation to social action. Cultural traditions became bases for nationalism when they effectively constituted historical memory, when they inculcated it as "habitus" or as "prejudice," not when (or because) their claims were accurate.[99] Conversely, not all "potential communities" based on common territory, language, or history have in fact been transformed into nationalities and nations. Some led to religious, ethnic, regionalist, or peasant-populist rather than national movements; some national movements and their creative political interventions failed.[100]

In this process, the actual symbolic birth of a nation has typically been rich in gendered political imagery. Feminist scholars have recently drawn attention to the tenacious influence of the classical understanding of the political as a realm arising from an act of generation by men that transcended and opposed physical—that is, womanly—generation.[101] In their different ways, as we have seen, the American and French revolutions have exemplified such acts of male symbolic creativity. First portraying themselves as Sons of Liberty, later as fathers of the republic, and eventually as Founding Fathers, American revolutionary leaders transformed themselves collectively from political youths into beneficent fathers of the new political nation, in part through mythologizing the figure of George Washington. In France, most representations of the republic were feminine—at times, as young mothers—yet it was the men of the French revolutionary leadership who were depicted as giving birth to the new, fraternal political order.[102] Such immaculate masculine conceptions of new nations and political orders would be repeated in many other countries in the course of the next two centuries; everywhere they were complemented by deep ambiguities about the status of women in the national community.[103]

The collective identities that emerged in the conflict-ridden course of forging nations from peoples who found themselves within the boundaries of any one state—or began to claim a state of their own—had a powerful influence on notions of individual identity, the more so because many traditional forms of community, such as kin and the village, parish, or guild, were increasingly eroded and disorganized. Indeed, the emergence of nationality—or the growth of a public for patriotic or nationalist discourse during the nineteenth century—can simultaneously be seen as the emergence of particular kinds of public spheres.[104] At least for some purposes, one was no longer a peasant and a native of Peronne but a citizen of France, not simply a bilingual shoemaker from Prague but a Czech nationalist, not just a Polish immigrant to America but a citizen of the United States.

As the politics of nationalism were transformed in the course of the nineteenth century, the individual identities of "them" and "us" were altered accordingly. Early nationalism was strongly identified with liberal and radical movements and with the tradition of the French Revolution.[105] In England, a legacy of radical patriotism stretching back to the English Revolution of the 1650s and beyond condemned tyrants (and Catholics) who wanted to sully the ancient (mythical) constitution of the land and impose fetters on free-born Englishmen such as parliamentary corruption, a large standing army, the slavery of the factory system, or the despotism of the New Poor Law. For the radicals, patriotism was a constantly reforged tool of opposition, a means of possessing the past. In the eighteenth and much of the nineteenth century, the government and its opponents claimed and reclaimed the vocabulary of patriotism, but it was not until the 1870s that the imagery of patriotism and national consciousness were decisively captured by the political right. Until then, the British ruling elite on the whole distrusted and discouraged nationalism for the masses, and passed over many obvious occasions around which it could be mobilized, fearing that it would support plebeian claims to citizenship. And indeed, almost all sectional interests used nationalist language and activism to legitimate their claims to wider social recognition. Thus working men used patriotism to underpin their claims to the vote, while the *nouveau riche* and the bourgeoisie set up memorials, art collections, and endowments as an opportunity to assert their parity with or superiority to the landed classes. Only after the 1870s did Britain's governing elite commit itself to patriotic, blatantly nationalist appeal. Not accidentally, this coincided with a massive extension of the franchise and the introduction of compulsory schooling.[106]

In France, nationalism during the French Revolution emphasized citizenship and popular sovereignty, but paid little attention to ethnicity or historical heritage as such. Indeed, one of the major emphases of the revolution was *breaking* with tradition—starting again, literally, from Year One. As the French Declaration of Rights put it, without specifying how "the people" was to be defined, "each people is independent and sovereign, whatever the number of individuals who compose it and the extent of the territory it occupies. This sovereignty is inalienable." In theory, at least, there was no logical connection between the nation as the body of citizens of a territorial state and some other criteria, such as linguistic or ethnic uniformity, which allowed that group to be identified as distinct. The revolutionary nation was constituted by the deliberate political choice of its potential citizens. Rather than arising out of some prior Frenchness, becoming a French citizen entailed new rights, duties, and responsibilities, among which happened to be the ability to speak French.[107] Indeed, many French revolutionaries believed that the revolutionary project and the spread of enlightenment would be furthered by a conscious effort to impose standard French—a "lofty and masculine language" [*langage mâle et sublime*]—on the territory of the Republic, and in the process eliminate local dialects and foreign tongues.[108]

There was nothing new, in world history, in subjugating some dialects and languages and elevating others to official status, even though the vernacular of the common people was usually a matter of indifference to their rulers, and a multiplicity of languages might at times be seen as desirable.[109] By the same token, there was no intrinsic reason why linguistic barriers should be seen to separate groups understood as potential nations or nationalities, rather than simply groups within one realm who had trouble understanding each other's words. When the French pioneered a new intention to get all citizens to speak a single national language, it was still unusual for a leading nation to actively attempt to suppress minor vernaculars and cultures.[110] By the end of the nineteenth century, a new, if not unprecedented, form of linguistic nationalism became common. All citizens of a nation, from the highest to the low, were now expected to learn, understand, and use—and often even read and write—a common language. Soon, lack of fluency in standard French, English, or German began to be translated into failure at school.

Such momentous transformation did not come easily. In many countries, the new "mother tongue" was incomprehensible to, or at least not routinely used by, the majority of the population. Although the French language became essential to the concept of France, on the eve of the revolution about half of French people did not speak it at all, and only some 13 percent spoke it "correctly." In northern and southern France, virtually nobody talked French, and even in the center it was often not used in the suburbs and the countryside.[111] By the early nineteenth century, the number of people speaking French increased dramatically, but instead of a planned democratization of the national language, literary French with a complicated grammar was enshrined as the norm.[112] By 1863, of all the men and women teaching in the public elementary schools in France, 65,338 instructors taught exclusively in French, 72 in patois, and 3,438 used both patois and French.[113]

In Italy at the time of unification in 1860, it was estimated that not more than 2.5 percent of the people actually used the Italian language for the ordinary purposes of life; the rest spoke in idioms so different that the schoolmasters sent by the Italian state into Sicily in the 1860s were mistaken for Englishmen.[114] Hungarian nationalism in the Kingdom of Hungary needed to take account not only of the fact that half of its subjects were non-Magyar, with only one-third of the serfs Magyar speakers, but also of the fact that the high aristocracy spoke French or German, and the bourgeoisie used dog Latin strewn with expressions from a dozen other languages. Similarly, when Russification became official policy in the 1890s, the Russian nobility spoke French, the bourgeoisie German, and the peasantry a great number of other separate languages. In Scotland, Ireland, and Wales, instruction in English (rather than Gaelic or Welsh) was inseparable from larger political issues. But even in England, where most people from most regions and classes had for a long time spoken in mutually comprehensible dialects, the introduction of "correct English" into schools presented problems to students and teachers alike. In some mining communities it was said that "the language of books is an unknown tongue to the children of the illiterate, especially in remote situations. It is utterly unlike their vernacular dialect, both in its vocabulary and construction, and perhaps, not less intelligible than Latin was to the vulgar in the middle ages."[115] "In the name of 'correct English,'" Raymond Williams remarked in 1961, "thousands of people have been capable of the vulgar insolence of telling other Englishmen that they do not know how to speak their own language."[116] Some fifteen years later, a new generation of feminist writers began documenting the vulgar insolence of male grammarians and legislators who decreed that male grammatical forms preceded, included, and were more comprehensive than the female ones in common usage. The resultant invisibility of women in much social discourse, it followed, could not be altered without "emasculating" the English language.[117]

In this complex process, schools would become indispensable, for through them alone the "national language" could actually become the written and spoken language of the people, at least for some purposes. This was not simply a matter of government expediency. According to Hobsbawm,

> As people from different homelands increasingly came into contact with each other, and the self-sufficiency of the village was eroded, the problem of finding a common language for communication became serious—less so for women, confined to a restrictive milieu, least so for those raising crops or livestock—and the easiest way of solving it was by learning enough of the (or a) national language to get by.

At the same time, direct bureaucratic government increasingly required the education of a quite substantial bureaucracy that routinely used the official language, and a population able to understand it. In turn, facility in the appropriate national language opened the door to a large area of potential employment—not only in schools, but in the rapidly expanding state bureaucracies, railways, and police forces as well. As a result, "for the lower middle classes rising from a popular background, career and vernacular language were inseparably welded together."[118]

As the century wore on, this process of eliminating local languages and dialects became increasingly problematic. Since the new, modern criteria of military and economic viability made virtually all states much larger than the boundaries of any one group based on common language, culture, and history, some ethnic groups, languages, and traditions (often recently invented) were promoted to the status of national heritage, while others were ignored, barely tolerated, or actively proscribed. More frequently, speakers of non-official vernaculars (and their men, in particular) became bilingual, using one language at home and another at school, the post office, the army, or the town hall. Yet many bilingual speakers from one of the non-official language groups began encountering systematic discrimination on the part of state officials. More and more often, some of these groups were denied the civil rights granted "real" citizens. At times they found themselves defined as the impure other against whom the pristine new nation was defined. The brilliant young radical-nationalist Hungarian poet Sándor Petöfi was not the first nor the last to refer to (non-Magyar) minorities as "ulcers on the body of the motherland."[119] In the Hapsburg Empire, it was a policy of the landed oligarchy of Hungary, to which Slovakia belonged, to immobilize the Slovaks politically by compelling all those who hoped for a post in any service to learn Magyar and turn themselves into Hungarians, just as the Czechs or Slovenes had to become German, or the Welsh, the Scots, and the Irish English. Some nations, it was becoming clear, were using the power of schooling to coerce other nations to abandon their aspirations by, for example, systematically Germanizing their children. In French, Dutch, Spanish, or English colonies, those who wanted to secure the confidence of the colonizers or get any of the jobs they dispensed had to learn the metropolitan language, cut themselves off from their people, and become black or Asian Europeans, without ever being accepted as real French, Dutch, Spanish, or English nationals—a privilege that was denied to most foreign-born whites as well.[120] In Australian schools, children began failing exams if they spoke with an Irish, Scottish, or working-class accent. Later still, "restricted codes" and bilingualism were defined as an educational disability.[121]

In response, some of the excluded groups managed to mount a successful campaign of counternationalism against what they began to interpret as forcible assimilation. In the West, nation-claiming nationalism was driven above all by the literate middle strata of societies, men—and to a lesser extent women—whose subsistence and everyday life revolved around the use of written language.[122] In Benedict Anderson's shorthand summary, new national languages and traditions were typically invented by a coalition of lesser gentries, academics, professionals, and businessmen, in which the first often provided leaders of "standing," the second and third myths, poetry, newspapers, and ideological formulations, and the last money and marketing facilities.[123] Romanticism and linguistic nationalism increasingly validated native tongues as the authentic voice of the *Volk,* and developed the claim, stemming partly from Herder, that language was a kind of collective cultural identity and history.[124] As many social groups stood to lose their "authentic voice," the rediscovery and re-creation of a "national language" could be at the heart of a popular movement of national emancipation. Ethnicity, particularly as defined by language, at times became the soul of the nation, and increasingly the crucial criterion of nationality.[125] The paradox of (linguistic) nationalism had been that in forming its own nation, it created the counternationalism of those whom it now forced into the choice between assimilation and inferiority.[126]

Language-based nationalism gained dominance just as western states began putting more and more emphasis on making citizens out of their inhabitants. A combination of factors—the profound changes in modes of governance, which brought individual (male) citizens more frequently into direct contact with agents of the state; the disruption of older worlds of social order; the need for large numbers of men to be conscripted or even to volunteer for army service in defense of the "nation"; the grudging extension of the franchise to new social strata; and, perhaps most important, the emergence of new forms of popular oppositional solidarity based on class, ethnicity, or religion—created a necessity to mobilize people's emotional commitment to their rulers' nation. As Hobsbawm put it,

> It became increasingly obvious, at least from the 1880s, that wherever the common man was given even the most nominal participation in politics as a citizen . . . he could no longer be relied on to give automatic loyalty and support to his betters or to the state. . . . States required a civic religion, patriotism, all the more because they increasingly required more than passivity from their citizens.[127]

The states' encouragement—or capture—of patriotism also coincided with the strengthening of the political right, the rise of scientific racism, and the flowering of biological theories of women's (and homosexuals') incommensurability with men. According to Hobsbawm, the time when the democratization of politics made it essential to "educate our masters," to "make Italians," to turn "peasants into Frenchmen," and to attach all to nation and flag, was also the time when popular nationalist sentiments, and those of national superiority, became easier to mobilize. The international situation that had previously made liberalism and nationalism appear compatible no longer held good. Until the depression of the 1870s, international peace and global free trade, while benefiting Britain, seemed to be in the interest of all. In the last two decades of the nineteenth century, the dominant view of international politics and economics changed. Global conflict came, once more, to be considered a serious, if not impending, possibility. This ideological transformation both bred and was encouraged by the movements of the political right, which held a particular appeal to the small traders, independent craftsmen, and farmers savaged by the economic decline.[128] Built on ideas of national superiority, xenophobia, and the idealization of national expansion, conquest, and the very act of war, they gave a new twist to the identification of politics with a particular form of belligerent masculinity. Only some inhabitants of a country, it now seemed, qualified as patriots; all others were branded as a menace or as traitors to the nation. In the age of imperialism, motherhood assumed a new significance—a prolific birthrate and scientific care of the right kind of racial stock became decisive in the new struggle for survival of the fittest nations.

*****

Even though their mixture, extent, and dynamics varied, the themes of racism, nationalism, language, masculine political birth, and patriotic motherhood can be identified in the nineteenth-century histories of all western nations. Nationalism was a powerful dimension of individual identity; it was also a major structuring force in the building of compulsory education systems. But it did not always displace or transform older loyalties and ways of thinking. As Hobsbawm notes,

> Contrary to common assumptions, the various principles on which the political appeals to the masses were based—notably the class appeal of the socialists, the confessional appeal of religious denominations and the appeal of nationality were not mutually exclusive. . . . Men and women did not choose collective identification as they chose shoes, knowing that one could only put on one pair at a time. They had, and still have, several attachments and loyalties simultaneously, including nationality, and are simultaneously concerned with various aspects of life, any of which may at any one time be foremost in their minds, as occasion suggests.[129]

CHAPTER FIVE

Worlds of Social Control
CIVILIZING THE MASTERLESS POOR

One can see the languor of those peasants forced to labour in the fields of their lords. One sees how much coercion is needed to make them fulfil their duties. Their sullen temperament breeds a contempt for their duties, so that all they desire to do is to work as little as the presence or absence of their overseer allows. . . . They have lost the desire to work even their own plots. Their miserable circumstances have made them vile and mean, living from day to day, immediately consuming whatever surplus they may have produced for themselves. Franz Anton Raab, 1777.[1]

These peasants have always been coerced; they have never learned to coerce themselves. Christian Garve, 1786.[2]

When hunger is either felt or feared the desire of obtaining bread will quickly dispose the mind to undergo the greatest hardships and will sweeten the severest labours. Joseph Townsend, 1786.[3]

We have lavished immense sums on the poor, which we have every reason to think have constantly tended to aggravate their misery. But in their education, and in the circulation of those important political truths that most nearly concern them, which are perhaps the only means in our power of really raising their condition, and of making them happier men and more peaceable subjects, we have been miserably deficient. Thomas Malthus, 1803.[4]

In the villages where there is no school human beings appear to differ from animals only in their shape. French Jansenist J. B. L. Crevier, 1760s[5]

For all the clergy you can dispatch, all the schoolmasters you can appoint, all the churches you can build, and all the books you can export, you will never do much good, without what a gentleman in [New South Wales] very appropriately called "God's police"—wives and little children—good and virtuous women. Caroline Chisholm, 1847.[6]

The story of the civilizing process, I argued in chapter 4, is not only gendered and differentiated by age; it also has a clear class dimension. Foucault notes that in each epoch, "the most rigorous techniques [the direction of consciences, self-examination, the entire long elaboration of the transgressions of the flesh, and the scrupulous detection of concupiscence] were formed and, more particularly, applied first, with the greatest intensity, in the economically privileged and politically dominant classes."[7] According to Elias, the members of a class that commanded the centralized means of violence were the first to develop self-command; the civilizing movement in peasant and worker strata emerged much more slowly and much later.[8] Similarly, Oestreich claims that Neostoicism was designed for and enthusiastically taken up by princes, officers, property-owning burghers, and other men of power and influence; Lipsius and his followers cared little for ordinary folk.[9] When, in the religious crises of the sixteenth century, a certain number of ancient practices of the self were reactivated to cope with individual responsibility to God, they were similarly adopted by only a minority of the elect. These same people, Ariès claims, were also the first to take up new definitions of childhood.

Certainly, over time, the poor in different regions may well have changed the way they thought and behaved, at times dramatically so. What was important was that their conduct bore little resemblance to the values and practices newly adopted by their betters. Laboring people, it appears, were among the last to abandon collective forms of subjectivity; frequently their world remained enchanted—seamlessly linked to a cosmos of supernatural forces—long after their betters became self-possessed. Time and again, historians note that their culture remained impervious to the logic of the market, calculating self-control, and Christian inwardness alike. By the late eighteenth century, in those regions still relying on unfree labor, many contemporaries became convinced that the peasants had gotten so lazy, stupid, and stubborn that serfdom was now a fetter on economic progress. Rural proto-industrial artisans, in spite of their exposure to market forces, seemed to show little capitalist rationality. The mass of propertyless people, no longer confined by the household discipline of their masters, were seen by their wealthy neighbors to present an increasingly menacing threat to social order. They begged and stole. In spite of widespread destitution, they were reluctant to work in factories. Elsewhere, wage workers were plentiful enough, but also prone to insolence, strikes, and other forms of insubordination. Nuisance, crime, and seditious ideas, it appeared, could at any moment turn to riot and insurrection. Finally, nothing seemed able to stop the poor from forming their own households and having children. And yet, wealthy commentators believed, most laboring men made appalling household heads, and their wives were manifestly unfit to be mothers.

Nineteenth-century educators, according to Richard Johnson, were appalled by just about every aspect of working-class life, from "coarse dialects," "vicious" amusements, and lack of "civility" to debauched meeting places, perverted religious and political ideas, and gross credulity. Importantly, many—perhaps most—of the failings that the inspectors perceived seemed to stem from some pathological tendency in domestic relations. From their accounts, Johnson notes, it is difficult to see how laboring families could perform the most elementary human functions with any degree of warmth or efficiency. The educators believed that both filial and parental duties were in crisis. The old were not looked after but were "cast" on poor relief. Money was not used for the purchase of necessities but was squandered. Homes were neglected, babies were uncared for, and children were not educated.[10] Even worse, lacking prudential constraints, the poor bred so fast that they flooded the labor market with new workers, underbid each other to get jobs, and thus perpetuated the spiral of misery and low wages.

The common denominator in various forms of the civilizing process among the privileged was rigorous self-command; one of the distinguishing features of plebeian (and "native") mentalities was considered to be a lack of it. For centuries, this distinction was built into conceptions of social order. "Subordination in the early modern world," Levine notes, "was formal—in the sense that 'consent' was externalised in public declarations of submission while being internalised in the private thoughts and deeds of only a minority, the so-called political nation."[11] To those on the receiving end of the masters' governance, service was a "constant, total, massive, non-analytical, unlimited relation of domination, established in the form of the individual will of the master, his 'caprice.'"[12]

Such personalized forms of mastery worked tolerably well in early modern Europe; they appeared less and less efficacious as patriarchalism began to falter, population multiplied, and new notions of privacy took hold among those who could afford them. Everywhere, the pressure of numbers lent urgency to schemes to control and to civilize impoverished families whose household heads seemed totally incapable of exercising the proper sort of patriarchal discipline. As social life was reorganized, fewer propertied masters aspired to control greater numbers of subordinates. Gradually and unevenly at first, state administration became more complex, the size of armies increased, workplaces became larger and more anonymous, and the number of students per teacher multiplied as more children went to school over a longer period. In the management of states and their armies, in the instruction of the young, in the supervision of production, the watchful eye of the master began to lose its power. How to restore or replace its effectiveness became one of the great questions of the age.

In *Discipline and Punish,* Foucault makes the audacious claim that the development and use of technologies of discipline went hand in hand with the development and use of technologies of production; in other words, "population thinking" was an indispensable component of the creation of modern industry:

> if the economic take-off of the West began with the technique that made possible the accumulation of capital, it might perhaps be said that the methods for administering the accumulation of men made possible a political take-off in relation to the traditional, costly, violent forms of power, which soon fell into disuse and were superseded by a subtle, calculated technology of subjection. In fact, the two processes—the accumulation of men and the accumulation of capital—cannot be separated; it would not have been possible to solve the problem of the accumulation of men without the growth of an apparatus of production capable of both sustaining them and using them; conversely, the techniques that made the cumulative multiplicity of men useful accelerated the accumulation of capital.[13]

Marxist accounts of the industrial revolution and the triumph of capitalism routinely make a similar point. The new mode of production created miraculous inventions and sources of wealth, and capitalist agriculture and industry could feed many more people than previously. But the expansion of capitalism could not occur without a revolutionary process of freeing up labor, which destroyed many of the old mechanisms of disciplining the poor. The new industrial order could survive only if other techniques of control replaced them.

A number of solutions thought up by contemporaries involved reorganizing the relations between rulers and the ruled. Bureaucracies developed to replace the master's supervision of everyday routine. Clerks, supervisors, and foremen began to supplement his oversight of the workshop. In schools, group teaching and monitorialism gradually replaced individual instruction, and a whole battery of techniques and instruments were developed to facilitate and speed up learning, measure time, keep discipline, and register the attainments and behavior of pupils. Other, more ambitious responses focused on changing the mentalities of common people themselves. Contemplating the mass of unreformed humanity, some far-sighted reformers speculated that the process of rule would be easier if subjects as well as their masters learned to exercise rigorous government of the self. Inspired by ascetic and introspective religious movements such as Puritanism, Pietism, and Jansenism, they explored techniques that would go beyond obedience to create self-discipline on the part of all—women as well as men, servants as well as masters, children as well as adults. What the seventeenth and eighteenth centuries anxiously called "a masterless man" need not be feared if he had become his own master. "If you were a servant," asked the American statesman Benjamin Franklin in 1758 in *The Way to Wealth,* "would you not be ashamed that a good master should catch you idle. Are you not then your own master, be ashamed to catch yourself idle." The child properly educated stands ashamed rather than guilty, because he has violated not a code imposed upon him but his own expectations of himself.[14]

The dreams of establishing universal self-mastery became more tangible in the context of new theories of what we would now call psychological development. Some of these ideas remained confined to small groups of scholars; others became familiar to various literate publics; yet others became part of the common sense of humble parents and teachers. Together, they can be seen as constituting crucial discursive—or conceptual—preconditions for the rise of mass schooling. Children's character, it was increasingly thought, was malleable rather than predetermined by God, and human intervention in its shaping was not only possible but desirable. What was more, habits and opinions formed in the first few years were likely to be felt throughout life: "The child was father to the man." To utilitarian thinkers such as John Locke, the mind was like a blank slate, a passive absorber of the facts presented by the surrounding world.[15] If true, such discoveries had far-reaching, even revolutionary, social implications. As Adam Smith put it in the *Wealth of Nations* in 1776, "The difference between a philosopher and a common street porter" arises "not so much from nature" as from "habit, custom and education." A few years earlier, the French philosopher Helvetius expressed it more concisely still: "Education can do everything."[16]

For a new generation of late Enlightenment thinkers, obscurantism—the desire to keep the poor ignorant—took on new meaning. Imbued with a new faith in the possibility of altering character through the transforming power of education, they believed that influences over youth were too valuable a form of power to be left to chance; doing nothing in fact meant doing quite a lot: "Simply abandoning the poor to their devices meant abandoning any effort to shape their direction, and ran the risk of letting the ambitious among them become a real threat." To neglect popular education was to forgo control over one of the most powerful tools at hand for influencing popular opinion and behavior.[17]

As Lutherans and Puritans had done before them, eighteenth- and nineteenth-century school promoters claimed that a respectable home with parents eager and competent to instruct their children in both secular and religious matters was preferable to outside educational agencies. "Were every parent able and willing to do his duty," an English reformer claimed, Sunday schools "would be useless, and might even be harmful; and it is only because parents *do not* or cannot fulfil their proper duties that these helps become necessary." But laboring men were too busy earning a living, and often too ignorant or lazy to do their duty: "though the Bible exhorts parents to teach their children, the poor are often unable to give them instruction and it is feared some have no heart for it." It followed that those who had both the requisite leisure and morality—men and women of the superior, wealthy classes—should step in and help with "unlearning the children much of what they have been taught," because "being from the lowest order of people they have not been taught to associate happiness with virtue." Repelled and terrified by the mass of working-class people, reformers hoped that Sunday schools would be able to "tame the ferocity of their unsubdued passions—to repress the excessive rudeness of their manners—to chasten the disgusting and demoralising obscenity of their language—to subdue the stubborn rebellion of their wills—to render them honest, obedient, courteous, industrious, submissive and orderly."[18] On their part, leaders of innumerable social movements became convinced that knowledge was power, and began struggling for appropriate educational media to impart this liberating knowledge to their brothers and sisters. Obscurantist opponents of popular schooling took arguments from each of these camps. Schools for the poor were credited with extravagant powers; the reformers' claims that they were able to harness these powers in the interests of social order were greeted with scorn. Teachers' intervention in the established, patriarchalist school of everyday life, they believed, would forever undermine the certainties of deference and subordination.

Until recently, many of these issues were conceptualized in terms of the Reformation precursors and the eighteenth-century "discovery of socialization."[19] Just as other scientists gradually discovered facts about the circulation of blood and the properties of gas, Enlightenment thinkers discovered and theorized what we now know to be natural human psychological attributes. As I noted in chapter 4, a number of scholars have interpreted these issues in a different way. Western subjectivities, they argue, are variable rather than stable; the modern conception of selfhood is a historical artifact. In writing about schools, Foucauldian theoreticians take this principle to its radical conclusion. The discourses apparently concerned with *describing* the dynamics of psychological development play a significant part in actually *constituting* subjectivities.[20]

*****

The first part of this chapter, concentrating on the agency of the power-ful, follows the Foucauldian trail and looks at how common schools were designed to produce self-governing subjects. The second part returns to more mundane—and often more effective—technologies of rule. It exam-ines how violence, deference, hunger, market forces, and family reform were employed to "civilize"—or make docile and industrious—the labor-ing poor.

PIETIST SCHOOLS, SELF-GOVERNANCE, AND ABSOLUTIST STATES

The first great wave of European interest in compulsory education, I argued in chapter 2, was designed to bolster patriarchalism in early modern Eu-rope. The second wave was closely linked to the dynamics of its eighteenth-century demise. By now, in the absolutist states of central and northern Europe, state authorities seriously limited the autonomy of both house-fathers and the nobility, the proportion of the masterless in the population increased considerably, the capacity of propertied households to absorb them appeared to have long since reached its limit, and in any case unfree labor began to seem a brake on economic progress. For Luther, successful schools would become redundant as masters assumed their rightful duties; for absolutist monarchs, schools might ease the transition to a society that could no longer be organized on patriarchalist principles alone.

In the sixteenth century, the building of schools was inspired by the Reformation and Counter-Reformation; the second wave of educational expansion was strongly influenced by reform movements within the re-formed churches themselves. Pietism, a seventeenth- and eighteenth-cen-tury reform movement within Lutheranism, proved particularly influential. To the Pietists, some of the trends today described as confessionalization had gone too far. Too much of religion was reduced to dry dogma, mindless conformity to regulations, and bureaucratic routine. Most humble parishioners went through the motions of what was required of them, but their hearts were not in it. On their part, in the midst of popular misery and desperation, courtiers and urban patricians flaunted their wealth far beyond the reasonable splendor necessary "so that the subject will venerate his lord more deeply."[21] Inspired by translations of English Puritan works, many educated Lutherans concluded that the earlier Reformation had not accomplished what its leaders had hoped. A spiritual renewal from within was far more important than passive, external observance of a rigid theological system. A true priesthood of all believers, informed by intimate personal knowledge of the whole Bible, would enable entire communities to be guided by the word of God and commit themselves to the exercise of Christian principles in everyday life.

Originally, the reform movement relied on conventicles, gatherings of small groups of believers who would clarify the meaning of the Scriptures among themselves, and then begin to reform others in their households and neighborhoods. This program of reform from below soon came up against strong opposition from church and state. In the Scandinavian countries, Pietism was eventually integrated into a state-sponsored system of household instruction. Elsewhere, Pietism revived after it secured an institutional base in Brandenburg-Prussia under the patronage of Frederick I (1688–1713) and his successor, the "sergeant-king" Frederick William I (1713–40). Frederick's support for the Pietists was dictated by politics, not spiritual affinity. To a Calvinist dynasty ruling a predominantly Lutheran population, Pietists not only provided congenial teachings on religious toleration, but furnished a useful counterweight to powerful provincial nobility; they later proved a natural ally of the austerity measures that Frederick William imposed on his court. From a movement emphasizing moral reform led by pastors within parish churches, Pietism in Prussia became a state-sponsored vehicle operating through established school systems.[22]

According to Melton, eighteenth-century absolutist reformers in fields as disparate as agrarian relations, theater, popular piety, manufacturing, and education shared concerns that were in some respects similar to those of the Pietists:

> What united these reformers was the conviction that the state, if it was to master social, economic and cultural change, had to redefine the manner in which power was displayed and exercised. Whether seeking to commute labour services, restrict pilgrimages, foster industry, ban burlesques or build schools, absolutist social policy in Prussia and Austria sought to strengthen moral pillars of authority by refining its exercise. Central to this refinement

was a shift in the technology of social discipline, whereby the locus of coercion was to be transferred from outside to inside the individual. Implicit in this attempted transformation was the belief that the extraneous, visible and objective forms through which authority had traditionally been exercised were no longer efficacious.[23]

Influenced by Foucault, Melton argues that a distinguishing feature of all these reform programs was stress on freely rendered rather than coerced obedience by which rulers would exercise their authority through love rather than force and subjects would submit themselves voluntarily and spontaneously. Schools based on the Pietist model became a central element of state policy precisely because they "offered an instrument for exacting obedience in a less coercive fashion"; the promotion of literacy became "a crucial means of cultivating the moral autonomy of the subject." Contemporaries seemed well aware that the state's monopoly on public violence increased the relative efficacy of moral compulsion; Prussia, the birthplace of Pietist schools, was also a region known for its reliance on violent means of social control. In the blunt words of the eighteenth-century cameralist von Justi, "In former times, before states had standing armies, mob rebellions were frequent. . . . But now that rulers have armies capable of imposing strict discipline and docility on the lower orders, religion and morality are sufficient for holding the mob in check. Since the common people know that the army can put down any popular disturbance, they rebel less frequently."[24]

First established in the Prussian city of Halle in the late seventeenth century, Pietist schools introduced a number of pedagogical techniques which are still in use today. These included formal training for elementary schoolmasters, normal schools, standardized textbooks, ability grouping of students, and simultaneous instruction. Some of these techniques had been developed earlier by the Brothers of the Christian Schools in France and may have been adopted from their methods; others, such as having pupils raise their hands to ask a question, were probably a Pietist innovation. Like the Puritans, Pietist teachers put great emphasis on introspection as a tool for developing self-discipline, often encouraging pupils to keep diaries in order to promote self-examination and reflection.[25]

Pietist pedagogy, like the Pietists' approach to faith more generally, stressed the distinction between outward compliance and inner conviction. As with any duty, the new schools enjoined pupils to perform their tasks freely and spontaneously: "not as if you were performing compulsory labour, but faithfully, diligently, and with relish." Pupils were to learn to obey their enlightened fatherly teachers just as they were to obey their rulers: out of love rather than compulsion. Yet at the same time, techniques such as daily evaluation of the progress and character of each pupil and strict control of his or her movements by compulsory attendance, diligent timekeeping, and constant supervision would, it was hoped, break the natural willfulness of the child. Pietists reconciled the paradox of cultivating free and active assent through breaking the child's will by seeing it in terms of a conversion experience. Only through self-abnegation could an individual become an instrument of God's will. Out of the depths of their innermost soul, the children should strive to please their fatherly schoolmaster, and beyond him, their worldly rulers and ultimately the patriarchal God in his heaven. False Christians, wrote Spener, "work purely out of necessity, so that they can have bread on the table," whereas true Christians labor "because they know they are fulfilling God's will."[26]

According to Melton, Pietist schools proved the single most powerful force behind the movement for compulsory schooling in eighteenth-century Europe. The adoption by Prussian rulers of Pietist educational reforms designed to inculcate self-discipline in the population culminated in Frederick the Great's historic compulsory school edict of 1763. The first such decree to apply to the entire monarchy, this legislation became a model for its age. The compulsory attendance provisions of earlier legislation were reasserted. In theory, at least, country schools came under full state jurisdiction, with Protestant and Catholic clergy delegated the task of supervising and inspecting classes for their parishioners. All instruction, hours, curricula, schedules, and texts were regulated by law. The legislation, which for many decades was only unevenly enforced, provided for free education for the poor, specific qualifications for teachers, graded classes, and uniform schoolbooks.[27] By 1794, it was supplemented by a state law code which, for the first time, recognized the state as the guardian of the child's right vis-à-vis the parents, and claimed that one of parents' responsibilities to their children was to raise them as good citizens.[28] Taking advantage of the huge sums of money and many buildings confiscated from the Jesuits, whose order was dissolved (and whose pedagogical style was discredited) by Pope Clement XIV, Maria Theresa adopted a similar reform program in Catholic Austria in 1773.[29]

MONITORIALISM AND THE LABORATORY OF POWER

Pietists built their education system around the individual power of a Christian father-teacher and his ability to imbue his charges with self-discipline. Other reformers put more emphasis on less personal methods. The same basic question must have occurred to countless reformers and educators faced with increasing numbers of scholars and meager resources: how to multiply the number of children who could be instructed simultaneously without diluting the effect of the master's will on individual scholars. By adopting a variety of techniques designed to facilitate group instruction, the Pietists themselves attempted to increase teachers' effectiveness. Taking such techniques one step further, some reformers began experimenting with measures that would make the teacher himself redundant, and turn the school into a type of machine.

The most influential institutions that bridged both models of instruction (and indeed were the source of some of the teaching methods used in Pietist schools) were the *Ecoles chrétiennes,* founded by Jean-Baptiste de la Salle in France in the late seventeenth century. In the words of Furet and Ozouf, this belated creation of the French Catholic Counter-Reformation gave birth to an utterly modern instrument which often appeared to the Enlightenment bourgeoisie as the very model of the useful school.[30] Just as military drill would make prideful, disciplined soldiers out of ungainly peasants, the myriad school rules and commands dreamt up and continuously perfected by Jean-Baptiste de la Salle would speed up the process of instruction and turn out Christian boys accustomed to ready obedience and with a keen sense of order and discipline.

In the growing number of schools developed and run by the Brothers in the 1680s, the classes (containing around one hundred boys) were to be held in silence. The master expressed himself through sign language, without having to give orders to be obeyed and understood.[31] "Whenever a good student hears the noise of the signal, he will imagine that he is hearing the voice of the teacher or rather the voice of God himself calling him by his name. He will then partake of the feeling of the young Samuel, saying with him in the depths of his soul: 'Lord, I am here.'"[32] The assiduity of the students was carefully recorded in an attendance register kept for each class; the system of punishments and rewards was meticulously elaborate.[33] The layout of the classroom and the position of the boys within it would indicate at a glance, as on a clock or in a statistical table, the boy's social rank, cleanliness, age, character, application, and attainment in a particular subject. The division of school time became increasingly minute and precise; activities at their correct times were governed in detail by orders that had to be obeyed immediately; every part of the body must be invested in each efficient gesture making up the act of writing, praying, or reading.[34] The teaching brothers themselves were trained in a special seminary; in their work, "uniformity must be the rule for all, without departing in any way from received practice"; identical timetables, lessons, signs, methods, and rules were to be used in all the institute's schools.[35] By the outbreak of the Revolution in 1789, the Brothers of the Christian Schools had become a major teaching congregation in France, with more than a thousand members.

The Brothers' emphasis on uniformity, drill, and order was designed to amplify the personal will of the master, to give it a direct and powerful effect on the innermost soul of each and every pupil. In an age increasingly impressed by scientific discoveries, some educators took the attempts to make teaching more effective one step further. Already in the 1650s, Jan Amos Comenius mused,

> As soon as we have succeeded in finding the proper method it will be no harder to teach schoolboys, in any number desired, than with the help of the printing-press to cover a thousand sheets daily with the neatest writing, or with Archimedes' machine to move houses, towers, and immense weights, or to cross the ocean in a ship, and journey to the New World. The whole process, too, will be as free from friction as a clock whose motive power is supplied by the weights.[36]

One and a half centuries after Comenius wrote down his technological dream, Andrew Bell, one of the rival self-proclaimed inventors of the monitorial system, noted that until recently,

> machinery has been contrived for spinning twenty skeins of silk, and twenty hanks of cotton, where one was spun before; but no contrivance has been sought for, or devised, that twenty children may be educated in moral and religious principles with the same facility and expense, as one was taught before.[37]

That was precisely what the monitorial system could achieve, according to its other inventor, Joseph Lancaster. It was a new plan "by means of which *one master* alone can educate one thousand boys, in Reading, Writing, and Arithmetic, as effectually, and with as little Trouble, as Twenty or Thirty have ever been instructed by the usual modes of Tuition."[38]

De la Salle and the Pietists, as I noted, went a long way toward making possible the *simultaneous* instruction of a large number of boys by one master. Bell and Lancaster became the best-known exponents of *mutual* methods of instruction and supervision, long recommended by educators such as Comenius as a commonsense expedient for masters charged with too many students.[39] Foucault notes that as French parish schools developed and the number of their pupils increased, the lack of methods for simultaneously regulating the activity of a whole class led to disorder and confusion. In his *Instruction méthodique pour l'école paroissiale* (1669), J. de Batencourt described how he selected from among the best pupils a whole series of officers to help the teacher—intendants, observers, monitors, tutors, reciters of prayers, writing officers, receivers of ink, almoners, and visitors. The tutors helped in instructing the pupils; the others were in charge of various practical tasks and different aspects of surveillance. A few decades later, C. Demia's *Règlement pour les écoles de la ville de Lyon* (1716) favored a similar hierarchy, but in most cases combined the pedagogical and surveillance functions: an assistant teacher taught the holding of a pen, guided the pupil's hand, corrected mistakes, and at the same time marked down troublemakers.[40]

The new educational machine derived some of its motive power from a source that had been perfected more or less independently by generations of princes, clerics, officials, commanders, reformers, and teachers: the visibility of individual scholars, subjects, and inmates. This technology of power, called panopticism by contemporary Foucauldian scholars, reached its most perfect expression in Jeremy Bentham's *Panopticon; or, The Inspection House,* published in 1787. Bentham's Panopticon was a circular structure with a central observation tower, designed so that every move of the individual inmates, who were segregated in separate cells on the periphery of the building, could be observed by guardians who themselves remained unseen. This laboratory of power, this utilitarian approximation of an all-seeing God, could be employed to many different ends—as a prison, a school, a workshop, a hospital.[41] As Bentham put it in the introduction to his book, "morals reformed—health preserved—industry invigorated—instruction diffused—public burthens lighted—. . . all by a simple idea in architecture."[42]

As is the case with many other modern "western" institutions, the first acknowledged monitorial school was developed in the colonies, as part of the effort to deal with people who threatened to blur racial boundaries between the colonizers and the colonized. It was organized in the 1890s in Madras by the Scots-born Anglican minister Andrew Bell, in an asylum for the orphaned Eurasian sons of British soldiers. Bell went to India not as a teacher but to make his fortune as a lecturer in science; his planned destination was not Madras but Calcutta. He took charge of the school by accident. Many of the boys were neither orphans nor of mixed race; and his monitorial system was not the result of theoretical analysis or classroom experiment, but sprang from a chance encounter with a traditional Indian open-air school. But Bell was profoundly influenced by his mechanic-scientist father, by Scottish Enlightenment thinkers, and by his university training in science. Soon he became obsessed with turning the school into an efficient scientific instrument for developing the innate abilities that he believed the supposedly inferior half-caste children possessed. After observing older boys in a local Hindu school teaching younger ones to write by tracing letters with their fingers in the sand, he tried to introduce the same method into the military orphanage. When the teachers failed to carry out his orders, Bell turned to one of the pupils. Eventually, all the adult teachers left or were dismissed, and by about 1894 the teaching of the entire school was given over to the boys themselves. Every boy was "either a master or a scholar, and generally both. He teaches one boy, while another teaches him." Soon the curriculum expanded beyond the three R's, with nearly half of the 280 pupils studying one or more subjects such as book-keeping, geometry, geography, navigation, mensuration, and astronomy.[43] Each day, each boy noted "the number of lessons said, pages written, sums wrought, etc" in a special book. Bell noted that "in the hands of the master the registers are instruments of discipline, and produce great precision and exactitude, enabling him to readily inspect, direct, conduct and control the respective classes." Already in India, Bell recognized the wide applicability and aesthetic appeal of his system. Self-instruction under surveillance was both a model of discipline and order and an engine of self-improvement and beneficial activity: it was "the principle on which every schoolroom, factory, workhouse, poorhouse, prison house, and every public or even private institution of any magnitude should be conducted."[44] Written up, transplanted to England, and combined with the methods more or less independently developed by the Quaker Joseph Lancaster, monitorial schools came to dominate British elementary schooling for nearly half a century.

Lancaster's London school, established in 1798, was similarly designed for the charitable instruction of poor children. It was held in one large hall with benches and desks in the middle and teaching materials posted around the walls. The eight hundred boys and two hundred girls on the rolls were divided into groups of ten pupils of equal attainment in particular skills, each group seated at a separate desk and allocated a monitor who taught them the task at hand, having earlier in the morning received instruction from the master himself. Other monitors were put in charge of tasks such as ruling paper, keeping slates and books in order, and inspecting scholars or the monitors themselves. The subjects taught were confined to reading, writing, arithmetic, needlework for girls, and non-denominational "leading and uncontroverted principles of Christianity." Lancaster, like Bell, broke with contemporary practice by teaching writing together with or even before reading, rather than as a separate and more complex craft reserved for more advanced (and better-off) boys and a handful of girls only after they had learned to read.

In Britain itself, the monitorial system spread under the auspices of the Anglican National Society for the Promotion of the Education of the Poor in the Principles of the Established Church, and the rival nonconformist British and Foreign School Society, and remained the chief means of providing elementary schooling for the working classes until the 1840s. The new technology of instruction soon spread around the world. By 1820, fifteen hundred monitorial schools were established in Paris and other large urban centers in France.[45] Sweden had nearly five hundred monitorial schools by 1841; in Denmark, nearly three thousand such schools were set up by 1831. Monitorialism was used extensively in Greece, Switzerland, Italy, Spain, Peru, Colombia, Panama, Russia, Canada, Australia, the United States, and Mexico; it reached as far as Ceylon, Haiti, Sierra Leone, Madagascar, and the Bahamas. For a whole generation of South Americans, education for the masses was virtually synonymous with the Lancastrian system.[46]

Monitorialism, lovingly compared by contemporaries to machines or well-drilled regiments, not only made abundant sense in commercial terms, it could well provide new techniques for maintaining discipline in other institutions. Just as entrepreneurs were attempting to do, monitorialism stretched limited resources by effecting economies in time, labor, and money; it promised to produce the largest quantity of a standardized product in the shortest time and with the least expense. Indeed, it accomplished something that other employers found much more difficult to do: it almost completely dispensed with paid teachers, relying instead on an army of unpaid assistants rewarded by a measure of "authority and prestige," badges of honor, or at best small prizes and occasional outings. In Bentham's blunt words, "Every professional teacher would need to be paid; no such scholar-teacher needs to be paid; or is paid."[47] Importantly, even the sole master of the school might eventually become redundant. As Lancaster noted in 1805,

> When the pupils, as well as the schoolmaster, understand how to act and learn on this system, the system, not the master's vague, discretionary, uncertain judgement, will be in practice. . . . In a school properly regulated and conducted on my plan, when the master leaves the school, the business will

go on as well in his absence as in his presence, because the authority is not personal. This mode of insuring obedience is a novelty in the history of education.[48]

Deeply impressed by monitorial schools, Jeremy Bentham spent some time systematizing the underlying logic of their operation, and devising a plan for extending the same principles to the systematic instruction of the middle and upper ranks of society in all branches of useful arts and sciences. As he described it in his *Chrestomathia* (1816), the finely tuned monitorial machine of ability grading, competition, mutual and simultaneous instruction, continuous activity, and discipline had at its heart a perfect engine of the utilitarian "felicific calculus" of maximizing pleasure and minimizing pain. While scholars would naturally want to minimize the discomfort caused by punishments finely calculated just to exceed the pleasure of particular transgressions, money could be saved if rewards for diligence and achievement consisted mainly of moving up one or several places on the bench where each class sat arranged according to merit. In this important work, P. J. Miller notes, Bentham uncovered the bedrock of administrative principles that still have resonance within schools today.[49]

This same engine of students' effort is the topic of an excellent (albeit gender-free) recent article by David Hogan. In attempting to streamline traditional education of the poor in Christian morality and useful skills, Hogan argues, Bell and Lancaster un-self-consciously transformed the psychological economy of the classroom. The school that Joseph Lancaster designed and built was not so much a church of piety, renunciation, social estates, subordination, and deference as it was a manufactory of desire and ambition, a marketplace of competitive individual achievement, and an engine of disciplinary power. Despite Lancaster's religious and conservative objectives, his school "was very much a pedagogical facsimile of the market revolution rather than a traditional institution of social control." Instead of asserting their absolute and coercive authority or relying on love, Lancaster urged educators to make a study of the passions of the human heart. The passions were to be employed, not repressed; stimulated to usefulness, rather than controlled; they were to be viewed as "auxiliaries, to assist us in great and beneficial designs." In the end, according to Lancaster, "the benefits resulting from a system of education which will create motives in the minds of youth, and induce them to exert their powers, is far superior to any benefit the exertions [of] their master can produce to them." In all, the inventors of the monitorial system bequeathed to the nineteenth-century world "a model of schooling organised around an individualised,

competitive, and meritocratic structure; a classroom psychology based on
scarcity, desire, ambition, shame, habituation, and the construction of a
new form of commercial sociability—the meritocratic achiever driven by
ambition to excel over others but yet needing their approbation; and a
highly rationalised structure of school authority and continuous surveillance."[50]

The emotional economy of monitorial classes, then, was considerably
different from that of Pietist schools, in spite of the similarity of many of
their teaching techniques. The Pietists strove to break the child's will in
order to produce free and spontaneous obedience to worldly and spiritual
masters, a calm and passive acceptance of one's lot in life coupled with
individual initiative and ceaseless activity in the exercise of one's Christian
vocation. In contrast, monitorial schools attempted to construct a secular
engine, harnessing individual passions in pursuit of an artificially created
scarcity of more or less tangible immediate rewards. Certainly, the curriculum in monitorial schools contained lessons in Christian docility, humility, and the virtues of hard work. But pupils' activism was to spring not from
abnegation to God's mysterious will and boundless love, but from a restless
striving to maintain and improve one's own place in a transparent hierarchy of achievement. The certainty of a finely graduated scale of reward
and punishment, and the ability to trade one against the other, came close
to creating a perfect model of commercialized capitalist morality. Paradoxically, this very fact proved to be a mixed blessing. Just as in other
areas where capitalist logic was taken to its logical conclusions, monitorial
schools threatened to wreak havoc with established social relations.

Sensitive to what they considered misuses of charity by the poor, pious
teachers and visitors to monitorial schools were scandalized "by the cynical
readiness of certain children to recite the Lord's prayer for a half-penny."[51]
Indeed, Lancaster's reliance on emulation and rewards was held to be
"unnecessary" and "mischievous, because thus to constantly hold out the
stimulus of gain is inconsistent with any system of sound morality, to say
nothing of Quakerism." Others were none too pleased to see children
habituated to promotion by merit, and regardless of social status. If the
system of motivation through meritocratic promotion really worked as well
as it was supposed to, it would give the children an altogether alarming
object lesson in unfettered meritocracy, which they then might want to
apply to the world outside the school. Lancaster's opponent Sarah Trimmer
warned that "boys, accustomed to consider themselves as the *nobles of a
school,* may in their future lives, from a conceit of their own *trivial merits,*
unless they have very sound principles, aspire to nobles of the land, and to

take the place of *hereditary nobility*."[52] In France, while the system's supporters claimed that "it disposes children to obey merit, to show no sur-
prise at seeing authority placed in the hands of their equal or even their
inferior, to respect this authority no matter who its repository may be, an
invaluable habit . . . preparing loyal subjects for the King, and useful
citizens for the State," better-off parents were distressed at "seeing their son
forced to obey a beggar's son, if he was a monitor."[53]

While some commentators alleged that the schools were too radical,
others believed they were not suitable to a new, democratic age. In the
United States, influential critics argued that while monitorial schools were
better than leaving pauper children to play in the gutters of English industrial towns, they were totally inappropriate for educating the enlightened
citizens of a proud democratic nation. The most valued accomplishments
of the system—its cheapness and machine-like regularity—were thrown at
it as insults:

> All self-exertion prevented; all responsibility lost; every generous feeling
> crushed; and the whole body taught to march on like a platoon of soldiers, as
> if they were moved by one spring and were parts of a single machine. . . . I can
> easily imagine that such a school may make excellent sailors and soldiers, for
> they are expected to be automatons. But for republicans, for freemen, for
> self-controlling, and elevated masters of their own destiny—it is not the
> place.[54]

Paradoxically, absolutist Prussia, not liberal England, was believed to provide the best model of liberal schooling.

Other critics, typically male heads of advanced schools for girls, questioned not so much the regimented appearance of monitorial schools, but
the very heart of their successful functioning: the restless competitive
striving to do better than one's fellows. According to Nancy Green, in the
antebellum United States, many educators felt that even if meritocratic
schooling (of which monitorialism was only the extreme example) was
appropriate for boys, it was likely to harm girls. "Hard study," many believed, fostered manhood. In the long term it might "unfit females for the
duties of their sex, encouraging boldness, vanity and selfishness at the
expense of humility, devotion to duty, and the desire to do right for its own
sake." Women, at least according to the men who wrote about them, were
naturally submissive, quiet, and self-sacrificing. But feelings of envy, selfishness, and aggressiveness, although unnatural, were easily acquired.
"The gentle promptings of women's sex" could easily be subverted by the

wrong influences, especially by a "discipline which has taught her to regard a station of inferiority as one of disgrace." The consequences of the wrong sort of female education could be devastating to a man. "Would the desire of distinction, or surpassing her friends," George B. Emerson asked in 1839, "be the most sure to suggest to a wife the numberless little kindnesses and attentions so essential to the happiness of a husband?" He feared not. A system built around emulation "tended to repress the gentle and retiring qualities which are the most beautiful in the female character, and to foster those which we should least wish a wife or a sister to possess."[55] As more girls began to attend schools, considerations such as these rekindled a long-standing debate on whether women should emulate men or forge a distinct identity of their own.

Indeed, what was harmful for women might not benefit boys either. According to Horace Mann, for example, if a teacher wishes his pupil to be "a great man rather than a good one; or that he should acquire wealth rather than esteem . . . then he will goad him on by the deep-driven spur of emulation . . . until he outstrips his fellows, at whatever peril to his moral nature. But if . . . the teacher . . . would see his pupils dispensing blessings along the lowliest walks of life," he will forgo emulation as an educational tool. Rather than applaud the fact that competitive schooling was in harmony with the logic of capitalist competition, critics complained that being rewarded with prizes in school would lead students into a sort of addiction to material rewards—"a morbid hankering . . . which cannot easily be eradicated." Once addicted, an individual was likely to carry into his life an excessive ambition, an inclination to drive ahead without regard to moral and religious precepts.[56] Not only did school competition have negative long-term effects on the students, but on a much more pedestrian level, it could be shown that this engine of the monitorial system had serious design faults: emulation reached only that small proportion of pupils who felt they had a good chance of winning, and produced ill-will and envy among the others; it focused attention on winning rather than learning, and rewarded natural ability rather than effort.

In the long run, however, probably the most telling criticism of the monitorial system was not that it embodied the wrong logic, but that it failed to live up to its promise. In exceptional circumstances, under exceptional masters, and in the presence of august visitors, the schools might have functioned like clockwork. The everyday reality was different, at least as judged by frequent comments such as the following observations of a girls' monitorial school in Birmingham:

Thirty-one girls read . . . to their monitor. The noise in the school was so great that as I sat by the monitor I could not hear the girl who was reading in the class. Several children were laughing to each other, others were inattentive; and the only symptom of reverence in the whole class was, that every time the name of our Lord was pronounced the whole class made a short rapid curtsey, occasioning along the whole class an irregular popping down, the effect of which, combined with their undisguised levity, was exceedingly unpleasant.[57]

Here and elsewhere, the monitors seemed to get their lessons hopelessly muddled; many of the words they were diligently repeating made no sense at all, or merely sounded similar to the ones originally intended. In a report on his educational tour of Europe, Horace Mann condemned the monitorial system in the strongest language he could muster:

One must see the difference between the hampering, blinding, misleading instruction given by an inexperienced child, and the developing, transforming, and almost creative power of an accomplished teacher;—one must rise to some comprehension of the vast import and significance of the phrase, "to educate,"—before he can regard with a sufficiently energetic contempt that boast of Dr. Bell, "Give me twenty-four pupils to-day, and I will give you back twenty-four teachers tomorrow."[58]

Just as Luther and most other Reformation thinkers abandoned their original enthusiasm about the humble master, Bible in hand, catechizing his family, so the idea that ordinary children could teach anything of value was abandoned in favor of expert guidance by a trained fatherly teacher.[59] And just as a "rational," finely graded, and invariable form of justice was for many decades strenuously opposed by the gentry as emasculating their own paternalist discretion, so replacing the master with a pedagogic teaching machine met with increasing opposition, not least from the male pedagogues themselves.

By the late 1840s, monitorialism went out of educational fashion, and the critics of emulation seem to have gained the upper hand in pedagogic discourse. (Indeed, as the evangelical spirit waned in the 1850s, educational solutions to social problems began to be seen as naive and impractical.) But in practice, condemnation by enlightened educators was not enough to reorganize the teachers' bag of tricks: teenage teachers in charge of classes of fifty or more were not always an improvement over monitors in charge of groups of ten; order, uniformity, and emulation still hold their appeal today. (Seating according to examination results was not uncommon in the 1950s.) As in many other battles for educational reform, "the reformers would appear to have won if we look at the educational journals, the most forward-looking schools, and what was taught at normal school; but in the long run . . . emulation lives on, though under a different name and with different prizes."[60]

THE MOTHER MADE CONSCIOUS

The late 1840s were a period when revolutions erupted—and were put down—in a score of European and South American countries. It was then that new definitions of separate spheres for men and women moved beyond the experiments and enthusiasms of Evangelical congregations and became the foundation of middle-class common sense. During the same period, the rate of children's industrial employment had passed its peak and begun to decline; capitalist economies throughout the West entered a period of unprecedented prosperity. A new science of education began to fire the imagination of social reformers. This time, it was based not on machinery or a master's judicious rule, but on systematic observation of what were considered to be the natural ministrations of a mother to her developing child. It too involved ceaseless monitoring of the child, but by the loving gaze of a motherly teacher rather than the dispassionate inspector and his administrative implements. In the words of Friedrich Froebel (1782–1852), the educational philosopher and founder of the kindergarten system, the ideal teacher of young children is like "a mother made conscious." Johann Pestalozzi (1746–1827), the Swiss philosopher and pioneer of education for the poor, similarly believed that "mothers are educators of their children, and we can learn from their methods."[61] Like that of the good mother, the role of the teacher must be one of "a continual and benevolent superintendence,"[62] but like a peasant mother, the teacher of young children need not be very clever; feeling, empathy, intuition, and sympathy, made more effective by expert training, should suffice.[63]

While monitorialism has today been consigned to the dark ages of schooling, the theories of Pestalozzi and Froebel continue to be taught in teacher education courses, and some of their ideas still underpin what is considered to be enlightened educational practice. In a series of imaginative essays, Carolyn Steedman has teased out some of the complexities of the now routinely made link between mothering and the teaching of young children. As we will see later, one of her arguments is that rather than mothers providing a model for women teachers, a particular form of feminized teaching eventually became a powerful model of "proper" mothering.[64]

Both Pestalozzi and Froebel based their theories on naturalistic observation of peasant mothers and their children. It was here, they thought, that the instinctual process of a mother's nurture of the slowly unfolding consciousness of the child could be seen in its purest form. Good mothers did naturally, "without any teaching, reminding or learning," what good teachers must extrapolate from their practice, make explicit, and use. Pestalozzi assumed that each individual had a nature that was inherently good, contained the necessary potential for moral and intellectual development, and stood in need of cultivation, which was best achieved by a bond of love, first between mother and child, and later between teacher and child. As a result, the child not only should be acted upon but, under the loving and careful supervision of its mother or a teacher, should also be the agent in its own intellectual education.[65]

Paradoxically, a pedagogy based on systematic study of the natural instincts of peasant mothers and children was most appropriately carried on away from the home, in classrooms where working-class children could be provided with the appropriate nurturing environment. Neither should these children be educated in dame schools, which most resembled the actual mothering that took place in laboring households—these schools, like the families who patronized them, were systematically condemned by state authorities. Rather, the newly conscious mother-teachers were ideally middle-class women specially trained in the complex science of their expert task. The philosopher Fichte, who popularized Pestalozzi's methods in Germany in the early 1800s, believed that contemporary laboring families were too flawed to perform their educational role, and therefore advocated the removal of their children to the purified environment of the school. "If complete reformation is intended, [the new generation] must once and for all be entirely separated from itself and cut off from its old life. Not until a generation has passed through the new education can the question be considered as to what part of the national education shall be entrusted to the home."[66] Similar sentiments would be repeated again and again over the following century. Pestalozzi himself set up an institute for the training of girls in child care next to his experimental school for boys at Yverdon. "What human being can speak the name of Mother," he wrote in 1806, "and not be aware of the high, developed strength which Woman needs so urgently for the early education of her child . . . and how few mothers can be to their children what they should be." According to Baroness Berthe von Marenholtz-Bülow, one of the most vigorous and influential propagandists of Froebel's kindergarten ideas, advanced child-rearing techniques could not be practiced by working-class mothers "because their work does not permit it and because at any rate they do not have the time." For the time being, at least, it was up to middle- and upper-class women to step into the breach. "Until the mothers of the lower orders are a better educated race, the education of their children must be the care of the educated class."[67]

The supervised educational freedom through which the "mother made conscious" facilitated the development of her child was, according to promoters of the new methods, ideally suited to producing orderly citizens of a democratic nation such as Germany promised to become in 1848. "The new political order, which grants political rights to every [male] citizen, requires an educated nation if it is not to degenerate into anarchy," ran a petition to the National Assembly in Frankfurt advocating the setting up of kindergartens, institutions that accustomed young children "to activity, to a sense of beauty, to law and order, to independence and social responsibility," providing a necessary antidote to tendencies such as "laziness, discontent, class conflict and egotism." Marenholtz explained that Froebel's ideas "were certainly very different from those of the youthful fanatics and agitators who sought to teach freedom by the overthrow of the national order." Rather, "the rough masses" must be made "capable of seeing that only self-restraint of individuals and their voluntary subjection to law makes greater freedom possible."[68]

Originally addressed to men and to the predominantly (in many places exclusively) male teaching profession, Froebel's kindergarten campaign was soon redirected to women, who gave it a far more enthusiastic response. Many women from better-off families glimpsed in the professionalization of motherhood a way out of the enforced idleness of the private sphere, a possibility of gaining the same status accorded male professionals. Froebel himself saw in the role of the educated mother—whether to her own biological family or to the spiritual family of the kindergarten— the fulfillment of women's demands for responsibility and respect. "It is a characteristic of our time," he declared, "to rescue the female sex from its hitherto passive and instinctive situation and, through its nurturing mission, to raise it to the same level as the male sex." Many female supporters of the kindergarten method justified their enthusiasm in a way that still finds resonance within the women's movement. Marenholtz specifically rejected emancipation, which she defined as the uncritical imitation of male behavior and values, and instead called upon women to regenerate a divided and demoralized society "in her true office in the great social household—namely as the educator of the human family."[69]

In practice, the ideas of Pestalozzi and Froebel (as well as of their intellectual predecessor Rousseau) had a strong if uneven impact on western schooling. In general, they were better received in Protestant than in Catholic countries, which objected to what they saw as a godless pedagogy. Neither was the educator's aim to replace mothers always welcomed by those in power. In ultra-conservative Prussia, kindergartens were banned between 1851 and 1860 as anti-family institutions. Girls from wealthy families often embarked enthusiastically on the scientific education intended for kindergarten teachers, but used it to gain independence and intellectual stimulation considered totally unsuitable to their intended duties. Indeed, the pay of kindergarten teachers was scarcely better than that of servants or factory operatives, and appealed more to daughters of skilled workers than to those of the "educated classes." Many actual kindergarten teachers were in fact unable to afford the full education originally intended for them; those who could frequently opted for the more lucrative position of a private governess. In many communities, only wealthy families were able to afford the fees that kindergartens usually charged. Yet even as dame schools for the poor were systematically weeded out of the education landscape and "mere accomplishments" for young ladies attracted increasing scorn, kindergarten methods and family-like schools continued to make themselves felt.

Indeed, students of western schooling can clearly discern a fault line running through different age-, gender-, and class-specific educational institutions and methods. On one side are military, bureaucratic, and industrial models and methods, on the other, familial ideals of the wise master/father and the loving mother made conscious. At times, in particular political climates, countries, and institutions, individual progression, understanding, and responsibility, family groupings, and nurturing of children's innermost faculties come to the fore (more frequently in theory than in practice); at other times, class instruction, rote learning of facts, competitive examinations, uniforms, and uniformity predominate. All too often, the fault line lies within the minds and bodies of the teachers themselves—and women teachers, in particular.

In a thought-provoking article, Grumet uses D. H. Lawrence's depiction of Ursula to explore the impossibility of combining the ideal of motherly love and selfless generosity with the brutal reality of classroom management. Ursula "dreamed how she would make the little ugly children love her. . . . She would make everything personal and vivid, she would give herself, she would give, give, give all her great stores of wealth to the children, she would make them so happy and they would prefer her to any teacher on the face of the earth." Her fellow teachers' cynicism and bitter hatred of the pupils, as well as the children's own fierce resistance, over-whelmed her. She began to feel the ghastly necessity of becoming the same: "put away the personal self, become an instrument, an abstraction, work-ing upon certain material, the class, to achieve a set purpose of making them know so much each day." After struggling for control, she thrashes a student who has defied her, subduing him after a desperate and vicious struggle. She has become a competent teacher, but at the price of searing her soul and destroying her motherly ideals.[70]

*****

The first part of this chapter looked at three distinct models of producing "civilized," self-governing subjects among the children of the poor. Pietists likened true education to a conversion experience. Under the guidance of a skilled fatherly master, children would embrace God's teaching. No longer needing to be coerced, they would scrutinize their own thoughts and behavior and joyously carry out their allotted duties in life. The inventors of monitorial schools hoped that children's mundane strivings to avoid pain and have the pleasure of doing better than their peers could power a mighty engine of instruction. Driven by emulation, kept in check by a Panopticon-like spatial organization, children could convert themselves into useful, industrious, and obedient citizens. Finally, "the mother made conscious," a trained kindergarten teacher, could sever the character of the new generation of laboring children from their tainted roots, and shape them through the sort of expert motherly love that the middle classes began imagining that the most virtuous women possessed. Chapter 6 looks at the way school systems were designed to put these ideals into practice; chapter 7 assesses their effectiveness. But first it is necessary to put the dreams of educators in the context of other technologies of power—other, and argu-ably more effective, ways of controlling the poor.

VIOLENCE AND DEFERENCE

According to Elias, the psychological apparatus of self-restraint among men of the nobility developed most closely with the emergence of institu-tions with a monopoly on violence. The concentration of physical force contributed to the disciplining of habits. The manners of the poor were a world away from the refinements of courtly society, but they too developed in the closest relationship with physical coercion. As many historians noted, the sanction of force and violence was never far beyond deference, master-and-servant relations, or orderly wage labor. Feminist analyses of women's subordination frequently make a similar point: the threat of violence constitutes the structural underpinning of relations between husbands and wives, parents and children.[71] Indeed, the state monopoly on the legitimate exercise of public violence did not lead to the complete pacification of social life. Rather, some forms of violence were proscribed, while others were given formal sanction; some categories of people lived in peace, while others coped as best they could with the constant shadow of physical coercion. In different regions, civilian life was to a greater or lesser extent militarized; uprisings, riots, and strikes were put down by the army; the poor were whipped, hanged, and branded for transgressions against worldly authority or for worshipping God the wrong way. The power of husbands, fathers, army corporals, employers and teachers to inflict "reasonable" corporal punishment on their children, wives, and servants was sanctioned by law, long after men's "public" rights to violence had been seriously curtailed.[72]

In absolutist Prussia, a region notorious for its prodigious use of overt state violence, Ludtke claims that "discretionary and violent police intervention had, inevitably, to be reckoned with by the poor, the propertyless wage labourers and those moving around the country. . . . With these subjects it was not even necessary for the police to establish the reason for the offence, they needed only to arrest arbitrarily those who crossed their paths." In the eighteenth and nineteenth centuries, there were a variety of mechanisms designed to legitimate "a violent practice of police [and military] power which . . . continually affected the entire daily life of the subjects."[73] Whipping and flogging was a routine part of police work directed at the majority of the population who were poor, whether used in questioning suspects, in restoring "public peace," or as punishment. In addition, more than half of civilian town-dwellers lived in garrison towns, where the guards were given powers to intervene at their discretion to restore public peace and order. Since "citadel practice" seemed to the authorities to be the only means to pacify the masses, consideration of alternatives was constantly blocked, and the immense social costs of the military appeared to be inevitable.[74] Even harsher powers than those formally accorded to the police or the military were left in the hands of country landlords and servants' masters. The majority of the population lived in the countryside; for rural day laborers, "a sound thrashing" from the landowners' agents was a constant and often realized threat. It was in the shadow of such violence that Prussia's admired school system, with its emphasis on internalized discipline, developed in the late eighteenth century.[75]

The monopoly on public violence secured by modern states did not rest merely on the size, centralized control, and bureaucratic efficiency of their armies. Crucially, it also depended on the perfectibility of the mass of lowly soldiers recruited among the poorest strata of society. The civilizing power of armies affected these men directly, with a relentless force. In the seventeenth century, the Dutch pioneered important improvements in army administration and routine, improvements that would later provide lasting models for other forms of social organization, factories and schools among them. In particular, the Dutch discovered that long hours of drill not only made soldiers easier to manage in the weeks and months between battles, but rendered them vastly more efficient in combat. For reasons only dimly understood, drill effected a remarkable transformation in the rank and file, even when the soldiers were recruited from the lowest ranks of society: prideful *esprit de corps* became a palpable reality to hundreds of thousands of human beings who had little else to be proud of.[76] Foucault describes this transformation in a brilliant and well-known passage:

> To begin with, the soldier was someone who could be recognised from afar; he bore certain signs: the natural signs of his strength and his courage, the marks, too, of his pride; his body was the blazon of his strength and valour. . . . By the late eighteenth century, the soldier has become something that can be made; out of a formless clay, an inapt body . . . posture is gradually corrected; a calculated constraint runs slowly through each part of the body, mastering it, making it pliable, ready at all times, turning silently into the automatism of habit; in short, one has got "rid of the peasant" and given him "the air of a soldier."[77]

In this process, armies began to lose their old image as uncontrollable bands of robbers, rapists, and murderers (from whose ranks they had often been systematically recruited), and came to be seen as instruments for the moral improvement of the people as a whole. In 1601, Maurice of Hesse described the three aims of the newly disciplined popular army as defense of prince and country, enhancement of esteem and reputation, and removal of the vices of "pernicious idleness, of disgraceful licence and excess in eating, drinking, dress and behaviour, of disorder and wickedness."[78] As Mannheim noted, "The army of the absolute states was the first great institution which not only devised rational methods for creating uniform mass behaviour artificially by means of military discipline and other means for overcoming fear, but also used these methods for educating large masses of men (who were taken for the most part from the lower classes) to act, and if possible to think, in the way prescribed."[79]

A well-drilled army, responding to a clear chain of command from a monarch claiming to rule by divine right to every corporal and common soldier, vastly increased the deadliness of military force per unit of expenditure, and constituted a more obedient and efficient instrument of policy than had ever been seen on earth before.[80] It was the effectiveness of these new armies, in which planning, complex chains of command, and blind obedience to orders of lowly recruits replaced the personal prowess and bravery of noble warriors and their retinues, that helped secure the monopoly on public violence and taxation of those rulers capable of financing the new military enterprise.

The sanction of physical force, immediately evident in Prussian "citadel" practice, could also take less direct forms. England was certainly not free from state violence. On many occasions, the momentous transformations accompanying the development of capitalism led to spectacular flare-ups. What was "moral," "legal," or "rational" in this new world was in the last instance frequently decided in armed conflict. As Christopher Hill put it (speaking of the seventeenth century),

> Rationality is a social concept, and social divisions in England (and elsewhere) were producing conceptions of what was "rational" which were so different that in the last resort only force could decide between them. The "reasonableness" of the sanctity of private property was imposed by the pikes of the New Model Army and by Dutch William's mercenaries.[81]

In the eighteenth century, when the enclosure movement reached a new peak, legislators redefined many customary rights as crimes. During the same period, capital punishment was introduced for a wide range of new property offenses. And yet, according to historians such as E. P. Thompson, throughout the eighteenth century ruling-class control was located primarily in a cultural hegemony, and only secondarily in an expression of economic or military power. Here, paternalism was as much theater and gesture as effective responsibility; far from a warm, household, face-to-face relationship, it was a studied technique of rule.[82]

Hay similarly argues that the quintessentially modern discipline of the capitalist market in England was, until well into the nineteenth century, complemented by an effective deferential dialectic, ostensibly built around pre-capitalist patriarchalist notions of reciprocal rights and duties and paternal benevolence.[83] Between 1688 and 1820, the number of statutes carrying the death penalty grew from about fifty to more than two hundred, with most of the new laws protecting the sacredness of every conceivable kind of private property. Yet in a period of rapidly increasing population, trade, and convictions for theft, the number of executions remained relatively stable, reduced by the increasing use of the royal pardon. According to Hay, this discrepancy, which others have sometimes interpreted as the sign of an unwieldy and irrational legal structure, in fact held the key to an effective system of class-specific justice and social control. The bloody penal code of eighteenth-century England was enacted and then manipulated to their advantage by an astute ruling class to maintain "the mental structure of paternalism." Where the law was ostensibly impartial and inflexible up to the point where a sentence was passed, men of property and influence were able to mobilize their resources to secure a pardon or a reduced sentence in circumstances of their choosing and for those they considered deserving, and to deliberately leave others to the full exemplary rigors of the law. Deference, then, was a tangible and powerful technology of rule, its efficacy often surpassing both random violence and "modern" rational bureaucratic (or market-based) systems of deterrence and punishment.

In a book on sexual assault, Anna Clark makes a parallel case with regard to women. In law, rape, like many forms of theft, was a capital offense, and could be punished by death. Many women believed that the law protected them as well as men, and they pursued their assailants through the courts. But while the law was often ruthless with "undeserving" teenage pickpockets, eighteenth- and nineteenth-century English judges and juries were notoriously reluctant to convict men for sexual assault; they almost never regarded the rape of an adult woman as a punishable offense. In a departure from the usual legal practice, the character of the woman victim, rather than that of the accused man, was the focus of proceedings. In a circular argument, a raped woman's irredeemable loss of her virtue made her evidence by definition flawed. Clark concludes that the law served the interests not only of the propertied classes but of men, helping to normalize men's sexual violence and to enforce women's silence.[84]

THE MARKET, HUNGER, POPULATION, AND WEALTH

The whole history of capitalist development, countless observers noted, has also been a relentless and frequently brutal process of education, its efficacy supplementing and at times replacing other modes of social control. This insight is central to Marx's understanding of capitalism. Once fully developed, he notes,

> The organisation of the capitalist process of production . . . breaks down all resistance. The constant generation of a relative surplus-population keeps the law of supply and demand of labour, and therefore keeps wages, in a rut that corresponds with the wants of capital. The dull compulsion of economic relations completes the subjection of the labourer to the capitalist. Direct force, outside economic conditions, is of course still used, but only exceptionally. In the ordinary run of things, the labourer can be left to the "natural laws of production" i.e. to his dependence on capital.[85]

The sheer force of this compulsion in the lives and mentalities of working people cannot be overestimated. Hunger drove people to work and deformed their bodies; it dominated their thoughts, killed their babies, and decimated their communities. And yet, to the chagrin of innumerable moralists and employers, the initial lessons of the market, which they themselves had learned so well, seemed to bypass whole communities of laboring people (just as they would later be lost on their "native" counterparts). Hans Medick, one of the many scholars who have commented on this fact, notes that the households of rural artisans in seventeenth- and eighteenth-century Europe offered a tenacious resistance to the work ethic that would subordinate the satisfaction of their immediate needs to that of long-range planning, hard work, and frugality. They worked hardest when they got hardly any returns for their labor, and slowed down or stopped altogether when the pay was good, leaving merchants with few supplies in a shortage and flooding them with products when there was a glut. The proto-industrial family continued to work until its subsistence was assured. It then gave in to leisure and worked to satisfy additional material or cultural needs, which always took precedence over an expenditure of work to gain a purely monetary surplus. These people knew little and practiced even less of deferred gratification. Since rural artisans did not see money as peasants saw corn, as a reserve for lean times, they would often suffer because of their lack of savings; some communities eventually starved because they could not or would not abandon their traditional ways.[86]

To pioneering entrepreneurs, a particularly vexatious aspect of this "traditional" mentality was a profound abhorrence of factory labor. "I found the utmost distaste," one English hosier who attempted to set up a factory reported in 1806,

> on the part of the men to any regular hours or regular habits. . . . The men themselves were considerably dissatisfied, because they could not go in and out as they pleased, and go on just as they had been used to do, and were subject during after-hours to the ill-natured observations of other workmen,

to such an extent as completely to disgust them with the whole system, and I was obliged to break it up.[87]

From experiences such as this, employers learned that men with no other incentive than punishment were virtually immune to work discipline.[88] Indeed, the men's refusal to be confined and ordered around explains much of the extensive use of orphans and destitute women and children in early factories.

By the 1830s and 1840s it was commonly observed that the English industrial worker was marked off from his fellow Irish worker not by a greater capacity for hard work, but by his regularity, by his methodical paying out of energy, and perhaps also by a repression, not of enjoyments but of the capacity to relax in old, uninhibited ways. Gradually, English workers stopped fighting *against* time, and began their struggle *about* time: for a shorter working day, overtime, and time off from paid work. The time discipline made necessary by steam-driven machinery in industrial operations, one old potter quoted by Thompson argued, had immense benefit for the workers, because the "calculating induced by the use of machinery" made them "keenly shrewd," and this helped them build up achievements such as cooperative societies.[89] But this is to anticipate.

A fully developed capitalist system, many contemporaries believed, would automatically guarantee rising profits and produce its own labor discipline through a surplus of workers and the resulting regime of low wages, unemployment, and destitution. Long before capitalism became dominant, however, the civilizing properties of hunger were rhapsodized by those who never felt it.

In feudal society, *households* had to produce a surplus to be of use to their lords. It was for this reason that local authorities attempted to preserve a favorable balance between population and resources, and restricted the marriages of the poor. Even as feudalism receded, tenants, smallholders, and sharecroppers paying productivity-linked rents and taxes were ideally well-fed and prosperous. Not only were impoverished, unproductive families a drain on communal resources, since they contributed little or nothing to rent or tax income, but they weakened both the local landholder and the realm. Not only were paternalist concerns with the well-being of one's subjects or parishioners—providing food in a famine, work and tax relief during hard times, charity to the unfortunate—pleasing to God and politically prudent, but they strengthened the rulers' power. Hobbes, writing in the seventeenth century, appealed to common sense (and what he hoped was the rulers' guiding interest) when he wrote, "The riches, power, and honour of a Monarch arise only from the riches, strength and reputation of his subjects. For no King can be rich, nor glorious, nor secure; whose subjects are either poore, contemptible, or too weak through want, or dissension, to maintain a war against their enemies."[90] The notions of "police" developed by cameralists and other contemporary thinkers similarly emphasized the maintenance of a sturdy and healthy working population as among the state's and ruler's major interests.

As wage labor and capitalist relations spread through Europe and its colonies, this logic began to change, typically first in the cities, followed by agricultural and industrial areas relying on wage labor. In capital-intensive regions, in particular, irregular labor rhythms and stubborn immunity of the poor to the hidden hand of the market, coupled with their reluctance to undertake particularly offensive forms of wage labor, provided the major motivation for mercantilist doctrines about the necessity of hunger and low wages to prevent idleness. As the ruling class derived benefit no longer from household surpluses but from wage contracts with individual laborers, poverty rather than the well-being of common people appeared to be a source of prosperity to their betters, and hunger was elevated to a mainspring of wealth. As the English agricultural writer Arthur Young put it succinctly, "Everyone but an idiot . . . knows that the lower class must be kept poor or they will never be industrious."[91] By the middle of the nineteenth century, the English social investigator Henry Mayhew defined poverty by the constant pain of hunger.

Certainly, it was morally awkward, even abhorrent, if large numbers of the poor died of starvation, and widespread misery might carry with it indirect political costs. But as long as there was an abundant supply of cheap labor (which impoverishment of the masses seemed to guarantee), the employers' own prosperity might in fact have an inverse relationship to that of wage workers. In Colquhoun's famous words (in 1806), "Poverty . . . is the source of wealth, since without poverty there would be no labour and without labour there would be no riches, no refinement, no comfort, and no benefit to those who may be possessed of wealth."[92] In early modern Europe, prudent husbanding of estate and national resources involved the integration of the masterless poor into wealthier households, and the careful safeguarding of economically secure holdings. In an increasingly capitalist world, both theory and practice pointed to the total expropriation of the laboring masses. Experience seemed to prove that only if they were completely stripped of productive property, and all other avenues of subsistence were blocked—only if they lost the last shreds of economic independence—would most of the poor willingly engage in wage labor. Within this logic, the old doctrines of obligations of the rich attendant upon rights of property no longer held; the meaning of police gradually changed to safeguarding individual property rights.

These ideas were expanded and reconceptualized in an influential series of essays by the English parson Thomas Malthus. According to Malthus, population had an underlying tendency to exponential growth, but the means of feeding it grew at best arithmetically. Only two things could restore a balance between people and resources: Either laboring people could restrict their own fertility by celibacy and late marriage (as had happened in previous centuries), or large numbers of them would have to die of starvation. In a situation where the poor had ceased to make prudent decisions about their own marriages and their numbers grew out of control, misdirected charity only made things worse. It depleted the resources of the rich, diverted them from funding productive employment, and eventually led to economic stagnation. At the same time, it enabled the poor to have even more children, thus only delaying the starvation of even greater numbers. In the present state of society, the well-being of the poor could lead only to social decay. Laws of nature, as instituted by God and perceived with awful clarity by Malthus, decreed that the rich must be cruel to be kind to the poor. Only the tangible threat of starvation, put in a proper perspective by judicious schooling, could bring home the prudential lessons of God's design of Nature and put in place new, voluntary restrictions on population expansion of the poor.[93]

In the early 1820s, Thomas Chalmers, minister of St. John's Church in Glasgow, published an influential three-volume work in which he argued that a combination of efficient religion, education, and political economy could bring individual working people to mend their ways so that capitalism could be peaceably improved. Malthus was right, Chalmers argued, when he said that the poor had only themselves to blame for their wretched condition. They bred so much that they flooded the market with new laborers, and then underbid each other in order to secure employment. Rational Christianity, by elevating the morality and self-respect of the common people, would get them to aim higher. They would postpone marriage and have fewer children so that they could live in greater comfort, and in this way, unknowingly, reverse the Malthusian curse, restrict the supply of labor, and, according to the economic laws elaborated by Adam Smith, be eagerly sought out by employers and offered higher wages—and all this without recourse to the absurdities of combination (trade unions).[94]

In Britain, most spokesmen of most of the major churches were converted to what they at first saw as Malthus's blasphemy and irreligion in the first decades of the nineteenth century.[95] The period of social unrest of the 1830s seemed to secure the support of many among the elites who until then had seen charity as an effective underpinning of the deferential dialectic that had served them so well.[96] In 1834, strongly influenced by Malthusian ideas, the New Poor Law radically restructured the existing system of poor relief, eliminating most forms of assistance to the "able-bodied" poor. In the United States, too, a crusade against outdoor relief was promoted by organized charity and some local poor-relief administrators. Outdoor relief was completely abolished in about half of major cities, and drastically reduced in others. In Canada, in contrast, a similar campaign had little effect on charity provision.[97]

The English legislature was less enthusiastic about the proposition of Malthus and his supporters that changing the morality of working-class children through schooling was a humane counterpart to the doctrine positing starvation, mandated by "natural" economic laws, as the price paid for the parents' imprudence. As one influential educator put it, "If the pauper child could be taught self-respect and self-reliance, even at the expense of the strict application of [poor-law regulations] the stigma of hereditary pauperism and the tendency for pauperism to generate itself, might be erased." Kay-Shuttleworth believed that the beneficial hidden hand of the market could not work properly if it was obstructed by moral and environmental impediments. Among the physical obstacles were slum housing and filthy sanitary conditions, "arbitrary" restrictions on trade and commerce, and the lack of an effective police force. Moral obstructions included the whole range of ignorance, barbarous manners, and faulty thinking of the poor. Slum clearance, enforcement of building codes, and the construction of sewers had the capacity to improve the physical environment; the New Poor Law and an efficient school system could mend popular morality.[98] Proper schooling would ensure that the lessons of poverty and of the market were read properly, resulting in docility, hard work, and prudent marriage rather than sensuality, riot, and insurrection.

MORALIZING THE HOME

While western countries differed in the actual treatment of the poor by private and state agencies, they long shared a profound distrust of laboring families, and a belief that defective household governance led to a range of social problems. In the first quarter of the nineteenth century, informal living arrangements among working-class couples came under renewed pressure from the propertied classes. Not only was casual cohabitation taken as a sure sign of incipient radicalism and defiant secularism, but the impoverished and depraved children of such unions, willing to take on any work at any price, would make it even harder for the swelling hordes of the poor to feed themselves. The rash of (largely ineffectual) legislation attempting to prevent marriages among the poor peaked in the 1830s; it was soon complemented and supplanted by massive campaigns directed at regularizing the cohabitation of working-class men and women. Throughout Britain and France, church and various other agencies embarked on a crusade to "tame the passions of the poor" and enforce "proper" marriage practices. In England, "by the 1840s, there were armies of volunteers engaged in this endeavour, from the City Missionaries who hunted out unwed couples and harried them to the altar, to the tens of thousands of 'lady visitors' who descended on working-class households to examine their moral condition; through to the Sunday Schools and Mechanics Institutes which constantly preached the virtue of stable family existence."[99]

In the new virtuous households, the theory went, women and children would of necessity attempt to safeguard the industriousness, frugality, and abstinence of their menfolk. English Evangelicals believed that in turn, domestic comfort and virtue would produce contented men happy to give up trade unions and political radicalism; in France, reformers dreamed that devout working-class mothers could "stamp out the spirit of independence in the working man" and extinguish the flames of class conflict.[100] Fully aware of women's power and influence, Chartist men in England put a lot of effort into winning women's support. "We cannot afford [women's] neutrality or hostility," one influential organizer put it in a speech to thousands of working women, "they must be our enthusiastic friends."[101] Revisionist historians such as Richard Johnson had eloquently described nineteenth-century educationists' attacks on laboring families, and their hopes that schools would destroy working-class culture.[102] Noting the importance of contemporary campaigns to moralize the working-class home, many feminist scholars similarly link them to the building of schools. Davin, Dyhouse, and Theobald all suggest that one of the major motivations for the establishment of mass schooling was an attempt to impose upon working-class children a middle-class family form of a male breadwinner and an economically dependent wife and mother—to make "good women" out of girls at risk of slothfulness and impropriety.[103] The actual impact of schools on family life will be considered in some detail in chapter 8. Here I will take up one example of a more general issue. In many instances, attempts to moralize the home further undermined the viability of laboring households.

A number of feminist commentators have noted that the New Poor Law in England was a powerful vehicle for imposing bourgeois notions of family life on the poor. The lawmakers assumed that a stable two-parent family dependent upon the father's wage was the norm, and they condemned and penalized those who did not conform to their preconceived notions. One of the most significant symbolic consequences of the act, according to Rose, was to strengthen an association that working men made between manliness and independence. Nevertheless, she also notes that the act forced people to work for wages that could not feed a family, and under conditions that ruined their health and thus their long-term capacity as breadwinners.[104] In *The Constitution of Poverty*, Dean makes an even stronger claim. Earlier gender-blind commentators on the poor laws had overlooked the important fact that the legislation helped *constitute* the male breadwinner family among the laboring poor, above all through removing the rights to outdoor relief of able-bodied adult men and all those seen as their natural dependents. Only if they entered a workhouse and submitted to its degrading discipline would such families get just enough food to avoid starvation. This sanction, it was hoped, would put a backbone of pride and manly independence into lazy and shiftless working-class men, gradually teaching them the virtues of prudence, hard work, and patriarchal responsibility.[105]

Whatever the long-term discursive effect of poor-law provisions, their immediate impact on families of the laboring poor was hardly in the direction suggested by Dean. Certainly, the commissioners waxed eloquent about the husband's manly independence and sacred duty to provide for his family; they were in complete sympathy with those wishing to moralize the working-class home. Indeed, by making it impossible for an unmarried mother to claim financial compensation or support from the child's father, the authorities eliminated one alternative to marriage. But the policies they actually implemented pointed to a fully proletarian family rather than one with a male breadwinner—indeed, that was often their explicit intent. In the early nineteenth century, according to official statistics, more than 10 percent of the total population was on some form of poor relief. Four out of ten of these were able-bodied adults and their children receiving wage subsidies, child allowances, and other support. As a rough rule, the larger and poorer the family, the more assistance it got. By the 1850s, the proportion of such men receiving outdoor support dropped to less than 1 percent of the total number of paupers.[106] In the period 1850 to 1910, the proportion of the population receiving poor relief fell from 5.7 percent to 2 percent, even as poverty levels remained the same or increased.[107] Low and intermittent male wages already made it necessary for wives and children to become supplementary—and sometimes the sole—breadwinners; the cessation of outdoor relief to husbands and fathers made this need even more pressing.

In addition, many English poor-law guardians remained skeptical about the benefits of formal education, however moral it might be. Ignoring an 1855 act that allowed them to pay the school fees of poor and destitute pupils, they continued to demand that the children of all those who applied for relief leave school to work.[108] Indeed, while English reformers eventually persuaded "the public" of the urgent need for popular schooling, they had much less success in raising cash for their educational ventures. Obscurantism might well have been defeated in England in the 1820s and 1830s, but voluntary contributions for elementary schools fell far short of the reformers' ambitions and demonstrated needs. The British state was among the last to become directly involved in the comprehensive management and financing of elementary schools.

Competing for his livelihood in a wildly fluctuating labor market, subject to the ravages of poverty and workplace injuries, for many decades forbidden to form trade unions, and denied most forms of charitable assistance, the working-class patriarch had ample opportunity to make the life of his wife and children a misery, but only rarely the positive power to provide them with a secure source of subsistence.[109] By refusing support to wives and children of drunk and violent men, or of husbands who deserted their families, the New Poor Law amplified the misfortune of an unhappy marriage. By denying aid to the dependents of unemployed and poorly paid workers, the law intensified the explosive family tensions that loss of productive property entailed, and magnified the disasters precipitated by illness, accidents, theft, economic slumps, and unruly lives of family members. As Lees put it, although poor-law officials continued to insist that families were obligated to provide for dependent members, both the theory and the practice of relief in London after 1834 helped dissolve kinship bonds and co-residence. Not only did relief policies discriminate against male-headed households and large families, and encourage child and female wage labor, but many officials believed that families of the poor were so bad that everybody would benefit if they were broken up.[110] From the other side, far from seeing the Poor Law as in any way assisting the formation of male breadwinner families, laboring men condemned Malthusianism, "a pretended philosophy [that] . . . crushes, through the bitter privations it inflicts upon us, the energies of our manhood, making our hearths desolate, our homes wretched, inflicting upon our heart's companions an eternal round of sorrow and despair."[111]

While the clergy, reformers, school teachers, and lady visitors every-where encouraged the poor to marry and lead virtuous lives, for more than half a century the poor of Britain lived in the shadow of Malthusian poli-cies. In France, the social landscape was different. Both urbanization and the proportion of proletarians were lower than in England. By the 1850s, only 14 percent of the French population lived in urban centers of more than ten thousand inhabitants, as opposed to some 40 percent in England. Unlike France, England had virtually no independent peasants. Its farmers no longer needed an extensive workforce, and the proportion of landless laborers in the population was the highest in Europe. While the population of England and Wales multiplied sixfold between 1750 and 1900, that of France increased by less than half.[112] Whereas labor discipline and over-population were a major concern in England, the danger of revolutionary outbreaks (France experienced three between the end of the old regime and 1848, as well as ten constitutional changes), falling birthrates, and the country's ability to produce sufficient numbers of healthy soldiers preoccu-pied social commentators in France. The ruling classes liked the idea of economic compulsion, and attempted to teach the poor to subsist at the least expense, but they were not prepared to risk social unrest by a whole-sale introduction of Malthusian policies. Throughout the nineteenth cen-tury, the system of poor relief, so eloquently described by Foucault and Donzelot, continued to put more emphasis on thorough policing of the poor than on regulating the labor market. Outdoor relief in France was never phased out, and social polices in the last part of the century actually attempted to increase population growth.[113]

French commentators first became concerned about depopulation when deaths exceeded births in 1854 and 1855. After France's ignominious de-feat in the Franco-Prussian War, these concerns intensified. In the minds of French politicians, demographers, and natalist propagandists, the dis-courses of depopulation and nationalism merged into one. According to Roberts,

> Although historians usually attribute France's humiliation in 1870–71 to ineffective and unimaginative military leadership, government officials ex-plained it in terms of declining population. Increasing awareness of demo-graphic decline coincided with the realization of France's worst nightmare: the rise of a united, aggressive enemy to the east. Politicians and propagan-dists transformed this temporal coincidence into causal determination, argu-ing that depopulation had, in fact, led simultaneously to the Prussian threat and French military vulnerability.[114]

Rachel Fuchs notes that in early-nineteenth-century France, the problem of the urban poor was equated with the fecundity of impoverished women who lacked morality and had children even though they could not support them or were not married. Illicit relationships were rampant in the cities, bourgeois citizens feared, generating urban malaise, immorality, deviancy, and threats to traditional values. The private religious charities that dominated the scene in the first seventy years of the nineteenth century put a lot of effort into creating and sustaining what they saw as proper families, and tended to aid only those legally married in a religious ceremony. To assist unmarried mothers and their illegitimate children, they believed, would encourage immorality and the breakdown of traditional patriarchal authority.[115] During this period, outdoor relief was restricted to those who followed the rules of a normal family pattern and moral character without blemish. The underlying principle was that "family bonds are not to be broken"; almost every article in the civil code relating to the family reinforced the power of the husband over his wife and children. But this form of bolstering of patriarchal authority was double-edged. Households receiving relief opened themselves up to extensive administrative scrutiny and intervention: "[male] workers who apply for relief put themselves into the position of minors, of necessity forsaking their rights as citizens, and as fathers."[116]

During the Third Republic (1870–1914), l'Assistance publique reversed many of the criteria previously stipulated by private charity. In a secularizing, anticlerical republic, concern with saving infants' lives through aiding their mothers as a means of combating depopulation took precedence over insistence on marriage and religion. Reformers and officials stopped criticizing the poor for having so many (mostly illegitimate) babies, and began to concern themselves with high infant mortality. In a sense, rather than mold women to the requirements of charity providers, assistance came to terms with the persistent realities of women's lives.[117] By the turn of the century, Mitchel and Koven argue, despite the weakness of the French women's movement, maternalist policies became part of the French welfare state; in England, which had a much stronger feminist presence, provisions for mothers and children lagged behind.[118]

* * * * *

The uneven dismantling of a patriarchalist social order in eighteenth- and nineteenth-century Europe was accompanied by the intensification of some old ways of controlling the poor and the invention of others; the development and use of new technologies of production indeed coincided with the development and use of new technologies of discipline. Foremost among these technologies of power was a new emphasis on creating a particular form of "civilized" self among the masses. The poor needed to govern themselves more than had ever been necessary, because in the new, more populous and vaster world, personalized forms of mastery were losing their effectiveness. Malthus, whose writings bridged the old and the new approach, hoped that hunger, its correct lessons interpreted by schoolmasters, would teach workers the virtues of prudence, celibacy, delayed marriage, and smaller families. In time, the resulting scarcity of workers would naturally push up wages. Workers themselves often short-circuited the process. Organization of labor, made strong by desperation born of hunger, could win better wages and working conditions. A male-dominated labor movement, hesitantly supported by women and some employers, added demands for male breadwinner wages and the exclusion of children and married women from the workforce. Eventually, the best-paid and most secure sections of the working class—rather than the most desperate—began limiting the number of their children, just as policy makers rediscovered the benefits of unchecked population growth. In the meanwhile, the poor everywhere used charity in ways that had little to do with the intentions of the donors.

CHAPTER SIX

Assembling School Systems

Knowledge, unless sanctified by religion, is an unmitigated evil.[1]

If we sow fools we shall reap vice; if we sow Larkins we shall reap criminals, but if we sow practical knowledge, we must reap power and riches.[2]

Taking children at random from a great city, undisciplined, uninstructed, often with inveterate forwardness and obstinacy, and with the inherited stupidity of centuries of ignorant ancestors; forming them from animals into intellectual beings, and . . . from intellectual beings into spiritual beings; giving to many their first appreciation of what is wise, what is true, what is lovely and what is pure.[3]

We are regulated in every way—in things we are perfectly well able to regulate ourselves.[4]

As a sex we are labouring under many and unreasonable handicaps. Men's interests are not women's interests, therefore there is a great need for solidarity amongst women. There are no prizes allowed us in the Education Department, we are excluded from all higher positions. As there is no valid reason why this inequality and discrimination should continue to exist, women teachers should demand, with one voice, that they be wiped away.[5]

The previous chapter described the schemes devised to civilize laboring people in and out of schools. Here I look at the process of implementing them. The first part of the chapter deals with problems of timing and uneven development. It addresses the fact that modern school systems were first established in relatively backward absolutist states, and examines the one area where this paradox was most apparent: the link between industrialization and mass schooling. The second part of the chapter is concerned with several key aspects of the building of educational systems: the interplay between local communities and the development of school regulations, the role of inspection and statistics in the accumulation of state knowledge, and the consolidation of gendered bureaucracies. Here again, I suggest, patriarchal dynamics play a crucial, but far from predictable, role.

*****

Just as they were in the forefront of educational experiments in early modern Europe, Germany and the Scandinavian countries were among the pioneers of modern schooling. Prussia legislated compulsory schooling in 1763. A Ministry of Education was established in 1808 to supervise all public education, merging in 1817 with the department overseeing church matters to become the Ministry of Education and Religious Affairs.[6] By 1826, all school teachers were required to be certified through a state examination. Almost one and a half million children were enrolled in these schools in 1822, double that number in 1867, and more than five million, or three-quarters of children aged five to fourteen, by the turn of the century. Sweden established a Ministry of Education and Church Affairs in 1809. In 1842, an elementary school act established a national system of schools and made education compulsory, without specifying the precise length of time children had to attend schools. In 1878, the compulsory school age was set at seven to thirteen years. By this stage, nearly three-quarters of those from five to fourteen were enrolled in school. In Denmark, the 1814 Public Education Act provided for the setting up of schools in all municipalities and for seven years of compulsory education for three days per week. In 1849, compulsory schooling was extended to cover a six-day week. Norway established permanent schools near every principal church in rural areas in 1827, and in 1848 made education for at least two months of the year mandatory for all children between seven years of age and confirmation. By 1870, almost 60 percent of children between the ages of five and fourteen were on the rolls.[7] Between 1869 and 1882, most western countries followed suit. Schooling was made compulsory in Ontario, British Columbia, and Manitoba, Canada; in fourteen U.S. states; in Victoria, South Australia, Western Australia, and New South Wales, Australia; and in New Zealand, Scotland, the fifteen crown lands of the Austrian Empire, Switzerland and Italy, the remaining lands of the German Empire, and France, England, and Wales.

In one country after another, the same basic pattern emerged. Local communities were encouraged, sometimes ordered, to set up elementary schools. At first, modest state subsidies supplemented income from school fees and local rates and taxes; as public funding expanded, so did the number of officials charged with oversight of schools and the complexity and ambition of their tasks. Within a few decades, complex (though by no means uniform) bureaucracies emerged in the space between local children, parents, and instructors and central authorities. First charged with physically locating schools and making sure that classes took place, inspectors began to examine individual students, check the qualifications of teachers, comment on their teaching style, certify that attendance rolls were accurately filled in, claim authority over the design of schoolrooms and school furniture, prescribe textbooks and suggest ways of using them, set curricula for different subjects, and ascertain whether detailed instructions had been followed. At first, parents were exhorted to send children to school; legislation eventually made attendance of those considered most in need of instruction compulsory for a part of the school year. Over time, more and more categories of children were caught in the net; more serious provisions were made for enforcement of the compulsory clauses, the period of mandatory school attendance expanded—and those deemed too young or too old (and at times those who were black) were excluded from the schools. The power of teachers over their charges increased inside the classroom and began to extend into the street; that of parents diminished. In theory, at least, the social space controlled by the state (at times in close cooperation with the church) expanded considerably. In those communities where cheap private schools survived alongside state-sponsored ones, more vigorous steps were taken to suppress them. As Simon Frith pointed out with regard to England, despite the existence of other models of schooling, for both the rich and the poor, by the late nineteenth century "the age-specific, teacher related process requiring full-time attendance at an obligatory curriculum" had come to be accepted as the only education worthy of the name.[8]

The mere enactment of compulsory legislation is not a reliable indicator of the proportion of children enrolled, and is an even less reliable indication of the number who actually attended school.[9] Neither can it be used to rank countries along one scale of social or economic development. In a schematic statistical overview, Soysal and Strang distinguish between three paths to the construction of educational systems. A statist construction of education (such as in Denmark, Norway, Prussia, and Sweden) was characterized by the early creation of education systems, both formally and organizationally, by the state. In contrast, a societal construction of education (for example, in France, the Netherlands, Switzerland, Britain, and the United States) involved a considerable expansion of schooling ahead of the state's involvement in education. Finally, a rhetorical construction of education occurred in countries such as Greece, Italy, Portugal, and Spain, where states were quick to legislate compulsory education but unable to realize it in actual schooling.[10]

Similarly, in the United States, Richardson identifies three distinct regional patterns which influenced the date of enactment of the compulsory laws, and the governing structures of state and local school systems. In the Northeast, with its autonomous towns characterized by sharp internal inequalities, compulsory schooling came after voluntary enrollments were built up. In the Midwest, in contrast, education systems were often built in anticipation of population growth, as one of the factors that would attract white settlers. Finally, in the South, early settlement on isolated farmsteads dispersed across large territorial areas was associated with sharp racial and class divisions. Such conditions fostered neither the spread of autonomous towns nor a commercial class capable of challenging the political dominance of a land-based elite. Here, legislation on compulsory schooling was delayed until after the racial segregation laws were passed around 1900.[11] Only then could whites be compelled to go to school and blacks be kept out.

Not only the timing of legislative change but contemporary measures of educational activity and expenditure must be treated with caution. Statistics have always been political artifacts, the more so since decentralized educational provisions in countries such as England, with its myriad competing and uncoordinated institutions and sources of private funds, were not easily compared to more closely controlled systems such as that in Prussia. For this and other reasons, both contemporaries and historians tended to underestimate private educational expenditure and activity in Britain. At the same time, then as now, arguments about the extent and comparative advantages of public and private provision were part of heated debates about the desirability of state intervention in public life. Most historians are all too aware that their arguments regarding the adequacy of public or private educational provision in the nineteenth century can be used to defend or to dismantle state schools and universities today—to condemn or to defend the privatization of public assets and services.

In the previous chapter, I noted that the Prussian school system became a model of enlightened educational practice throughout the western world. Many historians warn that the majority of *Volksschule* were not nearly as good as enthusiastic visitors of exceptional schools, keen to shame their own governments into action, reported. Many of the Prussian clergymen charged with inspecting schools had little sympathy for the newfangled ideas that teachers learned at the pedagogical institutes. Teachers aspiring to a new professional status claimed that only trained, full-time lay officers had the requisite expertise to guide them. Not least for reasons of cost, the government appointed such inspectors only in exceptional circumstances. In any case, state enthusiasm for educational innovation cooled considerably in the political unrest culminating in the 1848 revolution, in which many teachers took an active part.[12] "All the troubles which have overwhelmed Prussia during the past few years," Frederick William IV told a delegation of teachers in 1854, were due to an "irreligious mass education" which had "destroyed the piety and loyalty in the hearts of my subjects [and] turned them away from me."[13] In this period, interdenominational schools were discouraged or closed, the hours devoted to religious instruction were expanded, memorization rather than discussion was emphasized, and teacher training lost its previous broad curriculum and spirit of independence, self-reliance, and intellectual ambition.[14]

Wide disparities in available resources were also important. The most competent teachers and well-organized, adequately funded schools tended to be found in the towns and cities of the western provinces, the most impoverished ones in the east. Many village communities charged with financing schools were unable to find enough money to build or repair the schoolhouse and hire a trained teacher. Direct state contribution to schooling was small: in 1867, it amounted to only 4 percent of the total, growing to 12.2 percent in 1878. Even then, in the later decades of the nineteenth century, the government preferred to subsidize German Protestant schools in Polish-speaking areas rather than alleviate overcrowding in impoverished, predominantly Catholic regions. By the 1870s, many country teachers struggled with ungraded classes of a hundred or even a hundred and fifty students. At times they were required to deliver instruction in German to children who spoke only Polish at home; sometimes their schoolhouse was so small that they had to teach in three shifts.[15] And while Prussian schools were internationally famous for their sparing use of corporal punishment, biographers recalled the occasional teacher who did not beat his charges as an oddity.[16]

The fact remains that absolutist and semi-feudal rural Prussia pioneered an envied system of mass compulsory schooling, while in industrializing, highly urbanized Britain, the state assiduously avoided all involvement with common schools. According to Pollard, for example, Britain, with the poorest provision of public schools in the West, had the best industry, while the record of countries with good schools, such as Scandinavia and Prussia, was far less impressive. In the early nineteenth century, the learned consensus was that Prussian schools were excellent, most English ones a disgrace.[17] At the time, this fact was the subject of innumerable commentaries and debates; more recently it had become one of the explanations for Britain's decline as an industrial and political power. Prussia legislated compulsory schooling more than a century before England and Wales; in the early 1870s, seven out of ten children aged five to fourteen were enrolled in school in Prussia, half that number in England and Wales.[18]

While it has now become a commonplace that in their simple form, functionalist accounts of the links between industrialization and the rise of mass schooling are untenable, English-language histories of education, focusing as they do on national rather than comparative issues, rarely confront issues such as these head on.[19] Writers influenced by human capital theories routinely asserted that the need for new skills unleashed by the industrial revolution motivated the building of schools; others, following Durkheim and Parsons, emphasized the need for specialization and role differentiation in more complex urbanized, industrial societies.[20] Marxists amended this to argue that mass schooling had less to do with a need for skills than with class conflict, less with a necessity to master new bodies of knowledge than with reasserting mastery over the lower orders. The dispositions of wage workers, rather than book knowledge, were what mattered.[21] Even though their analysis of capitalist society differed considerably, a similar argument was made by Weberian scholars, who linked the need for schools with attempts to ameliorate the social disorder created by rapid urbanization and industrialization.[22] More recently, Foucault and others have reconceptualized these points to claim that new forms of governance, not just new forms of technology, had to be invented and policed during the age of revolutions. As Foucault put it, machinery capable of employing vast accumulations of people could become effective only to the extent that employers perfected techniques for controlling the bodies and populations of workers. A feminist account might add that a crisis of laboring families precipitated by rapid proletarianization contributed to a crisis of governmentality at all levels of society, and that the making of "good women" and virtuous families was seen as crucial to the securing of social order.[23]

Whatever they celebrate or criticize—urbanization, industrialization, liberalism, and capitalism—all of these explanations imply that schools were needed most in the most advanced, most modern regions. But if schools are essentially modern institutions, why did they develop first in semi-feudal states with strong absolutist histories, such as Prussia and Sweden? And if either the need for skills *or* the need for dispositions theory holds, why was the need not greatest where industry was most developed—or, in the feminist version, where the crisis unleashed by proletarianization was felt most keenly? Theories of uneven development, exemplified by arguments regarding capital- or coercion-intensive paths to state formation, might supply part of the answer. A rethinking of the modernity or otherwise of the British state, and of links between industrialization and the need for skills, illuminates other aspects of the problem.

ABSOLUTISM, CAPITALISM, AND MODERNITY

In the previous chapter, I drew attention to differences in family and population policies between France and England, and to the varying emphasis on violence, deference, and the market in England and Prussia. These issues illustrate a more general principle. Different jurisdictions afflicted local populations with different mixtures of public and private violence, capitalist markets, charity, and bureaucracy; gender, class, race, and age provided a different structure of constraints on individual people. According to Charles Tilly's useful typology, three different viable paths of European state formation had markedly different consequences for local technologies of rule. In "capital-intensive" regions (areas of many cities and commercial predominance, where markets, exchange, and market-oriented production prevailed), such as city-states, city-empires, and urban federations, rulers relied on compacts with capitalists to rent or purchase military force, and made war without building vast permanent state structures or conscript armies. The presence of capitalists, commercial exchange, and substantial municipal organizations set serious limits on the state's direct exertion of control over individuals and households, but facilitated the use of relatively efficient and painless taxes on commerce as a source of state revenue. States such as Genoa or the Dutch Republic could raise a lot of capital at short notice, had access to good credit, and easily drew taxes from customs and excise, all without a substantial central bureaucracy. Later, it was in regions characterized by a similar set of social relations that the invisible hand of the market could operate most smoothly. Areas of early urban dominance, with their active capitalists, produced very different kinds of states than did regions in which great landlords and their estates dominated the landscape.

In "coercion-intensive" regions (areas of few cities and agricultural predominance, where direct coercion played a major part in production), customs and excise yielded small returns in relatively uncommercialized economies, and rulers typically created ponderous fiscal machines to extract the means of war out of local populations. In these conditions, extensive power accumulated in the hands of armed landlords, nobility, gentry, village heads, and others who exercised intermediate control over essential resources. Not least because wage labor was scarce, peasants found it difficult to escape patriarchalist authority. In Brandenburg, Russia, Poland, and Hungary, powerful nobility and great landlords re-imposed serfdom on the rural populations at the close of the Thirty Years' War in 1648; in Poland and Hungary, the nobility retained sufficient power to continue to elect their kings. Two centuries later, in regions such as these, the compulsion of the market remained subordinate to direct coercion organized along patriarchalist lines.

Finally, in regions of "capitalized coercion," holders of coercion and capital—nobles and financiers—interacted on terms of relative equality. Rulers both built bureaucracies and depended on commercial taxes, but spent more effort on integrating capitalists and sources of capital directly into the structures of their states. Here, encroaching capitalism tended to undermine the patriarchalist structures of peasant families from below; bureaucracy eroded them from above. Tilly argues that it was this path, pursued by countries such as France, England, and Spain, that produced national states earliest, and which eventually proved to be most successful in waging war. By about the eighteenth century, other previously viable territorial units were under increasing pressure to adopt a similar form of state governance or suffer military defeat.[24]

Using a similar framework in their overview of different waves of social control in Europe between the sixteenth and the nineteenth centuries, Lis and Soly similarly stress the increasing divergence between capitalist and absolutist regions. In England and later the Netherlands, major emphasis was placed on policies directed at securing a cheap labor force for the growing number of capitalist ventures. In France, Germany, and other continental countries, where the rise of absolutist tax states (which supported peasant ownership) entailed greater reliance on punitive controls and penal policies, the weight of social control rested heavily on intricate bureaucratic regulation of public violence.[25]

Pursuing this line of argument, many historians conclude that in Britain, the Netherlands, and later the United States, people were exploited above all through economic means, the propertied classes taxed themselves and performed a substantial share of "public office" for free in their private capacity, and the remaining state offices were funded out of a portion of wealth skimmed off from gains accumulated in the "private" sphere by means of purely economic appropriation. In these countries, the state typically manipulated the relations between capital and labor as much as possible in favor of capital accumulation, but state agencies took little direct part in the restructuring of capital or the reorganization of production. In contrast, from the eighteenth century, absolutist states such as Prussia, Austria, and France became autonomous agencies of modernization and industrialization. They began fostering a form of bureaucratic capitalism, frequently combining serf labor with large-scale production for the market, and emphasizing aggressive defense and consolidation of their market advantages through measures such as direct subsidies to particular enterprises, tariffs, and monopolies.[26] Later still, industrialization on the Continent was to a greater extent led by the development of large and heavy industry encouraged by the state.[27]

Attention to different paths of state formation overlaps with debates regarding the relative "modernity" of different state institutions. As I have done in the preceding section, historians often draw attention to an apparent paradox. "Modern" institutions tended to develop in absolutist states, which were built around precapitalist modes of production, while Britain, where capitalism achieved its most "modern" form, for a long time retained seemingly archaic forms of governance. Indeed, at the height of its power as the greatest industrial, trading, and colonial nation on earth, with industry at a stage of development that many continental states would not attain for another half a century, Britain's government was routinely described as laissez-faire, weak, and old-fashioned by the majority of commentators, on both the left and the right.

This issue, which has been the subject of many learned debates, has recently been revisited with particular clarity by John Brewer in *The Sinews of Power* and by Ellen Meiksins Wood in *The Pristine Culture of Capitalism*.[28] Brewer notes the long tradition of describing (and often celebrating) the weakness of the eighteenth-century British state, but sets out to paint a radically different picture. According to him, the seventeenth and eighteenth centuries saw an astonishing transformation in British government, one that put muscle on the bone of the British body politic, increasing its endurance, strength, and reach, and creating what might be called a fiscal-military state. Britain was able to shoulder an ever more ponderous burden of military commitments thanks to a radical increase in taxation, the development of national debt on an unprecedented scale (to levels that would be unacceptably high by today's standards), and the growth of a sizable public administration devoted to organizing the fiscal and military activities of the state. As a result, the state became the single largest actor in the economy, its capital investments, running costs, labor requirements, and logistical problems dwarfing any contemporary civilian enterprise.[29]

In his argument, Brewer not only charts a radical increase in the external military and diplomatic might of the British state,[30] he also rejects the proposition that this strength was coupled with weak internal capacity to regulate the economy and govern its subjects. First, he qualifies the notion that the British regime, for all its military effectiveness, was characterized by a lightness of touch with regard to the administration of law and order: the heavy-handedness of British rule increased the further it extended beyond the metropolis. He then argues that the ability of government administrators to establish the routine by which revenues were collected, money was raised, and supply was requisitioned could make the difference between victory and defeat, and he claims that it was precisely such ability to mobilize England's wealth that explains how the nation was able to sustain such a powerful military effort.

Brewer attributes the ease with which substantial sums were raised to the existence of a powerful representative with undisputed powers of national taxation, a commercialized economy whose structure made it comparatively simple to tax, and the deployment of fiscal expertise that made borrowing against tax income an easy task. On all of these criteria, Brewer presents systematic comparative evidence in order to demonstrate that judged by the ability to take pounds out of people's pockets and put soldiers in the field and sailors on the high seas, Britain was one of Europe's most powerful states, one that had acquired prodigious powers over its subjects. The traditional view that England was lightly taxed was a myth: on average, per capita taxation in England in the eighteenth century was almost twice that of France. Moreover, between the late seventeenth and the mid-eighteenth century, the English state developed a civil administration characterized by a degree of professionalism every bit as rigorous as that of any body of officers in Europe. Indeed, tax collection in England was distinctive because it was to an unusually high degree in the hands of centrally appointed government bureaucrats (not private entrepreneurs or local government officials), whose number was large by contemporary standards. The tax system was not only exceptionally centralized, but also uniform in its legal incidence, with no region or rank exempt.

Last, Brewer gives due weight to the victories, limited though they were, of the proponents of small state and limited military involvement. The powers of the military over the civilian population were severely restricted, efforts to use civilian officers as a general police rather than merely tax gatherers were checked, and the bureaucracy's growth was limited to those circumstances necessary for its successful operation.[31] This lean administration with limited powers, according to Brewer, in fact made the eighteenth- and nineteenth-century state stronger and more effective, particularly since its limited powers could be used to full effect, with great legitimacy. Brewer concludes that, paradoxically, a strong parliament effectively resisting much that was proposed by government eventually produced a stronger state, one not burdened by the huge costs of sinecures and hereditary offices.

Venality, or the sale of government offices to private investors, is one of the starting points of Wood's essay on capitalism, absolutism, and modernity.[32] According to Wood, this "political mode of appropriation" typically produced a large and visible state bureaucracy, and this in turn has often been equated with a strong modern state. Indeed, she argues that although England was the world's first capitalist system, western culture has produced an image of capitalism to which England has failed to conform. The very features that have been ahistorically defined as the marks of modern capitalism might in fact be the tokens of its absence.

Wood's argument revolves around four key propositions. The first three reflect the starting point of scholars such as Perry Anderson who support the "archaic and weak British state" thesis; in the last she emphatically departs from their line of analysis and comes close to the "alternative form of strength" argument of historians such as E. P. Thompson, Brewer, Corrigan, and Sayer. First, capitalism in England developed slowly, organically, without pressing competition from more economically advanced rivals. Second, the organic development of capitalism within "archaic" institutions left these institutional forms in place instead of sweeping them away in a series of revolutionary onslaughts. Early English capitalism never faced the need to establish institutions or practices to enhance or accelerate economic development, and its slow and "natural" industrial revolution, unlike, say, the German process of industrialization, generated no need for innovations like the bureaucratic creation of a widespread, efficient system of technical education. Finally, English archaic institutional forms have gradually been transformed into more perfectly capitalist institutions: capitalism was more deeply rooted and unbridled in England, and its laws were more firmly established than in any other European country, transforming the substance while preserving old forms. Importantly, while this process established the reality of a unitary sovereignty in England, it contributed to making the stronger English state much less visible and less distinctly defined than was the case with continental absolutisms.[33]

SERFDOM, INDUSTRIALIZATION, AND SCHOOLS

Debates about uneven development and the modernity or otherwise of state institutions are relevant to discussions about the need for skills and the building of education systems: a resort to schools might indicate the relative *failure* of other forms of governance and social control. Not only was British industry, with all its problems, the most advanced in the world, it is possible to argue that the dull compulsion of its capitalist market was the most effective in producing adequate numbers of skilled and biddable workers. While this argument does not pretend to supply a comprehensive new grand theory of school expansion, it helps explain why it was the absolutist states of central and northern Europe that gave rise to the first forms of effectively enforced compulsory schooling.

Traditional historiography associates mass schooling with problems of urbanization and factory industrialization. According to Melton, the push for compulsory schooling in Prussia and Austria was, in contrast, linked to concerns with the breakdown of patriarchalist authority in rural areas undergoing proto-industrialization, a crisis in seignorial authority on the estates, and peasants' resistance to feudal obligations. Absolutist states such as Prussia and Austria, Melton notes, were economically backward countries with powerful state churches engaged in costly territorial wars. Under stress from more advanced capitalist economies, they attempted to transform their modes of governance and develop their economies along capitalist lines without jeopardizing the social hierarchy and the distribution of wealth. Military conquest followed by decades of sharpening exploitation precipitated widespread famines and left whole regions simmering with discontent. Tightening feudal obligations any further had no chance of increasing the landlords' returns. At best it would lead to debilitating poverty; more likely it would spark murderous uprisings. The only way out, it seemed, was to free the serfs, break up the estates, and commute labor services to money rents.

But only *after* the serfs internalized authority and learned to obey the profit motive, instead of responding only to the whip, would the nobles hazard abolishing serfdom and converting their estates to wage labor: "immediate freedom would be as destructive to agriculture as serfdom itself." As one contemporary put it,

> Hardly would the Bohemian peasant gain his freedom before he would begin to abuse it. . . . Fear, which at present is all that motivates the peasant and controls his behaviour, would disappear. Where virtue, honour, and the promise of prosperity can motivate a free individual, only the threatening whip of an overseer can motivate a peasant whose labour is coerced.[34]

At times drawing on cameralist doctrines that likened the prosperity of households, states, and estates, the enlightened reformers blamed the peasants' passivity and sullen obstinacy on the landlords' and government's careless housekeeping. Peasants rendering forced labor displayed "an almost bestial indifference to God and religion, a coldness towards their lords bordering on hate, and a stupid insensitivity to all morality. Neither disgrace nor honour can move their bitter hearts."[35] Most were so demoralized, they cared little for acquiring property; the blind greed of others threatened to undermine civic order.

In time, improved national housekeeping would both increase noble incomes and create respectful and happy peasant communities. For the time being, "the character of the peasant has been so neglected that the will and aptitude necessary for his self-improvement will require long and serious cultivation. In short, we must educate an entirely new generation."[36] According to Melton, those enlightened landowners who led the move for commuting labor services were also the ones who were most active in promoting schools on their estates. By promising to turn out masses of respectful, self-policing subjects amenable to the hidden hand of the market, Pietist schools could help accomplish a peaceful passage from feudalism to capitalism, from coercion-intensive patriarchalism to a new form of peaceable patriarchal order. Just as later it was claimed that a good schoolmaster had no need of corporal punishment, in the well-ordered village, a popular schoolbook promised, there was not even a jail. The old one had collapsed, and the lord refused to build a new one. "Jails are only for the wicked," said the lord, "and I have no wicked subjects."[37]

Paradoxically, while the creation of an orderly and diligent proto-industrial workforce during an acute shortage of labor was the main motivation for compulsory schooling legislation in late eighteenth-century Prussia and Austria, the very conditions that inspired this reform also stymied it. The policies designed to instill new work discipline in children were often resisted by both landlords and peasants because they disrupted household production by removing children from the labor market. Only in the rare cases where compulsory schooling was integrated into the structure of rural industry did the demands of state policy mesh with the labor needs of both noble landlords and rural households.[38]

* * * * *

How to expedite and make safe the transition to a new social order weighed heavily on the minds of Prussian reformers; how to deal with the problems and needs engendered by capitalism preoccupied those in England. Certainly, schools figured prominently in the civilizing schemes dreamed up by British reformers; the miraculous power of the monitorial system captured the imagination of a whole generation. Yet early industrialization coincided with a powerful wave of obscurantism. Industrialists themselves argued on occasion that Britain benefited from its neglect of elementary schooling. School attendance did not interfere with the supply of child labor; government expenditure, and therefore taxation, was kept to a minimum, and entrepreneurs and local gentry could contribute to schools in their localities if they felt they were needed. As late as the mid-1850s, the major argument against proposals to introduce mass compulsory schooling in England and Wales was that it would remove a cheap supply of labor and in this way "adversely affect the competitiveness of British manufacturers and thus the prosperity of the nation."[39]

In any case, the existing ramshackle provisions for transmitting basic literacy seemed to work. It has been estimated that industrialization requires a 40 percent level of literacy in the general population; Britain achieved this easily without state intervention in schooling. If we take the ability to sign one's name as a measure of basic reading ability, 60 percent of males and 35 percent of females in England were "literate" in 1750, 70 and 55 percent respectively in the 1830s, and almost 90 percent of both in 1869.[40] Indeed, there is some evidence that early factory industrialization was everywhere associated with a fall, rather than a rise, in local levels of literacy.[41] At the same time, while most debates on skills and industry focus on men, we saw that much of early industrialization relied on the extensive use of "unskilled" child and female labor. In England in the late eighteenth and early nineteenth centuries, even the advocacy of popular schooling as a vehicle for securing social order was a minority position. By the late 1820s, Tories compromised on the need to steer a careful course "between the Scylla of brutal ignorance and the Charybdis of a literary education." But while they ceased their *opposition* to "provided" schools, they remained convinced that the state should not be burdened with their funding.[42]

Throughout the nineteenth century, the majority of British industrialists maintained that the actual subject matter learned in elementary schools was of little or no value to industry. Yet most came to agree with the reformers, at least in theory, that mass schooling was valuable because it would moralize laboring families and instill in their members willingness to work, order, reliability, punctuality, "subordinacy," "receptivity to supervision," and a "sense of discipline and peaceful order." Workers who had attended an orderly Sunday or day school were believed to do more work for the same money, better, and with less trouble. As Henry Ashworth put it succinctly in 1880, "If they have been to school, they're obedient, they want less licking."[43] In practice, according to Vincent, employers welcomed the extension of compulsory schooling as an aid to the creation of a disciplined workforce, but almost invariably showed no interest in applicants' school attainment when they were hiring them, typically giving precedence to recommendations of workers already in the plant. Unlike teachers and reformers, who saw family as at best neutral and at worst utterly corrupting, employers believed that family and kin were the best placed to supply the "character" they were looking for: "first and foremost an approach to work—a sense of self-control, of moral probity, and of pride in workmanship."[44]

Elementary schooling for the mass of operatives was one thing; advanced education for the minority of skilled male workers, foremen, and engineers was quite another. But even here, the majority of early-nineteenth-century British businessmen and manufacturers, as well as most politicians, did not believe that national economic performance depended on education and training. Most historians agree. Hobsbawm, for example, argues that "whatever the British advance [in the industrial revolution] was due to, it was not scientific and technological superiority." This view was also held by the French and the Germans. Except for the Scottish universities and some of the dissenting academies, "English education was a joke in poor taste." There was nothing resembling the Prussian institutions of technical training, the Bergacademie, or the French Ecole Polytechnique.

> Fortunately few intellectual refinements were necessary to make the industrial revolution. Its technical inventions were exceedingly modest, and in no way beyond the scope of intelligent artisans experimenting in their workshops, or of the constructive capacities of carpenters, millwrights and locksmiths. . . . Even its scientifically most sophisticated machine, James Watt's rotary steam engine (1784), required no more physics than had been available for the best part of a century—the proper *theory* of steam engines was only developed *ex post facto* by the Frenchman Carnot in the 1820s—and could build on several generations of practical employment for steam engines, mostly in mines.[45]

Similarly, Pollard argues that "there is no evidence that Britain's smooth upward path of pioneering new technologies was at any time held up by weaknesses in the educational field, unplanned and uncoordinated though it was." According to him, links between formal education, bureaucracy, and industrialization could not be made tightly as long as production depended on

> the kind of skill which cannot be learnt out of books, nor even absorbed in a brief visit of inspection: the final filing of machine parts, the recognition, in

a moving piece of equipment, where the tension is too great or the play too loose, the almost instinctive knowledge when the wind is right for blowing in a furnace, or when the molten metal is ready for tapping. Even a skilled and experienced man might be lost abroad, for details which he had taken for granted at home, such as quality of ores or metals, or measurements, might be different and he would lack experience to deal with them, and the collaboration of other specialists might be missing.

In this period, methods were complex enough to exceed the experience of a single craftsman, and required the use of capital goods and other skills, but they had not yet reached the level at which technology could be systematized and transmitted in the abstract, without the personal experience of human agents.[46]

This point was attained during the second stage of industrialization in the 1860s. Dated from the huge railway-building boom of the mid-nineteenth century, this wave of industrialization was far more capital-intensive, associated as it was with the development of the capital goods sector, particularly steelmaking and precision engineering. In many of the most advanced sectors of industry, the mass of operatives, particularly children, began to be replaced by perfected machinery.[47] By now, industry was far more dependent on advanced technical training, which Britain had until then neglected without much detriment. From now on, the slow adoption of new technology and inferior technical training (hampered when provided by the poor literacy and numeracy skills of elementary school graduates) became identified as an important factor in Britain's gradual loss of world economic and political dominance.[48]

But even here, Pollard qualifies the case for a tight link between educational provision and economic development. In some branches of industry, most notably in precision engineering and chemicals, expansion was indeed linked to the availability of scientific research and highly trained men. Elsewhere the connection was not so clear. In particular, it might have made sense for the most advanced country to train its managers and skilled workers on the shop floor, where the latest equipment was being used and developed, rather than secondhand, as it were, from books in schools. Indeed, the need for an extensive network of technical schools might simply mean that students were reduced to learning from books what their competitors in more advanced countries were able to learn on site. In addition, Britain's unsystematic provision of technical education, dealing mainly with adult men, might have been more flexible and responsive to the needs of industrialists than centralized and orderly educational provision for boys. At the same time, if an attempt is made to count all the diverse endowments and other sources of private funding for scientific and technical education and research in Britain, and to add up actual enroll-ments in the bewildering range of institutions providing some technical and scientific training, the gap between Britain and Germany both in the proportion of domestic product devoted to technical training and in rel-evant enrollments is much reduced. Germany, although an economically backward country, is nevertheless remarkable for its educational achieve-ments. Finally, in those branches of the economy where technical training *was* necessary, such as the chemical industry, "it was not necessarily Great Britain which was the loser in a process in which the German government spent large sums to train chemists who then migrated to Britain."[49]

During this period, when British industrial superiority first began to falter, debates about formal education began to take a more familiar form. Time and again, "public opinion" was mobilized behind the idea that technical education of each and every (male) worker would not only safe-guard Britain's dominance and vastly increase the productivity of existing enterprises, but create industry where none had existed previously. In more sober times, it was acknowledged that only a minority of engineers, fore-men, and "captains of industry" needed specialized knowledge. Technical training was only one among many competitive factors, including availabil-ity of markets, cheap freights and raw materials, protective tariffs, commer-cial expertise, and, last but not least, low wages.[50]

While the links between technical training and industrial development have been widely canvassed, it was only recently that feminist authors drew systematic attention to the determined attempts of male workers to exclude women from work designated as skilled, and the concomitant attempts to construct and preserve the masculine ethos of technical and scientific courses.[51] More recent still are arguments that implicate technical training in the production of particular forms of working-class masculinity.[52] In-deed, debates about the education of girls and women were a microcosm of larger debates about their proper place in society. While reformers increas-ingly demanded complex preparation for boys and young men entering industrial occupations, training for women, when it was contemplated at all, tended to center on making them better homemakers.[53] Women them-selves picked and chose courses as it suited them, at times embarrassing their male colleagues by learning sewing and cooking in schools of mines, at other times flocking to commercial and telegraphy courses, which mor-alists would have preferred to reserve for men.

TRANSPORT AND THE TECHNOLOGICAL
TRANSFER OF SCHOOL KNOWLEDGE

The previous section presented some accounts of uneven development. Equally important was the fact that in the space of half a century, countries with considerably different histories, at different stages of political and economic development, and familiar with many models of instruction, developed remarkably similar systems of state compulsory schooling. Each locality had its own mixture of capital-intensive or coercion-intensive governance; prosperity or economic stagnation; political and religious conflict; effective, visionary, incompetent, and obstructionist men and women; powerful and ineffectual pressure groups; generous and inadequate budgets; social panics and industrial peace. The huge variety of regional economies, social climates, and local traditions provided individuals, families, and communities with different (and frequently incompatible) motives for the building of schools. Even if consensus emerged about the need for compulsory schooling, disagreements continued to simmer about the ways and means of achieving this goal.

As the wave of scholarization gathered force in the nineteenth century, however, these diverse conditions were increasingly seen through the same lenses. Politicians, reformers, newspaper editors, and state officials began to conceptualize schooling as a universal moralizing and modernizing agent, whose power and efficacy was not linked to specific social conditions. After their initial distrust of "provided" schooling, labor movements throughout the West similarly began to see schools as purveyors of knowledge and power. Just as today the same tractors, pumps, and generators are supposed to work in California, Java, Uganda, and Sicily, so the same technologies of school power were expected to succeed in Prussian and French villages, the urban slums of Chicago and Belfast, Swedish and American cities, and the Australian bush.

In his book on the industrialization of Europe, Pollard uses the example of transport to deal with similar issues: the same form of technology might serve markedly different uses and owe its existence to a range of diverse motives; a project that brings undoubted benefit to one region will not necessarily do the same elsewhere. It is axiomatic that the industrial revolution required at the same time a transport revolution, so mass-produced goods could reach distant markets. But the roads, waterways, and railway networks built in the nineteenth century did not merely reflect economic uses. They also served military and political purposes, and at times were a form of conspicuous consumption. Thus a French road was used to transport cotton goods to a seaport, but might also carry troops to the frontier, or the pomp and splendor of a royal procession. It will not be immediately obvious for which purpose the road had been built; in turn, military use might put a road in a place inconvenient to trade or ceremonial processions, and investment in a lavish transport system might preclude the funding of more productive projects. According to Pollard,

> While the different states of Europe, and their separate regions, will be at very different stages of economic development, and therefore require very different transport networks appropriate to them, their rulers will all want to live up to the same contemporary standard of what is expected of an absolutist sovereign. They will all want armies, and similarly equipped armies, even though the productive apparatus to feed, clothe, arm and pay them may be quite different. To allow them to march to the frontiers will require similar roads, but the additional uses to which these roads will be put, in the years of peace and behind the front lines in war, will be quite different. In some cases, as for example along the northern and eastern frontiers of France, they will carry traffic and yield high economic returns. In other areas, say along Austria's military frontier regions to the south east, they will be neglected and deserted.[54]

Whatever their provenance, new, miraculously faster means of transport made the nineteenth-century world smaller than ever before. In the 1760s, the journey from London to Glasgow still took ten or twelve days; by the end of the century, it was shortened to sixty-two hours. In 1840, there were 7,700 kilometers of railway lines in the world; by 1870 there were 210,000. Ten years later, trains between major European cities began to provide sleeping cars. In the United States, the railway network grew from about 60,000 to 320,000 kilometers between 1877 and 1890.[55] For those needing to travel even greater distances, steamships made sea travel more reliable and secure. And if their speed was not at first much superior to that of sailing ships, the opening of the Suez Canal in 1869 cut weeks off the journey between Australia and Europe. Even those too busy or too poor to leave home were informed in great detail, and from every conceivable political angle, by the mushrooming specialist literature, reports, and newspapers. And these messages now traveled faster and more reliably than ever before. The International Telegraph Union was formed in 1865, the Universal Postal Union in 1875. The world's main deep ocean telegraph cables were laid in the period 1866–76.

Modern technologies revolutionized the potential and reach of governmentality. In the educational field, they speeded up the dissemination of new theories and methods; they enabled educationists to keep up to date and maintain friendships and professional links.[56] The same steamship and railway companies that hauled cotton, iron, and coal around the globe in record time also carried, in first class, reformers, bureaucrats, and statesmen en route to inspect and learn from each others' schools, textbooks, factories, prisons, and hospitals, and to attend international exhibitions and conferences. In less comfortable circumstances, and sometimes gratis, traveled the various revolutionaries, radical preachers, feminists, blacklisted labor leaders, and trade union "martyrs" exiled, hounded, and deported from one country to another, setting out to convert or make formal links with new brothers and sisters, or simply trying to make a new beginning in a different corner of the world.

But more than that, there was a parallel between institutional innovation and the dissemination of new production methods:

> Aided by easy means of transport and simpler and non-vexatious passport and visa regulations, the men who had something to contribute to the industrial advance of Europe moved freely across the frontiers to learn, to teach and to build: east European students in German Technische Hochschulen; Italian engineers in the Balkans; German chemists in English works. As a result, there was not a single major sector of industry in a single major country or region which was not stimulated from a more advanced centre, by technicians, entrepreneurs, machines, capital or labour, and sometimes by all of them. . . . To be sure, the nature and duration of the influence across the frontiers differed greatly. . . . But everywhere it became increasingly clear that, economically speaking, there existed only a single European community.[57]

Nineteenth-century educators, keen to experiment with the most efficient "technologies of power," soon came to speak of educational methods in similar terms. According to John Dearness, speaking to the Ontario Educational Association in 1897,

> Sweden can lead us in physical and manual training, Britain in sanitation and the practical training of girls, Germany in deportment and compulsory attendance, France in agriculture and technical education, Nova Scotia will help us teach elementary science, while Manitoba has improved our own public school course eminently combining aims of utility and culture.[58]

As in the case of railways, such technological transfer was motivated by a variety of factors: an attempt to turn serfs into workers, workers into citizens, peasants into Frenchmen, and the desire to modernize a backward country or to attract immigrants by building a modern social infra-structure.

School promoters would typically be familiar with detailed descriptions of the "most advanced" educational systems and methods. In a private or public capacity, leading men and a few women would personally visit enlightened educators and famous schools and inspect a range of school systems, spending between three months to a year or more visiting class-rooms, asking questions of teachers and principals, and occasionally inter-viewing parents. A Canadian might visit neighboring provinces, several parts of the United States, England, Scotland, Germany, France, and sev-eral other European countries. A Frenchman would refer to Prussia and Boston. An Australian would be familiar with the education systems of other colonies and of Britain, but would also visit several continental European countries and perhaps the United States. An Englishman would have traveled to Scotland and Ireland, several European countries, and perhaps even farther afield. Their grand tour would result in a widely disseminated official report, of necessity presenting a selective reading of already selected evidence.[59] In introducing educational reforms, govern-ment ministers would draw on recommendations of committees of inquiry into the best educational practices at home and abroad, as well as on the report on the administrator's grand tour, and stress that many of their proposals had been successfully tried and tested elsewhere.[60]

BUILDING THE EDUCATIONAL STATE

In early modern Europe, schools might have been more effective in strengthening state power than in producing pious households ruled by wise and God-fearing masters. Similarly, nineteenth-century states not only built formal education systems, but were in some respects built through reformed schooling. At stake was not only the greater capacity of central agencies to see and to govern the periphery, but the increased density, even the building up, of the "local state." At times, this building process went more or less according to plan, controlled by powerful and capable men; in other localities it was a shambles, with no clear lines of authority and with disorganized and incompetent administration.[61] Everywhere, in addition, the local state was "actually constituted by the practical associational initia-tives of a new citizenry in the making, but as the unintended, rolling effect of structurally invited interventions, as opposed to the strategic results of a coherent design."[62]

Several studies of the interplay between school and state in what is now

Ontario, Canada, illustrate these issues with particular clarity.[63] Colonial education reforms, Curtis argues, were motivated by more than concerns with the literacy and morality of children. With the American Revolution (and the loss of colonial holdings that it entailed) fresh in their minds, British statesmen and administrators were profoundly concerned about the Rebellions of 1837–38 in the Canadas. The previous policy of fostering colonial rule by a home-grown aristocracy, appointed to office for life, had obviously failed. Not enough reliable men of quality could be found to carry on government business. Certainly, some families wielded formidable local power, particularly in the French provinces, where feudal forms of land tenure survived until the 1850s. But the masters were just as likely to clamor for independence as assist the government. In the meanwhile, His Majesty's decrees were flouted with impunity; circulars and questionnaires went unanswered. The government could not even find out what was going on in the locality, let alone punish the offenders. To inform themselves about local conditions, members of the executive were constrained to rely upon the work of irregular special commissions, supplemented by reports from such local correspondents as might choose to write. Instead of authoritative surveys backed by statistical tables, the Canadian Blue Books published lists of colonial officials from whom information might be sought, if any means of so doing had existed; for want of a better source of information, the British Colonial Office was sent local newspapers.[64] To resolve what they increasingly perceived to be a crisis, a number of British statesmen began to advocate a radical shift in existing colonial policy.

A network of orderly intermediate institutions must be established between the central government and the locality. Given a measure of autonomy, public health offices, registry bureaus, local government bodies, and school committees would enable the government to reach into and see the periphery, while insulating central powers from direct demands by disaffected groups. Equally important, such institutions would teach those who elected and served on them new forms of morality and behavior: order, constancy, regularity, and predictability, the willingness to cede legitimate political authority to representatives, to defer to experts, to follow detailed rules and procedures, to keep records, to respect the legitimate rights of others. In a series of articles on the reforms needed to make the Canadas governable, J. S. Mill noted that representative local government was "not only the grand instrument of honest local management, but the great 'normal school' to fit a people for responsible government."[65]

Among the first duties of local bodies was the oversight of schools. Eventually, schools would moralize the children; the orderly management of local education would prepare their fathers for responsible citizenship. School governing bodies were at times the first steps in transforming the messy landscape of local power; their reports, supplemented by those of the new school inspectorate, provided central authorities with some of their first systematic glimpses of local populations. Administrative practices such as auditing and examinations of officers pioneered in Canadian education were, over time, introduced to other local agencies. It was the education acts and the activities of the education office that led to the creation of the first corps of salaried traveling inspectors in Canadian administration. The changing character and organization of educational inspection contributed significantly to the growth of central government capacity in Canada West; education budgets soon became the largest item of social expenditure.[66]

Taking a lead from Foucault's emphasis on panopticism, Curtis pays particular attention to inspection and classification practices and their results. The ability to inspect and to see populations, he argues, was an essential part of modern systems of governance: "no central state agency could govern a population about which it was ignorant; inspection provided indispensable elements of intelligence to state agencies."[67] In the course of their work, inspectors did not simply report already existing, value-free facts waiting to be recorded; they engaged in a complex activity of identifying and categorizing that which merited attention. Identifying practices, Curtis notes, discipline the real by specifying administratively pertinent identities for people, social relations, and things. Administrative categories are politically selective, formative, and hence potentially violent (de-formative, deforming; figurative, thus potentially dis-figuring).[68]

This was particularly true of statistical information, which played such an important role in nineteenth-century debates about schools. In the period following the 1820s, many historians have noted, the western world was struck by a "proliferation," an "avalanche," an "explosion" of numbers. This flood of figures, generated by novel ways of categorizing and counting people and things, was a cosmological change, a fundamental transformation in the way the world's forces were conceived, apprehended, and lived, a transformation dubbed by one scholar "the taming of chance." Hazard and uncertainty, formerly the devil's playground, became probability, the essence of order, law, and rational calculation. Fed by the growth of international trade, the spread of capitalism (with its tendency to reduce everything to the exchange of equivalents in the market), the concomitant standardization of weights and measures, and, on a different plane, the rise of what Foucault called "population thinking," the avalanche of numbers also depended on the elaboration of new notions of citizenship. It is well known, Curtis notes, that the generalization of statistically governed political administration is impossible in societies where no practical notion of human equality exists. The census is impossible in its modern form in feudal societies, where lords and serfs are as different as horses and dogs. The same developments that (at least for some limited purposes) produced the notion of universal citizenship also made possible the promiscuous mingling of people in uniform statistical categories.[69]

In describing the building of a colonial education system in Canada West in the first half of the nineteenth century, Curtis brings out the complexity and contingency of the process of rule. Rather than smooth imposition of social control, the establishment of a modern school inspectorate was an enterprise full of conflict, confusion, incompetence, cheating, approximation, contradiction, compromise, and inventiveness. One of the first jobs the inspectors had to tackle was to actually find the schools they were to inspect, not an easy task on horseback, without accurate maps, on difficult roads in unfamiliar countryside, and following unreliable directions. It was only after the central office assembled the fragmented and primitive topographical and statistical knowledge—some won at great cost, and some made up with much personal discretion by the early inspectors— that it had any chance of detailed control of schooling.[70]

Educational inspectors, typically respectable Anglo-Saxon men of property, instinctively knew a good school when they saw one, and they felt eminently qualified to invent proper administrative procedures. Yet they often disagreed among themselves, some of them visited hardly any schools, and two or three absconded with the school moneys entrusted to them. These men were without formal qualifications for the work they were undertaking: they were, and saw themselves as, amateurs. Yet Curtis argues that the underlying common sense, aesthetic values, moral standards, and sense of justice they shared helped shape the standards, categories, criteria, and procedures that were later embodied in the more professional administration for which they helped establish the foundations. Paradoxically, the knowledge and experience imparted to the center by the early inspectors made these men themselves replaceable and allowed the center to curtail the very autonomy that made possible the gathering of educational intelligence in the first place—even as it gradually established more formal qualifications for the inspectors' less autonomous successors.[71]

In the 1830s, executive officials in Ontario had some sketchy information about numbers of schools and teachers, and knew roughly how much parliamentary money was appropriated for educational purposes. By the early 1850s, all this had changed. "The operation of educational inspection created relatively stable and normal connections between the central authority and local provision. The central authority could thus monitor local provision, identify centres of opposition and resistance to its policy, and intervene to resolve menacing disputes or contain threatening practices"; it could also defend educational practices in government on the basis of detailed local knowledge.[72] The intelligence-generating capacity of state agencies grew enormously; the cost of printing information alone had become the largest item of general parliamentary expenditure.[73] State servants learned how to conduct social inquiries: how to chart the domain of the social, how to place reliable informants in valuable viewpoints, how to design questionnaires, how to gather vital statistics, how to conduct censuses. As the technology of rule became more sophisticated and the right of the center to know local activity was accepted as legitimate, other mechanisms of administration, particularly financial accounting, began to displace inspectorial practice.[74]

* * * * *

While the process of building educational states was particularly pertinent to the colonies, the capacity of school officials to see local conditions was crucial in the colonial centers themselves. France and England might well have possessed a "dense and intelligent" community for centuries, but in the early nineteenth century their governments had no idea how many schools there were inside their frontiers, let alone what went on in them. In his perceptive work on the building of the French education system, Sharif Gemie notes that when Louis XVIII decreed in 1816 that all school teachers be authorized by the reconstituted Université, royal officials were left with a quandary. It was clear that there were already many teachers at work before the ordinance was enacted. How was the Université to make them conform? This issue led the authorities to face an even more basic problem: How was the Université to learn of the existence of unauthorized teachers? Since the few school inspectors had more pressing duties, committees of local notables were appointed to assist in the task of overview and encouragement of elementary schools. In the three decades of their operation, the committees' main function consisted in providing the Université with basic information on the simple existence of schools. In letters and circulars, this task was constantly compared to the act of seeing. The notables, it was hoped, would bring "to the eyes of government" information on villages "remaining in obscurity" and schools which were until then "covered in secrecy." Such turns of phrase, Gemie notes, reveal a profound contradiction between the Université's perceived role and its actual position: while claiming to control all schools, it was not even aware how many schools existed.[75] In practice, the modest tasks the notables were set produced disappointing results. Only about half of the required committees were established, and of these less than one in ten seemed to be actually working, producing only a fraction of the reports that they were required to write. Those reports that did turn up revealed at every step the difficulties of actually perceiving a school.

The notables were not given any working definition of an educational institution by the Université; educated by tutors before attending advanced schools, neither did they have personal experience of elementary schools. In the absence of clear guidelines, each group of notables had discussed the question "What is a school?" and then tried to apply their definition to the educational activities they discerned in their communes. Even though their criteria varied, Gemie argues that they were invariably based on the moral probity—and manliness—of the instructor, rather than on the school's role in transmitting literacy and numeracy. The committees had least trouble in seeing and recording thoroughly respectable male teachers, were doubtful about most women instructors, and explicitly excluded men who appeared to teach, but whose scandalous behavior—drinking, brawling, Jansenism, entertaining prostitutes—disqualified their establishment from what the notables defined as a school. Most women who taught perplexed the men entrusted with perceiving schools. As one mayor put it in 1819, "At the moment there is no teacher in the commune. . . . there's only the *desservant's* maid." Ten years later, another mayor was more explicit: "There are two other schoolmistresses, or rather women who give a few lessons. They could be seen as illegal teachers but it appears that they are not paid for their lessons. They are hardly educated, they only give a few lessons, and they do not merit any attention."[76] In their detailed statistical study of schooling in France, Grew and Harrigan note that the Guizot Law of 1833, which required every commune in France to establish a public elementary school (for boys), had less effect on the number of schools than is usually thought. Much of the apparent change resulted from counting, for the first time, girls' schools, which had previously not been thought to merit acknowledgment as educational institutions.[77]

Once all the "real" schools had been brought from obscurity into the light of state vision and registered with the Université, they needed to be inspected by one of its full-time officials in order to commence a process of linking them to the vital sources of central power. As Guizot put it in describing the first general school inspection of 1833,

In order to impress effectively into primary instruction a new potent momentum, to establish between authority and the teachers this universal link, these permanent connections which have been written into the law, and which are so difficult and yet so necessary . . . it is essential that some general measure should make the presence of central power felt everywhere, so that minds are struck by the spectacle of its activity, by the meaning of its intentions.[78]

In nineteenth-century England, according to Gardner, the various investigations and enumerations conducted by middle-class experts similarly tended not to classify working-class private schools as true schools. Teaching might have gone on in them, and the parents and children who patronized them might have believed it satisfactory, but to the expert eye it was worthless. Just like working-class households, the schools were cramped, dirty, badly ventilated, and dark. Children came and went as they (or their parents) pleased. The teachers had no special qualifications and often carried on other work while keeping school. Perhaps most important, there was no effort to teach religion or what the critics understood as morality. Pupils might have learned to read and write, but "the mass of the children cannot there learn their duties." Classes such as this could not be counted, for they were not, according to middle-class understanding, schools at all. In 1843, for example, one Lancastershire officer, having drawn up a complete table of the available schools in the district, mentioned in a footnote that "in addition to the above there are four or five (perhaps more) private schools for the poor, where reading and sewing are taught." Gardner's painstaking research suggests that official enumerations of schools left out a good proportion of the classes where poor people learned to read and write. In his recalculation, the population censuses suggest a possible total of 218 working-class private schools in the city of Bristol in 1851, with that number falling to 200 in 1861; the education census and the Newcastle commissioners indicate 126 and 139 respectively.[79]

BUREAUCRACY AND THE COMMUNITY

The building of state education systems, as the previous section argued, at the same time built the state. Looking at the same process from a different perspective, other scholars maintain that the educational bureaucracies themselves were constructed in part out of ad hoc responses to common, mundane, recurring problems and contingencies forcefully brought to their attention by local residents.[80] This process was particularly marked in struggles between administrators, teachers, and residents regarding administrative discretion. In the early nineteenth century, there existed a lively international debate about the relative merits of different approaches to educational inspection and administration. Two models in particular were singled out. In Prussia, it was believed, the education system was highly centralized and regulated in minute detail by statute. In a country with no republican institutions, ordinance and law were indistinguishable. In theory, at least, the minister of public instruction was informed by detailed inspectoral reports about local conditions and was thus able to direct the operations of the whole—including classroom layout and the amount of teachers' pay—from the center.[81]

In the Dutch republic, in contrast, the law provided for the barest of frameworks, and decisions about the actual conduct of schools were made by an expert education council, independent of both judicial and legislative interference. If education were regulated in detail by law, a perceptive critic noted, "the risk of having amendments inserted, during its discussion in a numerous assembly of men little conversant with such matters . . . would utterly destroy the best devised schemes."[82] Intense and detailed inspection in fact led to a particularly close regulation of Dutch schools. Yet the absence of detailed statutory definitions of educational authority gave the administrators ample room for maneuver, while making the "educational state" difficult both to define and to oppose.[83] It was this system that Egerton Ryerson, reformer and long-time chief superintendent of education for Canada West, explicitly favored. Teachers, parents, and local school committees, in contrast, demanded precision: they asked the central administration to adjudicate in local disputes, and insisted that clear and precise rules be formulated on a thousand and one contentious issues.

Institution-building in local communities where schooling had suddenly become everybody's business produced inevitable conflicts about issues such as the location of the schoolhouse, whether the school should be supported from general local taxes or from a tax on families with children, the nature of religious instruction, the range of curriculum to be offered (and therefore the cost of the teacher to be employed), and the role of local officials. What was to be done, correspondents typically asked, to ensure that justice and good sense prevailed? "Has a Son who is single and living with his Father in a House with two doors in it the right to vote at the School Meeting?" Could a school meeting legally be relocated to a pub? How could a challenge about decisions made at that meeting be resolved? Could the school committee sue those who refused to pay the school rate? How could school section boundaries be modified? What sort of record-keeping was necessary for local trustees to meet their own legal obligations? How could a teacher seek redress against the unjust cancellation of a teaching certificate by a local superintendent?[84] Could teachers legally beat students, given the department's repeated condemnation of corporal punishment? And if the regulations permitted teachers to use "reasonable force," such as might be employed by a "judicious parent," in disciplining students, how did this translate into the material and thickness of the instrument with which children could be struck? What parts of their bodies could be hit? And with what force? And how many times? Was whipping legitimate if it left marks on the body?[85]

None of these correspondents and petitioners, Gidney and Lawr note, advocated adopting bureaucratic procedure as a matter of principle. What people wanted was fair, efficient, lawful solutions to the particular problems they faced. But such demands were also demands for what are now defined as the classic modes of bureaucratic rule—for the delineation of explicit written rules of procedure; for the routinization of responsibility and an orderly hierarchy of control; for specialization and expertise on the part of administrative officers; for universalistic rather than particularistic criteria for rule-making; and for a style of decision-making that consists of applying general rules to particular problems. Rather than reflecting grand schemes of social control, the authors conclude, educational bureaucracy in Upper Canada grew out of ad hoc and incremental responses to the many problems thrown up from the school sections. While the central authority was ultimately responsible for the increasing bureaucratization of the system, the pace was forced by the pressures rising up from the localities.[86] But this, one can add, was precisely the "great normal school" of democracy in action. As Curtis put it, "All the fundamental questions concerning educational organisation—who needed to be taught, who could educate them, what they needed to know, how they should learn it, who should pay for it—these and other questions were answered only by answering at the same time questions concerning the state: who should rule, how, of what would rule consist, how would it be financed. The struggle over education was at once struggle over political rule."[87]

ENGENDERING BUREAUCRACY

Bureaucratic forms of governance, historians believe, were perfected in the military and later the railways, each underwriting the expansion of the other and necessitating control of vast numbers of men who could no longer be governed by face-to-face contact. By the late eighteenth century, armies expelled most of the women and children who had traditionally accompanied them, and devised new ways of dealing with the housework of war. Troops were divided into smaller, semi-autonomous units whose maneuverability and security depended on systematic and collective planning and coordination, based on more precise mapping, intelligence-gathering, and statistical knowledge. Officers lost the autonomy to recruit, pay, promote, and administer their units, and were transformed from a collection of ill-disciplined captains into an officer corps of a graded bureaucracy with its own corporate discipline. The summary authority of commanders was further limited by military academies that trained and certified a range of specialist personnel. At every level of authority, rational-legal authority replaced or at least severely circumscribed personalized patriarchalist powers, only partially replacing them with new forms of professional expertise.[88]

Nineteenth-century armies learned to depend on railways, and railway development owed a lot to military considerations. Here, too, the spatial dispersion and sheer numbers of employees, combined with the size and complexity of administrative tasks, led railway companies to search for new organizational forms for the command and control of large, complex enterprises. Where they were successful, their innovations pioneered major advances in the surveillance capacities of the capitalist firm. As in the case of the military, they facilitated the effective coordination of large-scale organizations without producing the attendant problems of unwieldiness or administrative overload. Dandeker suggests that nations and firms differed in bureaucratic inventiveness and in the speed with which they adopted particular administrative systems. Prussia, it seems, led the world with regard to bureaucratizing its army, the United States with regard to developing new bureaucratic structures for managing the railways. Education systems learned from both, while contributing their own administrative innovations. Indeed, next to armies, treasuries, and railways, education systems were among the largest arenas where masses of state employees were brought, with more or less success, under new forms of impersonal discipline.

The modern bureaucratic machines for the management of armies and railways were, however, also vast accumulations of males attempting to forge new forms of homosocial masculinity, marked, among other things, by an increasing proscription of homosexuality. Dandeker, like most of the authors he draws on, is systematically blind to gender issues. His index contains several references to patronage, but there is no entry on patriarchy, patriarchalism, gender, women, men, or sex. Yet both Weber and Foucault, on whom Dandeker relies extensively, provide openings for a gendered analysis of bureaucracy. Weber, indeed, explicitly defined bureaucracy as an alternative to the master's personal government of daily routine:

> Patriarchal power especially is rooted in the provisioning of recurrent and normal needs of workaday life. Patriarchal authority thus has its original locus in the economy, that is, those branches of the economy that can be satisfied by means of normal routine. The patriarch is the "natural leader" of the daily routine. And in this respect, the bureaucratic structure is only the counter-image of patriarchalism transposed into rationality.[89]

Similarly, as we have seen, Foucault in his later work notes that governing a state came to mean, among other things, a form of surveillance and control as attentive as that of a head of a family over his household and his goods.[90]

While most analyses of bureaucracy pay little attention to gender, feminist scholars have for some time been attempting to explicate the differently patriarchal nature of this new mode of social organization. Rosemary Pringle, for example, argues that while the rational-legal or bureaucratic form presents itself as gender-neutral, it actually constitutes a new kind of patriarchal structure. The apparent neutrality of rules and goals disguises the class and gender interests served by them. Weber's account of bureaucracy can be interpreted as a commentary on the construction of a particular kind of masculinity based on the exclusion of the personal, the sexual, and the feminine from any definition of "rationality."[91] Given the range of bureaucratic functions at different levels of authority (rank-and-file soldiers as opposed to strategic planners) and historical and cultural differences between different organizations, it is likely that specific bureaucracies foster not one but a range of masculinities and patriarchal relations.

* * * * *

The building of educational systems represents a particularly complex process of engendering bureaucracies. Everywhere, education departments were designed by men; for many years, men alone inspected the schools; men controlled the management of teacher-training colleges, even those for women.[92] Teaching was increasingly designated as a special calling that required prolonged specialist training in knowledge not otherwise available to ordinary people, and often inaccessible to women.[93] Yet a large proportion of scholars were below ten years of age, a constituency traditionally associated with women's work. This work could be re-gendered and valorized by converting the teacher into a professional. Indeed, the early stages of the reform process were usually accompanied by a marked masculinization of teaching as unofficial, part-time, casual, and unlicensed teachers, often women, were excluded or harassed, some convent schools were closed as nuns were replaced by lay teachers, and most of the new normal schools which trained teachers at first catered only to males. The new pedagogue, bringing reformed education to the people and helping to shape their moral character, was assumed to be a man, particularly when the task involved preparing boys for their future as responsible citizens.[94]

Yet the "masculine project of professionalism" was subverted at every point by the teachers' actual working conditions.[95] Teachers were instructed to acquire new expertise just as they became subject to increasing regulation in and out of school. They were expected to find new dignity in their status as servants of the state and to carry out their work without bowing to local opinion. Yet they were rarely freed from the menial housework of the school: scrubbing floors, cleaning latrines, chopping firewood, lighting fires in the morning; their pay was below that of a skilled workman. In states such as Prussia, where schooling and religion were closely linked, teachers for decades agitated against their duty to ring church bells, play the organ during service, and clean the church. Teachers frequently found themselves caught between various social and political interests in the locality, and without enough means or power to assert the authority they were supposed to have.[96]

In South Australia, when the education department was reorganized in the 1870s, inspectors were stunned to find their power and discretion delimited by minute regulations. "I regret to find it necessary to call attention again to the fact that in some cases reports as to smoky chimneys . . . are incorporated with the report of the Annual Examination," a letter from the Inspector General informed his subordinates in 1882. "I shall be glad if Inspectors will note that this is not to be done under any circumstances, nor are recommendations as to teachers' pay etc. to find a place there," the note concluded. An inspector could be admonished for failing to "see the defects of a school" or for coming to town on the goods train on Friday afternoon.[97] No wonder the senior inspector could say to the Education Commission, "Power . . . ? I do not know that I have any power. My business here is to inspect schools."[98]

The teachers themselves lost much of their former autonomy in day-to-day teaching. The department gradually colonized the power to decide on matters ranging from timekeeping and outside employment to the color of ink to be used in filling in returns, whether anything could be placed on top of the mantelpiece, and the size and precise location of the folder in which departmental correspondence was to be kept.[99] By 1891, one of the inspectors expressed "alarm and misgiving" at the proposal to allow the poetry to be taught to be selected by the teachers themselves. "I am not, as a rule, an advocate for cramping any teacher's individuality," he declared, but to allow teachers freedom in "a subject of so much importance to the rising generation" would allow "the unblessed and untrained blind . . . to lead the far greater portion [of children] into some doggerel ditch."[100] Experienced teachers complained that rather than helping them teach, regulations created work while hampering true education. Inspector General Hartley believed otherwise. "In a department like ours we cannot make rules to apply to one teacher and not to another," he explained.[101]

Examinations became the focus both of the department's attempt to discipline teachers and of the teachers' struggle for autonomy. Like Guizot in France, the administrators searched for "some general measure which would make the presence of central power felt everywhere." They believed they had found it in an adaptation of the English Revised Code of 1862. As one of the inspectors remarked, "The only way in which a large department can make its wishes known is by examination."[102] The new measures involved a yearly inspectoral "result examination" of each pupil in each state school in a list of prescribed subjects, as well as an assessment of discipline and drill. Rates of teachers' pay, security of employment, and promotion possibilities were all made partly dependent on the school percentages gained in these exams.[103] The inspectors believed that "payment by results . . . has been one of the most efficient factors in our system."[104] Teachers themselves testified that "the 'result' is present with the teacher everywhere—at his meals, when he rests at night, and in church."[105] With the advantage of hindsight, an inspector concluded in 1902 that "the result examination . . . has done more to stamp out the individuality of the teacher than anything else."[106]

Inspired and sometimes radicalized by the gap between the promises of professional status contained in educational rhetoric and their actual working conditions, male teachers began to organize. More frequently, they simply voted with their feet and found more congenial or better-paid work elsewhere. As the nineteenth century progressed, it became obvious that graded, stratified, "efficient"—and cheap—elementary schools could be made to work only by hiring large numbers of women. Many administrators were blunt about their preference for female teachers, at least in girls' and infant classes. In Canada, for example, "over and over again local as well as provincial officials explained that women teachers were not only as good as male teachers, but could be had 'at a saving of 50 per cent.'"[107] The chief superintendent of schools in Nova Scotia spoke for many of his colleagues when he wrote, in 1867, that "both by law of nature and of revelation" there was "a position of subordination and of dependence assigned to women," and that as a consequence there ought to be "situations in educational establishments better adapted to one sex than the other." Accordingly, it was generally admitted that the infant and primary departments of schools were "best fitted for the female," while "the head masterships, and the more advanced sections," ought to be reserved for male teachers.[108]

This process of incorporating women into mass education systems, often called, somewhat misleadingly, the "feminization of teaching," saw the proportion of women employed by some state educational bureaucracies rise to half and more of the teaching force by the turn of the century.[109] In England, women constituted the majority of elementary school teachers from the 1870s; by the beginning of the First World War, seven in ten teachers were female. In Scotland, women made up 35 percent of all teachers in 1851 and 70 percent by 1911.[110] Women constituted 60 percent of teachers in the United States by 1870, 80 percent by 1910.[111] In the predominantly French Catholic province of Quebec, more than half of government school teachers were women as early as 1851, and women constituted more than three-quarters of the teaching force by 1875.[112] In most other Canadian provinces, women had become the majority of elementary school teachers between 1845 and 1875. In the Australian colony of New South Wales, the feminization of public school teaching was not as pronounced as it was in North America and Britain, and was actively resisted at the political, bureaucratic, and ideological levels.[113] In South Australia, in contrast, the proportion of women employed by the Education Department rose from 44 to 70 percent of all teachers between 1875 and 1902. Hidden in the figures is the fact that the proportion of female head teachers fell from 29 to 10 percent of the total, and the proportion of women among the lowliest provisional teachers increased from about 55 to 85 percent.[114] In the few cases in which women inspectors were employed, they were paid less than the men, or even worked in an honorary capacity; they frequently dealt only with women teachers or with girls' subjects; unlike men, they were employed on short-term contracts; and they were retrenched at the first sign of financial stringency.

Figures on primary teacher-training schools similarly show increasing proportions of women, but also highlight substantial differences between countries. In Belgium, women accounted for 25 percent of all teacher trainees in 1854 and 50 percent in 1875. In France, the proportion of women rose from 29 percent in 1881 to 50 percent in 1896; in Switzerland it increased from 18 percent in 1871 to 43 percent in 1896. But in Italy, almost three-quarters of primary teacher trainees were women in 1870, and 93 percent by the turn of the century. In Prussia, in contrast, women constituted only 6.3 percent of teacher trainees as late as 1897. Similarly, in Sweden, 5 percent of trainees were female in 1871, 7 percent in 1876, 37 percent in 1881, and 41 percent in 1886.[115] The same military absolutist states that pioneered compulsory schooling, it seems, also built the most masculine education departments.

The differences in gendering of educational bureaucracies suggested by statistics such as these are underscored by the fact that even similar figures could hide substantial differences. According to Danylewycz, for example, in predominantly French Catholic Montreal in the early 1880s, the Catholic School Commission developed two separate forms of organization. The system of coeducational elementary Catholic schools, staffed by nuns and lay women, was informal and loosely organized, and offered no opportunity for advancement in the profession. Lay secondary schools for boys staffed by men, in contrast, were organized according to a formal and hierarchical structure that made professional advancement possible—and cost three to four times as much per pupil per year to run. In Montreal, a woman would achieve her career potential as a principal; for a man, being a principal was merely a stage in his upward track to the office of school commissioner. In nearby Protestant, English-speaking Toronto, on the other hand, headmasters gained status by presiding over large coeducational schools and hierarchies of female assistants.[116]

Theobald's work on the changing process of teaching in nineteenth-century Victoria, Australia, provides another excellent example of gender dynamics in a particular locality.[117] With the exception of modest dame schools and the handful of corporate colleges, teaching was traditionally a family enterprise. Families frequently built schools, in which the husband then ran the boys' department and the wife taught the girls, and their children or other relatives served as pupil teachers and assistants. A list of all teachers employed by the Board of Education in 1866, for example, reveals that well over half of the colony's schools were staffed in full or in part by teachers with the same surname. Such family ventures, particularly when managed with reasonable efficiency, were favored by parents who saw in the husband-and-wife team a guarantee that the school was conducted with the necessary moral propriety, and in particular that their daughters would not come to harm. By the time the Education Department was empowered to take over all schools receiving a public subsidy in 1872, many had been in continuous operation as "non-vested" schools for twenty or thirty years.

In this situation, building the educational state resembled a process of mutual colonization. The education department was keen to acquire the accumulated expertise, goodwill, and building stock; the bureaucracy it constructed was modeled in part on authority patterns in family-run schools where women and young people of both sexes labored under the direction of a judicious master. At first there were no restrictions on the employment of married women as teachers. While the gentlemen of the inspectorate preferred not to think of pregnancy and childbirth, neither was explicitly designated as an obstacle to the carrying out of teaching duties. On their part, teaching families desperately tried to preserve their livelihood and standard of living, and to find employment for wives and older children in the new departmental schools. Not surprisingly, there was ample scope for discord; at times a school embroiled in such conflicts became unworkable. There were many cases of harmonious schools that descended into bitter conflict when a newly married head teacher, or one whose children had grown up, attempted to replace his existing assistants with family members—or, alternately, when unrelated assistants became convinced that they should hold the place occupied by the head teacher's wife or daughter.

Many women demoted from the position of head of a girls' school refused to teach in mixed (coeducational) state schools, with a substantial drop in pay and under the direction of unrelated men; often they threatened to establish a rival private school and take most of the girls with them unless they received a better deal, and at times they did just that. Some aggrieved and litigious (though not necessarily the most competent) women teachers sued the department; when one Helena Mary Stark objected to her lowly position on the first classified teachers' roll of 1885, the case went all the way to the Privy Council in London, where a decision in her favor forced the department to reclassify and compensate a large number of female teachers.[118] And although women almost invariably lost pay, status, power, and security in the new bureaucracy, they now received a separate pay packet even when they worked in a school run by their father or husband. Over time, women teachers, too, became radicalized. Against the strenuous opposition of most male colleagues, many began to argue for equal pay, sometimes forming their own unions; a background in teaching was a common characteristic of many feminists.[119]

Education department officials almost invariably spoke of schools as if all the pupils and instructors were male; yet they taught both boys and girls and employed large numbers of women; they lamented a shortage of teachers even as they received many more applications from women than they were able to employ; they fully endorsed the ideology which decreed that only men possessed the "wholesome severity" and "habit of authority" necessary to hold responsible positions in the public sphere, and that women's fragility and moral sensitivity made their employment outside the home both impossible and undesirable, even as they commended mistresses who kept disciplined schools and investigated women teachers who mercilessly beat their students. The new regulations demanded that the private and the public be strictly segregated, that manliness should imbue the public space of the school. Yet departmental files indicate that the boundaries between the personal life of teachers and the work of schools remained permeable. In a period when the teacher's residence frequently adjoined the school, the headmistress would often step next door to nurse a child, give directions to a servant, or check the roast. When a woman teacher was in the final stages of pregnancy, it was customary for her to apply for three or four weeks of leave, and to find and pay a replacement teacher. A married woman giving birth every two years throughout her employment by the state might be a highly competent teacher and a good disciplinarian, but she could scarcely cultivate a character of sexless efficiency.[120] Gradually, as departmental routines ossified and the government's hold on schools became more secure, gender boundaries firmed. By the turn of the century, formal bars on the employment of married women were in place in most government bureaucracies.

Throughout this period, the fact that girls as well as boys were required to attend schools rendered the masculinity of their public space problematic. Indeed, the pervasive official rhetoric that held that the public school was a privileged vehicle for moralizing laboring families was undercut by a persistent discourse of moral danger. From the parents' point of view, manliness in a school was all too often accompanied by improper looks, words, and behavior between an unmarried male teacher and the older girls or women assistants; many withdrew their daughters from school at the slightest hint of scandal. In localities with significant numbers of cheap private schools, statistical returns consistently show that state schools catered to a higher proportion of boys, and private schools to a higher proportion of girls. Indeed, the very term "state school girl" often acquired some of the dubious moral connotations of "factory girl." The architects of public elementary schooling, Theobald concludes, had to contend with deep-seated fears of moral contamination if daughters left the protection of the private sphere of their homes. The imperative of moral guardianship and respectability demanded a female presence, which the department was obliged to purchase. Long before they learned to prize women for their natural endowments as caregivers to the young, or to appreciate their manifest availability as cheap labor, the men who administered Victorian schools employed women to moralize the school.[121]

*****

As in early modern Europe, nineteenth-century education systems helped accumulate state knowledge, build up local government, and engender intricate bureaucracies. Above all, however, they tried to moralize children. The next chapter discusses their success in this difficult task.

CHAPTER SEVEN

Social Movements, Individual Agency, and the School

The ideal economic man . . . is remarkable for his foresight and self-control; in the Residuum these qualities are entirely absent.[1]

It is indeed a sad and evil necessity, if the first lesson which they learn at school is to beware of their own parents and to look with disgust, if not horror at the filthiness and abomination of their own homes.[2]

[The teacher] is their over-looker; he is a spy upon them; his authority is maintained by his absolute power of punishment; the parent commits them to that power; to be taught is to be held in restraint; and, as the sparks fly upwards, the teaching and restraint will not be divided in the estimation of the boy.[3]

As I walk to and fro in Edgware Road, I cannot help sometimes wondering why these people exist. Watch their faces, and you will see in them a listlessness, a hard unconcern, a failure to be interested. . . . In all these faces you will see no beauty, and you will see no beauty in the clothes they wear, or in their attitudes in rest or movement, or in their voices when they speak. They are human beings to whom nature has given no grace or charm, who life has made vulgar.[4]

The inner life of the classes below us in society is never penetrated by us. We are profoundly ignorant of the springs of public opinion, the elements of thought and the principles of action among them—those things which we recognise at once as constituting our own social life, in all the moral features which give to it form and substance.[5]

What has helped to make the lower orders ignorant and vulgar? Is it not this same want of education? And why are we not educated? Because our noses are continually kept to the grindstone for a bare subsistence![6]

When I speak of a "disciplinary society" I do not mean a "disciplined society." When I speak of the spread of disciplinary techniques, it is not to claim
that "the French are obedient."[7]

Chapters 4 and 5 looked in some detail at the ways the aristocracy and
the bourgeoisie made and remade their mentalities between the sixteenth
and the nineteenth centuries, and at the different forms of mastery they
attempted to exert over laboring populations. "These peasants," an eighteenth-century Prussian commentator put it succinctly, "have always been
coerced; they have never learned to coerce themselves."[8] Surrounded by
slothful servants, rebellious journeymen, and surly peasants, and fearful of
hordes of masterless men, Pietist reformers dreamt of designing schools
that would teach children to "obey a given order with precision, without
being given a reason, promised a reward or threatened with punishment."[9]
While he does not ask explicitly whether the subjectivity of peasants in fact
changed as a result of the reformers' efforts, Melton is skeptical about the
practicality of most eighteenth-century educational ventures.

Corrigan, Curtis, and Lanning take a similar approach in writing about
nineteenth-century Canadian schools. Drawing on Foucault, they argue
that the educators were not interested merely in compliance with the rules,
but in what they called "cheerful" or "willing obedience": a state of mind in
which compliance would appear to the pupils as the exercise of free will,
and in which (and this seems to be a somewhat different matter) "proper"
habits would become so ingrained that they would sometimes make students act "even against [their] own decision."[10] In other words, while the
educators reserved the right to use their monopoly on physical violence in
maintaining order, they were far happier if the same aims were achieved
through the students' own "capacity for pleasure, desire, and self-control
or liberty." The best teacher would habituate the students to self-control
and obedience without diminishing the force of their wills.

Curtis develops this theme further in *Building the Educational State*.
Education, he argues, "was not a *means* to self government; education *was*
government: government of the self. The development of representative institutions demanded the development of individual self-government."[11]
Scottish writers and pedagogues, popularizers of Prussian schools, and
prominent educationists such as Kay-Shuttleworth and Horace Mann, Curtis notes, argued that teachers should reach their students' conscience and
rule their charges through love, pleasurable mental activity, and "agreeable
excitement" rather than force. The teacher who succeeded in securing the
love and affection of pupils would have unlimited control over their minds
and conduct, even when physically absent. Schools in which corporal

punishment was freely used, in contrast, helped produce the worst possible individual: the intelligent rogue, the sly deceiver—a person trained at school to dissemble, a liar equipped with the intelligence and ability derived from the course of study. In an ideal school, "the student's freely expressed emotions would be the basis of effective self-regulation, and educators could rest secure in the knowledge that they were not educating a generation of enemies of civilisation."[12] Those made to obey at school through physical force rather than moral discipline, in contrast, could not be trusted politically later in life. Curtis, too, does not examine whether schools managed to produce schooled subjectivities, but argues that this question can be assessed indirectly. To the extent that the practices of state schooling could be sustained only through the application of violence to a population deprived of the means of responding in kind, the promise of pleasurable teaching and learning failed.

In *Rethinking the School*, Hunter covers similar ground, but adds an important moral dimension to the argument. First, the collective attempt of social movements to reflect on, rationally comprehend, and transform their circumstances bears many similarities to the introspective selfhood favored by educationists and liberal theoreticians. They are both historical constructs, and neither should be accorded a privileged role in human development. Second, both forms of subjectivity are misrecognized as precious, fundamental human attributes by a social group that has a considerable vested interest in this fallacy. Marginalized by government but deriving moral authority, social prestige, and material benefits from their cultural capital as "virtuosi of self-reflective moral comportment," critical intellectuals forget that their particular moral type is largely the product of the school. Blind to their own past, intellectuals presume to judge state institutions by their capacity to nurture what they mistakenly understand to be universal human characteristics. In fact, however, the purported characteristics of the democratic public sphere, the radical social movement, the class-for-itself, are "thinly disguised surrogates for the pastoral intelligentsia's own ethical ideal: the self-realising personality."[13] Having satisfied himself that educational reformers wanted to produce a particular form of subjectivity, Hunter does not stop to ask whether they succeeded in their mission. Instead, he observes that citizenries did indeed become pacified and workers orderly, and he assumes, reasonably enough, that schools played an unspecified part in this process: "Far from repressing the collective personality of the working class, mass elementary schooling helped to create those commonalities of interest and comportment characteristic of national classes and national citizenries."[14]

There is, in brief, no doubt that influential eighteenth- and nineteenth-century educators set out to produce new forms of subjectivity in their charges, and devised a number of ingenious techniques for this purpose. The schools' civilizing mission among the poor, the heathen, and the savage became one of the major preoccupations of nineteenth-century liberal thought. But how can we assess the success of their projects? Schools, it is hardly necessary to say, even today find it difficult to measure the acquisition of facts and skills; they certainly have not invented a simple way to evaluate changing mentalities.

In writing about school curricula, historians frequently make a threefold distinction. What can be called *rhetorical curriculum* concerns the official pronouncements of leading educators. Here historians are able to examine easily accessible written documents, gain a measure of understanding of their authors' way of thinking, and reproduce particularly concise, belligerent, or striking passages for the reader. As any teacher would know, however, such prescriptions and descriptions need to be clearly distinguished from the *curriculum-in-use*. Were those in power persuaded by the reformers? Did the politicians and administrators actually implement the reforms they announced? Did teachers understand and carry out the regulations, instructions, and advice they received from higher up? Were they able to do so, given limited resources, difficult conditions, and finite energy and ability? Did classes, schools, and school systems differ in fundamental ways even though they were described in similar words?

These questions are further clarified if we differentiate between the *hidden* and *overt* curriculum: the things that schools, teachers, and textbooks explicitly set out to do, and those aspects of schooling that are no less powerful, but are implicit in the process of schooling. This distinction was employed with particular force by progressive teachers in the 1970s. Since then, its use has been complicated by the historians' insistence that different aspects of school curricula have been hidden at different times. Indeed, it is now commonplace to say that in the nineteenth century, much of what is today described as hidden curriculum was made perfectly explicit.

Although it is by no means easy to map out, much work has been done over the last two decades on a social history of (overt and hidden) curriculum-in-use. Inspectors' reports, statistics, teachers' and pupils' diaries and reminiscences, visitors' comments, legal cases, and teachers' correspondence have all been used, with great ingenuity and impressive results, by historians such as Theobald, Finkelstein, Grumet, Godsen, Cuban, and Hurt. Supplementing these sources with architectural drawings, paintings, photographs, physical remains of old schools and school implements, stockists' catalogues, advertisements, learned articles on school layout, and records of local disputes over smoky chimneys, smelly latrines, badly ventilated classrooms, and leaky roofs, other scholars have assembled detailed information on the physical environment of schooling.

Even if we manage to find out what was actually taught in particular settings, however, we cannot assume that it was identical to the *received curriculum*: the actual effectivity of educational schemes is an altogether more complex and difficult issue. Were the students learning roughly what the reformers or the teachers and school architects wanted them to learn? Or what their parents or they themselves wanted to find out? Or what could be expected given their health and the physical conditions of the schoolroom as reconstructed by the historian? Or something entirely different again? A handful of biographies, fragments of personal statements of anonymous parents and pupils, comments of visitors and locals from a higher social class, literacy statistics, print runs of newspapers, pamphlets, and books, court cases, charity records, contemporary and modern statistical reconstructions of attendance patterns, health status, and life expectancy, and evidence of industrial and political conflict are among the sources used, often to great effect, to answer these questions. Yet to a large extent, we will never know; in any case, historians and social theorists do not agree on what there is to tell.

The willingness of eighteenth- and nineteenth-century educationists to call a spade a spade when talking about their dislike of working-class mentalities makes it easy for historians to resort to explanations based on social control. The agency appears to have been with the masters and their surrogates; the subject populations suffered and at times resisted. Critical of such "reproduction" approaches, a number of sociologists and historians have developed alternative accounts of schooling. On the basis of participant observation of working-class youth, for example, in the 1970s a group of English sociologists offered an influential approach to students' resistance. Reproduction approaches argue that it is in part the appropriation and acceptance of bourgeois ideology taught in the schools that prepares working-class students for capitalist relations of production. Writers such as Willis and McRobbie showed, on the contrary, how a thorough *rejection* of all that the school stands for (parallel to shop-floor resistance to the prerogatives of management), combined with a profound sexism, prepared "the lads" for working-class jobs, and their sisters for the drudgery of impoverished motherhood.[15] Valuable as such studies have been, however, other critics have pointed out that this approach runs the risk of romanticizing resistance and ignoring the bulk of the students who sit through lessons without causing a stir.

Regardless of the approach used, one final problem confronts those who discover an increased incidence of introspective forms of subjectivity in particular populations. There is no *a priori* reason why the credit—or the blame—should go to schools. I noted earlier that there were systematic differences between different regions and social groups in the balance of deference, organized violence, private coercion, neighborly supervision, economic compulsion, class solidarity, and bureaucratic surveillance brought to bear on character formation. Children moved frequently between "efficient" and "inefficient" schools, educational fashions changed, and even in the same school, different teachers had different personalities and teaching styles. As most social historians know only too well, assessing the comparative psychic productivity of lifestyles and teaching methods is not likely to be easy.

Steering a careful path between different ways of understanding the psychological productivity of schools, this chapter focuses on some of the most problematic aspects of received curricula. Using different approaches to nineteenth-century working-class autobiography and recent work on public spheres and class formation, it suggests that the Enlightenment project did not belong to the bourgeoisie alone. Forms of it can be discerned in schemes for social emancipation of the powerless, and their uneven success was just as significant in the making of modern subjectivities as the strategies of the powerful.

BREAD, KNOWLEDGE, AND FREEDOM

David Vincent's studies of working-class autobiographies, literacy, and useful knowledge in England are a classic contribution to the understanding of working-class subjectivities.[16] For my purposes, Vincent's material has some limitations. Only 6 of the 142 autobiographies that form the basis of *Bread, Knowledge and Freedom* were written by women, and Vincent does not fully acknowledge the specifically masculine nature of many of his concerns. The study excludes those who moved out of the working class during their lifetime, among whom ordained ministers—the ones most likely to possess a self-scrutinizing, introspective self—were particularly significant. The book covers the period 1790 to 1850, when people's schooling, if they had any, was acquired during a time of profound educational change; they certainly did not all attend "efficient" schools. The narratives themselves were constrained by the writers' memory, their command of written English (rather than the dialects that they spoke), available forms of self-presentation, the restraints imposed by the form of publication and the nature of the intended audience, implicit rules of inclusion and exclusion suggested by the genre, and notions of propriety, relevance, and usefulness. And yet the biographies provide an invaluable corrective to descriptions of rhetorical and actual curricula. As Maynes notes in a different context, "Obviously autobiographies are not representative sources in the usual sense of the word. . . . Their evidence must always be read with caution and careful placement . . . however, far from being random or idiosyncratic reflections of their authors' individual trajectories, they are products of collective social, political, and cultural historical processes."[17]

Rather than problematize subjectivity, Vincent aims to make accessible a rich and relatively neglected source of social history. To some extent, his definition of autobiography already presupposes the personality form that he later reconstructs from the texts. Basing himself on Roy Pascal's *Design and Truth in Autobiography,* he notes that "'the most fatal error, in all types of autobiography, is not untruthfulness, but triviality of character.' What is required above all is energy of insight, an ability to comprehend fully the significance and coherence of past experiences, together with the literary skill to transmit the account in such a way as to make the widest connection with the experience and imagination of the readership."[18] Vincent in many ways outgrows the restrictions inherent in this model of personality, and his complex work can by no means be reduced to a single argument. One theme, however, recurs to organize and make sense both of his own and of the autobiographers' accounts: a specific form of a working-class Enlightenment project:

> Only by understanding himself could the working man understand the world in which he lived, and conversely, true self-knowledge was impossible without a comprehension of the structure and historical identity of the section of society in which his personality was formed. The search for such knowledge was both a precondition and a result of the growth of class consciousness. The more working men became aware of the historical significance of their actions, the greater was the necessity and the possibility of defining and controlling their historical identity.[19]

Even though she starts from a different perspective, Maynes similarly notes that a significant number of French and German working-class autobiographies were structured around a transition from a helpless object of history to an active subject through socialist militancy.[20]

Like other commentators, Vincent argues that middle-class reformers were increasingly keen to change the mentalities of the laboring poor, and were prepared to use the teaching of reading and writing, and the production and dissemination of edifying reading matter, as the vehicle for moralizing the working population. On their part, working people were greatly interested in morality, literacy, and useful knowledge, and their biographies frequently chronicle a profound psychological change attributed to the active use of literacy. Indeed, the very existence from the late eighteenth century of a fertile genre of working-class autobiography in itself bears witness to an increased level of individual self-awareness. But here the coincidences end. Fragments of literacy were picked up in a variety of settings, including schools, but the readers had to do a great deal of individual and collective learning to convert their rudimentary skills to practical use. In spite of the overwhelming importance the readers and biographers attach to moral education, few associate its acquisition with school, and even then the association is with a particularly important teacher rather than with the curriculum itself. (It is possible, of course, that the school exerted a moral influence on the child of which it was unaware, either at the time or later when an account came to be written.) In any case, the nature of school attendance was such as to make any systematic course of instruction all but impossible. Finally, working people made full use of cheap publications provided by their betters, and benefited indirectly from the rapidly falling costs of printing and distribution, but their understanding of useful knowledge was far removed from that of charitable societies, and their particular uses of literacy frequently landed them in jail.[21]

For Pietist, Puritan, Jesuit, and Methodist precursors of rational schooling, breaking the child's will to produce a cheerful obedience apparently springing from one's innermost soul was likened to a conversion experience. Vincent's readers and writers also spoke of awakenings and conversions, but of a markedly different kind. In recounting their lives, most adopted the vision of childhood as a period of wonder and innocence; all too often, this childhood innocence ended with a harsh awakening: the shattering realization, early in life, of their class position. "Sooner or later the 'blighting consciousness' that he was a member of the working class, and of a particular section of that class, would come upon each of these children. As he came to terms with his knowledge, the child gained a new regard for the period of innocence in which he had played and even worked in ignorance of his lot in life."[22] This first awakening was indeed often associated with schools—a painful and humiliating memory of an exclusion, a putdown, a slight. It appeared that whereas other people had command over their circumstances, the poor child was forever condemned to poverty. School was not needed to teach this lesson, but it was often a particularly painful setting for it. An effective moralizing school for the poor, in contrast, would presumably give children joy in their newly discovered humble status. However powerless they might appear, their diligent attention to duty had the capacity to please God as much as the grand gestures of the mighty. If they worked really hard, they were sure to win a modest competency.

The second awakening, as presented in the accounts of the autobiographers, was considerably different. Whatever they might have felt at different periods in their lives, these men and women rarely described strong emotion. Yet when they spoke of their encounters with literature, they used words such as "rapture," "wonder," "joy," "desire," "delight," and "pleasure."[23] What is more, their discovery of useful book knowledge often amounted to a secularized conversion experience that left no part of their lives untouched.[24] For weaver Ben Brierley, "it was in every sense a new light to me"; for the shepherd Robert Story, "the effect on my mind was magical"; when cabinetmaker Henry Price discovered the world of literature, "my eyes were opened it seemed for the first time in my life."[25] The shoemaker's daughter Mary Smith described how her earliest contact with literature "awakened my young nature." When Samuel Bamford first started reading, "faculties which had hitherto given but small intimation of existence suddenly sprang into action."[26] William Lovett, who became one of the best-known Chartist leaders, wrote about the momentous time in his life when "my mind seemed to be awakened to a new mental existence; new feelings, hopes and aspirations sprang up within me, and every spare moment was devoted to the acquisition of some kind of useful knowledge."[27]

Importantly, this momentous awakening had little to do with school. At best, teachers provided barely functional literacy; schools for the laboring poor neither intended to provide nor were practically capable of providing what the readers came to regard as useful literary knowledge. At the same time, while the first awakening revealed life-long bondage, the second provided the means of escape, of freedom. At first, much of this freedom was the freedom of thought: freeing oneself from superstition, accumulating untold riches of the mind, ranging freely through the ages, joining in imaginary conversation with the most fascinating thinkers and historical personages. Because of the biographers' straitened circumstances, much of this quest for intellectual freedom was of necessity conducted in the company of friends with similar interests—typically small groups of working men pooling their meager resources to buy books and rent a room in which to store and discuss them. However much some of these men wanted to be private, they were in turn enlisted to use their literacy in working-class struggles—as writers of letters and petitions, treasurers, secretaries, and spokesmen. Indeed, it was predominantly from these men that the leadership of working-class organizations was drawn.[28]

For all working-class readers, the pursuit of useful knowledge entailed rigorous self-control. Saving money for the purchase of precious books and newspapers, reading long into the night, forgoing rest, drink, and pleasurable pastimes with old friends for the company of books, attending to imaginary heroes and intellectual puzzles rather than to the day-to-day crises of family life, all came much easier to men, and implied powerful forms of self-mastery. But here again, the readers and biographers soon diverged from middle-class ideals. Vincent notes that for working men, increased understanding of one's world almost invariably entailed the realization that individual effort had a strictly limited capacity to achieve control of one's circumstances. In an age of rapid concentration of capital, low wages, and chronic insecurity, only fundamental social reforms achieved through collective action could reliably supply such basic needs as adequate food for one's family and physical safety at work.

While the biographers lend little credence to those who argue that schools produced pleasurable, willing obedience, they abound in stories of fear and punishment. One of the most graphic descriptions I found is contained in the adult recollections of a man who, at the age of eight, was sent to an English workhouse school. In commenting on the man's letter, the government official who included it in his annual report for 1873 noted that "it must not be considered in any way exceptional." After some traumatic experiences on admission to the workhouse, the boy threw a stone at the master and ran. To his horror, he found that there was no escape, no back door. The overwhelming effect of school discipline on a poor street boy, he concluded, was fear. "The utter impossibility of getting away, and the terrible certainty of the cane for misbehaviour, inspired me with terror. . . . It was no use trying to love the masters, I dreaded them."[29]

The construction of the national state, as I noted earlier, is often associated with a government monopoly over the means of violence. Curtis draws a direct parallel between this process and the building of educational bureaucracies. Any resort to violence by students, their parents, and school supporters was gradually outlawed; the teacher—in theory, at least —achieved a monopoly on the legitimate use of power. "You know," Curtis quotes the secretary of the British and Foreign School Society as remarking, "that if compliance with the just demands of government is refused, and resistance is sustained, force after force will be brought to bear upon you. . . . Such ought to be the character of all government."[30] A skilled teacher, however, just like a skilled ruler, would rarely or never need to resort to the naked power that buttressed his authority. Historical accounts of nineteenth-century schooling do contain a minority of such teachers, but against a backdrop of fear and violence.

Paying systematic attention to this issue, Maynes notes that in nineteenth-century Germany, most teachers seemed to rely not upon the internalized discipline of the psyche but on old-fashioned control through physical pain; the authoritarian, conservative, vindictive schoolteacher who kept order in the classroom through resort to the cane appears as a villainous character in the majority of the (working-class) men's accounts. One writer, born in Hamburg, contrasted his "genuine teacher" with the harsh and hated schoolmaster he knew was common: "What distinguished him was his great art or gift of pushing and teaching his pupils to do independent intellectual work. . . . Every pupil had open access to him and he took pains to create a humane atmosphere in the school, for which he was ridiculed by the schoolmasters. But I loved my teacher and remained bound to him into his old age."[31]

In France, such enlightened pedagogues were remembered more frequently. One son of day laborers in a small town in northern France, who attended school in the 1880s, recalled that his teacher "ran the school like a father, and he loved me like one of his children. It was he who gave me the books, the school supplies that my parents couldn't afford to buy and above all the good advice that was aimed at helping me to avoid suffering because of my situation." Several working-class French women similarly recalled their teachers with affection, praising their intellectual gravity, their physical beauty, and their emotional involvement with their pupils. Even in Germany, school seemed to have relatively more appeal to girls, who apparently received gentler treatment in the classroom than their brothers. Interestingly, as enlightened pedagogues lead us to expect, the boys who recall the most brutal treatment at school also tend to be those who became the most committed rebels and socialist activists.[32]

Not only their treatment at school but also their early deprivation radicalized many of the autobiographers. In Germany, recollections of working-class childhoods almost invariably contain boundless bitterness about the social conditions (particularly as brought home by their parents) that robbed the writers of the first golden years of life. Whether they adopted a vision of "real" childhood as a period of play and carefree happiness later in life, or glimpsed the lives of more privileged contemporaries, many of the biographers attributed their adult commitment to socialism to the terrible injustices of their youth. These children attended school but also had to continue working; their every waking moment was taken up with duties to the state or their family; the only free time they had was the breaks between lessons at school. Rather than reconcile them to a life of drudgery, school politicized them by bringing into sharp relief life as it was and as it could be. In France, in contrast, the relatively late enforcement of compulsory schooling meant that school and work were experienced as alternatives by the laboring poor. In these circumstances, while none of the biographers felt they were robbed of childhood, many were radicalized by what they experienced as a profoundly unjust necessity to choose work over education.[33]

In England, Vincent eloquently documents the many working-class uses of knowledge, but he uses the reports of exasperated school inspectors to suggest that, in terms of the educators' own criteria, the education system largely failed to transform working-class mentalities. Toward the turn of the century, report after report complained that pupils read without understanding, showed little conviction or enthusiasm, did not engage with the material, and failed to reveal their true selves for correction. Perhaps the style of teaching which could not produce "intelligence" in the children itself lacked intelligence and should be replaced. After decades of disappointing attempts at mass production of docile, introspective subjectivity, a new "synthetic method of learning" promised to endow the pupil with habits of self-discipline and intellectual inquiry. This would counteract the sensual tendencies engendered by the upbringing of working-class children and lay the foundation for a rational and moral approach to life outside school. And yet, while the inspectors complained about schools, for the first time in history full literacy became a reality, and virtually complete compulsory school attendance was achieved. The same period, Vincent notes ironically, also ushered in several years of massive union militancy.[34]

AUTONOMOUS SELF AND BODILY PAIN

Some of the themes suggested by Vincent's early work have since been explored more fully by other writers. Nan Hackett, in commenting on British writers, for example, argues that working-class autobiography did not conform to standard models of the genre because it chronicled the existence of a different form of self.[35] Rather than stressing introspection and self-discovery of a unique individual, it indicated the psychological and social effects of deprivation as well as a sense of communal consciousness. In many autobiographies, the authors provide an abundance of visual detail, list precious possessions, describe meager meals, note the titles of books read and articles written—but there is no plot, no dialogue, no action. Often a story is started but never completed; few reasons are given for what we would consider major alterations of belief; motives for particular courses of action are rarely discussed; the bystanders are in sharper focus than the ostensible subject of the narrative; spouses and children are mentioned in passing and rarely warrant more than a few paragraphs. Hackett notes that "Thomas Carter lists every book he read, but fails to record his wife's name. Timothy Claxton refers to his wife only in passing when he · remarks that after he moved to London, he acquired a 'lathe and a wife to assist him.'"[36] Maynes similarly notes that many workers' autobiographies have no sense of linear development, but are simply the chronological sequence of things that happened to or around them; others are structured around the *absence* of experiences (such as childhood) that they believed characterized "normal" lives.[37]

Like Hackett and Maynes, Regenia Gagnier starts from the premise that the rational, self-aware Cartesian subject is just one form of subjectivity and self-presentation among many, and notes that there is a clear class-based distinction between those British authors who claim an autonomous introspective self and those who do not.[38] This is not merely a matter of preference or cultural style. Gendered narratives of romance, of familialism, of a coherent progressive self and financial success were indeed at times employed by working-class women and men to make sense of lives of chronic poverty, un- and underemployment, aborted romance, non-familialism, and non-companionate marriage. The result was incoherence, confusion, and psychological disintegration. Narratives of relatively autonomous individuals in pursuit of chosen goals, which could successfully organize the experience of many middle-class people, were undermined at every point by the harsh economic realities of working-class life. Long hours of work, crowded housing, constant noise, and inadequate light made it difficult enough for workers to contemplate themselves; autobiographers also had to justify themselves as writers worthy of the attention of others. This was particularly difficult for women. "I have found it an interesting life to live," one woman wrote, "but I do not know whether it will be interesting to read." Elsewhere she says, "I have had frequent misgivings while writing this autobiography, for I know of no particular reason why it should have been written; and it has appeared very egotistic to do it." Even when the working-class autobiographers *did* establish their identity as separate from others, they often felt uneasy about their resultant "egotism," questioning the rightness of individualism and social distinction generally.[39] Many would have agreed with William Morris, who criticized the "hunters of introspection" and predicted that in the society of the future "you will no longer be able to have novels relating the troubles of a middle-class couple in their struggle toward social uselessness, because the material for such literary treasures will have passed away."[40]

The classical individual of the liberal tradition, Gagnier notes, is a rational being whose physical integrity is taken for granted and whose most valued attributes reside in the mind. Mental capacity is irreducible to and linked only contingently to the body; rationality is the property of individuals rather than groups. For the majority of nineteenth-century working people, in contrast, rationality was frequently experienced as a collective attribute, and consciousness was dominated by the experience of physical pain and privation. And bodily pain—caused by hunger, workplace injuries, and sickness, and aggravated for women by repeated pregnancies—made it impossible to construct a subjectivity on the basis of a confident prior assumption of bodily self-possession and integrity.

In the late eighteenth and the early nineteenth century, as I noted earlier, hunger was conceptualized by many bourgeois thinkers as a fundamental source of wealth and order. Only if they were driven by the spur of hunger, and motivated by the anticipated pleasure of a full stomach, would the mass of the poor work meekly and diligently for the benefit of their masters. The problem was that the poor themselves often constructed a different form of utilitarian calculus. Drink, many knew, was the quickest way out of Manchester. Open rebellion might secure better lives for their children. Hunger itself subverted the lessons of enlightened pedagogues, and undermined the long-term aims of civilizing the poor. Half-starved, sickly children who could be made to work for the promise of a few pence and the threat of a beating found it difficult enough to sit still, let alone concentrate on lessons and contemplate themselves. As teachers and school administrators increasingly realized, effective learning came easier to well-fed, healthy scholars.

The ever-present shadow of physical pain in working-class forms of self-presentation is particularly visible in Gagnier's commentary on Mayhew's famous surveys of London's poor. In the first letter to the *Morning Chronicle*, Mayhew identified the poor by the fact of their suffering, as "all those persons whose incomings are insufficient for the satisfaction of their wants —a want being contra-distinguished from a mere desire by a positive physical pain." Gagnier argues that at his best, Mayhew saw that the mind or personality, traditionally conceived as so unique and individual, was dependent upon communication with others, and was in fact the most shared aspect of "individual" identity. Alternatively, the body, so common that everybody had one, under conditions of deprivation became the most private and alienating aspect of identity. "Subjectivity cannot exist without intersubjectivity, whereas bodies in pain exist only as bodies in pain."[41] Like Vincent, Gagnier argues that for many working people, the achievement of a modicum of self-possession logically and immediately led to claims for social reform, even for revolutionary social change.

Certainly, not all laboring people were hungry or sick all the time, although contemporary health statistics which indicated that half the children of Preston machine operatives died before the age of five, that working-class girls were five and a half inches shorter than their wealthy counterparts, and that half the recruits for the Boer War from some districts had to be rejected on medical grounds, were grim enough. But it was in the lives of women that physicality predominated. Schools, we will recall, were expected to eradicate "sensuality" and foster in all pupils an inward-looking sense of individual self-scrutiny and self-control. In a particularly powerful section of her book, Gagnier argues that for most of their lives, the majority of pregnant and nursing working-class women were anything but self-possessed.[42] Their letters about the experiences of maternity complain of a debilitating lack of knowledge about their own bodies, the inability to obtain skilled advice and treatment that could have prevented terrible suffering, the necessity of incessant heavy work even when they knew that their lives were at risk or when a new baby was born, and totally inadequate nourishment for themselves and their children. The women record extreme physical abjection, or loss of boundaries, often starving themselves so that they could save for necessities. Often they were unable to sleep for days or weeks on end because of chronic pain. Far from providing a natural frontier of the self, one of the bases of conscious individuality, these women's bodies were a mystery to their unconscious owners, completely out of their control.

Gagnier's conclusions are abundantly supported by a closer reading of the letters themselves. The women's suffering was frequently aggravated by sexual abuse. Their husbands—worse than animals, several women suggested—forced them to have sex while they were pregnant, and again within days of confinement; others injured them through ignorance or selfish disregard.[43] The suffering of mothers, one woman wrote, would continue until men realize "that the wife's body belongs to herself" (27). Taken as a whole, the letters suggest that reproductive suffering was (but need not be) an essential component of the subjectivity in question: that is what it was like to be a working-class woman. "For twenty years I was nursing or expecting babies" (18–19); "for fifteen years I was in a very poor state of health owing to continual pregnancy" (61); "it is a time that women suffer terribly, yet it is a time when they get very little pity, as it is looked upon as quite a natural state of things" (79), wrote these working-class mothers.

A distinct sense of self was doubly submerged in physical suffering and responsibility for the everyday survival of the family. "I am afraid I cannot tell you very much, because I worked too hard to think about how we lived. . . . I was a particularly strong woman when I married. There is not much strength left" (110–11). "I am afraid many mothers, like myself, will find it almost impossible to explain our sufferings" (144). One woman, married at twenty-two and the mother of seven children—and "almost a mental and physical wreck" by the time she was thirty-two—wrote, "I am sure you will pardon me if I take the credit for bringing up such a family without the loss of even one, seeing that it entailed such a great amount of suffering to myself" (60–61). Un-self-consciously, the guild women wrote about behavior that could be described as iron self-control, but which they conceptualized in terms of simple necessity. Again and again they went without food, claiming that they had had their dinner before their husband came home, so that the little nourishment available would go further, "cutting and contriving" to make the weekly income go as far as they possibly could: "I looked after my husband and children well, but I often went short of food myself, although my husband did not know it. . . . I never worried him. He was very steady, and gave me all he could. . . . You may guess I was always scheming and planning to make ends meet. . . . But I always tried to keep a bright face, and make the best of things" (159).[44] "I was obliged to go without," "I was obliged to work before I was able," was a continuous refrain of the letters.[45] Was it this form of self-coercion, rather than an individual, self-scrutinizing self, that the reformers in fact had in mind, and that many historians misread?

Significantly, in the very act of writing about their suffering in response to a request for factual information, the guild women also hoped to use the compelling experience of their bodies to change society. The campaign in which they participated did in fact influence the establishment of maternalist policies in early-twentieth-century welfare states—even though there is evidence that statesmen's fears of falling birthrates, weakened economies, and military defeat were more effective in securing change than were feminist campaigns.[46] At the same time, many of the women recorded a dramatic transformation in their own consciousness over time. With changing

social attitudes and increased personal knowledge—and guild member-
ship—they would never again let themselves suffer as they had, and they
would make sure their daughters did not suffer either.[47] Their own enlightenment, and the power of informed collective action, had a realistic prospect of changing lives.

A working-class mother of five children, infected with a virulent skin
disease by a doctor who had attended her first birth, debilitated by pain and
exhaustion, with doctor's bills "growing like mushrooms," often crying "for
very weariness and hopelessness," at the age of forty-one years took stock
of her life. Her new self-understanding was typical of a large proportion of
the guild women in its chronicle of past suffering and future hope: "Working-class women have grown more refined; they desire better homes, better
clothes for themselves and their children, and are far more self-respecting
and less humble than their predecessors. But the strain to keep up to
anything like a decent standard of housing, clothing, diet and general
appearance, is enough to upset the mental balance of a Chancellor of the
Exchequer." This woman had three new dresses in fourteen years, could
not afford a doctor when she had her last baby (but did have enough for
sleeping pills to give her seriously ill husband so that he would not be
disturbed while she was giving birth), and eventually educated herself by
reading cheap editions of the classics, which she propped in front of the tub
on washing day. "I'd like to develop mentally," she concludes her letter,
"but I must stifle that part of my nature until I have made good the ills of
the past [paid off debts], and I am doing it slowly and surely, and my heart
grows lighter, and will grow lighter still when I know that the burden is
lifted from the mothers of the race" (44–48).

* * * * *

Labor historians have long argued that new technologies of (self-)disci-
pline were not the exclusive property of the rich and powerful; neither were
they all manufactured by the masters, the church, or the state. Disgruntled
soldiers were invariably to be found at the head of peasant uprisings;
common faith provided a source of strength to laboring communities in
their perpetual tug-of-war with the authorities, and helped fuel early nationalist movements. Literacy, the medium of converting peasants and
moralizing workers, was also the very stuff of which oppositional public
spheres were made. Many workers learned how to run a trade union in the
school of nonconformist religion; after 1839, the Chartists adapted the
Primitive Methodist camp meeting to overcome the banning and harass-

ment of mass demonstrations, infusing the agenda of hymns and sermons with a democratic and frequently anti-clerical content.

In addition, as E. P. Thompson, E. J. Hobsbawm, Barbara Taylor, and Richard Johnson all argue, the production and social organization that emerged in capitalist Europe *did* require different forms of mentality and culture among the laboring masses, and not simply because of upper-class fears of revolution and social unrest, or employers' desire for a docile, punctual, industrious workforce. New "moral" forces, an entirely novel set of cultural orientations, were needed for collective forms of social improvement, for self-advancement, and often even for sheer survival by the laboring people themselves. Overworked mothers, much as they loved their children, were strict in demanding obedience, self-control, and assistance; their cramped homes were completely unsuited to spontaneity and exuberance. Labor activists, too, knew the cost of blind lashing out and the effectiveness of disciplined action. Often, there was a very thin line indeed between swallowing bourgeois propaganda and using the new morality and discipline in organized struggle against the moralizers.[48]

Attention to the multiple sources, forms, and consequences of self-discipline in communities of laboring people remains one of the enduring strengths of E. P. Thompson's *Making of the English Working Class*. In one passage, limiting his observations to men, he notes that between 1780 and 1830, "the 'average' English working man became more disciplined, more subject to the productive tempo of 'the clock,' more reserved and methodical, less violent and less spontaneous. Traditional sports were replaced by more sedentary hobbies." But it would be foolish, he adds, simply to mourn the disappearance of old customs, many of which were neither idyllic nor quaint. "The passing of Gin Lane, Tyburn Fair, orgiastic drunkenness, animal sexuality, and mortal combat for prize money in iron-studded clogs, calls for no lament."[49] By the same token, neither Methodism nor the factory system could be given sole credit for these changes. Rather, many could be attributed to "a high degree of conscious working-class endeavour." A form of self-discipline was cultivated in fraternal craft organizations; it was an invaluable asset in hundreds of friendly societies organized by working men and sometimes women in the eighteenth and nineteenth centuries. "The discipline essential for the safe-keeping of funds, the orderly conduct of meetings and the determination of disputed cases, involved an effort of self-rule as great as the new disciplines of work"; to enforce appropriate behavior, regulations of friendly societies included "a list of fines and penalties more exacting than those of a Bolton cotton-master."[50] Other strands of self-discipline among laboring people could be traced to meetings of freethinkers and nondenominational Christians, yet others to union processions and Chartist mass meetings.

Hunter notes that Samuel Wilderspin, the famous English promoter of infant schools for the poor, planted the playgrounds of all his schools with fruit trees to instill in the children the self-restraint which he believed they lacked. In offering a continuous temptation to misconduct, the trees formed a constant incentive to self-reflection and self-regulation. The next time the child stops and looks at a fine cherry, Wilderspin reasoned, "he looks about to see whether there is anybody within view. Doubtless he is restrained from taking the cherry by fear, but in the process of time, by moving among restrained playfellows, he has that command over himself which enables him to resist temptation."[51] Working people were interested in similar skills. By the late 1830s, "tens of thousands of artisans, miners and labourers marched week after week in good order through the streets [of Newcastle] often passing within a few feet of the military, and avoiding all provocation. 'Our people had been well taught,' one of their leaders recalled, 'that it was not riot we wanted, but revolution.'"[52] Avoiding the provocation of hitting out at troops and that of reaching for forbidden cherries in the playground might well have involved similar technologies of the self, but such portability of skills would hardly have made Mr. Wilderspin happy.

Barbara Taylor similarly contrasts the Owenites' faith in the revolutionary power of correct character formation with bourgeois attempts to moralize the poor. To make socialism, one first had to make socialists, and nearly every item on the movement's internal agenda was geared to this task of cultural "elevation": a collective bootstrap-pulling operation on a grand scale. On the surface, the means of accomplishing this were strikingly similar to the moral reformation sought by other, bourgeois reformers of the working class: teetotalism, "rational recreation," and education. The aims, however, were altogether different. The one aimed to integrate working people peacefully, frugally, and industriously into the existing social order; the other aimed to transform that social order. The fiercely independent, class-conscious, democratic form of working-class respectability propagated by the Owenites soon became as abhorrent to their upper-class opponents as the cries of an angry rabble.[53]

Richard Johnson's articles on really useful knowledge take up these themes in the specific context of education.[54] Early-nineteenth-century working-class radicals, Johnson argues, took seriously the efficacy of "provided" education, the educational effects of established institutions, and the simple weight of the social order in training up people in docility and slavery. Ideas were not everything, of course, but how else was it possible to explain the continued dominance of an unjust and irrational social system? In their attempts to build a better society, the radicals engaged in a broad range of counter-educational practices. First, they produced a running critique of all forms of "provided" education—from Sunday schools and tracts to libraries and mechanics' institutes. At best, these were a waste of time, an irrelevant divergence offering useless knowledge. At worst, they were a species of tyranny, an outward extension of the power of the factory master, the priest, the corrupt state official. Middle-class educationalists, Cobbett was certain, "wish to make cheap the business of learning to read, if that business be performed in their schools; and thus inveigle the children of poor men into those schools; and there to teach those children, along with reading, all those notions which are calculated to make them content in a state of slavery."[55] More succinctly, William Goodwin charged that many of their supporters wanted Sunday schools to teach "a superstitious veneration for the Church of England, and to bow to every man in a handsome coat."[56]

Second, radicals developed a complex range of alternative educational goals, including their own definition of "really useful knowledge." Third, they conducted a vigorous debate about the place of various forms of education in the project of changing the world. Finally, they developed varied, lively, often powerful forms of alternative educational practice. While some radicals preferred schemes similar to the household-based instruction in the families of small masters that was so prominent in the popular ideologies of the Reformation, others supported a range of initiatives ranging from unstamped newspapers, plays, and itinerant lecturers to radical Sunday schools and Owenite Halls of Learning.[57]

At the heart of their critique, however, lay a powerful dilemma. On the one hand, the radicals valued passionately the acquisition of an extremely ambitious range of useful knowledge. Knowledge was power, and through early mastery of the habits of rational thought and scientific inquiry, working people could eventually become masters of their own destiny. On the other hand, they were keenly aware of the overwhelming material obstacles preventing working people and their children from getting any education whatsoever. While some, such as Cobbett, wanted to restore and strengthen the educational role of the family, many others concluded that long hours of work, hunger, cold, noise, incessant worry, tiredness, and ill health needed to be alleviated through political and economic means before educational schemes, good or bad, could take effect. Educational ideals are all well and good, most Chartist leaders argued, but limiting the people's struggle to what they began to call "knowledge Chartism" had no chance of success where political and economic struggles had failed. It risked moralizing the poor while perpetuating their slavery.[58] As Robert Owen put it, "While the labouring population are kept constantly immersed in pecuniary difficulties, struggling in a whirlpool of evils arising from intermittent employment, and low wages while in employment, the amelioration hoped for by the mere mental reformer can never be achieved."[59]

The almost unanimous early radical opposition to all forms of provided schooling, Johnson notes, "discouraged recognition of the difficulties faced by working people, especially working women, in obtaining education of any kind. The most important positive recommendation—'independence'—implied social conditions of its own, tended to individualism, and was beyond reach without communal provision."[60] Most oppositional educational strategies developed in England in the 1830s and 1840s were suitable to a rapidly shrinking minority of skilled male workers, independent craftsmen, and small masters, and were not really applicable to the majority of the laboring population, who found it difficult enough to find sufficient food to eat from day to day without committing time and resources to a steady program of educational self-improvement. These people were much more likely to support some forms of "provided" schooling, coupled with decent wages and living conditions that allowed for sustained attention to matters other than bare survival. As the workforce was transformed and fully proletarianized, Johnson speculates that "independence," whether at home or at work, became less and less realistic as a base of radical education. With improved economic conditions from the 1850s, the weakening of radical politics, and an increasing willingness to compromise on the part of the state, working-class activists gradually moved from unequivocal opposition to provided schooling to demands for access to state-funded schools. Throughout the world, free, universal, secular schooling became a standard part of the platforms of working-class organizations.

In her overview of schooling in western Europe, Maynes makes a similar point. Popular movements often produced alternative conceptions of what teaching and learning should be. And yet, "despite the evidence that class-conscious workers all over Western Europe were aware of the class character of the education their children were receiving in the public schools, organized political movements acting on behalf of the working classes rarely went beyond asking for higher budgets and more equal access [particularly by 'bright boys'], to the very schools they criticized." Indeed, many labor parties believed that fundamental educational change could occur only *after* workers had gained power. In the meanwhile, alphanumeric illiteracy gradually became a matter of shame among working people, and schooling helped shape an internal differentiation within the working class.[61]

We have seen that Vincent's autobiographies were set within a specifically working-class enlightenment project. Looking over his own work, Johnson reminds us that "one common tendency, across very different accounts, has been to treat early-nineteenth-century radicalism rather unproblematically as the politics of a class-conscious working class, made or in the making."[62] Both the self-presentation of labor radicals and historical characterizations of laboring people as a class in itself gradually forging the characteristics of a class for itself have used a questionable notion of individual and collective subjectivity. Instead of restraint and obedience based on self-scrutiny, we have self-discipline and effective organization for change based on a rational scrutiny of social conditions.

Hunter attributes the genesis of such subjectivities to churches, bureaucracies, and schools, and their celebration to the self-conceit of (genderless) armchair intellectuals. Other historians take a less categorical approach, and argue that the making of the working class during the early nineteenth century was nowhere near as comprehensive, rational, and complete as earlier analyses suggested. In recent years, there has been an important debate between those historians who put major emphasis on the material conditions of the social groups that formed the bases of nineteenth-century social movements and those, such as Stedman Jones and Joan Scott, who view radical traditions as political repertoires or discourses that were constitutive of political movements, not merely reflective of social conditions. Whatever their differences, the protagonists all agree that in both its social bases and its languages, radicalism was much more narrow than earlier historians were prepared to admit. As I argued in chapter 3, working-class activists and their ideologies tended at once to depend on and to marginalize and exclude the unskilled, the foreign, the female. The making of the working class was also the remaking of unequal gender relations, the consolidation of distinctions between the rough and the respectable, and a formalizing of political exclusions.

In his thoughtful critique of *The Making of the English Working Class,* for example, Eley notes that Thompson pays insufficient attention to the many divisions and contradictions *within* the early-nineteenth-century working class. While he correctly emphasizes "strongly-based and self-conscious working-class institutions—trade unions, friendly societies, educational and religious movements, political organisations, periodicals—working-class intellectual traditions, working-class community patterns, and a working-class structure of feeling," he fails to examine precisely which working-class interests such institutions embodied or excluded. Hierarchies of gender, skill, and status, as well as racial, ethnic, and religious diversity, within the laboring population gave rise to particularistic loyalties and preferences and a widely differing experience of everyday life. In this situation, the crucial strategic problem of the labor movement was (and still is) how to mobilize the maximum solidarity—a distinctively proletarian public—from a socially defined constituency that had no essential unity in the sphere of consciousness. One of the most successful periods when this was achieved in English history was during the Chartist era:

> Given the heterogeneity of situations, the unity of the working class could only be achieved indirectly in a coalition. . . . Only a broad and intense communicative system, continuously recharged via its own press, educational, protective, and fighting organisations, created a sufficient base for the articulation, exchange, examination, and further development of ideas. The right to communication was a central issue in the conflict between establishment and working-class movement. The flip side of *laissez faire* was a strict regulation of the freedoms of correspondence, speech, press, assembly, and association, which was exercised first by force and then by manipulation. But it was precisely the repression, above all the exceptional laws of 1792–1818, that taught the movement the necessity of greater cohesion.[63]

Significantly, this same period gave rise to some of the most unflattering comparisons between the educational systems of England and Prussia. By the mid-nineteenth century, the excellent and widely acclaimed Prussian system achieved a literacy rate (including reading and writing) of approximately 85 percent, compared to 61 percent for France (only reading) and 52 percent for England (reading and writing). While 91 percent of Prussian children aged six to twelve attended school at least 100 days per year, the comparable English figure (based, as Gardner showed, on dubious statistics) was 60 percent. Like many other commentators, Kay could not understand why his nation, "with the wealthiest and most enlightened aristocracy, the richest and most influential church, and the most enterprising middle class," should have the most ignorant population of any Protestant country in Europe.[64]

But it is possible to measure the progress of literacy and enlightenment in other ways. Barkin, perhaps underestimating the efficacy of Prussian censorship and political repression, notes that "one ostensible result of schooling mandated from above was the poor reading habits of Volksschule graduates. Prussia did not produce anything like the enormous pamphlet literature of late Georgian Britain, where private urban schools, however inadequate, flourished because of popular demand . . . the press runs of most published books in the Vormärz era were quite modest because of a limited reading public."[65] In England, in contrast, between 1830 and 1836, at the height of government attempts to suppress the "unstamped" press, at least 562 newspapers and journals, containing every sort of prose and poetry, were written, printed, published, sold, bought, and read by and to working men (and a much smaller constituency of women).[66] Indeed, according to Dorothy Thompson,

> In political terms . . . a formal national structure occurred earlier among working-class radicals [in England] than among the traditional political parties . . . such organisation owed nothing to middle-class encouragement or example. So far from national education preceding the growth of a working-class press and the spread of working-class literacy, it could be argued that the support which the movement for a national system achieved in the 1830s and 1840s was largely a response to working-class radicalism rather than to working-class illiteracy.[67]

* * * * *

Labor historians have long noted that oppositional forms of self-discipline made more sense to, and were more widespread among, the more skilled, better-off sections of the working class. Building on this work, recent feminist scholarship has begun to discern new patterns of gendered subjectivity among the laboring poor. To the extent that armed uprisings, riots, and crowd action gradually gave way to formal organization as the principal expression of people's power, solidarity, and discontent, and the emotional economy of the crowd was replaced by disciplined, rational discourse of oppositional public spheres, women were marginalized. Food riots, for example, were often instigated or led by women: "in matters of subsistence, women capitalised on their role as providers of food and care; violating codes of propriety, they vigorously protested social and economic injustices, establishing themselves as upholders of a rough and popular form of justice." In the course of the nineteenth century, subsistence issues became associated more commonly with the domestic sphere, and radical politics took on a more procedural form.[68] Masculine self-restraint on the part of male breadwinners—organizing, working for distant political goals, saving, attending technical classes, delaying marriage—became one of the foundations of the emerging labor movements. Increasing numbers of working-class men, building on their experience of the liberating power of disciplined thought, the self-restraint of temperance, organization, and self-education, began to understand themselves as autonomous moral agents and independent political beings. Combined with arguments built around property in (skilled) labor and the political rights of (white) household heads, this sense of individual agency complemented class consciousness to provide a powerful moral basis for the men's claims to full citizenship.

On their part, working-class mothers perfected the skills of "making do"—the self-restraint and ingenuity of budgeting on fluctuating and absurdly inadequate incomes, of denying themselves food so their children might survive and their husbands could cope with a day at the works, of keeping to themselves the sacrifices they made to keep the family together. But laboring women had far less access to technologies of the self (such as self-education) productive of a sense of individuality; neither were they seen by others as individual moral agents. As Hall noted, even female working-class activists positioned themselves, and were positioned by others, as wives, mothers, and sisters supporting the cause of working men. Some authors, indeed, have gone one step further and argued that the history of laboring women reveals distinctive moral behavior—"mutuality"—that starkly contrasts with the moral agent central to liberalism.

> For these women, "self" was often expressed and experienced as "jointness" rather than "oneness," as mutual rather than atomistic. Excluded from the citizenry, and indeed from any hope of inclusion in it, working-class women . . . defined and pursued moral activity in terms of family and religious sect. . . . They created "mutuality" as a form of individuality based in interdependence and the recognition of other agents as part of one's own agency.[69]

Interdependence and mutuality, indeed, were demanded by strategies of rough survival in poor neighborhoods and, however repugnant to the bourgeoisie or even to respectable craftsmen, were policed by moral codes just as rigorous as those that governed the world of bourgeois propriety.

*****

In their striving for pleasurable self-coercion of the poor, were the educationists really thinking of (manly) Cartesian individuals? Or did they wish to create in laboring people of both sexes an effeminate (or childlike) character driven by a spontaneous desire to do what their social superiors considered to be right? And how was this desire read in the context of the increasing manliness of the workers' movement? One is reminded of the gendered distinction in character formation so clearly delineated by Rousseau. A man should achieve self-mastery in order to be free, a woman in order to be subservient to propriety and to her husband: "she should learn

early to submit to injustice and to suffer the wrongs inflicted on her by her
husband without complaint." Rousseau added, "You will never bring young
lads to do this; their feelings rise in revolt against injustice; nature has not
fitted them to put up with it."[70] Many educators of the poor clearly felt more
optimistic.

Were the educators thinking of differently organized subordinate selves
which we cannot recognize, bound as we are by the conditions of our own
(class-and gender-and culture-specific) subjectivity? Or was there a double
case of misrecognition? In the nineteenth century, Gagnier notes, alternative forms of self-presentation could depict working-class selves with great
accuracy, even though the absence of an individual, introspective subjectivity that one can identify with makes them seem boring, ugly, worrying, or
unconvincing for readers whose selves are organized in a different way. The
insignificance of personal individuation is a constant in late Victorian
fictional representations of the working classes, finding its analogue in the
"social atom" phenomenon in working-class autobiographies. These books,
Gagnier notes, sacrifice the illusion that people living in conditions appalling to "us" could be "like us" or some part of "we." In turn, this absence of
individuation makes it difficult for contemporary readers, as for their nineteenth-century middle-class counterparts, to identify with any characters.[71]
Has the same problem afflicted historians of education writing about introspective subjectivity?

The pious, self-scrutinizing Christian was a rare but by no means unknown figure in eighteenth- and nineteenth-century Europe. Even in periods of intense religious fervor, it proved difficult to truly convert more than
small communities of a chosen few. Mass-producing such subjectivities
through schools was never going to be easy. A tangible fear of hell and
eternal damnation and love of God was only with difficulty secularized in
an increasingly "rational" age. Fear of corporal punishment and of the
inspectors' wrath, and love of the teacher, were but pale shadows of true
piety. Hunger, habit, fear, despair, deference, and ignorance were usually
enough to keep the poor in submission; self-scrutiny and self-control mixed
with literacy were just as likely to lead to organized insubordination as to
docility.

* * * * *

In this chapter, I have argued a largely negative case. Many social reformers, progressive educators among them, believed that the decline of patriarchalism and the rise of a new social order required the cultivation of self-

government among men, women, and children of the poor. For a variety of reasons, nineteenth-century schools proved incapable of mass-producing such subjectivities. But this does not mean that the schools had no effect at all. For many working people, schools provided the first prolonged encounter with new notions of childhood. As Maynes put it,

> Schools grouped children together on the basis of age, set them apart in space and function, and distinguished them from adults. The schools were increasingly organized on the basis of an assumption that children had psychological and social needs that were different from adults. Schools enclosed children and separated them, at least momentarily, from the activities and rewards, rigors and demands of the workaday world. In the schools, children pursued activities that were designed to correspond to their presumptive capacities *as children,* and that generally drew their significance from their contribution to a child's preparation for the future, rather than from their relevance to the present.[72]

Over time, the new institutions transformed the geography of everyday life and invested the bodies of working-class children with new disciplines. Out of everyday chaos and anarchy, at times emerged remarkable feats of order. In one South Australian school, children learned to march in and out of school to the "rhythmical recitation of the extended multiplication table forwards and backwards."[73] Visitors to a Boston classroom noted that "the movements and utterances of the class are as nearly simultaneous and similar as can be."[74] In New York, an observer described a classroom where

> they sat, the girls on the one side and the boys on the other, each with eyes fixed upon the wall directly in front. There was no motion . . . the rows of children, right and diagonal, were as regular as rows of machine-planted corn. A signal was given at which every face turned instantly, as though on a pivot toward the face of the directress. She bade them good morning, and, in one breath, the whole school responded. At another signal every face swung back on its pivot to the original position.[75]

Beyond the classroom, compulsory schooling became strongly associated with a historically unprecedented form of self-mastery. In all past known societies, fertility was controlled by increasing the spacing between births, or by delaying marriage. Now, for the first time in history, women began to stop having children long before they reached the end of their reproductive life. These momentous transitions will form the major theme of the last part of the book.

CHAPTER EIGHT

The Reconstruction of Private Life

Only a fool would take a wife whose bread would be earned solely by his own labour, and who will contribute nothing towards it herself. (1743)[1]

I ain't a child, and I shan't be a woman till I am twenty, but I'm past eight, I am. (1850)[2]

As a father is entitled to the services of his children, many of the rights which arise from the relationship of master and servant arise also in the case of parent and child. Thus a father may bring an action to recover damages for loss of service arising from personal injuries done to a child . . . or by a child being enticed away from home, or in the case of a daughter being seduced, but there must be some actual loss of service or implied service. (1909)[3]

We know there are countries where women marry with the oft-realised hope of having to work only in the house; in France there is nothing of the sort, precisely the contrary happens; my wife, like all other women of this country was raised to work in the fields from morning until night and she worked no less . . . after our marriage. (1885)[4]

To every right thinking man there must be a sense of degradation in being dependent upon the manual labour of his wife for support, unless unavoidable calamity is the cause. (1884)[5]

When a woman marries she ought to be dependent on her husband. (1895)[6]

We're a modern couple, we have no need for children. . . . Any idiot can have children, but it's better to have none. (c. 1917)[7]

Woman suffragists are either social despots or . . . the worst class of socialists. . . . Their idea of freedom is polyandry, free love, lease marriages and so on. Are these qualifications for the franchise? Are we going to allow women who would sap the very foundation of a nation to have votes? (1895)[8]

The first three chapters of this book traced the rise and decline of a patriarchalist social order, and its conflict-ridden replacement by new forms of patriarchal institutions. The next four chapters, dealing with mentalities and schools, looked at how this process affected the identities, organizations, and ideologies of the wealthy, informed the schemes they devised for civilizing the poor, and was taken up by laboring people themselves. This last chapter brings the argument to a close. Focusing on demographies, age relations, and families, it discusses the emergence of a new patriarchal equilibrium in nineteenth-century western societies. In each dimension of the new order, explicit and elaborate schemes were devised to transform working-class lives. Reformers designed and implemented policies to bring population numbers under control, to transform every feature of laboring families, and to make children more childlike and wives more womanly. The existence of these schemes, and the sheer virulence of many of them, makes it easy to reach for explanations based on social control. Seen from the vantage point of the present, the fact that demographic growth indeed slowed, that men attempted to become sole breadwinners and mothers dependent housewives, and that children went to school rather than to work suggests that this massive project of social control succeeded.

As in the rest of this book, I put forward a different story. Without diminishing the power of bourgeois discourses and the material constraints they helped build around working people's lives, I argue that the agency of those being reformed made a crucial difference to the process of reform and its outcomes. Whatever else detailed research shows, it is not a story of the smooth imposition of bourgeois schemes on working-class victims. To make the point in this concluding chapter, I deal in some detail with alternative explanations of demographic transition and family change.

UNDERSTANDING THE DEMOGRAPHIC TRANSITION

In the last decades of the nineteenth century, a quiet revolution swept across the western world. In the space of two or three decades, the number of children per family was almost halved. In England, women married in 1861–69 had an average of 6.16 children; those married in 1890–99 had 4.13; and the 1920–24 cohort had 2.31 children. Similarly, in Australia, the average completed family size dropped from 7.03 in 1891 to 5.25 in 1911 and 2.43 in 1954. Married women born in 1845 would bear, on average, 7 children, spaced over fifteen to twenty years. Those born thirty years later would have on average 4 children; those born in 1895, 3 children. In the United States, the birthrate of whites declined by almost 40 percent between 1855 and 1915.[9] Among women who ever bore children, the number of live births dropped from 7.04 in 1800 to 3.56 in 1900.[10] Marital fertility began to fall in France in the early nineteenth century, in England, Wales, and the Netherlands between 1871 and 1881, in Belgium between 1865 and 1880, in Germany between 1875 and 1880, in Australia between 1881 and 1891, in Italy and Spain before the end of the century, and in Portugal before the end of World War I.[11]

After more than a century of exponential population growth, the pressures eased as the proportion of children in the population began to fall. Dependency ratios became more favorable. For most twentieth-century mothers, childbearing became a far more concentrated activity than previously. In themselves, these changes were significant enough. They were supplemented by a historically unprecedented form of population control. Delayed marriage and increased spacing of births (a strategy of family limitation long employed in most western communities) was supplemented by "stopping," the cessation of childbearing long before the end of women's reproductive life.[12] Where earlier patriarchal restrictions on the *possibility* of marriage had played a key role in determining population numbers, now the limitation of childbearing *within* marriage became most important.[13]

Early in the nineteenth century, Malthus and his followers predicted that unrestrained population growth would lead to catastrophic social decay. While French and German statesmen were more concerned with raising plentiful armies, the social policy in Britain and the United States was profoundly influenced by Malthusian concerns. A century later, what we now identify as the demographic transition became the focus of a dramatic shift in population thinking throughout the English-speaking world. Many influential doctors, clergymen, politicians, and publicists became convinced that the decline in fertility, slow population growth, and rapid urbanization threatened the very survival of the Anglo-Saxon race; their concerns resulted in a number of widely publicized population commissions. These inquiries tended to share the same basic description and explanation of demographic change. The monied and professional strata first adopted more civilized—or selfish—behavior and limited the number of their children; they were gradually followed by those less privileged, educated, and skilled. For an influential group of eugenicists, this disparity in fertility rates between the rich and the poor was even more of a national disaster, as the least fit, breeding like rabbits, diluted the best racial stock constituted by the wealthy, who selfishly refused to have large families. For others, it simply indicated the cultural diffusion of prudent behavior first adopted by the most privileged.

Typical of similar inquiries elsewhere, the Royal Commission on the Decline of the Birth Rate was established in New South Wales in 1903 to investigate "the effects of the restriction of child-bearing on the well-being of the community."[14] In their report, the commissioners stated that the reduction in fertility was due to contraception and abortion and "pathological causes consequent upon both practices." According to the report, the four main motives for family limitation were an unwillingness to submit to the strain and worry of children; a dislike of the interference with pleasure and comfort involved in childbearing and child-rearing; a desire to avoid the actual physical discomfort of gestation, parturition, and lactation; and, finally, an increasing love of luxury and of social pleasures. All these reasons, the report suggested, "have one element in common, namely selfishness. They are, in fact, indicative of the desire of the individual to avoid his obligations to the community."[15]

In attributing the cause of falling birthrates to selfishness, the commissioners echoed the pronouncements of the clergy in particular. The decline of religion, "the weakening of the marriage vow, the facilities for obtaining divorce," and "the widespread unblushing impurity of life" were cited as especially important. In the opinion of the bishop of Carpentaria, "Impurity is eating out the heart and destroying the vitality of the Australian race." This "national sin" was responsible for the "alarming" decline in the birthrate and the increase in illegitimacy. The Anglican bishop of Melbourne spoke for many others when he condemned the fall in birthrates as an indication of deliberate "race suicide," of which the cause was "pure selfishness."[16] "What is the use of waving our flags . . . and making our patriotic speeches," another Anglican bishop proclaimed in his pastoral address, "when we are conscious of having this rottenness at our doors? . . . What is the use of augmenting our navy, when we are undermining our true source of strength? The palmy days of the Empire are numbered, and unless we mend our ways nothing can prevent us becoming an easy prey to any nation."[17]

The medical men who commented on the birthrate occasionally expressed similar views. In an address in 1907, one prominent Catholic doctor attacked the "lamentable Neo-Malthusian practice" of contraception. Prevention, he asserted, "may come from fashion, cowardice or shiftless poverty; it comes from the aimless dilettantism of women who will not mar their beauty, or disturb their patrician pleasures with the cares of maternity; it comes from too high a standard of living, which creates many artificial wants and demands many expensive luxuries."[18] The respectable woman, in the eyes of these critics, had no business being self-possessed; only a selfless offering of her body would satisfy national and moral imperatives. The chronically poor, some added, should be sterilized or incarcerated so that they could not "propagate their type."[19]

The first generation of post-Second World War demographers, extending their interest to contemporary third world countries, reverted to a positive valuation of family limitation. In their description of demographic change, however, they shared many assumptions with their predecessors, in particular by positing a model of gradual change initiated by the privileged, with other social strata following later. Strongly influenced by modernization theory, they hypothesized that increasing industrialization, urbanization, and levels of education and secularism led to family limitation within different countries and households. Like compulsory schooling, smaller families were posited as one of the markers of progress, civilization and modernity. The common set of forces responsible for the demographic transition in European countries were the key to predicting future developments in the rest of the world. As in the case of educational expansion, more detailed research on the demographic transition found modernization theory wanting.

The most comprehensive refutation of this theoretical model was supplied by a study originally designed around its assumptions. The massive European Fertility Project, conducted for more than twenty years by the Office of Population Research at Princeton University, mapped out a complex mosaic of fertility levels and trends in different provinces of Europe. Relying on aggregate statistics, the study found that while urbanization and industrialization played some role in accounting for local differences in fertility, it contributed little to explaining the timing of declines in specific localities. This was above all because the demographic transition occurred more or less simultaneously in regions with widely disparate economies, religions, and political systems: industrialized and urbanized Britain at much the same time as backward rural Hungary and Bulgaria.[20]

Over the last two decades, demographers, economists, historians of education, and social and feminist historians have all attempted to provide more precise descriptions and explanations of the demographic transition. The work of the small minority who have engaged in cross-disciplinary dialogue has been particularly useful.[21] In spite of their many differences, these scholars agree on the need to disaggregate demographic statistics so that different cultural and occupational groups, family types, and localities can be studied in more detail; on the value of combining qualitative and quantitative work; and on the benefits of interdisciplinary studies. "A good study on a single village," one reformed demographer noted, "could be worth a great deal; defective work on a nation could be dangerously misleading."[22] While the overall results in various regions and nation-states may be similar, detailed studies increasingly show that they were arrived at in quite dissimilar ways, embedded in different (though changing) "cultures of contraception" and infant care, which in turn tended to follow language and dialect boundaries established centuries earlier.[23] Taken together, the various analyses of the demographic transition suggest that there is no one causality responsible for declining fertility in western societies. Rather, three types of causal factors combine in different ways to produce a range of demographic transitions: the rise and diffusion of cultural norms (regarding sexuality, contraception, child care, mothering, respectability, morality, family size), the changing economic costs and benefits of having children, and the shifting balance of power between husbands and wives, and between the young and the old. In effect, the demographic transition is associated with redrawing the major axes of patriarchal relations.

The costs and benefits of children constitute the starting point of most contemporary analyses of the demographic transition. Economists in particular have argued that the decision to have fewer children is closely related to couples' calculation of the likely financial impact of extra babies. This in fact is also the much simplified conclusion of modernization theory. Children are more expensive to raise in cities, as they are compelled to attend school, and require more training. They contribute less as simple jobs are eliminated with industrialization, and as more elaborate standards of child care become the norm. A significant and influential variant of this hypothesis was developed by the Australian demographer John Caldwell.[24] In what became known as the new demographic transition theory, Caldwell expanded the individualist and economist assumptions of cost-benefit analysis to argue that what was at stake were wealth flows within households. By wealth he understood not only income, property, goods, and services, but also less tangible benefits such as deference and prestige accruing to patriarchal family heads. In each community, he argues, it is possible to discern a great divide—a point where the compass hesitatingly swings around 180 degrees—in the history of fertility. Before the compass swing, the logic of the family economy, whether in Europe or in Africa, encouraged high fertility; afterward it favored low fertility. Before the divide, the net flow of wealth within the family and the community in which it is set is toward the older generation, particularly the male household head. After the divide, the net flow of wealth changes direction toward the children, making low fertility economically rational.[25]

Importantly, Caldwell notes that changed wealth flows alone were not enough to transform procreative behavior; the "pre-transitional family" survived the early period of industrial capitalist development in the West. Rather, the onset of the demographic transition hinges on the gradual dismantling of an authoritarian, patriarchal form of "family morality of the type found in traditional cultures."[26] What demographers need to explain, he argues, is not so much why fertility fell, but why it took so long to do so after the economic logic had changed. The timing of the transition, he suggests, "is not merely dependent on the rate of economic or occupational change, but on the nature of the cultural superstructure and the family economics that superstructure helps to determine." The availability of alternative roles for women, the degree to which child-centeredness renders children relatively expensive, and the climate of opinion are all important.[27] The high-fertility regime survives until the traditional family morality and culture is undermined by the introduction of modern, western-type mass education, steeped in universalist, middle-class values, for both boys and girls. "Authoritarian" schooling would not have the same effect; neither would provision for boys only.

Schooling, according to Caldwell, affected the restructuring of family relationships, economies, the direction of the net wealth flow, and fertility through at least five mechanisms. It reduced the child's potential for work both inside and outside the home; it increased the cost of children as consumers; it created dependency inside the family and in the wider society as the child became identified as a future rather than a present worker; and it sped up cultural change and created new cultures by imposing middle-class and universalistic values in place of the older family culture and ties. In the contemporary developing world, schools served as the major instrument of westernization and the destruction of local cultures. These mechanisms, Caldwell asserts, made formal schooling, not widespread literacy, the engine of demographic change, initiating the decline in fertility.[28]

Even though they disagree with key aspects of Caldwell's thesis, many of the critics retain his emphasis on wealth flows, the lag between economic change and family limitation, cultural change, and formal schooling. Mark Stern, who has tested Caldwell's argument in a detailed analysis of individual-level data drawn from the manuscript census for New York State between 1850 and 1920, played down the *cultural* impact of schooling and argued that it can be integrated into an overall argument about economic strategies.[29] In Erie County, the new class of professionals and white-collar workers were the first to practice family limitation, followed by the old business class of merchants and manufacturers and the skilled workers in the early years of the twentieth century. The families of unskilled laborers were the last to make the transition to the small-family regime. The pattern varied not only by occupational group but by ethnicity, and was complicated by the fact that some groups limited their birthrate through the old methods of delaying marriage and spacing births, while others adopted the new practice of stopping. The explanation for this pattern, Stern argues, lies in the changing family economies and class structure in a society being transformed by the growth of corporate capitalism. Shifts in opportunity, even more than the breakdown of an older familial ideology singled out by Caldwell, altered the logic of family formation and child-rearing. Family limitation was not important as early for the established merchants and manufacturers who had the wealth to participate in the rising consumer culture and could pass on their capital to their children. White-collar workers and professionals, with little capital behind them, moved quickly to have fewer children and to send their sons and later daughters to school for an extended period of time. Within the working class, skilled workers followed soon after. The decline in apprenticeship made it more difficult for them to pass on their trades to their sons, while the rapid opening up of clerical positions, obtained through schooling, encouraged them to limit the number of their children. The laborers clung to the old demographic regime for the longest period because they were still dependent on income from their children's labor. In their households, the wealth flow was not reversed until well into the twentieth century. Importantly, economics alone did not explain fertility trends. Skilled workers' families moved to lower their birthrates *before* their poorer neighbors, and at a time when their standard of living—compared to that of laborers—was rising. As their lives became more secure and predictable, planning for the future and investing in education began to make sense, rather than being justifiably regarded as wishful thinking and a waste of time.

Stern agrees with Caldwell that education was important, but not because it emancipated children from the exploitation of their parents. Rather, he suggests, working-class families used education to adapt to changes in the labor market at the turn of the century, and fertility tumbled at the same time (between 1900 and 1915) as the attendance of skilled workers' children at high school rose dramatically. Those families who sent their children, especially their boys, to high school were those who lowered their fertility. For Stern, the connection between the two was sudden, simultaneous, and direct. The change in the family's opportunity structure with the rise of corporate capitalism wrought a profound and rapid change in the wealth flows and in fertility patterns.[30]

In an extended commentary on Caldwell's work, David Levine similarly questions the emphasis on cultural effects of schooling. Writing about England, he argues that the relationship between schools, fertility, and wealth flows within proletarian families worked the other way around.[31] Fertility did not decline because children acquired new morality when they started going to school; rather, families began sending children to school as part of their changed economic and procreative behavior. Above all, there is no evidence to suggest that the combination of rote learning and brutality common in most elementary schools somehow eroded working-class culture and replaced it with bourgeois, individualistic values—a parallel conclusion to that in chapter 7 of this book.[32] To drive home his point, Levine refers to studies of the small minority of working-class children who did make it through high school, and by definition accepted at least some of its values. Almost invariably, they were ostracized by local communities, and became strangers to their own families. Instead of new morality taught by the school, Levine argues that the fertility decline was ushered in by the dissolution of the family wage economy in the second phase of industrialization and the rise of new forms of working-class respectability built around the male breadwinner family.[33] Unlike Stern, Levine takes up Caldwell's concern with the patriarchal dimensions of families, but again reverses the logic of the argument. The new family form associated with family limitation was characterized by different, not decreasing, patriarchal power, as Caldwell suggested.[34]

The complexities of changing patriarchal relations within laboring families are the focus of recent feminist commentaries on the demographic transition. Their critiques tend to begin with a number of simple observations. It is not populations, social groups, or couples who have babies, but women. During a fertility transition, it is not fertility as such, or women's *capacity* to conceive and have babies, that falls, but their and their partners' willingness to bring children into the world and their ability to prevent further conceptions. Unlike most other economic decisions, those regarding the begetting of babies involve sex. Sex not only encompasses a range of cultural meanings and physical sensations, it is known to evoke different feelings and meanings for men and women. Indeed, "the social relations which govern human reproduction often reinforce the domination of women and the exploitation of women's labour," not least because western marriage laws traditionally guaranteed a husband's legal right to intercourse with his wife with or without her consent.[35] "What is a woman to do when a man's got a drop of drink in him, and she's all alone?" one mother, echoing the thoughts of countless others, asked a London settlement worker early this century.[36] While a number of neoclassical economists grant that household decisions may reflect differences in bargaining power between family members, and the wealth flows theory suggests how these change over time, both economic and sociological explanations typically exclude any explicit consideration of the complex power relations between husbands and wives that come into play in decisions regarding procreative sex.

This problematic is the focus of Wally Seccombe's important work "Starting to Stop." Influenced by Folbre's emphasis on changes in women's bargaining power, Seccombe complains that "sexual desire and conjugal power are largely absent from the standard accounts [of demographic transition]: it is as if demographers believed in Immaculate Conception—for everyone."[37] Much like Caldwell, Seccombe argues that for proletarian families, family limitation began making sense long before it was generally practiced, and he makes a distinction between a widespread desire to prevent further conceptions and the capacity to take effective action to this end. Unlike most demographers, however, Seccombe differentiates between the wishes and capacities of wives and husbands. Women, he argues, wanted to limit their families on both economic and health grounds first and most strongly. It was they who suffered the debilitating pain and injuries of childbirth, who cared for the children, and who managed the household budget. But it was men who held the responsibility for the main available forms of contraception—abstinence, withdrawal, or condom use. In these circumstances, "until such time as men came to fear the prospect of another child strongly enough to exercise sexual self-discipline, there was bound to be simmering tension, if not open conflict, between the spouses over the terms and conditions of intercourse."[38]

Other social historians confirm that for working-class mothers fending off hunger and destitution day by day, the extra expense and hardship of pregnancy was the subject of constant worry; during these months, motherhood hung over them "like a curse."[39] Ross, writing about late-nineteenth and early-twentieth-century London, notes that while middle-class observers recorded mothers' fatalistic statements about pregnancy and childbirth, working-class women's actual behavior suggests anything but universal resignation to repeated pregnancies. Women took many steps—many of them unsuccessful, to be sure—to control their bodies and to avoid motherhood at the several points where this was possible: avoiding sex or making sex "safe"; aborting pregnancies; and even—especially in the case of desperate single women—killing newborns or letting them die. Given the lack, in most regions, of popular and respectable language in which sex could be discussed, and the gulf between the men's and women's spheres in working-class families, she concludes, sexual intercourse was actually a fairly difficult point at which a woman could try to prevent conception.[40]

According to Seccombe, working-class women eventually did gain more bargaining power within their families in the early years of the twentieth century, and they then were able to assert their needs in a way not previously possible for a number of complex reasons. Doctors, who increasingly became involved in childbirth, frequently legitimated women's fears for their health. Unlike their mothers or grandmothers, many women came to feel that family limitation was within the realm of possibility. Often they were influenced by the example of wealthy families who had visibly limited *their* fertility, even as they denied contraceptive knowledge to the poor. The conventional wisdom among demographers is that improved literacy, especially among women, facilitates the spread and adoption of family-planning methods, but this was unlikely to have been a major direct cause in the late nineteenth century. There is compelling evidence that, initially, at least, contraceptives were too expensive for most working people, and that the main reduction in fertility was achieved through methods such as abstinence and withdrawal, whose effect had long been known.[41] A more tangible source of change in working-class women's consciousness, particularly in relation to conjugal rights, was contemporary feminism. Victorian middle-class feminists attacked the notion that a man had a God-given right to have sex with his wife whenever he felt like it, irrespective of her wishes, and many working-class women agreed.[42] As noted in chapter 7, many laboring mothers in England articulated their pain, loss of self, and despair so that their daughters would not have to suffer as they did, and in the process began transforming their own subjectivities; yet others were motivated by bitter memories of lost childhood. For all these women, liberation began with the ability to assert greater control over their own bodies and to have fewer children. It was these aspirations that statisticians, doctors, and clergymen at the turn of the century labeled as selfishness.

During this period, family limitation began to appeal to men as well. In earlier times, fecundity had been associated with male virility. By the early twentieth century, its excess was seen as a foolish, self-inflicted source of poverty. Sexual continence had long figured as a mark of respectability and self-control in the cultural world of the Victorian middle class. Now, for the better-off sections of the working class, at least, taking control of one's fertility similarly became a mark of self-reliance and respectability, while the prolific poor were pitied or ridiculed.[43] Malthusian arguments finally became a part of working-class common sense, almost a century after bourgeois reformers enthusiastically put them forward as a solution to the problems of poverty and trade unionism alike. Ironically, by then the same reasoning had lost much of its appeal to the rich and powerful.[44]

The simultaneous effect of different cultural and economic factors on the procreative behavior of men and women within different occupational groups has recently been taken up by Szreter in his massive reassessment of the 1911 census for England and Wales. A demographer widely read in social theory, feminist work, and social history, Szreter examines in detail the genesis of the statistical thinking that led to the formulation of census categories. Prior assumptions about a gradual "professional" model of demographic transition led by the privileged and educated, he concludes, shaped the outcome of the census, and confirmed what the enumerators expected to find.[45] Disaggregating the data for different occupational groups suggests an altogether different model of demographic change. Rather than a gradual process led by the professional strata and skilled workers, with the poor and the unskilled lagging behind the rest, the demographic behavior of different occupational groups was much more diverse. Szreter shows that the completed fertility of woolworkers was less than 5, similar to that of clerical and commercial occupations and somewhat higher than that of servants. Coal mining, one of the most skilled and best-paid occupations, had a completed fertility of 7.5 and over, considerably more than general laborers at around 6.5 and domestic, college, and club servants at around 4. Moreover, different occupational groups had different "cultures of contraception" and used different combinations of family limitation strategies: late marriage, delaying the start of childbearing, increasing the spacing of children, and ceasing to have children before the end of women's procreative life. Together with a number of other new demographers and social historians, Szreter concludes that quite different collections of constraints and strategies could go to make up similar outcomes; England witnessed not one but many demographic transitions.

Szreter posits the relative *perceived* costs of child-rearing as the single most powerful variable accounting for demographic change, but he also pays a lot of attention to gender-based power differentials in different types of laboring families. He agrees that married women's ability to stop having children increased over time, and that their bargaining power depended on the productive relations within households. But he pays much more systematic attention to a paradox that historians such as Levine note but treat as a special case. Children were usually perceived to be a greater burden in male breadwinner families than in those where all except the youngest worked for wages. But wives relying exclusively on the income of the male breadwinner were likely to have relatively *less* bargaining power than those in households where women as well as men habitually worked for wages, or where they shared the same task. Economic rationality varied in the opposite direction to women's conjugal power, and this was reflected in the fertility trends of key occupational groups.

Detailed historical studies, Szreter notes, show that miners and shipwrights worked in highly skilled and well paid all-male occupations supported by strong unions. Their exhausting and dangerous work, carried out in the company of large numbers of men, took a lot of emotional as well as physical energy; it bred a culture of manliness defined by bodily strength and the absence of all things feminine. Polarization of the worlds of male breadwinners and dependent wives and daughters was accentuated by the fact that there was little paid work for women in the locality. These men were even more likely than others to regard conjugal sex as their prerogative. Their wives bore disproportionate burdens of childbearing and child care, but were in no position to argue about their husbands' access to their bodies.[46] In the textile industry, in contrast, men were not paid enough to support a family. Teenage children often brought home enough supplemental income to free mothers from the necessity to go out to work; before they were old enough to do that, both partners earned similar wages and shared similar workday experiences. If babies were born too close together, the mother's income would be lost and the family plunged into poverty. This (and perhaps also the textile regions' religious nonconformity) arguably made men and women more equal partners in negotiating about marital sex, produced a greater degree of cooperation from husbands with regard to contraception, and in turn lessened the gap between economic rationality and demographic change.[47]

Szreter's re-reading of demographic indices for various European countries for the nineteenth and twentieth centuries suggests that not only occupational groups but also national populations exhibited contrasting sexualities and cultures of contraception. At one extreme, in France, the proportion of women married during their fecund years rose steadily from the 1830s, and marital fertility *decreased* at the same time, reaching one of the lowest rates in nineteenth-century Europe. In England (as well as in Australia and New Zealand), in contrast, the fertility decline occurred in part because women were spending less and less of their fecund years within marriage. Nineteenth-century France, many historians note, had a relatively sophisticated and widely diffused positive and hedonistic culture of both marital and non-marital sexuality. A sensually self-indulgent popular culture gave women and men enough knowledge and skill to restrict their fertility without having to abstain from marriage. In England, on the other hand, a culture of inhibited "Victorian" sexuality—sexual evasion, silence, and fear—played a key role. Those wishing most earnestly to avoid the burden of a large family began by remaining sexually abstinent for as long as possible, often by delaying marriage. After marriage, rather than contraception and non-coital sex, the principal methods of birth control were "a combination of attempted sexual abstinence, embarrassed and fumbling withdrawal when the will failed, and the resort to abortion when that failed, too." In other words, both the French and the English wanted smaller families, but the French were able to achieve this goal through positive sexual control, while the English relied above all on sexual repression.[48]

* * * * *

Schools, I argued in chapter 7, failed to produce in their charges the requisite form of self-scrutinizing mentality. On the basis of the demographic research presented above, neither did schools cause the demographic transition. Yet as an integral part of the comprehensive redrawing of social life in the late nineteenth century, compulsory schooling was closely implicated in the widespread adoption of more self-possessed and calculating procreative behavior.

Revisions of the demographic transition theory link the decline in fertility to changing wealth flows between the generations and between men and women, altered perceptions of childhood and motherhood, and new relations of power, dependence, and responsibility. The same problematic is at the heart of my argument about changing patriarchal regimes. The next section of the chapter will return more systematically to these issues, and discuss the difficult genesis of a family form that until recently dominated private life and public policy in the West. Even though male breadwinner families were not always the first to have fewer children, in time they became firmly associated with limited fertility.

MALE BREADWINNER FAMILIES AND SOCIAL STRIFE

In the early nineteenth century, as I argued in chapter 3, fully proletarian families were widely perceived to be caught in a profound and often violent crisis of domestic patriarchal relations. Husbands, wives, sons, and daughters at times competed, as individuals, in an overcrowded labor market. The material foundations of fathers' and husbands' authority were undermined: they neither owned productive property nor managed the labor of family members; at times they were financially dependent on their "dependents." Geographic mobility and the lack of material sanctions further loosened parents' influence over their children's future; this, and the lack of settled community life, made it difficult to hold young men to their solemn promise of marriage. Both women and the young, it was feared, were breaking out of customary restraints; they were becoming immoral, assertive, and economically independent. Demographic statistics show that a greater proportion of laboring people formed families, at younger ages, and had more children, fueling exponential population growth and widening the demographic pyramid at its base. Throughout the West, these conditions inspired innumerable schemes of bourgeois intervention. Importantly, they also became the focus of popular action. Not only did individual men and women of the working class urgently seek a resolution of the crisis into which their own families were thrown, but competing strategies designed to deal with contemporary challenges to gender and age relations formed an explosive core of nineteenth-century labor struggles.

By the end of the century, the crisis subsided. A new family form began to dominate working-class aspirations, union struggles, and political campaigns throughout the West; it made its way into an increasing number of reform programs and government policies. In male breadwinner households, women were expected to withdraw from the paid workforce on marriage, and children to enter it only after they finished their schooling. Only adolescent sons and daughters supplemented the father's wages, but even they did not have to remit all of their earnings.

In much of social theory, the rise of male breadwinner families among working people is explained through the agency of the rich. The new family form was discursively constituted by bourgeois reformers pursuing new strategies of social control. It was imposed on the poor by improving agencies, legislative interventions, and welfare measures. Alternatively, it percolated downward, in the form of more modern cultural forms, from higher social strata. Focusing on gender relations, an influential stream of feminist historiography emphasizes, in contrast, the agency of men and women themselves. The adoption of male breadwinner family ideals by the most respectable strata of the working class throughout Europe, these scholars suggest, developed less in emulation of middle-class attitudes and lifestyle than as a new historical compromise concerning gender and class relations. This difficult compromise favored men over women and the patriarchal interests of capitalists over their interests as employers. It can be seen as an attempt by laboring men to reestablish patriarchal control on a new basis—to recoup the earlier balance of sexual power by redefining the nature of women's work, by widening gender-based job segregation in the workplace, and by radically transforming the meaning of family life itself (and in particular women's role within the family) in a way that brought it much closer to the bourgeois ideal.[49] Focusing on age relations, a different (though in some cases overlapping) group of social historians chronicle struggles around the exclusion of "school-age" young people from the labor market and their redefinition as precious, dependent children. While historians dealing with gender relations usually situate their work in the context of debates about patriarchy, those working within a "history of childhood" tradition rarely do so.

Taylor's innovative work on the feminist component of Utopian Socialism in the middle decades of the nineteenth century is a model of an argument that brings out the many complex and unstable divisions and alliances between women, men, and employers. Concentrating on gender, she argues that Utopian Socialists and some other minority radical groups struggled for some decades to resolve the crisis of patriarchal relations within proletarian families by constructing a new, egalitarian gender order in place of the one that was so obviously disintegrating. Owenites in England and the followers of Saint-Simon, Enfantin, and Fourier on the Continent established model communities and attempted, unsuccessfully, to win the whole labor movement to a feminist solution: the unionization of women workers, the introduction of equal pay, the socialization of housework, universal franchise, and education built around the feminine virtues of caring and cooperation.[50]

In Britain in the 1850s, Chartism declined and working-class political organization weakened; on the Continent, the revolutions of 1848 were defeated. Capitalism survived, and a period of economic downturn gave way to several decades of economic prosperity. But even as political radicalism was pushed back, the economic organization of the working class strengthened, particularly among skilled male workers in expanding industries. Most labor organizations, drawing on traditions of guild intolerance toward working women and the exclusive masculinity of skilled work, excluded their remaining female members, proscribed apprenticeships for girls, and fought for adult male wages, conditions, and benefits sufficient to ensure financial security for a family, including a woman at home to provide all domestic comforts. But they could pursue these strategies only at the cost of distancing themselves and their unions from the bulk of the workforce—the unskilled or casually employed men who continued to rely on the income brought in by their wives and children to make ends meet, and the women and juniors who provided employers with a pool of casual labor at below-subsistence wages.[51] Only fifty years previously, most men would have adamantly defended their wives' right and duty to contribute to the family's income. Now they advocated the payment of a "living wage" to male breadwinners and the exclusion of women and children from the paid workforce, or at least their removal from "masculine" jobs, apprenticeships, and industries. Not only might women doing what was defined as a "man's job" become the target of industrial action, they also would, as Cynthia Cockburn has put it, "become unlovable."[52] In 1842, one Manchester Chartist told an audience of factory women, "If Charter became a legislative enactment tomorrow, I would not thank for it unless men were returned to Parliament who would make laws to restrict all females from working in factories . . . her place is in the home." Even though concerted moves to exclude married women from the paid workforce began in France and Germany some half-century later than in England, by 1866 members of the International Workingmen's Association (largely English, French, and Swiss artisans) passed by a large majority resolutions declaring that woman's place was in the home and man's role was to support her.[53]

Having lost the battle for equal pay (or even a living wage), excluded from most forms of skilled and well-paid work, and without any workable models of shared housework, many laboring women joined their menfolk in supporting the ideology of domesticity and pushing for a male breadwinner wage as the best in a very narrow range of unhappy options. It is not surprising that women tended to look toward a home-centered existence, supported by a reliable male breadwinner, as a desirable goal. After all, who would want to do two heavy and exhausting jobs when one was quite enough to destroy your health?[54] Indeed, given women's low wages and the complex and strenuous demands of frugal housekeeping, in all but the poorest families the standard of living usually improved if mothers worked only in the home.[55] Yet dependence on the uncertain employment prospects and individual discretion of a husband involved new dangers, tensions, and compromises. In any case, many women were painfully aware that they did not have husbands, lovers, or fathers who were willing or able to support them and their children. In the end, attitudes to women's employment tended to cut across gender lines. In the diminishing number of occupations where family subcontracting was still possible, working men and women defended the practice; as it gave way to individual wages, men often began demanding the exclusion of women.[56] While poor men defended their spouses' and sisters' right to work, the wives of artisans endorsed attempts to limit female access to their husbands' trades.[57]

The employers themselves were divided as well. Many large manufacturers and their liberal allies tended to support female labor, not least because of their anti-union stance. Women were cheap to employ, learned fast, and undercut the bargaining power of the men's trade organizations. Working women, many believed, should be protected, but through paternalism of bosses like themselves rather than through legislation. The parliamentary representatives of the landowning aristocracy tended to argue, in contrast, that protective legislation for both women and children was the proper responsibility of the state. A few political conservatives opposed female labor on moral grounds. Some small masters resisted the employment of women because they wanted to avoid the competition of cheaply made goods and to give their male employees and themselves decent income. Yet others, the Owenite minority, advocated equal pay for men and women as a solution to the problem. As the second stage of industrialization gathered steam in the later decades of the nineteenth century, many employers began replacing extensive exploitation of labor with more intensive forms. Rather than employ masses of women and juveniles over long hours and at starvation wages and put up with high labor turnover and exhausted workers, they provided better conditions and higher wages to a core workforce of married men. A "decent living wage" seemed to "bring out the best in the men and settle them down"; a supplementary floating population of secondary workers—juveniles, women, and single men—could be hired and fired as the need arose. A handful of industries, particularly in textiles, food, and clothing, continued to rely on female workers, but often made a point of not employing married women. Other entrepreneurs, profiting from the dearth of alternative employment opportunities for married women, built their livelihoods and fortunes out of indiscriminate use of home-based sweated labor.[58]

In a circular argument, women's low pay was often used as proof that their work was unskilled and of little value. Their domestic, industrial, and legal disabilities underpinned calls for their protection in the workplace. Most protective legislation applied to relatively well-paid jobs in male-dominated industries; work traditionally performed by women—whether in domestic service, on farms, or in shops, small workshops, and sweated homework—was typically left unregulated. Overall, one of its effects was to limit women's work opportunities and further depress their wages, providing additional proof of women's marginal status as workers.[59]

At the heart of the male breadwinner family that emerged out of these complex struggles was a doubly concealed form of unequal exchange.[60] On the one hand, as Marxists have argued for more than a century, the laborer seemed to have a fair contract with his boss, but in fact was paid less than the value of his labor. On the other hand, the price he received for subsistence appeared to belong only to him, and not to the wife (and children) who worked at home to reproduce his labor power. This analytical insight, for so long obscured in Marxist theorizing, was transparently clear to early-nineteenth-century feminists. Barbara Taylor quotes at length James Morrison, the editor of the Owenite paper *The Pioneer,* who in 1834 described the unequal bargain between husbands and wives:

> If a working man should make thirty shillings a week he may drink ten pints if he pleases; go to a coffee-house every night, and read the papers, and bring in fifteen shillings a week to keep home and pay the rent withal. *He has a right to do this,* for he makes the money. But what is the woman doing? She is working from morning till night at house-keeping; she is bearing children, and suffering all the pangs of labour, and all the exhaustion of suckling; she is cooking, and washing, and cleaning; soothing one child, cleaning another, and feeding a third. And all this is nothing; for she gets no wages. Her wages come from her husband; they are optional; he can give her either twenty shillings to keep house with, or he can give her only ten. If she complains, he can damn and swear, and say, like the Duke of Newcastle, "Have I not a right to do as I please with my own?" And it is high treason in women to resist such authority, and claim the privilege of a fair reward of their labour![61]

*   *   *   *   *

Not only gender but age relations within proletarian families became the focus of complex struggles. The making of the middle class in the late eighteenth and the early nineteenth century, we have seen, involved not only the creation of new separate spheres for men and women, but also the adoption of novel child-rearing practices, new relations between the young and the old. In many localities, the segregation of wealthy boys and girls from the world of work and adult concerns coincided with unprecedented intensification of labor for the sons and daughters of the poor. Some bourgeois reformers, frankly horrified at the evidence of children's working conditions, pressed for comprehensive reforms. Rejecting Malthusian and other justifications for ignoring the plight of the poor, a coalition of radicals and Tory paternalists campaigned for social regulation of the worst abuses of the new industrial system. In the 1830s, their "fury of compassion" resulted in a number of acts limiting various forms of juvenile labor, particularly in mines and factories.

Like compulsory education acts, the early child labor acts rarely provided effective means for implementation. In many regions, they were ignored by local authorities; in the United States, they were struck down by courts upholding what they saw as the sanctity of free market principles.[62] But this does not mean that the legislation—or the "fury of compassion" and labor agitation that inspired it—had no effect at all. Technology does not change of its own volition; neither does it solve technical puzzles alone. It was (and still is) commissioned, designed, purchased, and used with specific social conditions in mind, and these included the increasing proscription of child labor. Regional differences in labor relations, which affected the adoption of new technology and the organization of the labor process, were also important. According to Bolin-Hort, for example, child labor virtually disappeared in the 1830s in the Glasgow cotton district as a result of specific managerial responses to factory legislation and strained relations with local unions. Yet the very same legislation in the different social context of the Lancashire district allowed half-time child labor (and family subcontracting) to continue for another eighty years. In Massachusetts, employers disallowed subcontracting by midcentury and replaced child labor with juvenile operatives, but in the American South, extensive use of child labor persisted until the 1930s.[63]

If social order was to be secured, other reformers argued, the children of workers and peasants must be moralized by the schoolmaster, even if it compromised free market principles. Yet compulsory schooling was at first scorned by labor radicals, opposed by employers and families relying on child labor, and denied funding by niggardly and skeptical governments and local councils. Employers in trades and regions where jobs for young people were scarce tended to support protective legislation and tightened school attendance provisions; those who made extensive use of juvenile workers opposed them. In the last decades of the nineteenth century, a new wave of child saving emerged. Centered around Societies for the Prevention of Cruelty to Children, it further restricted the work that young people were allowed to do, this time as part of a comprehensive effort to reform the working-class experience.[64]

The reformers and their critics were not slow to realize that the regulation of children's time and labor represented a serious intrusion into parental prerogatives. While some hoped to break up the depraved households of the poor and destroy working-class culture, many politicians gave priority to what they understood as preserving the sanctity of the family, and opposed any measures that would curtail patriarchal powers. Prussian statesmen worried that kindergartens, instead of instilling proper manners in children of the poor, would destroy the mother's God-given nurturing role and produce a generation of radicals. Australian and English politicians believed that state intrusions into family life amounted to a covert acceptance of socialist principles. Free and compulsory education, many feared, would "weaken that most valuable of social virtues: parental responsibility," and tax the prudent for the sake of the improvident.[65]

On their part, working people desperately tried to keep their children away from the worst and most dangerous jobs.[66] They favored protective legislation, but not if it meant that their families went hungry. They pleaded for charity from child-saving agencies, but often used the gifts in ways totally incongruent with the intentions of the donors.[67] They demanded schools and spent precious money on school fees, but fiercely defended their right to send children to work or to keep them at home to help when needed. A 1909 investigation of cotton textile mills in the United States typically reported that "fathers and mothers vehemently declare that the State has no right to interfere if they wish to 'put their children to work,' and that it was only fair for the child to 'begin to pay back for its keep.'"[68] Many parents were keenly aware that the increased period of childhood dependency forced into paid employment women who had previously been able to make ends meet with the earnings of their sons and daughters. Gordon argues that such families overwhelmingly shared the social reformers' marked preference for the wife as a full-time housekeeper; they often considered it blasphemous that mothers should have to go to work if their able-bodied children were forced, by the very same reformers, to be "idle" at school. Issues such as these opened new lines of conflict not only between the working class and the bourgeois state, but, perhaps more important, also within the working class itself. Attitudes to schools, as chapter 7 noted, had long polarized working people; in some jurisdictions, the introduction of compulsory but not free education for some decades split the working class. In most countries, it was one of several measures that were welcomed by and benefited those better off, but entailed disproportionate sacrifices for the poorest groups.

*****

Tensions simmered not only between social groups that adopted or attempted to impose on others different moralities and strategies of economic survival, but also within individual households. Frequently, all family members agreed on the tasks to be done, contributed to the best of their ability to the household economy, and struggled through hardships with the knowledge that their sacrifice was shared by their loved ones. Working-class autobiographies abound in stories of women's heroic efforts to keep the family together, children's pride in being able to make things easier for their mothers, and men's desperate search for work. But this was not the only tale to be told. We cannot assume that household economies were homogeneous, and that decisions about economic strategies, contraception, and divisions of labor and of resources did not systematically benefit particular family members and disadvantage others. Indeed, the concept of household economy itself hides unequal exchange and contested relations between husbands and wives, parents and children, or sons, daughters, kin, and lodgers.

A few fathers terrorized their families and spent the meager earnings of their wives and children on drink. Even in the most respectable families, mothers had little idea of fathers' precise income, and fathers had even less understanding of household budgeting; their divergent plans and expectations of what should be done with the week's wages were a constant source of strain and conflict. As I noted in chapter 3, a husband's unemployment could create almost intolerable tensions in the household; the wife's "fierce questions and taunts" would frequently cast doubt on a man's very manliness if he could not provide for his family. Men, on their part, resorted to violence to assert authority that they were unable to enforce by economic means. Husbands and wives almost invariably had different opinions regarding the joys and drawbacks of sex, the costs and benefits of extra children, and the pleasures, dangers, and inconveniences of pregnancy. Fines for truancy accumulated because of a child's determined refusal to attend school could precipitate a disaster for the family budget. Conversely, a son's or a daughter's love of learning—or the offer of a scholarship—could provoke violent conflicts about financial priorities. By the time the eldest children were able to leave school, most laboring families desperately needed the extra income they could bring; they simply could not afford to support an unproductive child, however "bright," any longer. For many working people, exclusion from further learning was a source of pain and bitterness; for others it was a decisive moment on the road toward political critique or determined self-improvement.[69] But again, child labor was not simply a matter of need; it also depended on an understanding of obligations and responsibilities among household members. Gordon, writing about the United States at the turn of the century, for example, concluded that long before psychologists such as Hall conceptualized adolescence as a period of stress, the immigrant poor were experiencing intense conflicts between parents and children. Adults in a particular community frequently considered child labor proper and young people's refusal to work inappropriate, while many of their Americanized children refused to get a job, or kept their wages for themselves. Indeed, conflicts about children's work obligations accounted for the greatest number of reported child abuse cases before the Second World War.[70]

In those regions or social groups where compulsory schooling *was* effectively enforced long before the necessity for child labor subsided, women and children carried a double burden, visible to historians in their higher mortality and morbidity rates and bitter recollections of youth and married life. In the nineteenth-century German working-class autobiographies studied by Maynes, schooling is recalled as an obligation that interfered with the child's work, rather than, as some demographers suggest, preparation for the future. School attendance took up whatever play time the children had, and reduced the number of hours they could sleep. It became one more chore to be done in an overcrowded day, even though for many young people, school also provided the only respite from the treadmill of domestic manufacturing, service, and housework. "The greater demands of the family economy, coupled with the earlier and more insistent requirement of school attendance in central Europe, meant that for the Germans there was simply no time left for 'childhood.'" The conviction, later in life, that children had a right to childhood that they themselves had been denied was a powerful source of radicalism among the German biographers, and in turn constituted an important part of socialist critique (and probably contributed to the biographers' own efforts to have smaller families). "In later years," one woman wrote, "I was often overcome by a feeling of boundless bitterness because I had never enjoyed childhood pleasures or youthful happiness." Still, Maynes notes, "the undercurrent of bitterness and blame suggests that the authors were not entirely convinced that their parents were nothing more than victims of circumstance. Parents appear simultaneously as victims and as merciless taskmasters and petty tyrants."[71]

* * * * *

In attempting to resolve family strife, working people drew on whatever resources were at hand; increasingly these included the many charitable and improving agencies set up by the rich. They even made use of the police and the legal system—airing complaints against a violent husband or an abusive neighbor, attempting to discipline and reform errant children.

Ross notes that London magistrates in the 1860s and 1870s were so deluged with requests from parents to have wayward boys sent to reformatories that they retaliated by charging the parents a weekly maintenance fee for their children.[72] Bruce Bellingham pursues similar themes when he argues that the leading U.S. child-saving agency, the Children's Aid Society, which publicized itself as intervening against cruel, dissipated parents and rescuing "homeless orphan children," was in fact extensively and purposefully used by the working-class people themselves. In mid-nineteenth-century New York, at least seven out of ten children who lived with their own families before they were fostered out by the agency returned home later as family circumstances changed; about a third of the children used the society as an employment agency of sorts.[73] A detailed study of the State Industrial School for Girls in Lancaster, Massachusetts, similarly shows that between 1865 and 1905, more than half of the girls were sent to this institution on complaints from their families; the most common charge was "stubbornness." On many occasions, Brenzel shows, parents and relatives tacitly colluded with the authorities by labeling a range of disasters and misdemeanors in a way that would get the girls committed and provide them with food, clothing, and a roof over their heads.[74] The girls were charged with stubbornness or disobedience if they went to dances, refused to do what their mother or father said, ran away from employers, had an incurable skin complaint, kept bad company, were inconsolably distressed by the death of a parent, flirted with men, stayed out late or left home, were the victims of rape or sexual abuse, or simply had nowhere else to go. By claiming that their daughters were uncontrollable, parents obtained for them a free, secure home, however harsh the treatment meted out to them.[75]

As these examples show, the poor resorted to charity not only when they were cold and hungry, but also when they needed help with weaker or troublesome family members. Some of the complex issues at stake in such situations are elaborated by Linda Gordon in her work on family violence and child protection agencies in the United States. Gordon begins by noting the widespread incidence of strife within laboring families. Although men were the most frequent perpetrators of domestic violence, many serious conflicts flared up between mothers and children. The involvement of charitable and improving agencies in such conflicts, Gordon maintains, cannot simply be denounced as bourgeois social control.[76] Certainly, the records support historians' contention that the work of child-saving organizations such as the Society for the Prevention of Cruelty to Children represented an oppressive intervention into working-class families. The reformers attempted to force upon their clients a model of parenting that was not only culturally alien but sometimes also materially impossible. They often saw child labor as *prima facie* evidence of child cruelty, and prosecuted cases involving girls and boys who worked at home or on the streets instead of going to school. Unattended children, children playing in the street, or even those lodging with relatives or friends were considered by the agencies to be neglected. Rude language was seen as a form of cruelty to children; mothers were measured against a model of gentle, abstemious, non-Catholic domesticity; the smell of garlic indicated filthy domestic habits; while the fitness of fathers, regardless of the state of the local economy, was measured by their ability to provide a regular income.

In spite of this, Gordon agues that it would be wrong to condemn the reformers out of hand. To make her point, she outlines two typically complex case histories which show the difficulty of allocating guilt and virtue to the different protagonists. In the first case, an isolated, poverty-stricken immigrant widow was victimized by her patriarchal, hostile in-laws, but she herself exploited and physically abused her daughter. The daughter, in turn, could not make up her mind whether to stay with her mother; she was sent to an institutional home, where she was badly treated as well, and later joined with her mother to beat up and abuse her younger sister. In the second case, an Italian immigrant family got into trouble with the truant officer because one daughter helped her mother look after the younger children instead of going to school. The mother, in the meanwhile, made the rounds of various welfare agencies, seeking help in obtaining a divorce and getting her husband to stop beating her. While the father-in-law corroborated the woman's story and tried to get the husband's violence to stop, the relatives threatened to beat the wife themselves if she persisted in getting a divorce.

The reformers and social workers who were attempting to "save" the children were almost invariably biased against their clients. Yet they were confronted with communities in turmoil and cases where it simply was not possible to condone or advocate inaction, or to celebrate the failure of intervention. Poor women themselves often denounced the intervention of outsiders, but only when it suited them; at other times they eagerly used the agencies and asked them for help.[77] In the immigrant working-class neighborhoods of Boston, for example, six out of ten of the complaints of known origin that "the Cruelty" (as the MSPCC became known) dealt with came from family members, the overwhelming majority of these coming from women, with children following second. The requests for help came not only from victims but also from mothers distressed that they were not able to raise their children according to their own standards of good parenting. Indeed, "so many of the MSPCC's early 'interventions' were in fact invitations by family members that the latter were in some ways teaching the agents what were appropriate and enforceable standards of child care."[78] In addition, since there was no society for the prevention of cruelty to women, women often attempted to turn the SPCC into just that:

> A frequent tactic of beaten, deserted or unsupported wives was to report their husbands as child abusers; even when the investigators found no evidence of child abuse, social workers came into their homes offering, at best, help in getting other things women wanted—such as support payments, separation and maintenance agreements, relief—and, at least, moral support to the women and condemnation to the men.[79]

* * * * *

Working people made their own families, but they did not make them just as they pleased. They constructed them within material constraints over which they had little control, under the influence of traditions and institutions transmitted from the past, and in conflict with the interests and preferences of other family members. The last part of this chapter looks in more detail at some aspects of the new order. But first it is necessary to ask how widespread male breadwinner families and dependent children in fact were.

NATIONAL DECENCY AND STATISTICAL RETURNS

The first stage of industrialization, as I noted in chapter 3, was characterized by extensive and intensive uses of cheap female and child labor. Thousands of children were employed in early cotton, silk, and paper mills, in the tobacco industry, and in the potteries and brickworks. In 1816, one in five factory workers in the English cotton industry was under the age of thirteen; more than half were under eighteen.[80] In France in 1841, 12 percent of industrial laborers were under sixteen; in Belgium in 1846, 21 percent were under seventeen.[81] In French cotton and woollen textile mills in the mid-1840s, nearly one in five workers was under sixteen; in cotton blend textiles, almost one in four.[82] In the United States, the proportion of women and children in the whole manufacturing labor force in the northeast grew from 10 percent early in the nineteenth century to 40 percent in

1832. In 1820, children under the age of fifteen accounted for nearly a quarter of these workers; most worked in larger establishments and highly capital-intensive industries such as textile and paperworking. In cotton textiles, which employed more than half of all juvenile workers in 1820, more than 50 percent of employees in large firms were children.[83] Children were much less segregated by sex than were older workers; nevertheless, the gender ratios among young workers varied by industry: more girls were employed in textiles, more boys in agriculture.[84]

By the mid-nineteenth century, these trends began to change. In England and Wales, for example, official statistics show that 30 percent of children aged ten to fifteen were at work in 1851, 14 percent in 1911.[85] According to many scholars, the demand for those under twelve fell dramatically, in both absolute and relative terms, even before their employment was legally curtailed by the various Factory Acts in the 1830s and 1840s. Not only did new machinery mechanize most of the simple operations suitable for child factory workers, but the gradual elimination of family subcontracting and related forms of work discipline made the employment of those under twelve increasingly impractical.[86] Commenting on youth labor markets in the late-nineteenth-century United States, Hogan similarly notes that the introduction of automatic cigarette-making machines was credited with reducing the proportion of workers under sixteen in the tobacco industry from nearly 12 percent in 1894 to just over 1 percent in 1906. In the bookbinding trade, the introduction of folding machines replaced the labor of small girls; in city businesses, telephones replaced messenger boys; and pneumatic tubes in department stores made cash boys redundant.[87]

The uneven rise and destruction of domestic industries could also eliminate an important source of remunerative work for the young. In the English countryside in the second half of the nineteenth century, for example, labor-intensive home based industries were decimated by the introduction of sewing machines, imports of Chinese plaited straw and lace-making machines—and changes in fashion. According to one historian, "The eventual salvation of many children from long hours of illegal toil in the country workshops came not through a change of heart of either parent or employer, nor did it come from more effective administrative action. It came through technological innovation and other factors that made these rural crafts no longer economically viable."[88]

When diverse regional trends are averaged out, the statistical returns of most western countries show a steady decline in the proportion of children at work in the later decades of the nineteenth century. Importantly, young people's contribution to household economies did not stop at the regular paid work made visible by census statistics. Children assisted their parents at home as outworkers, ran errands, minded their younger brothers or sisters or the neighbor's baby, helped with a thousand and one chores at home and on the farm, delivered milk, stood in line for charitable offerings, carried their father's dinner to the factory or a customer's parcels home, assisted with the harvest, hawked papers, flowers, and sweets on the streets, did odd jobs for local shopkeepers, begged, hustled, scavenged, bartered, and stole.[89]

Historians of childhood in Britain note that by the late nineteenth century, working in their own homes, or doing housework and minding children for women of their own class for very low wages, was by far the most frequent occupation for working-class girls. According to a 1902 English report, for example, "The severest work, the longest hours, and the hardest conditions, are often to be found in the case of children who are employed without wages in doing housework in the homes of their parents." Girls in particular, according to the report, did an enormous amount of unpaid work that never appeared in any parliamentary return, for they were "more tractable than boys, and . . . more easily made into drudges."[90] In Germany, as we have seen, tighter enforcement of compulsory school attendance and stricter regulation of children's factory work drove more families to dependence on sweated domestic trades. At stake in the nineteenth-century reconfiguring of young people's lives was not only a reallocation of time and responsibilities, but also a redrawing of the categories used to describe their work.

In this context, the gradual elimination of child labor, one of the key goals of child-saving campaigns, cannot be seen as a simple exclusion of those below the school-leaving age from all gainful activity. Rather, what was at stake was the gradual definition of some activities as (good) child work, which helped boys and girls acquire proper morality and good habits, and others as (bad) child labor, which must be eradicated. Bad labor was done for wages in formal workplaces outside the home, or picked up on the street by casual child workers. Good, character-building work was performed at home or on the family farm; as such, it was not considered work in the census. As one American writer explained in 1924, "Work on the farm performed by children under parents' direction and without interference with school attendance is not child labor. Work performed by children away from home, for wages, at long hours and under conditions which endanger the child's health, education and morals is child labor."[91]

Statistical indicators of married women's work were affected by concerns about family propriety to an even greater degree. Just as early school inspectors found it difficult to classify classes for girls as real schools, the growing ideological dominance of the male breadwinner family made enumerators and respondents alike increasingly reluctant to designate what women did as work. Census reports in the later decades of the nineteenth century often reclassified farmers' wives and daughters as unproductive, and domestic workers as dependents along with infants, the sick, and the elderly. In Britain, according to Jane Lewis, the census of 1881 was the first to exclude women's household chores from the category of work; as a result of the new classification, female workforce participation was cut in half. Before then, men and women over the age of twenty were recorded as having similar levels of economic activity.[92] Similarly, in the Australian colony of Victoria, the colonial statistician explained that

> although no doubt female relatives of farmers, if living on the farm attend, as a rule, to the lighter duties of the poultry yard and the dairy, it was felt . . . that the statement that so many females were engaged in agricultural pursuits would create an impression elsewhere that women [in Australia] were in the habit of working in the fields as they are in some of the older countries in the world, but certainly are not in Australia. It was therefore decided not to class any woman as engaged in agricultural pursuits except those respecting whom words were entered expressing that they were so occupied, the others to be classed in the same way as other women respecting whom no employment was entered, under the head "domestic duties."[93]

Here and elsewhere, census figures systematically understated women's workforce participation for the sake of national decency.[94] Like other authoritative assessments, contemporary statistical indicators not only purported to describe the reordering of gender and age relations in nineteenth-century western societies, but their subsequent uses helped reinforce the trends they described.

Given these limitations, census figures suggest that in 1911, one in ten married women in England and Wales left home each day to work. In the United States, 4.6 percent of married women were recorded as participating in the workforce in the 1890 census, 5.6 percent in 1900, and 10.7 percent in 1910.[95] If agricultural employment is excluded from these figures, even fewer wives were officially perceived to work: 3.3 percent were recorded as participating in the non-agricultural labor force in 1890, 3.9 percent in 1900, and 6.8 percent in 1910.[96] In Ontario in 1921 (the first date for which statistics differentiated by marital status are available), 50 percent of all single women, almost 20 percent of all widows, but only 2 percent of all married women received an income from their work.[97] In the same year in

Australia, the labor force participation rate of married women was recorded as 4.4 percent. In France, traditionally high rates of married women's workforce participation proved more resistant to change: in 1906, 20.2 percent of married women were counted as employed.[98]

In addition to regular paid employment (which in many districts was in short supply), married women sought a great variety of more or less legal and respectable casual work in order to make what was often a crucial contribution to the household income. In the country, whatever statisticians and moralists decreed, women continued their backbreaking work on the land. In towns and cities, they worked in a range of home industries and sweated trades, hired out as charwomen, took in lodgers, collected and sold firewood and engaged in other forms of petty trading, cleaned and babysat for others, mended clothes, and took in washing. Mindful of the new standards of respectability, they often went to great lengths to conceal such activities from their husbands and neighbors. One Welsh woman revealed just how invisible such work could be to enumerators—or even to her—when, in describing her married life in the 1920s, she said:

> No, never worked no more. Oh—I went out working in *Houses* to earn a *few* shillings, yes, I worked with a family, my mother's and my sister's, and took in washing. . . . And then when a shop would go idle and they were letting it to somebody else. I done it in several places, we'd have perhaps fifteen shillings—and I scrubbed 'em. . . . And I'd do *anything* to earn money.[99]

For some localities, at least, another source of evidence overcomes some of the limitations of census data. Quantitative analyses based on compilations of late-nineteenth- and early-twentieth-century working-class budgets give us a clearer idea of the changing reliance on child and female labor and the uneven adoption of male breadwinner norms by different social groups.[100] These studies all seem to agree on several basic points. In the first place, in a period of increased regulation of young people's lives, when work opportunities for children began to decline and married women's participation in the paid workforce fell, male heads of working-class families rarely provided the whole of family income. In early industrial families, the father's labor might contribute as little as a quarter of the total income. Husbands most commonly brought home 60 to 80 percent of household earnings, although their contribution could be as low as 55 percent. The male head of the family was the sole breadwinner in 40 to 70 percent of families in the different studies. The larger the family, the lower the proportion of total income contributed by the male head. The higher the family income, the less likely was the wife to work for wages, but the more likely were the children to work. Rises in real wages and more regular male employment were seen as reducing the necessity for both children and wives to work outside the home. However, statistical averages tend to even out sharp differences in the respective contributions of men, women, and children over a family life cycle, and to underestimate the magnitude of children's share of the household income.[101]

The second point of agreement was that throughout the period under examination, children's monetary contribution remained crucial to the family income. It rose as parents got older, and was more important when fathers were not in secure, well-paying jobs. All the studies show that the lower the income of the family head, the more important were the wages of sons and daughters. In a study of ethnic groups in Philadelphia in 1880, for example, Goldin found that among two-parent families with fathers fifty to seventy years old, Irish children contributed from 38 percent to 46 percent of total family income, German children contributed from 33 percent to 35 percent, and native-born children's contributions ranged from 28 percent to 32 percent. Boys worked for wages more often than girls, and older children more often than younger.[102] The local demand for child labor made considerable difference to family strategies. In England in 1880, by the time fathers were over fifty, children earned an average of 38 percent of total family income among wool and coal workers, 36 percent among those in cotton, and 29 and 25 percent, respectively, among those in steel and bar iron. Ten years later, the early entry of children into the labor force remained a normal part of working-class life. In families in the woollen industry who had children ten years of age or older, 83 percent of the young people were employed. Conversely, of the co-residing children aged ten to fourteen, 94 percent in steelworkers' families, 76 percent in ironworkers' families, and 76 percent in woollen workers' families, but only 51 percent of the children of cotton workers, were still in school.[103]

Finally, the paid labor of children could substitute for mothers' wage contribution, or the income from boarders and lodgers, and vice versa. To a considerable extent, the balance between these income strategies depended on the cultural preferences and work opportunities of different ethnic groups in different countries. In every industry surveyed, far more children than wives worked. However, the six-nation study of budgets conducted in 1890 showed that in the five European countries, levels of female work outside the home were somewhat higher than in the United States, and the levels of child labor-force participation were considerably higher: 41 percent for Europe compared to 29 percent for the United States. The inci-

dence of boarding varied in the opposite direction: 17 percent of families
in the United States kept boarders, compared to only 6 percent in Europe.[104] In the United States itself, there were marked differences between
the experiences of black and white families, and first- and second-generation immigrants from different countries. In some urban areas, a majority
of black married women worked for wages. A lower proportion of white
immigrant women were in the workforce, but even here the percentages
could be very high: 36 percent for Italian wives in New York City in 1911,
28 percent for Irish wives in Philadelphia in the same year. The ethnic
patterns of child labor were the opposite of those for working mothers:
black children were less likely to be working for wages (not least because
most factories refused to employ them) and more likely to attend school
than white immigrant children.[105] On the whole, working-class mothers in
those years were most likely to get jobs when there were young children in
the home, and to withdraw from the labor force when adolescents could
take their place.

Hogan's data on Chicago similarly show that immigrant men earned less
of the family income than white native-born men, but that the family
distribution of labor, and the sources of supplemental income, followed
divergent patterns. In 1894, investigators from the U.S. Department of
Labor concluded that in Chicago's slums, foreign-born children were more
than four times more likely than native-born children to be at work. In
1907, more detailed statistics again revealed sharp differences in the family
strategies of different ethnic groups. In German families, just over half of
the family income was provided by the husband, more than a third from
children, and a negligible 2.7 percent from boarders and lodgers and 1.2
percent from wives. One in thirteen of the wives but almost half of the
children had a job, and one in twenty-two families had lodgers. In contrast,
husbands in Slovak families provided 68 percent of the family income, and
lodgers most of the rest, with children contributing 1.2 percent and wives
1.9 percent. More than three-quarters of these families kept lodgers, but
only one in thirty-two sent children and one in twenty-two sent wives to
work. In native-born white families during the same period, husbands
contributed 78 percent of household income, wives 0.8 percent, children
8.8 percent, and lodgers 7.8 percent.[106] Hogan concludes that patterns of
child labor and school non-attendance reflected working-class strategies of
economic survival. These strategies varied from one nativity group to another, and among first- and second-generation immigrant families. Some
immigrant groups preferred to send their children to work, others to take in
boarders and lodgers. Small though variable percentages of households of

immigrant backgrounds included working wives. After 1900, other strategies of survival, based on home ownership or school attendance, were added.[107]

* * * * *

Drawing on practices first established among a minority of well-paid skilled craftsmen, working-class communities began to adopt new understandings of family life. By the turn of the century, the male breadwinner family became the pivot of working-class respectability. In practice, both qualitative and quantitative evidence indicates that only a minority of married men were able to secure wages high enough to become sole breadwinners, and that only during periods of relative prosperity. Even then, the labor of their wives and children was as likely to be redefined as non-work as it was to be eliminated. Immigrant families trying to establish themselves in a new country, and often drawing on different notions of morality, frequently found their alternative economic strategies stigmatized as uncivilized. Black households coping with ingrained racism faced even more difficult issues. In this situation, the enforcement of compulsory schooling, and the associated redistribution of paid work between mothers and their "school-age" children, assumed heightened significance.

SCHOOLING THE FAMILY

Between the sixteenth and the nineteenth centuries, as I noted in chapter 5, philosophers, princes, statesmen, and prelates throughout the West became convinced of the usefulness, even necessity, of universal elementary schooling. And yet, until well into the nineteenth century, "only a person with immense local authority or with a political talent for coordinating all the opposing tendencies could occasionally bring a limited degree of success."[108] By itself, the building of schools, even the passage of compulsory attendance legislation, was not enough. The law could be passed and remain a dead letter for decades; it might contain no provisions for actual enforcement, or simply prove impossible to enact. The obscurantism of the rich and powerful, the opposition of employers, the antagonism of the church, the incompetence of regional administrators, the hostility or indifference of local householders, the magistrates' refusal to prosecute, the simple lack of secure sources of funding, all stood in the way of successful scholarization. Even when ordinary people believed (as they increasingly did) that schools were of value, for a long time they had little time or resources to make much use of them.

Children's need to contribute to household economies was the most important of these factors. As long as the demands of work and school both remained flexible, an increasing proportion of boys and a smaller proportion of girls were able to accommodate a period of intermittent schooling in between other demands on their time, and more urgent uses of school fees. Indeed, whenever economic conditions improved and men's wages rose or became more regular, the supply of child laborers fell—and school attendance increased. Nevertheless, contemporary observers, inspectors, and reformers, narrative histories, and multivariate statistical analyses of attendance records all agree that high levels of child employment, whether in the formal or the informal economy, made universal, day, year-long schooling almost impossible.[109] In addition, the poorest children, invariably considered by reformers to be most in need of instruction, were precisely the ones whose circumstances made school attendance least likely.

Against the continuity of economic necessity, however, it is possible to discern a fault line of qualitative change. By the early nineteenth century, young people in much of Europe, Canada, the United States, and Australia attended school sporadically for two or more years, but the rhythm of work continued to dominate the rhythm of school. Beginning in Prussia, the Scandinavian countries, and the rest of Germany, this relationship was gradually reversed. By the late nineteenth century, compulsory education became a reality for whole populations. Child labor and family life would thereafter be constrained by the rhythms of school. As Houston and Prentice put it with regard to Canada, "When once the time spent at school was fitted around the demands of family time, now the situation was reversed. Increasingly, the regulated hours of the school day, week, and year would dictate the routines of family life."[110] At the beginning of the nineteenth century, the most accurate general description of a twelve-year-old was as a young servant; at the century's close it was as a pupil at school.

Davey's study of a working-class community in Adelaide, South Australia, provides one typical example of the complex interplay between gender, class, and school during the process of transition.[111] In this corner of the British Empire, limited compulsory legislation for children between seven and thirteen years of age came into force in 1875, with thirty-five days' mandatory attendance out of each quarter of about fifty-five days. It took almost forty years, however, before most children began to experience the stage of prolonged institutional dependency in their teenage years that we associate with adolescence today. Using a combination of statistical, archival, and oral history sources, Davey shows that parents jealously asserted the right to control their children's time. While most aimed to satisfy the minimal requirements of the act, they kept children out of school to help at home or in the workshop, or sent them out to earn money in the variety of casual laboring jobs that flourished in the urban areas and the market gardens surrounding them. Many children, particularly before education was made free, began their school careers in one of the small local dame schools, and continued to move from school to school—and from job to job—as their parents shifted from one neighborhood to another. If the demands on children's time were greater, they could always attend one of the small, cheap private schools whose attendance requirements were more flexible than the severely supervised regime of the state system. Most children left school willingly as soon as they were able to do so, not least because their irregular attendance had marked them as failures. In any case, they knew that school knowledge and certificates had little relevance for most of the jobs on offer. The abolition of fees in 1891, restrictions on the hours that school-age children could work and on the type of work they were allowed to do, and the tightening of compulsory attendance requirements to four out of five days a week in 1905 and full-time attendance until the new leaving age of fourteen in 1915 still did not make schooling essential to most people's lives. It did, however, decisively transform the pattern of working-class childhood.

Compulsory schooling, technological change, protective legislation, and a plethora of child-saving and -improving institutions all affected the distribution of work and resources within working-class households and communities; over time, they helped put in place a new ideology and experience of childhood. Importantly, the same institutions also began affecting the rhythm and content of women's domestic work. The explicit lessons in proper femininity contained in textbooks, home economics classes, and gender relations within schools were supplemented by more tangible pressures. As the time of older children was monopolized by "efficient" schools, mothers lost their traditional entitlement to sons' and daughters' help and earning capacity. At the same time, schools (supplemented by various child-saving, welfare, and public health organizations and legislation) created more work for mothers by demanding new standards of dress, manners, cleanliness, and punctuality. Indeed, teachers, administrators, and school boards were often explicit in their hope that stricter school routines would teach mothers how to care for their children "properly"—that is, with expenditure of more time and energy than they had been able to afford.

From the 1870s, Ross notes, London mothers with young children became more dependent on husbands' earnings, and on their own poorly paid employment. But it was they who had to shoulder the added burdens of keeping children clean, clothed, healthy, and on time for school. Given the absence of running water (let alone hot water) in working-class homes, keeping boys' trousers clean and patched, dressing girls in starched white pinafores, and keeping the long hair of several daughters clean, curled, and free of lice—on pain of humiliating "special treatment" at school—was a major and demanding undertaking. In some impoverished London neighborhoods, several houses shared a single water tap and toilet; one of these, Collingwood Place, had only one pump and tub for twenty-three households, the tub serving for washing people and clothing as well as the flowers, fish, and other produce sold by the court's population of hawkers.[112]

The heroic mothers who figure in innumerable family histories and contemporary accounts literally battled against death as they watched over feverish children ill with typhoid, whooping cough, or scarlet fever. Conditions that brought children only discomfort, Ross notes dryly, made little claim for heroic treatment. By ignoring them themselves, parents taught children to ignore toothaches, itchy skin rashes, runny noses, infected sores, and bad eyes; perfect health was a state the mothers never imagined. Chronic pain, after all, was the distinguishing feature of poverty for commentators such as Mayhew. After infancy, working-class people shared the rigors of the family economy, and few grew up to believe in a right to relief from the discomfort of hard work, lack of sleep, scanty food, and chronic ailments. As working-class mothers saw it, in applying extravagant standards of child care, the reformers simply demanded that the fixed amount of household resources be shifted from some family members to others. The mother's own food, money, rest, and health had to be curtailed in order to provide non-essential goods and services for her children. On their part, school and medical authorities demanded that parents deal with the ailments they identified. Remembering their own secure childhoods, they were outraged when they encountered evasion and noncompliance.[113]

By calling for more work and new legal responsibilities for mothers, the educators helped make motherhood more burdensome. Together with infant welfare workers, particularly nurses and doctors, they communicated both directly and by inference their certainty that a woman could never adequately care for more than three or four children, and that each child was a major commitment. Such state intervention in motherhood, though it was not specifically intended to lower fertility rates, was nonetheless predicated on women's having fewer, more intensely mothered children;

it helped produce that "selfishness" that population inquiries condemned. Anna Martin, a suffragist London social worker at the turn of the century, argued eloquently and bitterly that much of this intervention represented a *political* alliance between organized working-class men and upper-class male legislators to establish elements of the welfare state on the cheap by squeezing more money and work out of the disenfranchised poor wives of Britain. The price of noncompliance with the new laws and regulations was not only "countless humiliations" but also fines, jail sentences, or the loss of child custody. To be a mother in these circumstances, Martin pointed out, was to be little more than "the unpaid nursemaid of the state."[114]

In searching for the origins of "proper" mothering, Caroline Steedman has taken the relationship between school and the work of mothering one step further. The very ideal of mothering developed as the keystone of "the cult of domesticity," she argues, was modeled in part on the full-time attentive child care provided by paid teachers and governesses in wealthy families. In "Prisonhouses," she suggests that the usual assumed relationship between the primary classroom and mothering should be reversed: "In classrooms, and in the middle-class nurseries of the nineteenth century, the understood and prescribed psychological dimensions of good mothering have been forged—and forged by waged women—by nurses, nannies and primary school teachers. . . . The classroom may be one of the places where the proper relationship between mothers and children [promoted with particular aggression after the Second World War] has been culturally established."[115] In all these cases, the rhythm of school began to set the rhythm not only of work for children, but also of the work of mothering for women.

FROM YOUNG SERVANT TO A PRICELESS CHILD

Master-and-servant statutes, described at some length in chapter 1, applied indiscriminately to children, apprentices, and household servants, and overlapped with provisions regulating the relations between husbands and wives. They accorded masters the power of judicious control, correction, and chastisement of their legal dependents, gave them property in their labor, and enabled them to forcibly return any servants or apprentices who absconded. Expanded and redefined in the eighteenth and nineteenth centuries, master-and-servant statutes became the basis of general relations between employers and wage workers. But while the courts reinvented the employer's mastery in the workplace, they began to restrict his use of force and violence. Corporal punishment, once considered a necessary underpinning of *all* master–servant relations, was gradually redefined as a corollary of the father's or his deputy's duty to nourish and educate infants. By the early nineteenth century, American courts began to affirm that for white adults, at least, the state would not countenance the forceful detention of workers unwilling to complete labor contracts.[116] The situation of propertyless minors was different. As late as 1897, a Supreme Court decision included apprenticeship as one of those "descriptions of servitude which have always been treated as exceptional," and to which the involuntary servitude clause of the Thirteenth Amendment did not apply. It was also good law at this time that farmers had the right to beat their minor resident servants, although in many American states the employers failed (in the letter of the law, at least) to have this right extended to their jurisdiction in factories.[117]

The overlapping status of father and master enshrined in master-and-servant laws affected relations between the generations in other important ways. As Simpson put it in his *Treatise on the Law and Practice Relating to Infants*, "As a father is entitled to the services of his children, many of the rights which arise from the relationship of master and servant arise also in the case of parent and child. Thus a father may bring an action to recover damages for loss of service arising from personal injuries done to a child . . . or by a child being enticed away from home, or in the case of a daughter being seduced, but there must be some actual loss of service or implied service."[118] In cases of wrongful death, lawyers meticulously worked out compensation due the father or his widow as the sum the child would have earned between death and the age of majority, minus the cost of its keep. Moral and sentimental concerns, however, were explicitly excluded: "The jury are not entitled, in assessing damages, to take into account the feelings of the survivors as distinct from their pecuniary loss; the damage must be actual pecuniary damage." In 1891, for example, after a seven-year-old girl was killed in a railroad accident in Indiana, the jury was instructed to consider the monetary value of "all acts of kindness and attention . . . nursing of sick members of the family . . . attending to the other children . . . which are reasonably expected to be performed by a daughter . . . and they are of value to the father, for, if not performed by her, other help must . . . be provided to perform them."[119]

As Zelizer showed in her pathbreaking book *Pricing the Priceless Child*, in the United States these principles were applied to give laboring men substantial damages for the death of a sturdy son or a daughter in service. Only token compensation, however, was awarded for the wrongful death of a "priceless but useless" child of the rich. Under existing common law, indeed, such a death appeared as a net benefit to the parents: these children made a negligible economic contribution to their families, and consumed considerable resources for their upkeep, entertainment, and education. While most awards for sons or daughters of working men and poor widows ranged between two and five thousand dollars, in a series of sensationalized cases around the turn of the century, judges awarded bereaved middle-class parents sums ranging from one cent to ten dollars for the wrongful killing of *their* children. In the full glare of publicity, legal principles were gradually brought into line with a social revaluation of children pioneered by the wealthy. Rather than calculate the monetary value of children's lives in terms of their potential economic contribution, judges began to estimate the parents' sentimental investment in a sacred, economically useless but emotionally priceless child. During this period, mothers' legal custody rights over their children were, for the first time, recognized to be the same in law as those of their husbands. Zelizer notes that while the economically useful child was legally "owned" by the father, the priceless child came to be considered the mother's sentimental asset.[120] As a more cynical feminist commentator put it, women gained legal control over their children just as the young lost their value as an economic resource and became a drain on the parents' income.[121]

The distancing of the legal status of child and servant was not accompanied by an emancipation of young people from masters' and parents' authority. Rather, the relationship was psychologized. Children and adolescents, experts increasingly thought, required judicious adult control not because they were young workers in need of supervision, but because their excitable and fraught natures required it for proper development. The conviction that many parents could not be trusted to carry out their parental duties, however defined, nevertheless led to protracted struggles about who precisely had authority over the young. Everywhere, these struggles resulted in a marked expansion of state jurisdiction over infants—and a corresponding diminution of paternal rights. In early modern Europe, the everyday rule of a monarch's subjects was delegated to patriarchal households. Now the scope of governmentality expanded considerably. Although the state lost the ability to prevent marriages among the poor, it gained increasing powers to control their children.[122]

In Europe, Australia, and North America, the passage of school, industrial, and protective legislation entailed expanding the theoretical power of the crown as *parens patriae* into detailed authority over particular categories of children. In England, the crown's traditional jurisdiction over propertied infants was expanded in 1847 when a landmark judgment of the Chancery Court held that "the cases in which the Court interferes on behalf of infants are not confined to those in which there is property. The Court interferes for the protection of infants by the virtue of the prerogative which belongs to the Crown as *parens patriae*." Almost forty years later, the same court still showed reluctance to interfere with fathers' "natural" patriarchal rights:

> When by birth a child is subject to the father, it is for the general interest of the families, and for the general interest of the children, and really for the interest of the particular infant, that the court should not, except in very extreme cases, interfere with the discretion of the father but leave to him that power which nature has given him by the birth of the child.

Only in 1892 was the state finally given explicit legal power of guardianship of all infants: "The Chancery Court was put to act on behalf of the Crown as being the guardian of all infants, in place of a parent, and as if it were the parent of the child, thus superseding the natural guardianship of the parent."[123]

In the United States, to give another example, the introduction of the ancient English equity doctrine of *parens patriae* into criminal law sanctioned the right of government to act as super-parent for children whose moral and physical well-being was considered to be jeopardized by their natural guardians. According to one judge, "The juvenile court laws are usually so broad that the State, in its capacity of *parens patriae* . . . will take jurisdiction over practically every significant situation where it appears it should do so in the interests of the child." The Juvenile Court Act (1899) gave the court the power to re-educate families through the intervention of probation officers, who could "go into the home and demand to know the cause of the dependency or the delinquency of the child" and, using threats if necessary, teach the family "lessons of cleanliness and decency, of truth and integrity." Alternatively, the court could incarcerate the child in an institution, or place it with a different (healthy and decent) family, "by legal adoption or otherwise."[124]

Like compulsory schooling, progressive innovations of the criminal system such as juvenile courts were more problematic than their enthusiastic supporters acknowledged. Juvenile justice made young people subject to "paternal" rather than punitive correctional measures while denying them access to some of the legal safeguards of criminal law, such as *habeas corpus* and trial by jury. Most fourteen-year-olds were no longer imprisoned with adult criminals but were sent to reformatories or industrial schools. By the same token, an offense that would earn an adult a three-month sentence or a fine could see them incarcerated, "for their own good," for several years. Schlossman notes that even at the time they were set up in the United

States, juvenile courts proved controversial. Some lawyers argued that many of the provisions of juvenile law represented class-biased legislation, led to indiscriminate punishments, and were in any case unconstitutional because they conflicted with the Bill of Rights guarantees. The courts' casual application of *parens patriae* to their overwhelmingly poor clientele would never be tolerated if applied to the well-to-do. The worst single abuse, the critics argued, was treating children merely suspected of crimes the same as those actually convicted of having committed them.[125]

In many instances, such as in the forcible removal of black children from their families or the sterilization of young people who fell afoul of eugenic categories of virtue, the new civic parent was guilty of what many today regard as criminal conduct. In other cases, as I argued earlier in this chapter, intervention, conflict, and resistance were more complex, and moral judgments are less easy to make. Still, it is reasonable to ask, as Hendrick does, why

> the reformist acts nearly always restrict the ability of young people to do so many activities, ranging from wage-earning to what was known as "dangerous play"? Why did the legislation seek to protect children from certain kinds of physical abuse and neglect, while simultaneously institutionalising other forms of physical violence in schools and reform homes? And why was there a shift away from the view of the child as an active member of society (though too often abused and exploited), to one that emphasised the child's ignorance, incompetence and passivity?[126]

*****

In early modern Europe, age, gender, and class relations overlapped in masters' household rule. Two centuries later, the trajectories of workers, wives, and children began to diverge. During the same period in which young people began attending school and became subject to juvenile courts, middle-class women began challenging laws formulated in "person" terms to be allowed to enter the professions, study at universities, and practice medicine.[127] Working women organized for equal pay, for maternity benefits, for fair union representation. The citizenship rights of white men became more secure, and the emerging women's movements registered their first political and industrial victories. In New Zealand, Australia, Finland, Norway, and eleven of the separate states of the United States of America, women's suffrage was granted before the First World War. Britain, Germany, the Netherlands, Canada, Austria, Czechoslovakia, and

Poland followed after the war. Women were enfranchised at the same time as working-class men in some countries, decades later in others. In France, women gained the right to vote in 1946, sixty-two years after all men did.

Certainly, the twentieth century has not been an era of steady progress. In many nations, men got the vote as part of an effort to enlist them in the war effort; in Europe, democratic gains were rescinded with the rise of Fascism; the Great Depression wiped out many of the achievements of decades of labor struggles. A number of the Australian women telegraphists who in 1902 won equal pay were dismissed a couple of years later when the Commonwealth Public Service blocked the employment of married women; by 1918, the living wage for females was set at half the male rate. An anti-feminist backlash followed most advances by women into the public sphere; hard-won maternalist policies could be used to undermine women's demands for civil equality with men, or be harnessed to Nazi propaganda.

The women's movements themselves combined demands based on women's unique role and their essential difference from men with calls for equal treatment and status; their rights, like those of men, were frequently built on racial and ethnic subordination and exclusion. Nevertheless, while adults debated and strove for equality, histories of growing up in the twentieth century chronicle struggles about who should control the young, or celebrate their gradual liberation into proper childhood.

Mothers and fathers not only behave, they signify; we not only think about but think with the family, using it as an object of our cultural work of self-definition.[128] By the turn of the century, familial metaphors began to carry new meanings, not only for bourgeois "publics" but for working-class constituencies. Household relations had long since ceased to provide a conceptual model of state power; now they began losing relevance to theoretical models of productive relations. The economic invisibility of unpaid labor, previsaged so clearly by Owenite writers, continues to have enormous implications, and not only for women's relations with their husbands and housewives' lowly social standing in increasingly monetized economies. In capitalist economies dominated by market imperatives, calculations of utility, efficiency, need, and sustainability revolve around paid labor and its products. Unpaid work, however useful, rarely appears in national accounts. When its productivity rises, governments and stock markets do not become more optimistic. When it is wasted on a massive scale, statistical indicators remain silent.[129] These issues are fragments of another story, that of the rise and decline of fraternal forms of governance.

Conclusion

I have worked on this book for ten years, and it is now time to stop. A project such as this could take forever. There are always new articles to read, details to correct, new theoretical angles to consider. But there are also other researchers who have been struggling with similar issues and who might find this contribution useful in their own work. But before I hand it over to others, it is necessary to recapitulate the main lines of my argument.

DISCONTINUITIES

It has been one of the commonplaces of sociology that throughout the modern era the western family gradually lost judicial, religious, protective, and later economic and some socializing functions, as church or state institutions took over tasks previously consigned to the household, and production was removed from the home. While some scholars lamented that the resulting "emasculation of fathers' authority" eventually weakened trade unions and produced the authoritarian personality and narcissism, others celebrated the rise of egalitarian families, or at least endorsed any erosion of patriarchal power and exploitation. Complementing these approaches is a wealth of non-feminist (or pre-feminist) historical literature on patriarchalism. Weber, Schochet, Stone, Gillis, Gordon Wood, and Fliegelman are just a few of the writers who have contributed to this tradition, often with much insight. Some of these studies concluded that patriarchalism was not defeated with Locke's symbolic victory over Filmer, but survived well into the eighteenth century, as "part of a deep-rooted Toryism that still gripped the minds of Englishmen despite all its inconsistencies and lack of first-rate theorists."[1] In spite of the multiplicity of their approaches, these authors have one thing in common: they all assume that patriarchalism ended, more or less peacefully, sometime between the seventeenth and nineteenth centuries, and are systematically blind to the differently patriarchal character of modern social relations.

A similar discontinuity appears in the work of Marx and Engels. According to them, the growth of capitalism undermined the material bases of the patriarchal family among the proletariat. Dispossessed of private property, men lost their leverage over women and parents over children. Working-class women, forced to enter the labor force, would in time lose their economic dependence upon men; patriarchal control over children would weaken as young people received their own wages. While Marx and Engels were correct in noting that capitalism threw existing age and gender relations into crisis, they were wrong in thinking that the outcome would be the defeat of domestic patriarchy. In his own work, Engels did not foresee the possibility that patriarchal interests might inform employer, union, and government policies, and help structure women's paid work. He also ignored the possibility that wage labor would not replace household production and child-rearing, but would simply increase the length of women's working day.[2]

Alongside and overlapping these traditions, Foucauldian and other scholars have analyzed the flowering of disciplines, the surge in governmentality, the augmented power of surveillance, the increasing effectiveness of control over populations, the growing capacity of discourses to constitute and reshape subjectivities. Although occasional links between the weakening of one and the strengthening of the other form of governance are made, the overwhelming impression is of populations ever more intensively controlled. In his later work, Foucault himself provides brilliant insights into forms of governance both before and after the great divide of modernity, but typically pays little attention to how the earlier patriarchal forms survive and are re-created in the modern era.

CONTINUITIES

Authors within the Marxist tradition frequently make the point that while "relics" of feudalism may be discerned in some types of modern wage labor, the dominant tendency within capitalism is the gradual replacement of older forms of unfree labor by "free" contracts and more modern technologies of power. In one useful (pre-feminist) counterargument, Philip Corrigan makes two important points. First, most workers in Britain and other western countries were *de jure* servants until the late nineteenth century and beyond, and *de facto* servants until after the First World War. Domestic and agricultural servants formed one of the largest occupational groups, particularly among women; in master-and-servant laws, the legal status of household dependents and wage workers overlapped. Second, seen from a world perspective, many forms of "free labor" not only coexist with but often depend on one variant or another of coerced or semi-coerced semi–wage labor.[3] This is not confined to early capitalism, but is crucial to contemporary high-technology areas such as the European car industry.

On their part, feminists have unearthed and traced a myriad of patriarchal continuities in the development of western societies. Domestic violence and the marriage contract in particular are frequently analyzed in terms of the survival of patriarchalist social relations into the modern era. Equally if not more important are those feminist contributions that chart the many ways in which novel forms of patriarchal governance were invented, challenged, and put into practice, even when they used some recycled materials and were wrapped in familiar language. Thus in the age of democratic revolutions, middle-class men were enfranchised through practices and institutions built around the categorical exclusion of women; bureaucratic efficiency came to depend on the elimination of what was designated as emotional, arbitrary, irrational ways of thinking and behaving elsewhere associated with women; armies were disciplined through the imposition of new models of Stoic masculinity. At times, such feminist work ignores those aspects of patriarchy that do not concern gender, such as relations between masters and servants and adults and children. However, it again points to a form of analysis that sees unfree labor and sexist workplace practices both as relics of feudalism and patriarchalism, and as the inventions and achievements of a new social order.

Drawing on this work, I have argued that significant aspects of the transition from patriarchalism to fraternal bureaucratic states should be conceptualized not only as *increases* in forms of social control but also as *transfers, mutations, rediscoveries, and recaptures* of powers previously wielded by household heads. A despot, Giddens correctly notes, had in a certain sense extreme power over his subjects—the power of life and death—but he did not have the capacity to administer directly the day-to-day lives of his subjects, which were largely ordered by local traditions and practices.[4] But this did not mean, as some have interpreted this statement, that the lives of slaves, serfs, wives, children, or farm servants were free and unsupervised: their world was circumscribed by the master's will and everyday discipline, and almost invariably also by grinding poverty, hunger, violence, filth, and disease.[5] As governmentality increased and a number of other institutions gained detailed powers over people's everyday lives, they drew freely on the patriarchal aspects of the local traditions and practices that they undermined and displaced.

By the end of the nineteenth century, most of the structures of patriarchalism were transformed. In spite of the tenacity of patriarchalist legal conventions, the absolute authority of the father as the legal head of the household was curtailed, and significant aspects of jurisdiction over children were transferred from the family to the state. During the same period, Foucault notes, Freud discovered the awesome power of the Oedipus complex in structuring what he described as people's subconscious mind.[6] The family lost its preeminent position as the key location of social order. In rhetoric, at least, it had become a private rather than a public institution, although enlightened reformers had high hopes for the policing powers of virtuous wives and little children.[7] A prolonged crisis of patriarchal relations in people's everyday life was resolved as laboring men and women adopted, for better or worse, new family strategies. Eventually, a proletarian family built around male breadwinners and housewives and children excluded from paid labor emerged as a new basis for workers' aspirations and government policy. Labor and familial relations had become radically distinct, even though master-and-servant statutes began to be repealed only in the late nineteenth century, paternalism persists in many workplaces, and unpaid domestic labor continues to be hidden in wage calculations. On the political front, a series of democratic revolutions contributed to the creation of citizenship modeled on a fraternity rather than a patriarchal household, but patronage and inherited wealth continue to play an important part in politics. Bureaucracy replaced patriarchalism as the dominant mode of governing states, but the instrumental rationality of bureaucratic organizations hides (and is sometimes subverted by) a sexual and gendered politics.

UNEVEN DEVELOPMENT

The slow and complex process through which various forms of territorial governance in early modern Europe converged toward national states took markedly different forms in different regions; to some extent, traces of these differences persist today.[8] Different family forms, modes of production, and paths to state formation not only coexisted, they frequently depended on each other. The growth of industrial regions in northwestern Europe was fueled by trade with refeudalized provinces in eastern and central Europe. In some localities, proto-industrial production never took hold; in others, its development was accelerated and compressed into a few short decades. The early cotton industry in England depended on the slave plantations of the American South; the railway boom that fueled the second industrial revolution employed thousands of men with picks and shovels; established centers of industrial production were abandoned as employers sought a cheaper and less organized workforce elsewhere; the contemporary fashion industry in Australia relies on the sweated labor of immigrant women outworkers; and the Japanese electronics industry assembles components produced in thousands of small family workshops.

Not only was it common to find differently organized households in different regions and ethnic and occupational groups, but even the ascendancy of a particular form of household relations in a particular locality did not mean that all people now lived and thought the same way. Certainly, men, women, and children were influenced by the thousand and one cultural practices associated with newly dominant social institutions. Yet detailed studies of laboring communities show that a range of household arrangements and fertility regimes coexisted. Everywhere, young people moved between childish submission in school and adult responsibilities at work. Travel accounts, in both spatial and class geography, emphasize the uneven spread of dependent childhood. While cumulative statistical measures indicate that children's and married women's labor-force participation rates gradually fell—and fertility declined—as the nineteenth century drew to a close, averages tend to hide systematic differences in household strategies. In many communities, it was only between the wars that the male breadwinner model took hold; for some social groups, it became feasible only in the 1950s. Yet others, from choice or necessity, followed other strategies while being stigmatized as "rough" or deviant. For all these reasons, theories of modernization, with their emphasis on a single direction of change and the gradual replacement of older institutions by more modern ones, are unsatisfactory.

AN UNFINISHED PROJECT

My insistence on regional diversity and uneven development does not preclude the recognition of powerful systems of social relations. These systems can be seen as constituting a particular form of impermanent hegemony. In a useful passage, Raymond Williams defined hegemony as "in the strongest sense a 'culture,' but a culture which has also to be seen as the lived dominance and subordination of particular classes. . . . It is the whole body of practices and expectations, over the whole of living: our senses and assignments of energy, or shaping perceptions of ourselves and our world."[9] Williams went on to stress that hegemony was not a thing but a process, and a contested one at that. "In practice . . . hegemony can never be singular . . . it does not just passively exist as a form of dominance. It has continually to be renewed, recreated, defended and modified. It is also continually resisted, limited, altered, challenged by pressures not at all its own."[10] Levine, after commenting on similar issues from a Foucauldian perspective, concluded that although a powerful range of modern institutions and discourses do drive citizens into an administrative grid, enormous countervailing forces—ecology, demography, economic crises, and new nationalism among them—disrupt the process of normalization and at times subvert it altogether.[11] In this book I have argued that the transitions from patriarchalism to a fraternal social contract did not occur without conflict; they involved a process of contested social creativity, and the final results typically opened new avenues of emancipation to previously excluded groups, new possibilities for challenge and contestation.

AGENCY

Throughout, this book emphasizes that historical agency was not limited to ruling-class men and their schemes of social control. In the first place, the proletariat made itself in a demographic sense; modern concerns with controlling "biopower" were formulated in the context of population growth that seemed to be out of control. Certainly, the rich and powerful never ceased to assert what they perceived to be their interests, and to impose them on others. But even the same "man" could have conflicting interests as a son, father, employer, subject, burgher, Lutheran, and philanderer. In some cases, the interests of the prince, church, and householders overlapped; in many others, they clashed.

The technologies of rule themselves were partly forged by those subject to them, in a continuous process of negotiation, conflict, bargaining, compromise, and give-and-take. Participating in historical action ranging from armed struggle, strikes, and court cases to rules of etiquette, budgeting on a tight income, and gossip about "keeping oneself right," men and women, children and old people, rich and poor rethought social categories, common interests, and ways of doing things. In this process, literacy, diligence, self-reflection, and punctuality could be used to subvert as well as strengthen the sinews of state power. Of the minority of self-taught laboring men who learned to think of themselves as autonomous moral agents, a number began plotting against the established order. Disciplined working-class movements at times came close to revolution; many self-possessed women challenged patriarchal privilege.

CHILDHOOD

The history of childhood is often considered to be a quaint historical backwater replete with toys, games, and swaddling clothes. Even the conceptual revolution brought about by Ariès's *Centuries of Childhood* has not altogether integrated the field into the mainstream of history and social science. In British social anthropology, age relations take center stage in descriptions of "primitive" societies; they tend to be relegated to the sidelines in western social history. Much of the material presented in this book, in contrast, suggests that struggles about the respective characteristics, powers, duties, and disabilities of infants and adults, masters and dependents, fathers and sons, mothers and children, were at the very center of political life. On many issues, age relations were the stuff of which social conflict was made. In an age when household governance served both as a metaphor for political authority and as the actual locus of social power, many political and economic issues were thought out and struggled over in terms of appropriate models of child-rearing. Treating children too leniently, a "domestic republicanism," would surely lead to social disorder and a disrespect for all government. American colonies needed to liberate themselves from the authority of a despotic father. The brotherhood of men needed to assert their healthy virility against a licentious, effeminate, and impotent absolute monarchy. Journeymen had to win a status that clearly differentiated them from judicial infants and social children. At a particular chronological age, men with property in their own labor had to be recognized as citizens with full adult rights, regardless of the amount of money they had. The class relationship between employers and employees needed to be clearly distinguished from domestic relations between parents and children, masters and servants. Where such distinction was too difficult to make, women—or blacks—should take over the most servile jobs. In English-speaking countries, male servants were among the last men to gain the right to vote; during the same period, "service" became feminized.

For women, discussions about age relations were just as important. Could a lady grow up to assume adult status, or did she remain an infant all her life? Conversely, could a lady ever behave like a child and still preserve her virtue? Did a woman's biology make her a permanent child? Could a woman ever become a citizen, given that she was naturally dependent on others? Could a wealthy woman command grown men? Or did this threaten to emasculate men, just as when they were ordered around by a small boy or a girl? Did women forfeit their femininity if they insisted on assuming adult roles? Did women's claims to citizenship depend on the special role they played in the lives of their infants? And did this mean that the nature of childhood itself had to be redefined? And what about the original inhabitants of Europe's colonies? Were native peoples congenitally childlike? Could black men ever attain full legal majority and become citizens? Or were racial groups inevitably ranged in a hierarchy of mental development, with western men at the apex and the black races not exceeding the mental capacity of white children? And did this make it acceptable for white women to command adult black men?

In all these cases, notions of infancy and adulthood become crucially important as soon as we give up the exclusive focus on age categories and take notice of *relations* between different groups. Certainly, all infants need looking after, and toddlers of five are not capable of the same work as people of sixteen. But how toddlers are treated and age categories are defined tells us a lot about different cultures, and is an important topic of social history. It is when we pay simultaneous attention to social and biological childhood in their relation to adulthood that we learn most about different societies. Just as gender relations and patriarchy are not only about women, so age relations concern both the young and the old.

SCHOOLS

Schools cut across a number of these issues. Debates about the desirability of universal school attendance are also debates about the nature of childhood appropriate for different social groups. The attempts to confine schooling to those of "school age" contribute to the increasing overlap of chronological and social childhood. Legal redefinitions of childhood frequently begin with questions about the relative jurisdiction of parents, teachers, and magistrates. Do fathers—or parents—have an inalienable natural authority over their children? Does this authority extend to the school or workplace? Or, conversely, should the *in loco parentis* power of teachers extend out into the street and even the home? Should government assume the power to arbitrate on age relations and proper parenting? Do fathers forfeit their claims to citizenship (and manliness) if they do not earn enough to support sons and daughters while they attend school? Do women jeopardize their custody of children (and femininity) if they have a paid job outside the home? Should the state step in if parents do not treat their children as children should be treated? Who can legally beat boys and girls, and how much? Should young people have the same legal standing before the courts as adults? Does due process have to be followed in cases brought against them? Or should the judiciary and their educational surrogates have the wide discretion normally granted to parents? And can this discretion stand up against a legal challenge from the children's "real" parents?

The first great wave of European scholarization was arguably part of attempts to consolidate patriarchalism in early modern Europe; the second was closely linked to the dynamics of its eighteenth-century demise. Aiming to strengthen the authority of housefathers, experiments with compulsory schooling in early modern Europe were more effective in shoring up the authority of regional powers at the expense of household rule. New forms of state knowledge were at times gained through education-related practices such as literacy and catechism examinations and the collection of educational statistics. Nineteenth-century educational bureaucracies pioneered some "masculine" administrative techniques later employed in other state agencies, but were also among the first to employ large numbers of potentially disruptive women. Through a range of manifest and hidden curricula, schools tried to foster patriotism, deference, self-control, frugality, and industry, but they also provided working men and women with some of the inspiration and tools for opposing the system. Whatever the effect of reformers' speeches and texts, or the outcome of heated exchanges between mothers, teachers, and government officials, schooling began to take up an increasing amount of space in people's early lives. In time, the compulsion to send children to school significantly limited the authority of household heads. The prolonged experience of age-graded institutions, with their special rules, social divisions, and separations from the street, began to craft new social categories—such as the concept of measurable intelligence or women's "stupidity" at mathematics—out of the fabric of people's everyday lives. Some early-nineteenth-century reformers hoped (prematurely, as it proved) that schooling would reduce the birthrate by fostering prudential restraint among the poor. By the late nineteenth century, prolonged schooling helped transform the roles of men, women, and children within domestic economies; it became associated with the demographic transition.

* * * * *

In the process of reading all this, as I frequently was in the process of writing it, some people will at times be seized by blind terror. It is hard enough to make sense of one area of social life; this book seems to argue that one has to know everything about everything to appreciate what is going on. Not so. My intention throughout has been to redraw maps, sharpen questions, provoke debates. These can, in the last instance, be resolved only by theoretically informed empirical work. It is the accumulation of such historical work that has enabled me to indulge my ten-year flight of fancy. It is to these social historians (whose ranks I plan to rejoin) that I dedicate this book.

Notes

Introduction

1. Quoted in Robert J. Steinfeld, *The Invention of Free Labor: The Employment Relation in English and American Law and Culture, 1350–1870* (Chapel Hill: University of North Carolina Press, 1991), p. 146.

2. As Outram put it with regard to the French Revolution, "Whatever discursive transformations occurred [during this period] did not affect all French men and women equally. In fact it would appear that the changes in discourse had been so *unequal* that they had not produced a new, common discourse but rather a cleavage in language and reference so great that violence was at once the only means of control and the only means of negotiation in this complex situation of mutual incomprehension." Dorinda Outram, "Revolution and Repression," *Comparative Studies in Society and History* 34, no. 1 (1992): 64.

3. In focusing on the *changing articulation* of gender, age, class, race, and other relations, even as these categories are themselves being constructed and redefined, I sidestep recent feminist debates about whether gender and productive relations should be conceptualized separately or as a single system of power.

4. This view was originally associated with radical feminists (such as Mary Daly), but it also applies to others, such as Lacanian-influenced theoreticians who see patriarchy as a relatively autonomous structure of psychic relations responsible for the production of sexed subjects.

5. The different name tags given to these forms of gender relations often reflect judgments regarding the politics of theoretical language, rather than deep-seated disagreements about the content of the analysis.

6. Bruce Curtis, "Representation and State Formation in the Canadas, 1790–1850," *Studies in Political Economy* 28 (1989): 61.

7. M. Ignatieff, "State, Civil Society and Total Institutions: A Critique of Recent Social Histories of Punishment," in S. Cohen and A. Scull (eds.), *Social Control and the State* (Oxford: Basil Blackwell, 1985), p. 96.

8. Michel Foucault, "Governmentality," in G. Burchell, C. Gordon, and P. Miller (eds.), *The Foucault Effect: Studies in Governmentality* (London: Harvester/Wheatsheaf, 1991), pp. 102–103.

9. Quoted in Constance Jordan, *Renaissance Feminism: Literary Texts and Political Models* (Ithaca: Cornell University Press, 1990), p. 150.

10. J. Fitz, "The Child as a Legal Subject," in R. Dale et al. (eds.), *Politics, Patriarchy and Practice* (London: Falmer Press, 1981), pp. 287–88.

1. The Consolidation of Patriarchalism in Early Modern Europe

1. According to Robisheaux, for example, in the mid-sixteenth century German princes, Lutheran pastors, and villagers struggled, each in their own way and

following their divergent interests, to bring order and stability to their society. In this process, no path proved more important than the effort to reform the family, to bolster patriarchal authority, and to introduce a strict marital discipline. Thomas Robisheaux, *Rural Society and the Search for Order in Early Modern Germany* (Cambridge: Cambridge University Press, 1989), pp. 95–96.

2. According to Weber, "Patriarchalism means the authority of the father, the husband, the senior of the house, the sib elder over the members of the household and sib; the rule of the master and patron over bondsmen, serfs, freed men; of the lord over the domestic servants and household officials; of the prince over house- and court-officials, nobles of office, clients, vassals; of the patrimonial lord and sovereign prince over the 'subjects.'" Max Weber, "The Social Psychology of the World Religions," in H. H. Gerth and C. Wright Mills (eds.), *From Max Weber: Essays in Sociology* (London: Routledge and Kegan Paul, 1970), p. 296. See also Jordan, *Renaissance Feminism*, p. 3.

3. Even though Stone's controversial conceptualization of this period is in many ways different from the one presented here, he makes a parallel argument in *The Family, Sex and Marriage in England:* "A diffuse concept of patriarchy inherited from the middle ages that took the form of 'good lordship'—meaning dominance over kin and clientage—was vigorously attacked by the state as a threat to its own authority. Patriarchy was now reinforced by the state, in the much modified form of authoritarian dominance by the husband and father over the woman and children within the nuclear family. What had previously been a real threat to the political order was thus neatly transformed into a formidable buttress to it." Lawrence Stone, *The Family, Sex and Marriage in England, 1500–1800* (London: Weidenfeld and Nicolson, 1977), pp. 153–54.

4. I have taken up Tilly's distinction between *nation-states*, rare entities that consist of only one nationality contained within the geographical boundaries of one state, and the much more common *national states*, whose boundaries encompass regions inhabited by several different ethnic groups. C. Tilly, *Coercion, Capital and European States, 990–1992* (Oxford: Blackwell, 1992), pp. 2–3.

5. For Weber's definition of patrimonialism, see M. Weber, *Economy and Society* (Berkeley: University of California Press, 1978), p. 643.

6. See, for example, Perry Anderson, *Lineages of the Absolutist State* [1974] (London: Verso, 1989), pp. 401–409, 412. There were other corporate bodies besides nobles who held such powers, such as imperial cities, some urban communes, or religious houses.

7. Tilly, *Coercion,* pp. 69, 184–85; Norbert Elias, *The Civilising Process: The History of Manners* (Oxford: Basil Blackwell, 1978), pp. 65, 201. For a recent overview of the violent regime of rule during this period, see T. N. Bisson, "The 'Feudal Revolution,'" *Past and Present* 142 (1994).

8. William McNeill, *The Pursuit of Power: Technology, Armed Force and Society since A.D. 1000* (Oxford: Basil Blackwell, 1983), pp. 125, 142.

9. Geoffrey Parker, *The Military Revolution: Military Innovation and the Rise of the*

West, 1500–1800 (Cambridge: Cambridge University Press, 1988), p. 24. According to Hacker, a 40,000-man imperial army in 1648 might have been accompanied by, and depended on, some "100 000 soldiers' wives, whores, man servants, maids and other camp-followers." B. Hacker, "Women and Military Institutions in Early Modern Europe: A Reconnaissance," *Signs* 6, no. 4 (1981): 648.

10. McNeill, *Pursuit*, p. 117.

11. Norbert Elias, *The Civilising Process: State Formation and Civilisation* (Oxford: Basil Blackwell, 1982), p. 202.

12. In the fifteenth century, for example, the newly perfected cannon for a while proved capable of destroying the mightiest fortifications. By the 1520s, ramparts on the new Italian model were again quite capable of resisting even the best-equipped attackers. But the cost of these fortifications, and of the guns needed to protect them, was enormous, and only the wealthiest states and cities could afford them. This put the weaker ones at a great disadvantage, but it also was a significant factor in preventing the unification of Europe into a single imperial unity just as this became conceivable with the enormous territory assembled by Charles V (1500–1558) as emperor of the Holy Roman Empire. McNeill, *Pursuit*, p. 90.

13. David Kaiser, *Politics and War: European Conflict from Philip II to Hitler* (Cambridge, Mass.: Harvard University Press, 1990), pp. 19, 23–24.

14. Anderson, *Lineages*, p. 49.

15. Parker, *Military Revolution*, pp. 42–43.

16. McNeill, *Pursuit*, p. 139. In sharp contrast, the local economies and peoples on Europe's periphery, or in lands that became the targets of European expansionism overseas, *were* devastated.

17. Elias, *The Civilising Process: State*, p. 11.

18. Tilly, *Coercion*, pp. 103–104.

19. Ibid., pp. 69, 184–85.

20. Hobsbawm, *The Age of Revolution* (London: Abacus, 1977), pp. 113–14. See also Anderson, *Lineages*, pp. 37–39.

21. C. Tilly, "Cities and States in Europe, 1000–1800," *Theory and Society* 18, no. 4 (1989): 573.

22. Wally Seccombe, *A Millennium of Family Change: Feudalism to Capitalism in Northwestern Europe* (London: Verso, 1992), pp. 126–30.

23. Ibid., pp. 133–66.

24. Ibid., pp. 146–61.

25. Ibid., p. 190.

26. Ibid., pp. 138–40.

27. P. Kriedte, *Peasants, Landlords and Merchant Capitalists: Europe and the World Economy, 1500–1800* (Cambridge: Cambridge University Press, 1983), pp. 21–22.

28. Ibid., p. 43.

29. S. Pollard, *Peaceful Conquest: The Industrialisation of Europe, 1760–1970* (Oxford: Oxford University Press, 1986), pp. 192–93, 199.

30. C. Tilly, "Demographic Origins of the European Proletariat," in D. Levine

(ed.), *Proletarianization and Family History* (New York: Academic Press, 1984), p. 33. These figures should be taken as rough estimates; relatively reliable statistics of the kind we now use are a recent historical artifact. For many purposes, however, order of magnitude and direction of change are more important than precise figures.

31. J. de Vries, *European Urbanization, 1500–1800* (Cambridge, Mass.: Harvard University Press, 1984), p. 36.

32. Wally Seccombe, "The Western European Pattern in Historical Perspective: A Response to David Levine," *Journal of Historical Sociology* 3, no. 1 (1990): 66.

33. Colin McEvedy and Richard Jones, *Atlas of World Population History* (Harmondsworth: Penguin Books, 1978).

34. Tilly, "Demographic Origins," pp. 32–36.

35. D. Levine, "Industrialisation and the Proletarian Family in England," *Past and Present* 107 (1985): 170–71.

36. Kriedte, *Peasants*, p. 150.

37. D. Levine, "Punctuated Equilibrium: The Modernisation of the Proletarian Family in the Age of Nascent Capitalism," *International Labour and Working Class History* 39 (1991): 9.

38. Tilly, "Demographic Origins," pp. 33–34.

39. In early modern Germany, for example, "some areas of Bavaria . . . were characterized by systems of impartible inheritance, large homesteads, and multigenerational households. . . . But these were pockets of peasant-household prosperity in the midst of regional varieties that encompassed, by the late seventeenth century, fully developed commercial agricultural estate economies . . . with their mixed populations of bound peasants, cottagers, and landless laborers; the tiny 'handkerchief plots' of the southern Rhineland resulting from generations of overpopulation and subdivision; and the putting-out industrial villages of the river valleys and mountainous regions of western and central Germany. Preindustrial family life . . . can hardly be spoken of in terms of generalizations." Mary Jo Maynes and Thomas Taylor, "Germany," in J. M. Hawes and N. R. Hiner, *Children in Historical and Comparative Perspective: An International Handbook* (New York: Greenwood Press, 1991), p. 307.

40. See H. Medick, "The Proto-Industrial Family Economy," in P. Kriedte, H. Medick, and J. Schlumbohm, *Industrialization before Industrialization: Rural Industry in the Genesis of Capitalism* (Cambridge: Cambridge University Press, 1981), p. 76.

41. Seccombe, *Millennium*, p. 184.

42. J. R. Gillis, *For Better, for Worse: British Marriages, 1660 to the Present* (New York: Oxford University Press, 1985), chap. 2.

43. Merry E. Wiesner, *Women and Gender in Early Modern Europe* (Cambridge: Cambridge University Press, 1993), p. 60.

44. Seccombe, *Millennium,* pp. 38, 140.

45. Patrimony can be understood "as a flexible instrument for disciplining one generation into assuming responsibility and another into dying off. Parents had a long period between the marriage of their offspring and their own retirement to

teach them the terms of obligation. And property came from them at the rate they were prepared to give it up." David Warren Sabean, *Property, Production, and Family in Neckerhausen, 1700–1870* (Cambridge: Cambridge University Press, 1990), pp. 18, 422.

46. David Sabean, *Power in the Blood: Popular Culture and Village Discourse in Early Modern Germany* (Cambridge: Cambridge University Press, 1984), p. 173.

47. Lyndal Roper, *The Holy Household: Women and Morals in Reformation Augsburg* (Oxford: Clarendon Press, 1989), pp. 31, 59.

48. Gillis, *For Better,* pp. 11, 15, 57.

49. For a discussion of the overlapping status of servants and youth, see Michael Mitterauer, "Servants and Youth," *Continuity and Change* 5, no. 1 (1990): 11–38.

50. Christopher Tomlins, *Law, Labor and Ideology in the Early American Republic* (Cambridge: Cambridge University Press, 1993), pp. 234, 243, 247. See also Christopher Tomlins, "Subordination, Authority, Law: Subjects in Labour History," *International Labor and Working-Class History* 47 (1995): 56–90, and Steinfeld, *Invention.*

51. Steinfeld, *Invention,* pp. 38–40, 43, 50, 114–16; Tomlins, *Law,* pp. 235–36.

52. A. H. Simpson, *A Treatise on the Law and Practice Relating to Infants,* 3rd ed. (London: Stevens and Haynes, 1909), pp. 129–30, 206.

53. Ibid., p. 37. No such provision applied to propertyless infants.

54. Ibid., p. 127.

55. L. Holcombe, "Victorian Wives and Property: Reform of the Married Women's Property Law, 1857–1882," in M. Vicinus (ed.), *A Widening Sphere* (Bloomington: Indiana University Press, 1980), pp. 4–8. In the colonies, even the wealthy were often denied the use of equity law. Few lawyers were experienced in equity principles, and in any case such agreements were often juridically unenforceable because in many localities there were no equity courts. C. B. Backhouse, "Married Women's Property Law in Nineteenth-Century Canada," *Law and History Review* 6, no. 2 (1988): 211–57.

56. Quoted in R. Harrison and F. Mort, "Patriarchal Aspects of Nineteenth-Century Class Formation: Property Relations, Marriage and Divorce, and Sexuality," in P. Corrigan (ed.) *Capitalism, State Formation and Marxist Theory* (London: Quartet Books, 1980), p. 87. See also Susan Staves, *Married Women's Separate Property in England, 1660–1833* (Cambridge, Mass.: Harvard University Press, 1990).

57. Nicole Arnaud-Duc, "The Law's Contradictions," in G. Fraise and M. Perrot (eds.), *A History of Women in the West,* vol. 4: *Emerging Feminism from Revolution to World War* (Cambridge, Mass.: Belknap Press, 1993), p. 106.

58. Quoted in A. Stanley, "Conjugal Bonds and Wage Labor: Rights of Contract in the Age of Emancipation," *Journal of American History* 75 (1988): 477. See also Carole Pateman, *The Sexual Contract* (Cambridge: Polity Press, 1988), pp. 126–27.

59. P. Corrigan and D. Sayer, *The Great Arch: English State Formation as Cultural Revolution* (Oxford: Basil Blackwell, 1985), pp. 35–36.

60. Until 1884 in Britain, a wife could be jailed for refusing conjugal rights; until 1891, husbands were empowered to imprison their wives in the matrimonial home to obtain their rights. Pateman, *Contract,* pp. 123, 127.

61. Frances E. Dolan, *Dangerous Familiars: Representations of Domestic Crime in England, 1550–1700* (Ithaca: Cornell University Press, 1994), pp. 21–22, 33.

62. Quoted in A. Fletcher and J. Stevenson (eds.), *Order and Disorder in Early Modern England* (Cambridge: Cambridge University Press, 1985), pp. 1, 14.

63. G. S. Wood, *The Radicalism of the American Revolution* (New York: Vintage Books, 1991), p. 84.

64. Douglas Gorsline, *What People Wore: A Visual History of Dress from Ancient Times to the Twentieth Century* (London: Orbis Publishing, 1978), p. 43.

65. G. S. Wood, *Radicalism,* pp. 25–28, 33, 235.

66. James A. Brundage, *Law, Sex and Christian Society in Medieval Europe* (Chicago: University of Chicago Press, 1987), pp. 488, 498–99; Robisheaux, *Rural Society,* p. 98.

67. Roper, *Holy Household,* p. 17; Christopher Hill, *Society and Puritanism in Pre-revolutionary England* (London: Secker and Warburg, 1964), p. 488; Stone, *Family,* p. 135.

68. Roper notes that the first generation of Protestant clergy, including Luther, found marriage very difficult to get used to. Lyndal Roper, *Oedipus and the Devil: Witchraft, Sexuality and Religion in Early Modern Europe* (London: Routledge, 1994), pp. 18, 43.

69. See Hill, *Society,* chap. 13; C. Jordan, *Renaissance Feminism,* p. 54.

70. Quoted in Hill, *Society,* pp. 444–45. See also R. Po-Chia Hsia, *Social Discipline in the Reformation: Central Europe, 1550–1750* (London: Routledge, 1989), p. 148.

71. Quoted in Thomas Robisheaux, "Peasants and Pastors: Rural Youth Control and the Reformation in Hohenloe, 1540–1680," *Social History* 6, no. 3 (1981): 287.

72. Brundage, *Law,* pp. 552–53.

73. It was published in England in 1612. Quoted in S. D. Amussen, *An Ordered Society: Gender and Class in Early Modern England* (New York: Blackwell, 1988), pp. 37–38.

74. Quoted in Hill, *Society,* p. 447.

75. According to Schochet, Quakers attributed to Satan himself the notion that fathers were entitled to special treatment. Gordon J. Schochet, "Patriarchalism, Politics and Mass Attitudes in Stuart England," *Historical Journal* 12, no. 3 (1969): 420.

76. Roper, *Holy Household,* pp. 1–2.

77. In 1529, for example, the Memmingen city council forbade women to discuss religion while drawing water at neighborhood wells. Evidently no German government went as far as King Henry VIII of England, who in 1543 forbade women to read the Bible altogether. Merry Wiesner, "Women's Response to the Reformation," in R. Po-Chia Hsia (ed.), *The German People and the Reformation* (Ithaca: Cornell University Press, 1988), p. 161.

78. Keith Thomas, "Women and the Civil War Sects," *Past and Present* 13 (1958): 42–62.

79. Roper, *Holy Household*, p. 267; Hill, *Society*, pp. 124–44.

80. Roper, *Holy Household*, p. 3.

81. Strauss, for example, one of the first scholars to systematically examine the Reformation in rural Germany, argued that because Lutheranism was pitched at the solid burgher, the peasants, who saw little in the new creed to attract them, were indifferent to it. Gerald Strauss, *Luther's House of Learning: Indoctrination of the Young in the German Reformation* (Baltimore: Johns Hopkins University Press, 1978), p. 307.

82. Robisheaux, "Peasants and Pastors," p. 299. As he put it, "Patriarchy, Protestantism and the control of wealth and property were all inseparable from one another in a land like Hohenloe." Robisheaux, *Rural Society*, p. 106.

83. Robisheaux, "Peasants and Pastors," pp. 283, 298–99.

84. S. Ogilvie, "Coming of Age in a Corporate Society: Capitalism, Pietism and Family Authority in Rural Württemberg, 1590–1740," *Continuity and Change* 1, no. 3 (1986): 321–22.

85. Wiesner, "Women's Response," p. 155; Stone, *Family*, chap. 5. Such legal reforms were frequently accompanied by protracted struggles between church, commune, and larger civil authorities over who exactly had jurisdiction over family matters, infringements of peace, and moral transgressions.

86. Brundage, *Law*, pp. 563–65; Robisheaux, "Peasants and Pastors," p. 299; S. Hanley, "Engendering the State: Family Formation and State Building in Early Modern France," *French Historical Studies* 16, no. 1 (1989): 15.

87. Robisheaux, *Rural Society*, chap. 4.

88. Ogilvie, "Coming of Age," pp. 302, 321.

89. Others brought for correction included those who transgressed simply by being vagrants or beggars; those who played dice, cards, or other "illegal games"; women who scolded and brawled with their husband and neighbors; those who allowed their children to run around the church during sermons, sat in the wrong seat in church, or argued with others about who should sit where; and the poor who insulted their superiors, or who refused to behave reverently in church or fell asleep during sermons. Ingram argues that in spite of their many problems and imperfections, in the period between 1570 and 1640 the church courts were effective, and in many respects worked harmoniously with their common-law counterparts. M. Ingram, *Church Courts, Sex and Marriage in England, 1570–1640* (Cambridge: Cambridge University Press, 1987).

90. Stone, *Family*, p. 175. Only a small number of young people probably were executed for such crimes. The death penalty was repealed in 1681, but the basic legal form (the criminal prosecution of children whose parents could not control them), much altered during the years, remained in effect in that state until 1973. Linda Gordon, *Heroes of Their Own Lives: The Politics and History of Family Violence* (London: Virago, 1989), p. 190.

91. S. Hanley, "Family and State in Early Modern France: The Marriage Pact," in M. Boxer and J. Quataert (eds.), *Connecting Spheres: Women in the Western World, 1500 to the Present* (New York: Oxford University Press, 1987).

92. Hanley, "Engendering."

93. M. Foucault, *Discipline and Punish* (London: Penguin, 1979), p. 214. The storming of the Bastille in the first year of the French Revolution freed a large proportion of the persons imprisoned on paternal orders under the *lettres de cachet de famille.* Jacques Donzelot, *The Policing of Families* (New York: Pantheon Books, 1979), pp. 49–51. See also Arlette Farge and Michel Foucault, *Le désordre des familles. Lettres de cachet des Archives de la Bastille* (Paris: Gallimard, 1982).

94. Robisheaux, *Rural Society,* chap. 4.

95. Merry E. Wiesner, "Spinning Out Capital: Women's Work in the Early Modern Economy," in R. Bridenthal et al. (eds.), *Becoming Visible: Women in European History,* 2nd ed. (Boston: Houghton Mifflin, 1987), p. 227; Hill, *Society,* p. 434.

96. Fletcher and Stevenson, *Order,* p. 34.

97. Amussen, *Ordered Society,* p. 48.

98. Steinfeld, *Invention,* p. 58.

99. Wiesner, "Women's Response," p. 167; Wiesner, "Spinning," p. 5.

100. W. Monter, "Protestant Wives, Catholic Saints, and the Devil's Handmaid: Women in the Age of Reformations," in R. Bridenthal et al. (eds.), *Becoming Visible: Women in European History,* 2nd ed. (Boston: Houghton Mifflin, 1987), p. 209.

101. H. Rebel, *Peasant Classes: The Bureaucratization of Property and Family Relations under Early Habsburg Absolutism, 1511–1636* (Princeton: Princeton University Press, 1983), pp. 145, 148–49. One result of this policy was a high rate of illegitimacy, which in some regions exceeded 80 percent. These children, born to agricultural laborers or servants without their own homes, spent a considerable proportion of their early life being passed from one relative or acquittance to another, before becoming "unhoused" laborers and servants themselves. Richard L. Rudolph, "The European Family and Economy: Central Themes and Issues," *Journal of Family History* 17, no. 2 (1992): 119.

102. Sabean, *Property,* p. 429.

103. Roper, *Oedipus,* p. 46.

104. Roper, *Holy Household,* pp. 5, 165, 205. For another example, see Ogilvie, "Coming of Age."

105. Corrigan and Sayer, *Great Arch,* p. 40; Hill, *Society,* p. 448.

106. D. E. Underdown, "The Taming of the Scold: The Enforcement of Patriarchal Authority in Early Modern England," in Fletcher and Stevenson, *Order and Disorder.*

107. Quoted in Amussen, *Ordered Society,* p. 201.

108. Roper, *Oedipus,* p. 94.

109. Seccombe, *Millennium,* pp. 184, 191; P. Laslett, K. Oosterveen, and R. M. Smith (eds.), *Bastardy and Its Comparative History* (Cambridge, Mass.: Harvard University Press, 1980).

110. Seccombe, *Millennium,* pp. 162, 165, 166–67.

111. Ibid., pp. 194–95, 197. According to Tilly's "informed guesses," in contrast, while dispossession of the peasants was important, natural increase played the major role in the growth of the European proletariat from the 1500s, although it accelerated appreciably after 1800. Tilly, "Demographic Origins," p. 52.

112. Ellen Meiksins Wood, *The Pristine Culture of Capitalism* (London: Verso, 1991), p. 25.

113. Hill, *Society,* p. 459; Andrew Vincent, *Theories of the State* (Oxford: Blackwell, 1987), p. 47.

114. C. Jordan, *Renaissance Feminism,* p. 62.

115. Hsia, *Social Discipline,* p. 148. See also Hill, *Society,* p. 459.

116. Schochet, "Patriarchalism," p. 434–35. See also Steinfeld, *Invention,* pp. 57–59.

117. Hill, *Society,* p. 461.

118. Quoted in Amussen, *Ordered Society,* pp. 37–38.

119. Schochet notes that Filmer's *Patriarcha* gained the status of official doctrine on royal power with the trial for treason of one of Filmer's opponents. G. J. Schochet, *Patriarchalism in Political Thought* (Oxford: Blackwell, 1975), pp. 16, 80, 193, 276. See also Pateman, *Contract,* p. 24.

120. Stone notes that Filmer deliberately omitted the words "and Mother" from his rendition of the Fifth Commandment. Stone, *Family,* p. 152.

121. Quoted in T. A. Brady, "Luther and the State: The Reformer's Teaching in Its Social Setting," in J. D. Tracy (ed.), *Luther and the Modern State in Germany* (Ann Arbor, Mich.: Edwards Brothers, 1986), p. 36.

122. Quoted in Schochet, "Patriarchalism," p. 433 (original spelling retained).

123. Quoted in Hill, *Society,* p. 459.

124. Hanley, "Engendering," pp. 4–27. In a speech at the 1537 Lit de Justice assembly, avocat Jacques Cappel, for example, declared, "By its nature, the crown is inalienable. . . . The sacred patrimony of the prince cannot be divided among men. [Rather,] it is transmitted to the king alone, who is the husband and political spouse of the chose publique which brings to him at his sacre and coronation the said domain as the dowry of his crown. . . . Kings swear solemnly never to alienate that dowry." S. Hanley, *The Lit de Justice of the Kings of France* (Princeton: Princeton University Press, 1983), p. 91.

125. In *The Pristine Culture of Capitalism* (p. 25), Wood argues that it was in France and in the German states, which for a long time retained feudal parcelization of power, that theories of state sovereignty received their greatest elaboration. In England, in contrast, there was much less interest in theories of the state, precisely because the problems of fragmented sovereignty they were designed to solve had long since been brought under control.

126. A. J. La Volpa, "Review of Keith Tribe, *Governing Economy: The Reformation of German Economic Discourse,*" *Journal of Modern History* 62, no. 4 (1990): 879; Gerhard Oestreich, *Neostoicism and the Early Modern State* (Cambridge: Cambridge University Press, 1982), p. 196; Tomlins, *Law,* chap. 2. This notion of police

was fundamentally transformed with the triumph of capitalism and the ideology of the free market.

127. Foucault, "Governmentality," pp. 90, 92.

128. James Van Horn Melton, *Absolutism and the Eighteenth-Century Origins of Compulsory Schooling in Prussia and Austria* (Cambridge: Cambridge University Press, 1988), pp. 109–15.

129. K. Blaschke, "The Reformation and the Rise of the Territorial State," in Tracy, *Luther*. The expropriation of church lands was a complex process which predated the Reformation. A. G. Dickens and J. Tonkin, *The Reformation in Historical Thought* (Cambridge, Mass.: Harvard University Press, 1985), pp. 340–43.

130. Michael Mann, "European Development: Approaching a Historical Explanation," in Jean Baechler et al. (eds.), *Europe and the Rise of Capitalism* (Oxford: Basil Blackwell, 1989), p. 10.

131. Seccombe, *Millennium*, pp. 71–72. In the High Middle Ages, the church owned about a third of all the land in some regions of Europe. Dickens and Tonkin, *Reformation*, p. 341.

132. Robisheaux, *Rural Society*, pp. 2–3.

133. A. Vincent, *Theories*, p. 67.

134. G. Strauss, "Lutheranism and Literacy: A Reassessment," in Kaspar von Greyerz, *Religion and Society in Early Modern Europe* (London: Allen and Unwin, 1984), p. 201.

135. Strauss, *Luther's House*, p. 260.

136. J. Obelkevich (ed.), *Religion and the People, 800–1700* (Chapel Hill: University of North Carolina Press, 1979). In a recent overview of these debates, Scribner warns against interpreting the Reformation in terms of a "disenchantment of religion," and argues that for both Luther's and Calvin's generation, the reformed religion intensified perception of the world in terms of a cosmic struggle between the divine and the diabolical. "Protestant belief did not hold that the sacred did not intrude into the secular world, simply that it did not do so at human behest and could not automatically be commanded." Robert W. Scribner, "The Reformation, Popular Magic, and the 'Disenchantment of the World,'" *Journal of Interdisciplinary History* 23, no. 3 (1993): 484.

137. Geoffrey Parker, "Success and Failure during the First Century of the Reformation," *Past and Present* 136 (1992): 43–82.

138. Ian Hunter, "The Pastoral Bureaucracy: Towards a Less Principled Understanding of State Schooling," in D. Meredyth and D. Tyler (eds.), *Child and Citizen: Genealogies of Schooling and Subjectivity* (Brisbane: ICPS, Griffith University, 1993), p. 257. See also Ian Hunter, *Rethinking the School: Subjectivity, Bureaucracy, Criticism* (Sydney: Allen and Unwin, 1994).

139. See Hsia, *Social Discipline*. For an earlier and more extensive overview of historical writings on the Reformation, see Dickens and Tonkin, *Reformation*.

140. Foucault, "Governmentality," pp. 87–88, emphasis mine.

141. Quoted in C. Lis and H. Soly, "Policing the Early Modern Proletariat, 1450–

1850," in D. Levine (ed.), *Proletarianization and Family History* (New York: Academic Press, 1984), p. 172.

142. Oestreich, *Neostoicism*, p. 269.

143. Scribner, "Reformation," p. 486.

144. Oestreich, *Neostoicism*, p. 265 and passim. According to Oestreich, the horrors of the religious civil wars led a generation of humanist scholars such as Lipsius to seek the source of worldly peace and security outside of religion, which was so clearly used in sectional conflicts. Lipsius's wide knowledge of classical authors allowed him to formulate the solution in terms of a selective reading of their works. A strong and just ruler imbued with a sense of justice and self-discipline, manly courtiers actively working for the welfare of the community, and an efficient, well-disciplined army could succeed where church alliances failed, and bring peace to the community.

145. Roper, *Oedipus*, p. 40. See also Lis and Soly, "Policing."

146. H. Schilling, "The Reformation and the Rise of the Early Modern State," in Tracy, *Luther*, p. 25. See also Strauss, *Luther's House*, chap. 12.

147. Corrigan and Sayer, *Great Arch*, p. 50.

148. C. Tilly, *Coercion*, p. 107; Bengt Sandin, "Education, Popular Culture and the Surveillance of the Population in Stockholm between 1600 and the 1840s," *Continuity and Change* 3, no. 3 (1988): 357–90.

149. Hsia, *Social Discipline*, pp. 2–3; Schilling, *Reformation*; Blaschke, "Reformation."

150. Oestreich, *Neostoicism*.

2. Patriarchalism Challenged

1. The defenders of women routinely drew attention to some aspects of women's power, and then criticized their lack of formal, political authority to publicly use this power. C. Jordan, *Renaissance Feminism*. See also J. Kelly, "Early Feminist Theory and the Querelle des femmes, 1400–1789," in *Women, History and Theory* (Chicago: University of Chicago Press, 1984).

2. Hill, *Society*, p. 465.

3. Robisheaux, *Rural Society*, p. 104. In Hohenloe, the visitation of 1556 revealed that about half the pastors were completely incompetent in doctrinal matters; one was unable to recite the Lord's Prayer and did not know where it was written; elsewhere, boys who had been attending catechism classes for many years did not realize that they were Christians. Robisheaux, "Peasants and Pastors," p. 286; Susan C. Karant-Nunn, "The Reality of Early Lutheran Education: The Electoral District of Saxony—A Case Study," in *Responsibility for the World: Luther's Intentions and Their Effects, Lutherjahrbuch* (Göttingen: Vandenhoeck and Ruprecht, 1990), p. 143.

4. Strauss, *Luther's House*; Gerald Strauss, "The Social Function of Schools in the Lutheran Reformation in Germany," *History of Education Quarterly* 28, no. 2 (1988): 191–206.

5. Strauss, *Luther's House,* p. 13; Wiesner, *Women and Gender,* p. 121.

6. Although there is wide agreement that girls received less schooling and were generally excluded from the more advanced and prestigious Latin schools, some historians offer a more optimistic reading of their opportunities than others. Green, for example, argues that Luther and his followers took an unusually positive interest in the education of women and girls, and that this was translated into actual schools and regulations; Karant-Nunn claims that, in Saxony, at least, the Reformation disrupted existing provision of girls' schooling and restricted the curriculum available to them. Lowell Green, "The Education of Women in the Reformation," *History of Education Quarterly* 19, no. 1 (1979): 129–43; Karant-Nunn, "Reality."

7. Quoted in Strauss, "Social Function," p. 192.

8. Strauss, *Luther's House,* pp. 6–7, 11; Strauss, "Social Function," p. 193.

9. Quoted in Strauss, *Luther's House,* p. 9.

10. Quoted in Strauss, "Lutheranism," p. 113. Although Luther originally translated the Bible into vernacular German, he now believed that it should be read in Greek, Latin, or Hebrew so that it could be understood properly.

11. Quoted in Richard Gawthrop and Gerald Strauss, "Protestantism and Literacy in Early Modern Germany," *Past and Present* 104 (1984): 35.

12. Strauss, *Luther's House,* p. 123.

13. Ibid., pp. 119, 130.

14. Ibid., pp. 258–59, 261.

15. In Catholic Tyrol in the 1570s, the government of Archduke Ferdinand II compelled parishioners to obtain "confession receipts" from their priests. The names of recipients were transmitted to the local district chief, who kept a list of them and sent a copy of it to the central administration in Innsbruck, where officials stood ready to go after slackers and resisters. Strauss, "Social Function," pp. 202–203. The archbishop of Milan organized his visitations like a military operation, with his staff preparing detailed maps and plans of every parish to be inspected. Parker, "Success and Failure," p. 71.

16. Strauss, *Luther's House,* pp. 262, 303–304; Strauss, "Social Function," p. 195.

17. It was well into the nineteenth century, however, before the world of ordinary people became "disenchanted." Scribner, "Reformation."

18. Parker, "Success and Failure," pp. 45–46, 51.

19. Quoted in Strauss, "Social Function," pp. 208–209.

20. Melton, *Absolutism,* p. xiii.

21. Strauss, *Luther's House,* pp. 19, 23; Karant-Nunn, "Reality," pp. 133–34, 136.

22. *The First Book of Discipline* of the Laudian Church, for example, stated, "Every master of a household must be commanded either to instruct, or cause to be instructed, his children, servants and family in the principles of the Christian religion," without the knowledge of which none would be admitted to communion. Heads of households who failed to carry out this duty were to incur ecclesiastical and civil penalties. Hill, *Society,* p. 448, chap. 12.

23. Hill, *Society,* pp. 454–55, 466. In turn, the multiplicity of denominations could have some quite serious anti-patriarchal implications, as when masters

belonged to a different faith from that of their sons or daughters, or wanted pious servants to break the Sabbath. Puritans took these problems with them when they departed for the New World in 1630.

24. Egil Johansson, "Literacy Campaigns in Sweden," in R. J. Arnove and H. Graff (eds.), *National Literacy Campaigns: Historical and Comparative Perspectives* (New York: Plenum Press, 1987), pp. 65–98, and Egil Johansson, "The History of Literacy in Sweden," in H. J. Graff (ed.), *Literacy and Social Development in the West* (Cambridge: Cambridge University Press, 1981), pp. 151–82. See also R. A. Houston, *Literacy in Early Modern Europe: Culture and Education, 1500–1800* (London: Longman, 1988), p. 199.

25. On a more technical level, the case demonstrates the problem of tying together the abilities to read and to write. In Sweden, Denmark, Norway, Finland, and Iceland, a nearly universal ability to *read* was achieved by the eighteenth century. This achievement was remarkable for its time, but remained invisible to many scholars who took the widespread inability to *sign* as a mark of total illiteracy.

26. Sandin, "Education," pp. 357–90.

27. Johansson, "Literacy Campaigns," p. 81.

28. Sandin, "Education," p. 359.

29. Parker, *Military Revolution,* pp. 53–54.

30. Sandin, "Education," pp. 359–62.

31. Perry Anderson notes that in the mid-sixteenth century, the existence of a free peasantry allowed the Swedish king, alone in Renaissance Europe, to raise a conscript army, because the legal and material conditions of free peasants, unlike those of the serfs, were compatible with loyalty in the field. P. Anderson, *Lineages,* p. 182, chap. 7.

32. Sandin, "Education," p. 364.

33. Strauss, *Luther's House,* pp. 118–19.

34. Sabean, *Property,* p. 34.

35. Rebel, *Peasant Classes,* pp. 195ff.

36. Robisheaux, *Rural Society,* pp. 121, 225.

37. Hsia, *Social Discipline,* p. 6.

38. Tilly, *Coercion,* pp. 61, 135–36.

39. Hobsbawm, *Age of Revolution,* pp. 21–22.

40. Foucault, "Governmentality," pp. 97, 99.

41. E. M. Wood, *Pristine Culture,* p. 46. Similarly, in Germany, "just as each village had a slightly different system of weights and measures, a slightly different law prevailed in each community." Ogilvie, "Coming of Age," p. 287.

42. Oestreich, *Neostoicism,* pp. 263–64. Oestreich notes that it was only in the age of enlightened despotism that this sphere was invaded by the central government.

43. G. S. Wood, *Radicalism,* pp. 62, 71–72, 82–85, 89.

44. Robisheaux, *Rural Society,* pp. 3–4.

45. E. P. Thompson, "Eighteenth-Century English Society: Class Struggle without Class?" *Social History* 3, no. 2 (1978): 163.

46. Lyndal Roper, "'The Common Man,' 'the Common Good,' 'Common Women':

Gender and Meaning in the German Reformation Commune," *Social History* 12, no. 1 (1987): 20.

47. All the authors quoted in this section concentrate on secular associations. Religious fraternities need to be investigated as well.

48. Michael Mitterauer, *A History of Youth* (Oxford: Blackwell, 1993), chap. 4.

49. John R. Gillis, *Youth and History: Transition and Change in European Age Relations, 1770 to the Present* (New York: Academic Press, 1981), pp. 22–33, 83, 86; my emphasis.

50. Mary Ann Clawson, "Early Modern Fraternalism and the Patriarchal Family," *Feminist Studies* 6, no. 2 (1980): 371.

51. Mary Ann Clawson, *Constructing Brotherhood: Class, Gender and Fraternalism* (Princeton: Princeton University Press, 1989), p. 47.

52. Merry E. Wiesner, "Guilds, Male Bonding and Women's Work in Early Modern Germany," *Gender and History* 1, no. 2 (1989): 125–37; Merry E. Wiesner, "Wandervogels and Women: Journeymen's Conceptions of Masculinity in Early Modern Germany," *Journal of Social History* 24, no. 4 (1991): 767–82. In addition, dishonor attached to prostitutes, gypsies, people of servile origin, or those who had to do with the theater, and those who performed obviously distasteful work, such as the hangman or the skinner.

53. Jean E. Quataert, "The Shaping of Women's Work in Manufacturing: Guilds, Households, and the State in Central Europe, 1648–1870," *American Historical Review* 90, no. 5 (1985): 1122–48.

54. Roper, *Oedipus*, p. 46.

55. Wiesner, "Wandervogels," p. 776. Wiesner notes that there are no reliable statistics which would indicate whether the hostility to marriage on the part of the journeymen actually led to life-long celibacy. The masters, who might have been paragons of civic decorum and disciplined moderation in the town hall, were frequently as rowdy and disorderly as the young men; what was more, the town frequently depended on the brute fighting force of all its male citizens for its sheer survival. Roper, *Oedipus*, chap. 5.

56. Tomlins, *Law*, pp. 114–24.

57. Ibid., p. 118.

58. See Gillis, *Youth*, pp. 77–80; G. S. Wood, *Radicalism*, pp. 223–24; Clawson, *Constructing Brotherhood*.

59. This view is associated particularly with Augustin Cochin and François Furet. J. A. Goldstone, "Reinterpreting the French Revolution," *Theory and Society* 13 (1984): 701–702.

60. Sarah Maza, "Politics, Culture and the Origins of the French Revolution," *Journal of Modern History* 61, no. 4 (1989): 715; Jürgen Habermas, "The Public Sphere," *New German Critique* 3 (1974), and *The Structural Transformation of the Public Sphere* (Cambridge: Polity Press, 1989). See also the comprehensive commentaries on these works in C. Calhoun (ed.), *Habermas and the Public Sphere* (Cambridge, Mass.: MIT Press, 1992).

61. Guilds typically held a number of designated positions on city councils.

Females could not be councilors, and so the few women's guilds were denied direct political representation.

62. Quoted in Wiesner, "Guilds," p. 134.

63. Shanley argues that in their debates with social contract theorists, royalists introduced and at first profited from an analogy between the marriage contract and the initial contract between a sovereign and his people: both were in essence hierarchical and irrevocable. Mary Lyndon Shanley, "Marriage Contract and Social Contract in Seventeenth-Century English Political Thought," *Western Political Quarterly* 32 (1979): 79–91.

64. Jay Fliegelman, *Prodigals and Pilgrims: The American Revolution against Patriarchal Authority, 1750–1800* (New York: Cambridge University Press, 1982); G. S. Wood, *Radicalism,* pp. 147–65. While many educational practices helped build state capacities, educational theorizing at times helped build state theory. Lynn Hunt similarly argues that during the French Revolution, new social structures were frequently imagined and thought through in terms of familial relations.

65. See, for example, Pateman, *Contract;* Mary Lyndon Shanley and Carole Pateman (eds.), *Feminist Interpretations and Political Theory* (University Park: Pennsylvania State University Press, 1991); C. Pateman, "The Fraternal Social Contract: Some Observations on Patriarchal Civil Society," in J. Keane (ed.), *Civil Society and the State: New European Perspectives* (London: Verso, 1988). While later commentators tended to develop a remarkable blindness to the patriarchal features of political theory, Filmer and his contemporaries were not slow to draw attention to what they saw as a fundamental flaw in the expositions of social contract.

66. John Locke, *Some Thoughts Concerning Education,* ed. J. W. and J. S. Yolton (Oxford: Clarendon Press, 1989), p. 103.

67. John Locke, *Second Treatise on Civil Government: An Essay Concerning the True Original Extent and End of Civil Government* [1690], in *Social Contract: Essays by Locke, Hume and Rousseau* (London: Oxford University Press, 1966), para. 82, p. 68.

68. Ibid.

69. For a pioneering essay on this topic, see Elizabeth Fox-Genovese, "Property and Patriarchy in Classical Political Theory," *Radical History Review* 2–3 (1977): 36–59. See also Shanley, "Marriage Contract."

70. Locke, *Second Treatise,* para. 87, p. 71.

71. Fliegelman, *Prodigals,* p. 30.

72. Jean Jacques Rousseau, *The Social Contract* [1762], in *Social Contract: Essays by Locke, Hume and Rousseau* (London: Oxford University Press, 1966), p. 248.

73. Rousseau adds a few pages later "you will never bring young lads to do this; their feelings rise in revolt against injustice; nature has not fitted them to put up with it." Jean Jacques Rousseau, *Emile* [1762] (London: Everyman's Library, Dent, 1963), pp. 332–33, 359.

74. Ibid., p. 328.

75. A major weakness of Hunter's argument in *Rethinking the School* is his failure to differentiate between these two forms of self-control.

76. Pateman, *Contract,* chap. 5.

77. C. B. Macpherson, *The Political Theory of Possessive Individualism: Hobbes to Locke* (London: Oxford University Press, 1962), p. 124.

78. Hill, *Society,* p. 478.

79. Locke, *Second Treatise,* pp. 69–70. The same principles were expressed in Blackstone's famous eighteenth-century *Commentaries,* which grouped the duties and obligations between master and servant with those between husband and wife, parent and child, and guardian and ward, to make up what he referred to as the private economical relations of persons.

80. Macpherson, *Political Theory,* pp. 221–22.

81. Quoted in Pateman, *Contract,* p. 169.

82. Adam Smith, quoted in J. Rendall, "Virtue and Commerce," in E. Kennedy and S. Mendus (eds.), *Women in Western Political Philosophy: Kant to Nietzsche* (Brighton, Sussex: Wheatsheaf Books, 1987), pp. 59–60.

83. Gillis, *For Better,* p. 13; Kriedte, *Peasants,* p. 68.

84. Gillis, *For Better,* pp. 13, 98–99.

85. Kriedte, *Peasants,* pp. 159–60.

86. P. Kriedte, "The Origins, the Agrarian Context, and the Conditions in the World Market," in Kriedte et al., *Industrialization before Industrialization: Rural Industry in the Genesis of Capitalism* (Cambridge: Cambridge University Press, 1981), p. 23.

87. Kriedte, *Peasants,* p. 133. The term "proto-industrialization" was first used by Franklin Mendels in "Proto-Industrialisation: The First Phase of Industrialisation," *Journal of Economic History* 32, no. 1 (1972): 241–61.

88. P. Kriedte, H. Medick, and J. Schlumbohm, "Proto-Industrialisation Revisited: Demography, Social Structure, and Modern Domestic Industry," *Continuity and Change* 8, no. 2 (1993): 223–25; S. C. Ogilvie, "Proto-Industrialization in Europe," *Continuity and Change* 8, no. 2 (1993): 159–79. See also other articles in this issue of the journal. An earlier useful summary of these debates is provided in Pollard, *Peaceful Conquest,* pp. 69ff. For a systematic overview of proto-industrial production in the United States, see Steven Hahn and Jonathan Prude (eds.), *The Countryside in the Age of Capitalist Transformation: Essays in the History of Rural America* (Chapel Hill: University of North Carolina Press, 1985). Kriedte et al., "Proto-Industrialisation Revisited," note that although the household was where production took place, it was not always organized as a production unit with a division of labor between family members. At the same time, the availability of waged work for young boarders meant that marriage and household formation was not always a precondition for earning an independent income.

89. In England and western Europe, where feudal restrictions were weaker, proximity of markets, transport routes, and raw materials played a larger part in the emergence of proto-industrial regions.

90. D. Levine, *Reproducing Families: The Political Economy of English Population History* (Cambridge: Cambridge University Press, 1987), p. 124.

91. Gillis, *For Better,* pp. 116–17.

92. Kriedte, *Peasants,* p. 65.

93. H. Medick, "The Proto-Industrial Family Economy," in Kriedte et al., *Industrialization before Industrialization,* p. 56.

94. Quoted in ibid., p. 57.

95. Gillis, *For Better,* chap. 4. In some regions, however, many young people worked as lodgers in the households of others, and families were less dependent on the labor of their own children. Kriedte et al., "Proto-Industrialisation Revisited."

96. H. Cunningham, "The Employment and Unemployment of Children in England c. 1680–1851," *Past and Present* 126 (1990).

97. Quoted in Gillis, *For Better,* p. 119.

98. Quoted in Medick, "Proto-Industrial Family Economy," p. 58.

99. Seccombe, *Millennium,* p. 207. According to Minge-Kalman, for example, children worked from the age of four in the textile cottage industries. Wanda Minge-Kalman, "The Industrial Revolution and the European Family: The Institutionalization of 'Childhood' as a Market for Family Labor," *Comparative Studies in Society and History* 20, no. 3 (1978): 454–68.

100. The increased childhood mortality was partly linked to the increased potential for self-exploitation among proto-industrialists compared to guild-controlled crafts and also most peasants. The merchant could deduct from the price of labor power that which the family earned from their little garden or field. The workers were compelled to accept any piece wages offered to them; otherwise they would get nothing at all, and they could not live from the products of their agriculture alone. In addition, they could not go and look for employment elsewhere because their cottage and little piece of land chained them to the spot. Medick, "Proto-Industrial Family Economy," pp. 43, 51, 88.

101. Maxine Berg, "What Difference Did Women's Work Make to the Industrial Revolution?" *History Workshop Journal* 35 (1993): 31, 39.

102. J. H. Quataert, "Teamwork in Saxon Homeweaving Families in the Nineteenth Century," in R. B. Joeres and M. J. Maynes (eds.), *German Women in the Eighteenth and Nineteenth Centuries* (Bloomington: Indiana University Press, 1986), p. 15.

103. Quoted in Medick, "Proto-Industrial Family Economy," p. 62. See also Seccombe, *Millennium,* pp. 207–208.

104. Quoted in Medick, "Proto-Industrial Family Economy," p. 63. See also Underdown, "Taming."

105. Gillis, *For Better,* p. 118.

106. E. P. Thompson, "Rough Music: *Le charivari anglais,*" *Annales, ESC* 27, no. 2 (1972): 285–312.

107. Medick, "Proto-Industrial Family Economy," p. 77. Medick argued that it was increasing fertility (matched by relatively high rates of mortality) that was responsible for the population growth, rather than a fall in mortality. This was a comparatively recent view among historians, who for a long time attributed the increase in European population to falling mortality rates as a result of better

nutrition, sanitation, and medical advances, and believed that this fall occurred against fertility rates which were relatively stable until the demographic transition in the late nineteenth century.

108. Kriedte, *Peasants,* p. 104.

109. Seccombe, *Millennium,* pp. 205, 212–25. See also the debate in *Continuity and Change* 8, no. 2 (1993).

110. Maynes and Taylor, "Germany," pp. 305–31; Kriedte et al., "Proto-Industrialisation Revisited," pp. 223, 225.

3. Revolutions

1. For an overview and critique of these arguments, see M. Berg and P. Hudson, "Rehabilitating the Industrial Revolution," *Economic History Review* 45, no. 1 (1992): 45–50; D. Cannadine, "The Past and the Present in the English Industrial Revolution, 1880–1980," *Past and Present* 103 (1984): 149–58.

2. See, for example, Maza, "Politics," pp. 704–23; Goldstone, "Reinterpreting," pp. 697–713; Outram, "Revolution"; "The Origins of the French Revolution: A Debate," *French Historical Studies* 61, no. 4 (1990).

3. Dorinda Outram, *The Body and the French Revolution: Sex, Class and Political Culture* (New Haven: Yale University Press, 1989), p. 971.

4. G. S. Wood, *Radicalism,* p. 5.

5. For an overview of women's presence in the different democratic revolutions, see H. B. Applewhite and D. G. Levy (eds.), *Women and Politics in the Age of the Democratic Revolution* (Ann Arbor: University of Michigan Press, 1990).

6. Pollard, *Peaceful Conquest,* pp. 12, 26.

7. S. Pollard, *European Economic Integration, 1815–1970* (London: Thames and Hudson, 1974), p. 14.

8. Kriedte, *Peasants,* p. 152.

9. Berg, "What Difference," pp. 27, 29.

10. Pollard, *Peaceful Conquest,* pp. 39–40; Kriedte, *Peasants,* p. 158; Hobsbawm, *Age of Revolution,* p. 214.

11. Pollard, *Peaceful Conquest,* p. 20.

12. For one interesting contribution to the debate, see J. Baechler et al. (eds.), *Europe and the Rise of Capitalism* (Oxford: Basil Blackwell, 1988).

13. E. Mandel, *Marxist Economic Theory* (London: Merlin Press, 1968), pp. 443–44.

14. Seccombe, *Millennium,* pp. 239–40.

15. Hobsbawm, *Age of Revolution,* p. 365.

16. Pollard, *Peaceful Conquest,* pp. 39–40, 109.

17. On the other hand, some of the latecomers, such as the Scandinavian countries, managed to avoid the worst of the pollution, ecological devastation, and child labor of the first stage of industrialization. Pollard, *Peaceful Conquest,* pp. v, 86.

18. Pollard, *Integration,* pp. 15–17, 23.

19. Hobsbawm, *Age of Revolution*, p. 51.

20. Pollard, *Peaceful Conquest*, p. 24.

21. R. Samuel, "Workshop of the World: Steam Power and Hand Technology in Mid-Victorian Britain," *History Workshop* 3 (1977): 6–72; Wally Seccombe, *Weathering the Storm: Working-Class Families from the Industrial Revolution to the Fertility Decline* (London: Verso, 1993), p. 24; Levine, "Industrialization," p. 177. See also Michelle Perrot, "On the Formation of the French Working Class," in I. Katznelson and A. R. Zolberg (eds.), *Working-Class Formation: Nineteenth-Century Patterns in Western Europe and the United States* (Princeton: Princeton University Press, 1986).

22. Samuel, "Workshop"; W. Lazonick, "Industrial Relations and Technical Change: The Case of the Self-Acting Mule," *Cambridge Journal of Economics* 3, no. 3 (1979): 231–62.

23. Kriedte, *Peasants*, p. 144.

24. Samuel, "Workshop."

25. Pollard, *Peaceful Conquest*, p. 122.

26. A. J. Scott and M. Storper (eds.), *Production, Work, Territory: The Geographical Anatomy of Industrial Capitalism* (Boston: Unwin Hyman, 1986), p. 309.

27. Quoted in Kriedte, *Peasants*, p. 112; Hobsbawm, *Age of Revolution*, p. 362.

28. E. Hobsbawm, *The Age of Capital: 1848–1875* (London: Sphere Books, 1985), p. 27. Hobsbawm, *Age of Revolution*, p. 193.

29. Wally Seccombe, "Patriarchy Stabilised: The Construction of the Male Breadwinner Wage Norm in Nineteenth-Century Britain," *Social History* 11, no. 1 (1986): 66.

30. Lazonick, "Industrial Relations," p. 249; Seccombe, *Weathering*, p. 120.

31. Quoted in Eric Hopkins, *Childhood Transformed: Working-Class Children in Nineteenth Century England* (Manchester: Manchester University Press, 1994), p. 64.

32. J. Humphries, "'The Most Free from Objection . . . ': The Sexual Division of Labour and Women's Work in Nineteenth-Century England," *Journal of Economic History* 47, no. 4 (1987): 938, 947.

33. It is important to keep in mind, however, that in the larger cities the typical working-class household residing in one rented room with a minimum of belongings called for different forms of ingenuity, local knowledge, and housework skills than would have been practiced in households with land or servants.

34. Quoted in Seccombe, *Weathering*, p. 74.

35. In many regions, early factories were associated with prisons, workhouses, and orphanages. Seccombe, *Weathering*, p. 28; Hobsbawm, *Age of Revolution*, p. 253; Judy Lown, *Women and Industrialization: Gender and Work in Nineteenth-Century England* (Cambridge: Polity Press, 1990).

36. Louise A. Tilly and Joan W. Scott, *Women, Work and Family* (New York: Holt, Rinehart and Winston, 1979), p. 76. Ure evidently tended to employ similar reasoning as promoters of computers do today, and did not take into account machine breakdowns and repairs, problems caused by bad materials, labor disputation, and

other factors that reduced the theoretical benefits of new technology. See Lazonick, "Industrial Relations."

37. Frederick Engels, *The Condition of the Working Class in England* (London: Panther Books, 1969), pp. 173–75. To his credit, Engels added that "so total a reversal of the position of the sexes can have come to pass only because the sexes have been placed in a false position from the beginning. If the reign of the wife over the husband, as inevitably brought about by the factory system, is inhuman, the pristine rule of the husband over the wife must have been inhuman too." See also Sonya O. Rose, *Limited Livelihoods: Gender and Class in Nineteenth-Century England* (Berkeley: University of California Press, 1992), p. 127.

38. Barbara Taylor, *Eve and the New Jerusalem: Socialism and Feminism in the Nineteenth Century* (London: Virago Press, 1983), p. 264; Seccombe, *Weathering*, pp. 54–60.

39. Quoted in I. Pinchbeck, *Women Workers and the Industrial Revolution, 1750–1850* [1930] (London: Virago, 1981), p. 197.

40. Engels, *Condition*, p. 171.

41. Jutta Schwarzkopf, *Women in the Chartist Movement* (London: Macmillan, 1991), chap. 4.

42. Pinchbeck, *Women Workers*, p. 313.

43. Seccombe, *Weathering*, pp. 55–56.

44. Gillis, *For Better*, p. 119.

45. Quoted in Seccombe, *Weathering*, pp. 120–21.

46. As in all cases concerning social panics, historians are confronted with a series of daunting questions. It would be difficult to find a period in history when *nobody* was worried about insubordinate youth and women. When do worries turn into a panic? To what extent does the panic reflect "reality"? Did the actual practices of those being observed change, or was the change confined to the perceptions of outsiders? Does a social panic have to have a basis in "fact" before it can serve as a basis for legislative and other interventions?

47. Joan W. Scott, "The Woman Worker," in G. Fraise and M. Perrot (eds.), *A History of Women in the West*, vol. 4: *Emerging Feminism from Revolution to World War* (Cambridge, Mass.: Belknap Press, 1993), p. 404.

48. See, for example, Michelle Perrot, "The Three Ages of Industrial Discipline in Nineteenth-Century France," in John M. Merriman, *Consciousness and Class Experience in Nineteenth-Century Europe* (New York: Holmes and Meir, 1979), pp. 153–55.

49. See, for example, Lazonick, "Industrial Relations," p. 236; W. Lazonick, "The Subjection of Labor to Capital: The Rise of the Capitalist System," *Review of Radical Political Economics* 10, no. 1 (1978): 9; Judy Lown, "Not So Much a Factory, More a Form of Patriarchy: Gender and Class during Industrialisation," in E. Gamarnikov et al. (eds.), *Gender, Class and Work* (London: Heineman, 1983).

50. C. Hall, "The Home Turned Upside Down? The Working-Class Family in Cotton Textiles, 1780–1850," in E. Whitelegg et al. (eds.), *The Changing Experi-*

ence of Women (Oxford: Martin Robertson, 1982), p. 25. See also Seccombe, *Weathering*, pp. 60, 114; and Pinchbeck, *Women Workers*, pp. 197–99.

51. See Seccombe, *Weathering*, pp. 57–59, 62–63.

52. For the incidence of family violence in Britain, see B. Taylor, *Eve*, p. 111; N. Tomes, "'A Torrent of Abuse': Crimes of Violence between Working-Class Men and Women in London," *Journal of Social History* 11, no. 3 (1978): 328–45; E. Ross, "'Fierce Questions and Taunts': Married Life in Working-Class London, 1870–1914," *Feminist Studies* 8, no. 3 (1982): 575–602. James Hammerton, *Cruelty and Companionship: Conflict in Nineteenth-Century Married Life* (London: Routledge, 1992). For the United States, see Gordon, *Heroes*. But how does one measure the incidence of family violence? Even today, such an enterprise is fraught with difficulties. In past times, such problems are compounded. As with social panics, any arguments regarding levels of family violence will have to deal with the question of simultaneously changing practices and perceptions of what was normal and acceptable to both participants and observers, as well as ecological variables, such as residential segregation, which made the classes more or less familiar and visible to each other.

53. Levine, *Reproducing*, p. 152.

54. E. P. Thompson, *The Making of the English Working Class* (Harmondsworth: Penguin, 1968), pp. 370, 384.

55. Seccombe, *Weathering*, pp. 71–78, 236, note 164. See also R. Floud, A. Gregory, and K. Wachter, *Height, Health and History: Nutritional Status in the United Kingdom, 1750–1980* (Cambridge: Cambridge University Press, 1989); W. Coleman, *Death Is a Social Disease: Public Health and Political Economy in Early Industrial France* (Madison: University of Wisconsin Press, 1982).

56. Seccombe, *Millennium*, p. 228. See also Laslett et al., *Bastardy*.

57. B. Taylor, *Eve*, pp. 195–96; Donzelot, *Policing*, p. 34; J. R. Gillis, "Peasant, Plebeian and Proletarian Marriage in Britain, 1600–1900," in Levine, *Proletarianization and Family History*, p. 144.

58. A typical reason was given by a woman who "didn't choose to be knocked about, nor to see her children treated bad, neither!" Quoted in I. Minor, "Working-Class Women and Matrimonial Law Reform, 1890–1914," in D. E. Martin and D. Rubinstein (eds.), *Ideology and the Labour Movement* (London: Croom Helm, 1979), p. 114; Donzelot, *Policing*, p. 35.

59. Seccombe, *Weathering*, p. 54.

60. Gillis, "Peasant, Plebeian," pp. 156, 153.

61. Seccombe, *Weathering*, p. 59.

62. Edward Countryman, *The American Revolution* (London: Penguin, 1991), pp. 55–56.

63. G. S. Wood, *Radicalism*.

64. Ibid., pp. 96, 176.

65. Quoted in Countryman, *American Revolution*, p. 138.

66. A. F. Young, "The Women of Boston: 'Persons of Consequence' in the Making

of the American Revolution," in H. B. Applewhite and D. G. Levy (eds.), *Women and Politics in the Age of the Democratic Revolution* (Ann Arbor: University of Michigan Press, 1990), pp. 181–226.

67. Countryman, *American Revolution,* pp. 200–201.

68. S. Coontz, *The Social Origins of Private Life: A History of American Families, 1600–1900* (London: Verso, 1988), pp. 128–29, 137, 146. See also Joan R. Gundersen, "Independence, Citizenship, and the American Revolution," *Signs* 13, no. 1 (1987): 37–58.

69. Countryman, *American Revolution,* pp. 189, 150, 152–53.

70. Ibid., pp. 191–213.

71. Karen Orren, *Belated Feudalism: Labor, the Law, and Liberal Development in the United States* (Cambridge: Cambridge University Press, 1991).

72. Coontz, *Social Origins,* p. 151.

73. G. S. Wood, *Radicalism,* p. 294.

74. Coontz, *Social Origins,* pp. 133, 138.

75. See, for example, D. Hay, "Property, Authority and the Criminal Law," in D. Hay et. al., *Albion's Fatal Tree: Crime and Society in Eighteenth-Century England* (London: Allen Lane, 1975), pp. 17–63.

76. Tomlins, *Law,* pp. 223–31, 236–38; Steinfeld, *Invention,* pp. 115–16.

77. Douglas Hay quoted in Steinfeld, *Invention,* pp. 230, 243.

78. Until legal changes in 1880, the common-law rule was that the master was not liable for injuries occurring to his servant in the ordinary course of his employment. Simpson, *Treatise,* p. 97. See also Tomlins, *Law,* chap. 10.

79. Orren, *Belated Feudalism,* pp. 8, 29, 60.

80. Tomlins, *Law,* pp. 261, 269, 291.

81. Quoted in Steinfeld, *Invention,* pp. 127–28. See also David R. Roediger, *The Wages of Whiteness: Race and the Making of the American Working Class* (London: Verso, 1991).

82. Ruth H. Bloch, "The Gendered Meaning of Virtue in Revolutionary America," *Signs* 13, no. 1 (1987): 56.

83. Quoted in G. S. Wood, *Radicalism,* p. 204.

84. L. K. Kerber, "'I Have Don . . . Much to Carrey on the Warr': Women and the Shaping of Republican Ideology after the American Revolution," in Applewhite and Levy, *Women and Politics,* pp. 232, 235, 250–51.

85. G. S. Wood, *Radicalism,* pp. 216, 218.

86. Quoted in ibid., p. 296. In their own homes, of course, women were supposed to remain altruistic.

87. Coontz, *Social Origins,* p. 131. Tocqueville commented that what held this diverse, restless, rootless people together was interest: "That is the secret. The private interest that breaks through at each moment, the interest that, moreover, appears openly and even proclaims itself as a social theory." Quoted in G. S. Wood, *Radicalism,* pp. 336, 359.

88. Bloch, "Gendered Meaning," pp. 52, 56.

89. G. S. Wood, *Radicalism*, p. 357.

90. According to Wood, "In the three or four decades following the Revolution, newly independent men and women came together to form hundreds and thousands of new voluntary associations expressing a wide array of benevolent goals . . . indeed societies for just about anything and everything that was good and humanitarian." Ibid., p. 328.

91. Mary P. Ryan, *Cradle of the Middle Class: The Family in Oneida County, New York, 1790–1865* (Cambridge: Cambridge University Press, 1981), pp. 236–38.

92. David Philips, "Good Men to Associate and Bad Men to Conspire: Associations for the Prosecution of Felons in England, 1760–1860," in D. Day and F. Snyder, *Policing and Prosecution in Britain, 1750–1850* (Oxford: Clarendon Press, 1989). It is important to note that while the phrase captures my meaning, it is quoted out of context. Philips writes about England, and the associations were not directly concerned with unions.

93. Tomlins, *Law*, pp. 125, passim. Woodiwiss notes that in the 1820s and 1830s, judges held that the rights granted to individuals under the Constitution were not transferable to collectivities, except where the ends of the collectivity were "virtuous." Anthony Woodiwiss, *Rights v. Conspiracy: A Sociological Essay on the History of Labour Law in the United States* (New York: Berg, 1990), p. 23.

94. By 1842, the courts conceded the right of trade unions to exist: working people were no longer held to commit a crime by the simple fact of forming an association for mutual protection. An extremely wide interpretation of the enticement provisions of master-and-servant laws, however, still secured prosecutions against an extremely wide range of union actions. Tomlins, *Law*, chap. 6, p. 125.

95. Orren, *Belated Feudalism*, p. 3. In Britain, the Employer and Workman Act replaced many provisions of the master-and-servant laws in 1875.

96. Hobsbawm, *Age of Revolution*, pp. 73–75.

97. Lynn Hunt, *The Family Romance of the French Revolution* (Berkeley: University of California Press, 1992), pp. 4–5, 203–204.

98. Ibid., p. 40. "After having made man free and happy in public life, it remains for us to assure his liberty and his happiness in private life. You know that under the Old Regime the tyranny of parents was often as terrible as the despotism of ministers; often the prisons of the state became family prisons. It is suitable therefore to draw up, after the declaration of rights of man and citizen, a declaration, so to speak, of the rights of spouses, of fathers, of sons, of parents, and so on." Deputy Gossin, speaking on 5 August 1790, quoted in ibid., p. 17. See also Joan Wallach Scott, "French Feminists and the Rights of 'Man': Olympe de Gouge's Declarations," *History Workshop* 28 (1989): 2.

99. Outram notes that it has long been a commonplace of French history that counterrevolution was a movement in which women played an important and enduring role, far more than they did in the revolution itself. Women's devotion to the throne and the altar during the revolution set the stage for the decisive separation between men's and women's politics that occurred in the course of the

following century. This led to the formation of radically different attitudes between the sexes on such crucial issues as the fate of the Church and of republicanism, with men tending to reject the programs and the language of the Church and most women tending to reject the programs and language of secular republicanism. Dorinda Outram, "Le langage mâle de la vertu: Women and the Discourse of the French Revolution," in P. Burke and R. Porter, *The Social History of Language* (Cambridge: Cambridge University Press, 1987), pp. 129, 133.

100. Quoted in Scott, "French Feminists," p. 6.

101. Hunt, *Family Romance*, p. 118.

102. Karen Offen, "The New Sexual Politics of French Revolutionary Historiography," *French Historical Studies* 16, no. 4 (1990): 920.

103. Quoted in Hunt, *Family Romance*, p. 43.

104. Several writers have noted the importance of political pornography in this context. Lynn Hunt, for example, argues that "democracy was established against monarchy through pornographic attacks on the feminization of both the aristocracy and monarchy. . . . The fraternal bonds of democracy were established—in pornography, at least, and perhaps more broadly—through the circulation of images of women's bodies, especially through print media and the effect of visualization through pornographic writing." Lynn Hunt, "Pornography and the French Revolution," in Lynn Hunt (ed.), *The Invention of Pornography: Obscenity and the Origins of Modernity, 1500–1800* (New York: Zone Books, 1993).

105. Outram, "Le langage mâle," pp. 127–29. By the 1790s, the male revolutionary leadership in America changed its image from that of political youths to that of a beneficent political father. In revolutionary France, in contrast, the sacred body of the king would initially be replaced by collective representations of revolutionary fraternity. Hunt, *Family Romance*, p. 72.

106. As Hunt notes, the French king and French fathers had such extraordinary powers under the old regime that the position of father was itself called into question by the revolution. Until Napoleon organized his own cult, the French did not mythologise a living leader. Hunt, *Family Romance*, pp. 13, 71–73, 83.

107. "We want to naturalise the family spirit in France," decreed the 1795 constitution. "No one is a good citizen if he is not a good son, good father, good husband." Quoted in ibid., p. 163. The constitution required all members of the upper house to be either married or widowed.

108. Outram, *The Body*, p. 126. See also J. W. Scott, "French Feminists."

109. The General Assembly, however, voted on December 31, 1793, that at civic ceremonies patriotic women were to have a special place, "where they will be present with their husbands and children and where they will knit." Carol Blum, *Rousseau and the Republic of Virtue: The Language of Politics in the French Revolution* (Ithaca: Cornell University Press, 1986), pp. 213, 215.

110. By 1793, the revolutionary government outlawed all women's clubs and popular societies and eventually all political association by women. J. B. Landes, *Women and the Public Sphere in the Age of the French Revolution* (Ithaca: Cornell University Press, 1988).

111. D. Levy and H. Applewhite, "Women and Political Revolution in Paris," in R. Bridenthal et al. (eds.), *Becoming Visible: Women in European History*, 2nd ed. (Boston: Houghton Mifflin, 1987), p. 300.

112. Hunt, *Family Romance*, p. 158.

113. K. Marx, *Capital* [1867], vol. 1 (New York: International Publishers, 1967), p. 741.

114. Jacques Donzelot, *L'Invention du social: Essay sur le déclin des passions politiques* (Paris: Fayard, 1984), pp. 142–49. Similarly, a Napoleonic edict of 1810 made the concession of national mineral rights to private enterprise conditional on the obligation of the entrepreneur to ensure "good order and security" among the "mass of men, women and children" needed for their exploitation. Quoted in Colin Gordon, "Governmental Rationality: An Introduction," in G. Burchell, C. Gordon, and P. Miller (eds.), *The Foucault Effect: Studies in Governmentality* (London: Harvester/Wheatsheaf, 1991), pp. 26–27.

115. By 1817, of a population of some thirty million, about ninety thousand French men were able to vote, and less than seventeen hundred were entitled to stand for election. Roger Price, *A Social History of Nineteenth-Century France* (London: Hutchinson, 1987), p. 358. Universal male franchise was reintroduced in 1848, but the jurisdiction of parliaments was limited under a series of authoritarian regimes. But in 1908, a contemporary would still write of "the shocking contrast between man as voter and man as worker. In the polling booth he is a sovereign; in the factory, he is under the yoke." Quoted in C. Gordon, "Governmental Rationality," p. 32.

116. Perrot, "Three Ages."

117. Hobsbawm, *Age of Revolution*, pp. 140–41.

118. Serfdom in Russia and Rumania lasted until the 1860s; in the rest of western and central Europe it was abolished in the French revolutionary and Napoleonic period. Hobsbawm, *Age of Capital*, chap. 1.

119. Habermas, "Public Sphere," p. 49.

120. Geoff Eley, "Nations, Publics and Political Cultures," in Craig Calhoun (ed.), *Habermas and the Public Sphere* (Cambridge, Mass.: MIT Press, 1992), pp. 304–305. See also Geoff Eley, "Edward Thompson, Social History and Political Culture: The Making of a Working-Class public, 1780–1850," in H. J. Kaye and K. McClelland (eds.), *E. P. Thompson: Critical Perspectives* (Cambridge: Polity Press, 1990).

121. Eley, "Nations," p. 306.

122. See, for example, J. W. Scott, "French Feminists," pp. 4–5; Landes, *Women*, p. 46; Eley, "Nations," pp. 309–15.

123. Eley, "Nations," pp. 297–98.

124. Dorothy Thompson, "Women and Nineteenth-Century Radical Politics: A Lost Dimension," in J. Mitchell and A. Oakley, *The Rights and Wrongs of Women* (Harmondsworth: Penguin, 1976). See also Schwarzkopf, *Women*; and S. O. Rose, "Gender and Labour History: The Nineteenth-Century Legacy," *International Review of Social History* 38, Supplement (1993): 145–62.

125. Eley, "Edward Thompson," pp. 31–32.

126. Schwarzkopf, *Women*, chap. 4; J. W. Scott, "On Language, Gender and Working-Class History," in *Gender and the Politics of History* (New York: Columbia University Press, 1988), pp. 62–65.

127. Catherine Hall, "The Tale of Samuel and Jemima: Gender and Working-Class Culture in Nineteenth-Century England," in H. J. Kaye and K. McClelland (eds.), *E. P. Thompson: Critical Perspectives* (Cambridge: Polity Press, 1990), p. 82.

128. Quoted in E. P. Thompson, *Making*, p. 464.

129. D. Thompson, "Women," p. 137.

4. State Formation, Personality Structure, and the Civilizing Process

1. J. and S. Morse, *A New System of Geography* [1828], quoted in B. Finkelstein, *Governing the Young: Teacher Behavior in Popular Primary Schools in Nineteenth-Century United States* (New York: Falmer Press, 1989), p. 83.

2. Sir Thomas Elyot, *The Book of the Governor*, quoted in K. Hodgkin, "Thomas Whythorne and the Problems of Mastery," *History Workshop* 29 (1990): 21.

3. Rousseau, *Emile*, p. 332.

4. Ibid., p. 324.

5. *South Australian Parliamentary Papers*, 1883–84, no. 27a, p. 31/7367.

6. Karl Marx, "Introduction" to *A Contribution to the Critique of Political Economy* (1859), quoted in T. B. Bottomore and M. Rubel (eds.), *Karl Marx: Selected Writings in Sociology and Social Philosophy* (Harmondsworth: Penguin, 1963), p. 67.

7. Quoted in L. Schiebinger, "Skeletons in the Closet: The First Illustrations of the Female Skeleton in Eighteenth-Century Anatomy," in C. Gallagher and T. Laqueur, *The Making of the Modern Body: Sexuality and Society in the Nineteenth Century* (Berkeley: University of California Press, 1987), p. 70.

8. For some famous examples, see Sabean, *Power*; R. Darnton, *The Great Cat Massacre and Other Episodes in French Cultural History* (New York: Vintage Books, 1985); E. P. Thompson, "Patrician Society, Plebeian Culture," *Journal of Social History* 7, no. 4 (1974): 382–405.

9. Buddhism, to take just one sharply contrasting view, held that the idea of the self is "an imaginary, false belief which has no corresponding reality, and it produces harmful thoughts of 'me' and 'mine,' selfish desire, craving, attachment, hatred, ill-will, conceit, pride, egotism, and other defilements, impurities and problems." Quoted in S. Lukes, "Conclusion," in M. Carrithers, S. Collins, and S. Lukes (eds.), *The Category of the Person: Anthropology, Philosophy, History* (Cambridge: Cambridge University Press, 1985), p. 291.

10. One of the most useful texts dealing with "the individual" is Charles Taylor, *Sources of the Self: The Making of the Modern Identity* (Cambridge: Cambridge University Press, 1992). For an introduction to a Foucauldian approach, see Michel Foucault, "On the Genealogy of Ethics: An Overview of Work in Progress," in Paul Rabinow (ed.), *The Foucault Reader* (Harmondsworth: Penguin Books, 1986).

11. One brilliant discussion of these issues, which has strongly influenced my own approach, is the Introduction to Roper, *Oedipus*.

12. Ibid., p. 12. In contrast, the inhabitants of contemporary western societies are frequently depicted as complex exemplars of multiple discourses bereft of individual agency.

13. This argument is common in late-nineteenth-and early-twentieth-century social theory.

14. Regenia Gagnier, *Subjectivities: A History of Self-Representation in Britain* (New York: Oxford University Press, 1991), pp. 138–39.

15. Jock McCulloch, *Colonial Psychiatry and "the African Mind"* (Cambridge: Cambridge University Press, 1995).

16. A good summary of feminist debates about Kohlberg's work is in R. Tong, *Feminist Thought* (London: Unwin Hyman, 1989).

17. Anne Laura Stoler, *Race and the Education of Desire: Foucault's History of Sexuality and the Colonial Order of Things* (Durham, N.C.: Duke University Press, 1995).

18. Taylor, *Sources*.

19. For a classic study, see Natalie Zenon Davis, "Hosts, Kin and Progeny: Some Features of Family Life in Early Modern France," *Daedalus* 106, no. 2 (1977).

20. Elias, *Civilising Process: Manners*, p. 200.

21. Elias, *Civilising Process: State*, pp. 235, 242, 286.

22. P. Anderson, *Lineages*, p. 48.

23. Elias, *Civilising Process: State*, p. 304, passim.

24. Hunt, *Family Romance*, pp. 96–97.

25. Quoted in Elias, *Civilising Process: State*, p. 272. Klein quotes an early eighteenth-century author according to whom "*Politenesse* may be defined as a dextrous management of our Words and Actions, whereby we make other People have better Opinion of us and themselves." Lawrence Klein, "The Third Earl of Shaftesbury and the Progress of Politeness," *Eighteenth-Century Studies* 18, no. 2 (1984–85): 190. I am indebted to Liam Leonard for this reference.

26. Albert O. Hirschman, *The Passions and the Interests: Political Arguments for Capitalism before Its Triumph* (Princeton: Princeton University Press, 1977).

27. Later still, the principles of economic interest were applied to informing the conduct of common people as well. "As the physical world is ruled by the laws of movement so is the moral universe ruled by laws of interest," Helvetius proclaimed in 1748. Quoted in Hirschman, *Passions*, p. 43.

28. Oestreich, *Neostoicism*, pp. 28–35, 53.

29. Ibid., pp. 68, 271.

30. Quoted in Joan Kelly-Gadol, "Did Women Have a Renaissance?" in R. Bridenthal et al. (eds.), *Becoming Visible: Women in European History*, 2nd ed. (Boston: Houghton Mifflin, 1987), p. 195. Laqueur similarly notes that Castiglione's book was rampant with anxiety, expressed in the language of the body, that men engaged in the skills of courtesy, dress, conversation, and self-fashioning will to all

intents and purposes turn into women. Thomas W. Laqueur, *Making Sex: Body and Gender from the Greeks to Freud* (Cambridge, Mass.: Harvard University Press, 1990), p. 125.

31. John Brown's 1757 *Estimate of the Manners and Principles of the Times* singles out music dwindled into "an eunuch's effeminate trill," the habit of traveling by "the effeminate covering and conveyance of an easy chair," and that "fountain of weakness and disease," a heated nursery, for particular condemnation. Linda Dowling, "Esthetes and Effeminati," *Raritan* 12, no. 3 (1993): 54, 56–57. I owe this reference to Liam Leonard.

32. G. S. Wood, *Radicalism*, pp. 12, 14, 36, 196, 202.

33. Lynn Hunt, "The Unstable Boundaries of the French Revolution," in M. Perrot (ed.), *A History of Private Life*, vol. 4: *From the Fires of Revolution to the Great War* (Cambridge, Mass.: Belknap Press, 1990), pp. 16–18.

34. Gorsline, *What People Wore*, pp. 67–68, 100–101.

35. S. F. M. Grieco, "The Body, Appearance and Sexuality," in N. Z. Davis and A. Farge (eds.), *A History of Women in the West*, vol. 3: *Renaissance and Enlightenment Paradoxes* (Cambridge, Mass.: Belknap Press, 1993), pp. 63–64.

36. See G. S. Wood, *Radicalism*, pp. 285–86; L. Davidoff and C. Hall, *Family Fortunes: Men and Women of the English Middle Class, 1780–1850* (London: Hutchinson, 1987), p. 445; and Klein, "Third Earl," pp. 202–203. This issue is a subsection of Weber's famous question in *The Protestant Ethic*: How did commercial, banking and similar money-making pursuits become honorable after having stood condemned or despised as greed, love of lucre, and avarice for centuries? See also Hirschman, *Passions*, p. 9.

37. Quoted in G. S. Wood, *Radicalism*, p. 37.

38. Ibid., pp. 26, 285.

39. Jan Cohn, *Romance and the Erotics of Property: Mass-Market Fiction for Women* (Durham, N.C.: Duke University Press, 1988).

40. Kelly, "Early Feminist Theory," pp. 65–109; Wiesner, "Women's Response," p. 168.

41. Hacker, "Women." It was only gradually that the armed forces managed to dispense with women and indeed depend, for much of their discipline and legitimation, on stressing the exclusive masculinity of war.

42. Kelly, "Early Feminist Theory," pp. 56, 85–86.

43. Dowling, "Esthetes," p. 56.

44. M. Weber, *The Protestant Ethic and the Spirit of Capitalism* (London: Unwin, 1930). See also A. Gamble, *An Introduction to Modern Social and Political Thought* (London: Macmillan, 1981), pp. 156–57; and J. Morgan, *Godly Learning: Puritan Attitudes towards Reason, Learning and Education, 1560–1640* (Cambridge: Cambridge University Press, 1986), chap. 2.

45. N. Abercrombie, S. Hill, and B. S. Turner, *Sovereign Individuals of Capitalism* (London: Allen and Unwin, 1986), pp. 50–57. See also Roper, *Oedipus*, p. 39.

46. T. L. Haskell, "Capitalism and the Origins of the Humanitarian Sensibility,"

pts. 1 and 2, *American Historical Review* 90, no. 2 (1985): 339–61; 90, no. 3 (1985): 547–66.

47. Ibid., p. 550.

48. H. A. Oberman, *Luther: Man between God and the Devil* (New Haven: Yale University Press, 1989), pp. 272–77.

49. Roper, *Oedipus*, pp. 22–23.

50. L. A. Hall, "Forbidden by God, Despised by Men: Masturbation, Medical Warnings, Moral Panic and Manhood in Great Britain, 1850–1950," in J. C. Fout (ed.), *Forbidden History: The State, Society and the Regulation of Sexuality in Modern Europe* (Chicago: University of Chicago Press, 1992).

51. Davidoff and Hall, *Fortunes*; C. Hall, "Missionary Stories: Gender and Ethnicity in England in the 1830s and 1840s" and "Competing Masculinities: Thomas Carlyle, John Stuart Mill and the Case of Governor Eyre," in *White, Male and Middle Class: Explorations in Feminism and History* (Cambridge: Polity Press, 1992).

52. Davidoff and Hall, *Fortunes*, pp. 110, 205, 413. See also Klein, "Third Earl," and Dowling, "Esthetes."

53. Davidoff and Hall, *Fortunes*, pp. 445, 74.

54. In his *Dictionary*, Samuel Johnson defined "club" as "an assembly of good fellows, meeting under certain conditions." Phillips, "Good Men," p. 121.

55. Davidoff and Hall, *Fortunes*, p. 416. Importantly, the increasingly solid and elaborate public sphere gradually decreased men's dependence on the moral capital produced and maintained by women in the private sphere. Acceptance into polite society was still important, but men now had myriad new bases for claims to social distinction which, far from openly depending on women, explicitly excluded them.

56. Indeed, in something of a coup, bourgeois statisticians managed to designate personal occupation (rather than rank) as the fundamental criterion of social identity, at least for purposes of government enumeration—ostentatiously classifying those living off private means and returning no personal occupation alongside paupers in a residual category, designated as the unproductive class. S. Szreter, *Fertility, Class and Gender in Britain, 1860–1940* (Cambridge: Cambridge University Press, 1996), pp. 122–23, referring to a new classification in the 1861 Census of England and Wales. Ironically, as soon as they made enough money, many British industrialists retired from active business life and became rentiers, affecting the life of leisured gentry. D. Levine, "Production, Reproduction and the Proletarian Family in England, 1500–1851," in Levine, *Proletarianization and Family History* (New York: Academic Press, 1984), p. 182.

57. See for example J. A. Mangan and J. Walvin (eds.), *Manliness and Morality: Middle-Class Masculinity in Britain and America, 1800–1940* (Manchester: Manchester University Press, 1987).

58. See, for example, Leonore Davidoff, *The Best Circles* (London: Hutchinson, 1986).

59. Ehrenreich and English note that while sickness, injury, exhaustion, and undernourishment were routine in the lives of working-class women, in the

nineteenth-century United States the medical profession believed that it was affluent women who were most delicate and most in need of medical attention. According to them, civilization had made the middle-class woman sickly; her physical frailty went hand in hand with her superior modesty and refinement. Working-class women were robust, just as they were supposedly coarse and immodest. B. Ehrenreich and D. English, *For Her Own Good: 150 Years of the Experts' Advice to Women* (London: Pluto Press, 1979), pp. 101–103.

60. Mrs. S. Stickney Ellis (1839), quoted in Davidoff and Hall, *Fortunes,* p. 315.

61. Davidoff and Hall, *Fortunes,* p. 315.

62. Ibid., pp. 274–75.

63. Marjorie R. Theobald, "The Accomplished Woman and the Propriety of Intellect: A New Look at Women's Education in Britain and Australia, 1800–1850," *History of Education* 17, no. 1 (1988): 25.

64. Quoted in ibid., p. 33. The lovely young woman was entirely out of place in a capitalist economy driven by individual selfishness. As Adam Smith put it, "It is not from the benevolence of the butcher, the brewer, or the baker, that we expect our dinner, but from their regard to their own interest. We address ourselves, not to their humanity but to their self-love, and never talk to them of our own necessities, but of their advantages. No one but a beggar chooses to depend chiefly upon the benevolence of his fellow citizens. . . . Every individual is continually exerting himself to find out the most advantageous employment for whatever capital he can command. . . . The study of his own advantage leads him necessarily to prefer that employment which is most advantageous to the society." Quoted in Gamble, *Introduction,* p. 44.

65. Just as educated women seeking equality with men were ridiculed, so men defending women's rights (and even worse, the rights of emancipated slaves) were increasingly described by their opponents as emasculated, passionless paragons of dry reason. Hall, "Competing Masculinities."

66. Quoted in Karin Hausen, "Family and Role-Division: The Polarisation of Sexual Stereotypes in the Nineteenth Century—An Aspect of the Dissociation of Work and Family Life," in R. J. Evans and W. R. Lee, *The German Family: Essays on the Social History of the Family in Nineteenth- and Twentieth-Century Germany* (London: Croom Helm, 1981), p. 57.

67. Quoted in Schiebinger, "Skeletons," p. 69. The eccentric Victorian diarist Arthur Munby realized that matters were more complicated. "Are the relations of the sexes really inverted," he mused, "when three men sit at table, with hands delicate and jewelled, and a woman stands behind and waits, offering the dishes with so large [and] coarse a hand that makes her master's look almost lady-like: And is it the proper thing, that the *women* should sit as at a ball supper, drawing the gloves from their dainty fingers, and waited on by *men* whose hands that seemed so ladylike by comparison with Molly's, look sinewy and labourious by the side of Blanche's tender tips? If *this* is right for one class is that for the other? In short, what, in the Equation of Life, is the respective value of the terms *sex* and *station*. " Quot-

ed in L. Davidoff, "Class and Gender in Victorian England," in J. L. Newton, M. P. Ryan, and J. R. Walkowitz (eds.), *Sex and Class in Women's History* (London: Routledge and Kegan Paul, 1983), p. 62.

68. On occasion, it was believed, "women have changed into men" when "the heat, having been rendered more vigorous, thrusts the testes outward." Laqueur, *Making Sex*, p. 127.

69. Thomas Laqueur, "Orgasm, Generation, and the Politics of Reproductive Biology," in Catherine Gallagher and Thomas Laqueur (eds.), *The Making of the Modern Body: Sexuality and Society in the Nineteenth Century* (Berkeley: University of California Press, 1987), pp. 18, 24.

70. Ibid., pp. 31–32.

71. Even Darwin concluded that natural selection, reinforced by sexual selection, had favored man, who "became superior to woman." Using similar reasoning, the anarchist philosopher Pierre-Joseph Proudhon, who strenuously campaigned against women's rights, wrote in 1875, "The difference of the sexes establishes a difference between them of the same magnitude as that which difference of breeds establishes between the animals." Quoted in Geneviève Fraise, "A Philosophical History of Sexual Difference," in Geneviève Fraise and Michelle Perrot (eds.), *A History of Women in the West*, vol 4: *Emerging Feminism from Revolution to World War* (Cambridge, Mass.: Belknap Press, 1993), pp. 68, 73.

72. Quoted in Schiebinger, "Skeletons," p. 69.

73. Some men justified this with reference to the "physiological feeble-mindedness of women." Hausen, "Family," p. 62.

74. Barbara Taylor, quoted in Scott, "French Feminists," p. 6.

75. Ruth Courtauld, quoted in Lown, *Women*, p. 2.

76. Davidoff and Hall, *Fortunes*, pp. 322, 395.

77. Carroll Smith-Rosenberg, "The Female World of Love and Ritual: Relations between Women in Nineteenth-Century America," *Signs* 1, no. 1 (1975): 1–29. For a debate, see *Feminist Studies* 6, no. 1 (1980): 26–64.

78. R. M. George, "Homes in the Empire, Empires in the Home," *Cultural Critique* 26 (1993–94): 96–97.

79. Philippe Ariès, *Centuries of Childhood* (Harmondsworth: Penguin, 1973).

80. Maynes and Taylor, "Germany."

81. DeMause, Stone, and Finkelstein are among the scholars associated with this tradition, also known as psychohistory.

82. S. Ryan Johansson, "Centuries of Childhood/Centuries of Parenting: Philippe Ariès and the Modernization of Privileged Infancy," *Journal of Family History* 12, no. 4 (1987): 343–65.

83. For a rebuttal of some aspects of the Ariès thesis, see Stephen Wilson, "The Myth of Motherhood a Myth: The Historical View of European Child-Rearing," *Social History* 9, no. 2 (1984): 191–98. For a critique of Ariès influenced by sociobiology, see Linda A. Pollock, *Forgotten Children: Parent-Child Relations from 1500 to 1900* (Cambridge: Cambridge University Press, 1983). For an incisive critique of

Pollock and a careful evaluation of Ariès, see S. R. Johansson, "Centuries." See also Roper, *Oedipus*, pp. 1–3.

84. Stone notes that in England, much of the fierce determination to break the will of children, and to enforce their utter subjection to the authority of their elders, masters, and parents, can be traced to the Puritans, who regarded children as the unreformed bearers of original sin. Similar precepts and practices, however, seemed to exist throughout western Europe. Stone, *Family*, p. 162.

85. Ariès, *Centuries*, p. 251.

86. Stone, *Family*, pp. 163–70.

87. G. S. Wood, *Radicalism*; Fliegelman, *Prodigals*; Ryan, *Cradle*, p. 232. In both cases, it is necessary to distinguish between social prescriptions of appropriate behavior and the way people actually behaved.

88. Joseph F. Kett, "Curing the Disease of Precocity," and C. F. Kaestle and M. A. Vinovskis, "From Apron Strings to ABCs: Parents, Children and Schooling in Nineteenth-Century Massachusetts," both in J. Demos and S. S. Boocock (eds.), *Turning Points: Historical and Sociological Essays on the Family* (Chicago: University of Chicago Press, 1978).

89. Kett, "Curing," p. S202.

90. D. Tyler, "The Case of Irene Tuckerman: Understanding Sexual Violence and the Protection of Women and Girls, Victoria, 1890–1925," *History of Education Review* 15, no. 2 (1986): 52–67. Feminist scholars have similar reservations about the applicability of concepts such as "youth" and "adolescent" to young women.

91. Hobsbawm, *Age of Capital*, p. 97. At the beginning of the nineteenth century, "Germany" was made up of roughly eighteen hundred more or less autonomous political units. J. Kocka, "Problems of Working-Class Formation in Germany: The Early Years, 1800–1875," in I. Katznelson and A. Zolberg (eds.), *Working-Class Formation* (Princeton: Princeton University Press, 1986), p. 283.

92. "Historians of nationalism agree to differ in their estimates of how much (and what sorts of it) already existed in the Atlantic world of 1785. They are at one in recognising that that world by 1815 was full of it, and that although each national variety had of course its strong characteristics, those varieties had enough in common for it to constitute the most momentous phenomenon of modern history." Quoted in Craig Calhoun, "Nationalism and Ethnicity," *Annual Review of Sociology* 19 (1993): 213.

93. Charles Tilly, "Review" of *Nationalism in the Age of the French Revolution, Journal of Modern History* 62, no. 3 (1990): 575. According to Tilly, the word "nationalism" refers to two different phenomena: (1) the zealous pursuit of an existing state's interest, or national-interest nationalism, and (2) claims to a distinct state for a set of people who do not have one, which can be called state-claiming nationalism.

94. Benedict Anderson, *Imagined Communities* (London: Verso, 1991), pp. 6–7. Anderson uses the word "fraternity" un-self-consciously; feminist critics have not been slow to point out that the imagined community is indeed an overwhelmingly masculine product.

95. See, for example, E. J. Hobsbawm, *Nations and Nationalism since 1780* (Cambridge: Cambridge University Press, 1990); and E. Hobsbawm and T. Ranger (eds.), *The Invention of Tradition* (Cambridge: Cambridge University Press, 1983).

96. Hobsbawm and Ranger, *Invention,* pp. 1–2, 7.

97. E. J. Hobsbawm, *The Age of Empire, 1875–1914* (New York: Vintage Books, 1989), p. 146–47.

98. Geoff Eley, "Nationalism and Social History," *Social History* 6, no. 1 (1981): 91.

99. Calhoun, "Nationalism," p. 222.

100. Eley, "Nationalism," p. 90.

101. Pateman, *Contract,* p. 89. Pateman notes that according to Plato, some men, unlike those who turn to women, "conceive in the soul . . . the most beautiful [conception] . . . that which is concerned with the ordering of cities and homes, which we call temperance and justice."

102. Several contemporary satirical prints derided Deputy Guy Target for *literally* giving birth to the constitution of 1791. Hunt, *Family Romance,* p. 99. See also Vivian Cameron, "Political Exposures: Sexuality and Caricature in the French Revolution," in L. Hunt (ed.), *Eroticism and the Body Politic* (Baltimore: Johns Hopkins University Press, 1991), pp. 98–100.

103. When the Australian nation was born in the popular imagination in the landing at Gallipoli during the First World War, for example, the bloody and costly military campaign (in which no Australian women except army nurses were allowed to serve) had been a failure resulting in an inglorious retreat. Yet it was hailed at one and the same time as the achievement of Australian manhood and the nation's birthplace. In this powerful mythmaking, "the blood women shed in actually giving birth—their deaths, their courage and endurance, their babies— were rendered invisible. In determining the meaning of men's deeds . . . women's procreative capacities were at once appropriated and erased. Men's deeds were rendered simultaneously sacred and seminal. Though women gave birth to the population, only men it seemed could give birth to the imperishable political entity of the nation." P. Grimshaw et al., *Creating a Nation* (Melbourne: McPhee Gribble, 1994), p. 218.

104. Eley, "Nations," p. 296.

105. Hobsbawm, *Age of Empire,* p. 143.

106. Raphael Samuel (ed.), *Patriotism: The Making and Unmaking of British National Identity,* vol. 1 (London: Routledge, 1989); Linda Colley, "Whose Nation? Class and National Consciousness in Britain, 1750–1830," *Past and Present* no. 113 (1986): 97–117.

107. Hobsbawm, *Nations,* pp. 19–20, 88.

108. Others were busy making sure that all revolutionary decrees were translated into as many languages as was necessary. P. Higonnet, "The Politics of Linguistic Terrorism and Grammatical Hegemony during the French Revolution," *Social History* 5, no. 1 (1980): 42, 55; J. Langins, "Words and Institutions during the French Revolution," in P. Burke and R. Porter (eds.), *The Social History of Language*

(Cambridge: Cambridge University Press, 1987), p. 137. French emphasis on the voluntary aspects of citizenship was not universal. In Germany, for example, nationalists emphasized ethnic rather than civic criteria for inclusion in the nation; these differences are felt even today, as in the ease with which "foreigners" can acquire citizenship. Calhoun, "Nationalism," p. 221.

109. Victor Kiernan, "Languages and Conquerors," in P. Burke and R. Porter, *Language, Self and Society: A Social History of Language* (Cambridge: Polity Press, 1991), p. 207. Stephen, later sanctified as the first king of Hungary, believed that "the utility of foreigners and guests is so great they can be given a place of sixth importance among the royal ornaments. . . . For, as the guests come from various regions and provinces, they bring with them various languages and customs, various knowledges and arms. All these adorn the royal court, heighten its splendour, and terrify the haughtiness of foreign powers. For a country unified in language and custom is fragile and weak." Quoted in B. Anderson, *Imagined Communities*, p. 109.

110. Hobsbawm, *Nations*, pp. 51, 36.

111. Ibid., p. 60.

112. Higonnet, "Politics," pp. 66–69.

113. R. Grew and P. J. Harrigan, *School, State and Society: The Growth of Elementary Schooling in Nineteenth-Century France—A Quantitative Analysis* (Ann Arbor: University of Michigan Press, 1991), p. 150.

114. Hobsbawm, *Age of Capital*, pp. 20, 110–11; Hobsbawm, *Age of Empire*, chap. 6. In the extreme case of the Jewish state, nobody spoke Hebrew for everyday purposes before it was reconstructed as the national language from ancient texts.

115. Patrick Joyce, "The People's English: Language and Class in England c. 1840–1920," in Burke and Porter, *Language, Self and Society*, p. 157.

116. Raymond Williams, *The Long Revolution* (Harmondsworth: Penguin, 1965), p. 247.

117. See, for example, Dale Spender, *Man Made Language* (London: Routledge and Kegan Paul, 1980).

118. Hobsbawm, *Nations*, p. 115, and *Age of Empire*, p. 156.

119. Quoted in B. Anderson, *Imagined Communities*, p. 103.

120. Ibid., pp. 82, 87. On the American continent, the Creole descendants of the colonizers themselves were not accepted as equal in the metropolitan countries, a deeply felt injustice which activated their own wave of nationalism early in the nineteenth century, well before nationalism developed in most of Europe. See also Eley, "Nationalism," p. 98.

121. P. Miller, *Long Division: State Schooling in South Australian Society* (Adelaide: Wakefield Press, 1986), pp. 43–46; C. Steedman, "'Listen How the Caged Bird Sings': Amarjit's Song," in C. Steedman, C. Urwin, and V. Walkerdine (eds.), *Language, Gender and Childhood* (London: Routledge and Kegan Paul, 1985).

122. Hobsbawm, *Age of Empire*, pp. 146–47.

123. B. Anderson, *Imagined Communities*, p. 79.

124. Roy Porter, "Introduction," in Burke and Porter, *Language, Self and Society,* p. 10.

125. Hobsbawm, *Nations,* p. 95. Hobsbawm adds that "very few modern national movements are actually based on a strong ethnic consciousness, though they often invent one once they have got going, in the form of racism." In addition, "visible ethnicity tends to be negative, inasmuch as it is much more usually applied to define 'the other' than one's own group." Ibid., pp. 65, 66.

126. Hobsbawm, *Age of Capital,* p. 20.

127. Hobsbawm, *Nations,* pp. 83, 85.

128. Ibid., p. 91; Hobsbawm, *Age of Empire,* p. 159.

129. Hobsbawm, *Nations,* p. 123.

5. Worlds of Social Control

1. Quoted in Melton, *Absolutism,* p. 162.

2. Quoted in ibid., p. 145.

3. Quoted in Lis and Soly, "Policing," p. 191.

4. T. R. Malthus, *An Essay on the Principle of Population* [1803] (Cambridge: Cambridge University Press, 1992), p. 276.

5. Quoted in Mary Jo Maynes, *Schooling in Western Europe: A Social History* (Albany: State University of New York Press, 1985), p. 41.

6. Quoted in A. Summers, *Damned Whores and God's Police* (Ringwood: Penguin, 1975), p. 11.

7. M. Foucault, *The History of Sexuality,* vol. 1: *An Introduction* (Harmondsworth: Penguin, 1981), p. 120.

8. Elias, *Civilising Process: State,* p. 295.

9. Oestreich, *Neostoicism,* p. 35.

10. Richard Johnson, "Educational Policy and Social Control in Early Victorian England," *Past and Present* 49 (1970): 105–107.

11. Levine, "Punctuated Equilibrium," p. 14.

12. Foucault, *Discipline,* p. 137. "Prompt complete respectful and easy obedience" was expected of servants (and wives) until well into the twentieth century. L. Davidoff, "Mastered for Life: Servant Wife and Mother in Victorian and Edwardian Britain," *Journal of Social History* 7, no. 4 (1974): 412. As Melton notes, this does not mean that Lutherans, or late medieval Catholics, did not to some extent rely on internal modes of control. Melton, *Absolutism,* pp. xx–xxi.

13. Foucault, *Discipline,* pp. 220–21. For a discussion of these claims, see Levine, "Punctuated Equilibrium."

14. Quoted in Fliegelman, *Prodigals,* pp. 33–44.

15. Maynes, *Schooling in Western Europe,* pp. 39–44.

16. David Hamilton, *Learning about Education: An Unfinished Curriculum* (Milton Keynes: Open University Press, 1990), pp. 14, 48. As Kett put it, "Where character had traditionally been viewed as innate and where the events of childhood had traditionally been looked on as no more than remote foreshadowings of adult-

hood, progressive educators of the late eighteenth and early nineteenth centuries decreed that the experiences of childhood determined those of adulthood, and that adult character was forged rather than foreshadowed in childhood." Kett, "Curing," p. S197.

17. Maynes, *Schooling in Western Europe*, pp. 43–44, 39.

18. Instructions to Lincolnshire Sunday school teachers, quoted in E. P. Thompson, *Making*, p. 441.

19. See, for example, F. O. Ramirez and J. Boli, "The Political Construction of Mass Schooling: European Origins and Worldwide Institutionalization," *Sociology of Education* 60, no. 1 (1987): 10, 12; R. O'Day, *Education and Society, 1500–1800* (London: Longman, 1982), p. 243.

20. See, for example, J. Henriques et al., *Changing the Subject: Psychology, Social Regulation and Subjectivity* (London: Methuen, 1984), p. 1.

21. Quoted in Melton, *Absolutism*, p. 27.

22. Gawthrop and Strauss, "Protestantism," p. 48, passim; Melton, *Absolutism*, pp. 32–33.

23. Melton, *Absolutism*, p. xix.

24. Quoted in ibid., p. xxi.

25. Ibid., p. 42.

26. Ibid., pp. 40–44.

27. H. S. Graff, *The Labyrinths of Literacy: Reflections on Literacy Past and Present* (London: Falmer Press, 1987), pp. 183–87.

28. Maynes, *Schooling in Western Europe*, p. 49.

29. Melton, *Absolutism*, pp. xiii, xix–xxiii, 41, 210.

30. François Furet and Jacques Ozouf, *Reading and Writing: Literacy in France from Calvin to Jules Ferry* (Cambridge: Cambridge University Press, 1982), p. 78.

31. James Bowen, *A History of Western Education*, vol. 3: *The Modern West, Europe and the New World* (London: Methuen, 1986), pp. 118–19.

32. La Salle, quoted in Foucault, *Discipline*, p. 166. The signal was a small wooden contraption for attracting pupils' attention.

33. Furet and Ozouf, *Reading*, p. 79; Foucault, *Discipline*, pt. 3.

34. Foucault, *Discipline*, pp. 147, 150, 152.

35. Furet and Ozouf, *Reading*, p. 79.

36. Quoted in Carl F. Kaestle (ed.), *Joseph Lancaster and the Monitorial School Movement: A Documentary History* (New York: Teachers College Press, Columbia University, 1973), pp. 9–10.

37. Bell, 1807, quoted in P. J. Miller, "Factories, Monitorial Schools and Jeremy Bentham: The Origins of the 'Management Syndrome' in Popular Education," *Journal of Educational Administration and History* 5, no. 2 (1973): 11.

38. Lancaster, 1806, quoted in ibid., p. 11.

39. Kaestle, *Lancaster*, p. 3.

40. Foucault, *Discipline*, pp. 175–76.

41. Ibid., pp. 200–209. The invention of the Panopticon is attributed to Jeremy

Bentham's brother Samuel, who was interested in problems of prison design. P. J. Miller, "Factories," p. 15.

42. Quoted in P. J. Miller, "Factories," p. 15.

43. Phillip McCann, "The Indian Origins of Bell's Monitorial System," in *International Currents in Educational Ideas and Practices,* Proceedings of the 1987 Annual Conference of the History of Education Society of Great Britain, University of Hull, Evington, Leicester, 1987.

44. Bell, 1797, quoted in K. Jones and K. Williamson, "The Birth of the Schoolroom: A Study of the Transformation in the Discursive Conditions of English Popular Education in the First Half of the Nineteenth Century," *Ideology and Consciousness* 6 (1979): 73–74.

45. Bowen, *History,* pp. 297, 298–99; Furet and Ozouf, *Reading,* p. 135.

46. Bowen, *History,* pp. 300–301; McCann, "Indian Origins," p. 29; Kaestle, *Lancaster,* pp. 32–34. The Church of England National Society, however, continued to dominate English schools. In 1860, it owned nine out of every ten elementary schools and enrolled about three-quarters of all schoolchildren. David Rubinstein, *School Attendance in London, 1870–1904: A Social History* (New York: A. M. Kelley Publishers, 1969), p. 1.

47. P. J. Miller, "Factories," pp. 13–14, quoting Bentham's *Chrestomathia* [1816], p. 46. About 16 to 22 percent of the budget of Lancaster's Borough Road Free School was expended on prizes and rewards; half or more was spent on the master's salary. Bowen, *History,* p. 294.

48. Lancaster, 1805, quoted in Kaestle, *Lancaster,* pp. 13–14.

49. P. J. Miller, "Factories," pp. 13–17.

50. David Hogan, "The Market Revolution and Disciplinary Power: Joseph Lancaster and the Psychology of the Early Classroom System," *History of Education Quarterly* 29, no. 3 (1989): 384, 397–98, 400, 414. While Hogan acknowledges his debt to Foucault, his essay is concerned with Foucault's *neglect* of the relationship between the disciplinary revolution and the market revolution.

51. Jones and Williamson, "Birth," p. 88.

52. Quoted in Hogan, "Market Revolution," pp. 406–407.

53. Quoted in Furet and Ozouf, *Reading,* pp. 134–35. These perceived problems would have been made more serious by the presence of girls.

54. *New England Magazine,* Boston, 1832, quoted in Kaestle, *Lancaster,* pp. 182–83.

55. Nancy Green, "Female Education and School Competition, 1820–1850," *History of Education Quarterly* 18, no. 2 (1978): 133–36.

56. Ibid., p. 136.

57. Quoted in June Purvis, *A History of Women's Education in England* (Milton Keynes: Open University Press, 1991), p. 23. Lancaster himself complained that the nation was suffering under the consequences of the "basest impositions" by untrained teachers keen to make money off the popularity of the Lancastrian system. Quoted in Kaestle, *Lancaster,* pp. 90–91.

58. Mann, 1846, quoted in Kaestle, *Lancaster,* pp. 184–85.

59. Maynes notes that one French communard mused in his memoirs that monitorial schools did not teach much, but "the habit of teaching, contracted at [a monitorial] school by a lot of children of my generation," might have produced "this seedbed of workers who prepared, in their associations and public meetings, the downfall of the Empire." Maynes, *Schooling in Western Europe,* p. 150.

60. N. Green, "Female Education," pp. 137, 138.

61. Quoted in Carolyn Steedman, "'The Mother Made Conscious': The Historical Development of Primary School Pedagogy," *History Workshop* 20 (1985): 149, 153. Froebel knew Pestalozzi's work, had spent some time at his experimental school at Yverdun, and developed a similar educational philosophy based on a naturalistic observation of peasant mothers and their children.

62. Pestalozzi, quoted in Bowen, *History,* p. 231.

63. Steedman, "Mother," p. 160.

64. Carolyn Steedman, "Prisonhouses," *Feminist Review* 20 (1985): 13.

65. Bowen, *History,* pp. 225, 231.

66. Quoted in Ann Taylor Allen, "Spiritual Motherhood: German Feminists and the Kindergarten Movement, 1848–1911," *History of Education Quarterly* 22, no. 3 (1982): 323.

67. Quoted in ibid., pp. 321, 327.

68. Quoted in ibid., pp. 324, 326.

69. Quoted in ibid., p. 327.

70. D. H. Lawrence, *The Rainbow,* quoted in Madeleine Grumet, "Pedagogy for Patriarchy: The Feminization of Teaching," *Interchange* 12, nos. 2–3 (1981): 177. See also M. R. Grumet, *Bitter Milk: Women and Teaching* (Amherst: University of Massachusetts Press, 1988).

71. See, for example, Jalna Hanmer, "Violence and Social Control of Women," in G. Littlejohn et al. (eds.), *Power and the State* (London: Croom Helm, 1978), p. 229.

72. For a debate on whether wife-beating in early modern Europe was permitted and desirable, see, for example, C. Jordan, *Renaissance Feminism,* esp. pp. 287–303.

73. Corporal punishment by police was formally abolished in 1848. Alf Ludtke, "The Role of State Violence in the Period of Transition to Industrial Capitalism: The Example of Prussia," *Social History* 4, no. 2 (1979): 196–97, 182.

74. Ibid., pp. 195, 214.

75. In spite of their early reputation, Prussian schools in the second half of the nineteenth century relied on prodigious amounts of corporal punishment. Mary Jo Maynes, *Taking the Hard Road: Life Course in French and German Workers' Autobiographies in the Era of Industrialization* (Chapel Hill: University of North Carolina Press, 1995), pp. 86–91.

76. McNeill, *Pursuit,* p. 133.

77. Foucault, *Discipline,* p. 135. Similarly, a contemporary noted that "where a few days and a good drill sergeant might suffice to train a reasonably good

arquebusier, many years and a whole way of life were needed to produce a competent archer." Quoted in Parker, *Military Revolution*, p. 17.

78. Parker, *Military Revolution*, p. 52; Oestreich, *Neostoicism*, pp. 84–85.

79. Quoted in Oestreich, *Neostoicism*, p. 270. Mannheim neglects to note that these techniques were pioneered in the non-absolutist Republic of the (Dutch) United Provinces.

80. McNeill, *Pursuit*, pp. 117, 133.

81. Quoted in Corrigan and Sayer, *Great Arch*, p. 94.

82. E. P. Thompson, "Patrician Society," pp. 387, 397. See also E. P. Thompson, "Eighteenth-Century English Society."

83. Hay, "Property."

84. Anna Clark, *Women's Silence, Men's Violence: Sexual Assault in England, 1770–1845* (London: Pandora, 1987). This situation was similar to that in Australia, but seemed to differ markedly from that in Ireland. See J. A. Allen, *Sex and Secrets: Crimes Involving Australian Women since 1880* (Melbourne: Oxford University Press, 1990); and C. A. Conley, "No Pedestals: Women and Violence in Late Nineteenth-Century Ireland," *Journal of Social History* 28, no. 4 (1995): 801–18.

85. Marx, *Capital*, vol. 1, chap. 28, p. 737.

86. Medick, "Proto-Industrial Family Economy," pp. 64–73. E. P. Thompson similarly argued that even in England, the birthplace of industrial capitalism, alternate bouts of intense labor and of idleness were the norm, and it was only from the second half of the eighteenth century that "normal" capitalist wage incentives became effective for any sizable sectors of the population. E. P. Thompson, "Time, Work-Discipline and Industrial Capitalism," *Past and Present* 38 (1967): 56–97.

87. Quoted in Lis and Soly, "Policing," p. 192. As late as 1907, leatherworkers in Gentilly, near Paris, walked out of their workshops because employers sought to impose fixed work schedules; in the same year, the nailmakers of Revin struck for more than a hundred days against a regulation that fixed arrival and departure times and prohibited workers from going out to "refresh themselves" in the neighborhood tavern. Perrot, "Formation," p. 83.

88. Lis and Soly, "Policing," p. 193.

89. Ironically, whenever any group of workers passed into a phase of improving living standards, the acquisition of timepieces was one of the first things noted by observers. E. P. Thompson, "Time," p. 70.

90. Hobbes, *Leviathan* [1651], quoted in Hirschman, *Passions*, p. 97.

91. Quoted in G. S. Wood, *Radicalism*, p. 34. Laws setting maximum wages for different sorts of wage labor, and compelling the propertyless to enter service on pain of severe punishment, were common throughout early modern Europe.

92. Quoted in Mitchell Dean, *The Constitution of Property: Toward a Genealogy of Liberal Governance* (London: Routledge, 1991), p. 145. Not all political thinkers agreed. According to Adam Smith, for example, "What improves the circumstances of the greater part [of society] can never be regarded as an inconveniency to the

whole. No society can surely be flourishing and happy, of which the far greater part of the members are poor and miserable. It is but equity, besides, that they who feed, clothe, and lodge the whole body of the people, should have such a share of the produce of their own labour as to be themselves tolerably well fed, clothed and lodged." Adam Smith, *Wealth of Nations* (London: J. M. Dent, 1937), vol. 1, chap. 8, p. 70.

93. Malthus, *Essay.*

94. Thomas Chalmers, *The Christian and Civic Economy of Large Towns,* vol. 1 (Glasgow: Chalmers and Collins, 1821), pp. 1–3.

95. Levine, *Reproducing,* pp. 68–72; Dean, *Constitution,* pp. 93–94.

96. Lis and Soly, "Policing," pp. 187, 195–97.

97. Ann Shola Orloff, *The Politics of Pensions: A Comparative Analysis of Britain, Canada and the United States, 1880–1940* (Madison: University of Wisconsin Press, 1993), pp. 132–33.

98. R. Johnson, "Educational Policy," p. 111. This is a different argument from that in an influential early article by Jones and Williamson ("Birth"), which argues that environmental arguments *superseded* moral ones. See also Szreter, *Fertility,* p. 88.

99. B. Taylor, *Eve,* p. 200; Seccombe, *Weathering,* pp. 50–54; Lis and Soly, "Policing," p. 205.

100. One well-known proposal was put forward by Caroline Chisholm in 1847 in *Emigration and Transportation Relatively Considered* (1847). See also Schwarzkopf, *Women,* p. 107; Donzelot, *Policing,* p. 36; and Linda L. Clark, *Schooling the Daughters of Marianne: Textbooks and the Socialization of Girls in Modern French Primary Schools* (Albany: State University of New York Press, 1984), pp. 34–35.

101. Quoted in Schwarzkopf, *Women,* p. 210.

102. Richard Johnson, "Notes on the Schooling of the English Working Class, 1780–1850," in R. Dale et al. (eds.), *Schooling and Capitalism* (London: Routledge and Kegan Paul, 1976).

103. Anna Davin, "'Mind You Do As You Are Told': Reading Books for Board School Girls, 1870–1902," *Feminist Review* 3 (1979): 89–98; Purvis, *History,* p. 31; Marjorie Theobald, *Knowing Women: Origins of Women's Education in Nineteenth-Century Australia* (Cambridge: Cambridge University Press, 1996).

104. Pat Thane, "Women and the Poor Law in Victorian and Edwardian England," *History Workshop* 6 (1978): 29–51; Rose, *Limited Livelihoods,* pp. 52–55.

105. Dean, *Constitution.*

106. Ibid., pp. 97–99, 170–71.

107. Orloff, *Politics,* p. 131.

108. In 1858, for example, Newcastle commissioners concluded that poor children should work rather than be compelled to go to school: "Independence is of more importance than education; and if the wages of the child's labour are necessary, either to keep the parents from the poor rates, or to relieve the pressure

of severe and bitter poverty, it is far better that it should go to work at the earliest age at which it can bear the physical exertion than that it should remain at school." Quoted in Rubinstein, *School Attendance*, p. 5. See also Hurt, *Elementary Schooling*, p. 58.

109. Malthus [1798] himself argued that for a man with a large family, "any ill luck whatever, [and] no degree of frugality, no possible exertion of his manual strength, could preserve him from the heart-rending sensation of seeing his children starve, or of forfeiting his independence, and being obliged to the parish for their support." Quoted in Dean, *Constitution*, p. 79.

110. L. H. Lees, "The Survival of the Unfit: Welfare Policies and Family Maintenance in Nineteenth-Century London," in P. Mandler (ed.), *The Uses of Charity: The Poor on Relief in the Nineteenth-Century Metropolis* (Philadelphia: University of Pennsylvania Press, 1990), pp. 79–80. Similar effects have been attributed to the abolition of outdoor relief in the United States. Orloff, *Politics*, pp. 133–34.

111. A letter from George Harney to Yorkshire Chartists, *Northern Star,* 1838, quoted in Anna Clark, "The Rhetoric of Chartist Domesticity: Gender, Language, and Class in the 1830s and 1840s," *Journal of British Studies* 31, no. 1 (1992): 62. The forcible separation of families in workhouses, one of the most bitterly resisted aspects of the New Poor Law, inspired some of the many Poor Law riots.

112. Massimo Livi-Bacci, *A Concise History of World Population* (Cambridge, Mass.: Blackwell, 1992), p. 6.

113. Lis and Soly, "Policing," pp. 200–207.

114. Mary Louise Roberts, *Civilization without Sexes: Reconstructing Gender Relations in Postwar France, 1917–1927* (Chicago: University of Chicago Press, 1994), pp. 99–100. See also Anne Cava, "French Feminism and Maternity: Theories and Policies, 1890–1918," in G. Bock and P. Thane (eds.), *Maternity and Gender Policies: Women and the Rise of the European Welfare States, 1880s–1950s* (London: Routledge, 1991).

115. Rachel G. Fuchs "Preserving the Future of France: Aid to the Poor and Pregnant in Nineteenth-Century Paris," in Mandler, *Uses of Charity,* pp. 93–94, 110.

116. Quoted in Lis and Soly, "Policing," p. 203.

117. Fuchs, "Preserving," pp. 93–94, 110. According to Fuchs, public officials in Paris had no interest in taking children away from mothers; on the contrary, they went to considerable lengths to prevent abandonment, and usually did not stop aid to a single mother even if they disapproved of her morals. Indeed, if in the first part of the century most aid to mothers went to those in legitimate marriages, after 1870 most went to unmarried mothers, and might even have discouraged marriage because a husband's (but not a lover's) income could not be concealed from the authorities and would lead to the loss of benefits.

118. S. Koven and S. Mitchel, "Womanly Duties: Maternalist Politics and the Origins of Welfare States in France, Germany, Great Britain, and the United States,

1880–1920," *American Historical Review* 95, no. 4 (1990): 1076–1108. See also S. Koven and S. Mitchel, *Mothers of a New World: Maternalist Politics and the Origins of Welfare States* (New York: Routledge, 1994).

6. Assembling School Systems

1. Sir Robert Inglis, quoted in Hopkins, *Childhood*, p. 133.

2. *Register,* South Australia, 24 April 1873.

3. Boston School Committee, 1857–58, quoted in M. B. Katz, *The Irony of Early School Reform: Educational Innovation in Early Nineteenth-Century Massachusetts* (Cambridge, Mass.: Harvard University Press, 1968), p. 120.

4. *South Australian Parliamentary Papers,* 1881, no. 122, p. 147/2994.

5. Victorian Lady Teachers' Association, Australia, 1880s, quoted in Theobald, *Knowing*, p. 164.

6. Marjorie Lamberti, *State, Society and the Elementary School in Imperial Germany* (New York: Oxford University Press, 1989), p. 14.

7. Peter Flora, *State, Economy and Society in Western Europe, 1815–1975: A Data Handbook in Two Volumes* (Frankfurt: Campus Verlag, 1983).

8. Simon Frith, "Socialization and Rational Schooling: Elementary Education in Leeds before 1870," in P. McCann (ed.), *Popular Education and Socialization in the Nineteenth Century* (London: Methuen, 1977), p. 80.

9. The distinction between school enrollment and attendance is important. The fact that a child's name appeared on a school roll tells us little about the time she actually spent in school; it might have been one day in the year or two hundred. Problematic as they are, attendance statistics are a much more reliable guide to the actual use of schools.

10. Y. N. Soysal and D. Strang, "Construction of the First Mass Education Systems in Nineteenth-Century Europe," *Sociology of Education* 62, no. 4 (1989): 277–88.

11. J. G. Richardson, "Variation in the Date of Enactment of Compulsory School Attendance Laws: An Empirical Enquiry," *Sociology of Education* 53, no. 3 (1980): 153–63; J. G. Richardson, "Settlement Patterns and the Governing Structures of Nineteenth-Century School Systems," *American Journal of Education* 92, no. 2 (1984): 178–206; J. G. Richardson, "Historical Sequences and the Origins of Common Schooling in the American States," in J. G. Richardson (ed.), *Handbook of Theory and Research in the Sociology of Education* (New York: Greenwood, 1986).

12. Maynes, *Schooling in Western Europe,* p. 70; Kenneth Barkin, "Social Control and the Volksschule in Vormärz Prussia," *Central European History* 16, no. 1 (1983): 36.

13. Quoted in A. T. Allen, "Gardens of Children, Gardens of God: Kindergartens and Day-Care Centres in Nineteenth-Century Germany," *Journal of Social History* 19, no. 3 (1986): 440.

14. Barkin, "Social Control," p. 51.

15. Lamberti, *State.*

16. Maynes, *Taking the Hard Road,* p. 88.

17. Pollard, *Peaceful Conquest,* p. 159. In his later work, Pollard modifies this claim by noting that German elementary schools were not nearly as good, and that English ones were nearly as bad, as contemporaries claimed and historians repeated. See also Barkin, "Social Control."

18. Flora, *State,* vol. 1, pp. 586, 628.

19. Recent exceptions are Margaret Archer, *The Social Origins of Educational Systems* (London: Sage Publications, 1979), and Andy Green, *Education and State Formation: The Rise of Education Systems in England, France and the USA* (London: Macmillan, 1990).

20. Human capital theories, attempting to explain economic differences between "developed" and "underdeveloped" countries and better- and worse-paid segments of the workforce, were particularly influential in the 1960s and 1970s.

21. See S. Bowles and H. Gintis, *Schooling in Capitalist America* (London: Routledge and Kegan Paul, 1976); R. Johnson, "Notes."

22. For a classic statement, see Randall Collins, "Functional and Conflict Theories of Educational Stratification," *American Sociological Review* 36, no. 6 (1971): 1002–1019.

23. See, for example, P. Miller and I. Davey, "Family, Schooling and the Patriarchal State," in M. R. Theobald and R. J. W. Selleck, *Family, School and State in Australian History* (Sydney: Allen and Unwin, 1990); Ian Davey, "Capitalism, Patriarchy and the Origins of Mass Schooling: The Radical Debate," in Ali Rattansi and David Reeder, *Rethinking Radical Education: Essays in Honour of Brian Simon* (London: Lawrence and Wishart, 1992).

24. C. Tilly, *Coercion,* pp. 14, 54.

25. Lis and Soly, "Policing." See also C. Lis and H. Soly, *Poverty and Capitalism in Pre-industrial Europe* (Brighton: Harvester Press, 1982).

26. See, for example, Rebel, *Peasant Classes,* pp. 137, 22; Kocka, "Problems," p. 289.

27. E. M. Wood, *Pristine Culture,* p. 105.

28. Particularly notable are debates around Perry Anderson and Tom Nairn's "Origins of the Present Crisis," *New Left Review* 23 (1964): 26–53, and E. P. Thompson's "The Peculiarities of the English," in E. P. Thompson, *The Poverty of Theory and Other Essays* (London: Merlin Press, 1978).

29. John Brewer, *The Sinews of Power: War, Money and the English State, 1688–1783* (London: Unwin Hyman, 1989).

30. In a related argument, Eldridge draws attention to the fact that in the half-century between 1815 and 1875, an era of free trade when Britain (according to the majority of historians) was supposedly not interested in imperialism, the empire expanded by an average of about 100,000 square miles a year. C. C. Eldridge (ed.), *British Imperialism in the Nineteenth Century* (London: Macmillan, 1984), p. 29. By 1933, the British Empire covered 23 percent of the land surface of the globe and ruled a quarter of the world's population.

31. Much "policing" in Britain was regionally or privately funded and controlled, and as such was not counted in conventional statistics on taxation or state expenditure. Voluntary and localized initiatives ranged from justices of the peace and schools to local police forces and the East India Company with its private armies.

32. E. M. Wood, *Pristine Culture,* pp. 22–23, 61. See also P. Anderson, *Lineages,* p. 97.

33. E. M. Wood, *Pristine Culture,* pp. 15, 34, 48, 117. Even though they do not focus on comparative issues, Corrigan and Sayer develop a parallel argument in their study of the cultural processes associated with English state formation. Corrigan and Sayer, *Great Arch.*

34. Quoted in Melton, *Absolutism,* p. 163.

35. Quoted in ibid., p. 162.

36. Quoted in ibid., p. 165.

37. Quoted in ibid., p. 168.

38. One successful system-wide experiment was implemented in late-eighteenth-century Bohemia. Children were taught reading, writing, arithmetic, and religion in the morning, and spinning in the afternoon. Attendance was encouraged by paying the children cash for their homespuns rather than by imposing fines on parents who kept their sons and daughters at home. Because of the desperate shortage of spinning labor, noble landlords readily provided the raw wool, cotton, or flax, which they then purchased from the schools after it had been spun. By 1790, spinning classes had been introduced into five hundred parish schools, almost 25 percent of all schools in Bohemia, and were attended by around 75 percent of the school-age population. Melton, *Absolutism,* pp. 131, 138, 231–32.

39. Jones and Williamson, "Birth," p. 100.

40. Sidney Pollard, *Britain's Prime and Britain's Decline: The British Economy 1870–1914* (London: Edward Arnold, 1989), p. 125.

41. For a survey of evidence that literacy preceded factory industrialization, and that early industrialization and the urban growth that accompanied it were associated with initial falls in levels of literacy, see Maynes, *Schooling in Western Europe,* chap. 7.

42. Hopkins, *Childhood,* p. 133. In the United States, according to Kaestle, the argument that mass elementary education would spread dissent among the lower orders and make *white* workers unfit for their station in life was almost unheard. Opposition to education was substantial and effective on only one issue: the schooling of slaves. Carl F. Kaestle, "'Between the Scylla of Brutal Ignorance and the Charybdis of a Literary Education': Elite Attitudes toward Mass Schooling in Early Industrial England and America," in L. Stone (ed.), *Schooling and Society* (Baltimore: Johns Hopkins University Press, 1976).

43. Pollard, *Britain's Prime,* p. 139.

44. David Vincent, *Literacy and Popular Culture: England, 1750–1914* (Cambridge: Cambridge University Press, 1993), pp. 121–22.

45. Hobsbawm, *Age of Revolution*, pp. 45–46.

46. Pollard, *Peaceful Conquest*, pp. 125, 147–48.

47. In Britain, with its huge surplus of cheap labor combined with relatively effective union opposition to many forms of new technology, this process proceeded more slowly than elsewhere. According to Samuel, even the "railway mania" of 1845–47 employed some 300,000 men with picks and shovels. Samuel, "Workshop," p. 28.

48. For a classic statement, see D. S. Landes, *The Unbound Prometheus: Technological Change and Industrial Development in Western Europe from 1750 to the Present* (Cambridge: Cambridge University Press, 1969), p. 344. For a comprehensive reexamination of the case, see Pollard, *Britain's Prime*, chap. 3.

49. Pollard, *Britain's Prime*, p. 200.

50. Ibid., chap. 3; P. Miller, *Long Division*, chap. 6.

51. See, for example, Rose, *Limited Livelihoods*; June Purvis, "Working-Class Women and Adult Education in Nineteenth-Century Britain," *History of Education* 9, no. 3 (1980): 183–212. In his overview of education, science, and technology, Pollard simply states that "the education of girls and women will be largely ignored, as it has been omitted in most of the relevant literature." Pollard, *Britain's Prime*, p. 116.

52. See, for example, C. Cockburn, *Brothers: Male Dominance and Technological Change* (London: Pluto Press, 1983).

53. Purvis, "Working-Class Women"; Carol Dyhouse, "Towards a 'Feminine' Curriculum for English Schoolgirls: The Demands of Ideology, 1870–1963," *Women's Studies International Quarterly* 1, no. 4 (1978): 297–311; C. Dyhouse, "Social Darwinistic Ideas and the Development of Women's Education in England, 1880–1920," *History of Education* 5, no. 1 (1976): 41–58; John R. Rury, "Vocationalism for Home and Work: Women's Education in the United States, 1880–1930," *History of Education Quarterly* 24, no. 1 (1984): 21–44.

54. Pollard, *Peaceful Conquest*, pp. 123–24.

55. Hobsbawm, *Age of Revolution*, pp. 21–22; D. Hamilton, *Towards a Theory of Schooling* (London: Falmer Press, 1989), p. 122.

56. On personal links and friendships between different reformers, inspectors, and school administrators, see, for example, Curtis, "Representation," especially notes 3, 11, and 53.

57. Pollard, *Integration*, pp. 90, 97.

58. Quoted in P. Corrigan, B. Curtis, and R. Lanning, "The Political Space of Schooling," in T. Wotherspoon (ed.), *The Political Economy of Canadian Schooling* (Toronto: Methuen, 1987), pp. 36, 38.

59. Barkin, "Social Control," pp. 38–39.

60. Richardson, "Variation," p. 155.

61. Kay-Shuttleworth in England, Guizot in France, Ryerson in Canada West, Wilkins in New South Wales, and Hartley in South Australia were all men who managed to assemble great personal power and used their considerable ability to

construct sturdy and effective educational bureaucracies. For an example of administrative chaos, see Denis Grundy, "The Formation of a Disordered Teaching Service in Victoria, 1851–1871," *History of Education Review* 18, no. 2 (1989): 1–20.

62. Eley, "Nations," p. 292.

63. See in particular Bruce Curtis, *Building the Educational State: Canada West, 1836–1871* (London: Falmer Press, 1988); Bruce Curtis, *True Government by Choice Men: Inspection, Education and State Formation in Canada West* (Toronto: University of Toronto Press, 1992); R. D. Gidney and D. A. Lawr, "Bureaucracy vs Community? The Origins of Bureaucratic Procedure in the Upper Canadian School System," *Journal of Social History* 13, no. 3 (1980): 438–57.

64. B. Curtis, "The Canada *Blue Books* and the Administrative Capacity of the Canadian State, 1822–1867," *Canadian Historical Review* 74, no. 4 (1993): 535–65.

65. J. S. Mill, 1833, quoted in Curtis, *True Government*, p. 26.

66. Curtis, *True Government*, p. 32.

67. Ibid., p. 30.

68. Bruce Curtis, "Gender in the Regime of Statistical Knowledge/Power," ANZHES Conference, Melbourne, 1993, typescript, p. 8.

69. Curtis, "Canada *Blue Books*."

70. Curtis, *True Government*, p. 30.

71. For a similar process in South Australia, see P. Miller, *Long Division*, pp. 49–56.

72. Curtis, "Representation," p. 79.

73. B. Curtis, "Révolution gouvernementale et savoir politique au Canada-Uni," *Sociologie et sociétés* 24 (1992): 169–79.

74. Curtis, "Representation," p. 81.

75. Sharif Gemie, "What Is a School? Defining and Controlling Primary Schooling in Early Nineteenth-Century France," *History of Education* 21, no. 2 (1992): 134–35.

76. Ibid., pp. 136–39.

77. Grew and Harrigan, *School*, chap. 2.

78. Quoted in Gemie, "What Is a School?" p. 144. In their search for this miraculous general measure, many countries adopted annual external examinations of all pupils.

79. Phil Gardner, *The Lost Elementary Schools of Victorian England* (London: Croom Helm, 1984), pp. 48, 62, 165.

80. See in particular Gidney and Lawr, "Bureaucracy." In Australia, a similar approach has been used by Malcolm Vick.

81. Curtis, *True Government*, pp. 47–51. Lamberti quotes a contemporary who wrote, "In the [Prussian] state government under Frederick William III and just as much in the school administration, public agitation had no significant effect on the decisions of officials. Minister von Altenstein could still reign over the whole [education] system like a grand seigneur. . . . Beginning in 1840 all this changed; the political movements in public life did not go without a noticeable effect on the

school system. . . . Following the civil code's conception of the school as an institution of the state, there came next political parties with their claims to the school; it has remained ever since then an arena of conflict between various and often conflicting principles and interests." Lamberti, *State*, p. 26.

82. Victor Cousin, quoted in Curtis, *True Government*, p. 50.

83. Ibid., p. 51.

84. Gidney and Lawr, "Bureaucracy," pp. 438, 442, 444–45, 448.

85. Curtis, *Building*, chap. 8.

86. Gidney and Lawr, "Bureaucracy," p. 448.

87. Bruce Curtis, "Preconditions of the Canadian State: Educational Reform and the Construction of a Public in Upper Canada, 1837–1846," *Studies in Political Economy* 10 (1983): 103–104.

88. This and the following paragraphs are based on Christopher Dandeker, *Surveillance, Power and Modernity: Bureaucracy and Discipline from 1700 to the Present Day* (Cambridge: Polity Press, 1990), pp. 68–101, 167–73.

89. Weber, *Economy and Society*, vol. 2, chap. 14, p. 1111.

90. Foucault, "Governmentality," p. 92.

91. Rosemary Pringle, *Secretaries Talk: Sexuality, Power and Work* (Sydney: Allen and Unwin, 1988), p. 88.

92. J. Burstyn, "Women's Education in England during the Nineteenth Century: A Review of the Literature," *History of Education* 6, no. 1 (1977): 13.

93. Kindergarten methods, with their special reliance on women, became influential only later in the century, and even then were only rarely taken up.

94. Maynes, *Schooling in Western Europe*, pp. 62–63, 71.

95. Theobald, *Knowing*, p. 149.

96. Maynes, *Schooling in Western Europe*, p. 70.

97. B. Condon (ed.), *The Confidential Letterbook of the South Australian Inspector General of Schools, 1880–1914* (Adelaide: Murray Park CAE, 1976), letters no. 60, 104, 147.

98. *SAPP*, 1882, no. 27, p. 86/4807.

99. B. K. Hyams, "The Teacher in South Australia in the Second Half of the Nineteenth Century," *Australian Journal of Education* 15, no. 3 (1971): 288.

100. *SAPP*, 1891, no. 43, p. xvi.

101. *SAPP*, 1882, no. 27, p. 203.

102. *SAPP*, 1898–99, no. 44, p. 15.

103. The Revised Code, introduced as both a cost-saving and a control measure, was strongly opposed by leading educationists for the same reason it was later condemned in South Australia. Importantly, according to Vincent, its introduction was influenced by persistent demands of working-class parents for quick and efficient teaching of the 3Rs. D. Vincent, *Literacy*, p. 54.

104. *SAPP*, 1881, no. 122, p. 27/528.

105. *SAPP*, 1882, no. 27, p. 74/4533.

106. *SAPP*, 1902, no. 44, p. 23.

107. A. Prentice, "The Feminization of Teaching," in S. M. Trofimenkoff and A. Prentice, *The Neglected Majority: Essays in Canadian Women's History* (Toronto: McClelland and Stewart, 1977), p. 52.

108. Quoted in ibid., p. 61. There is some evidence, at least in Canada, that any enthusiasm the leading promoters of school reform might have had regarding the superior educative and nurturing qualities of the schoolmistress had come only grudgingly, and only when the numerical dominance of women in the state elementary schools was already a reality. A. Prentice and M. Theobald (eds.), *Women Who Taught: Perspectives on the History of Women and Teaching* (Toronto: University of Toronto Press, 1991), p. 6.

109. The term "feminization of teaching" is misleading because eighteenth- and nineteenth-century women had already taught—"as mothers and female relatives in the home, as governesses . . . in a variety of dame schools; in Catholic convent schools; in middle-class ladies academies. . . . The recruitment of women as teachers by the state signalled a shift of location, a transformation of their teaching labour, a loss of autonomy, but not a radical new departure in the history of women's work." Prentice and Theobald, *Women Who Taught*, p. 9.

110. Steedman, "Mother," pp. 158, 163.

111. Grumet, "Pedagogy," pp. 173–74.

112. Prentice and Theobald, *Women Who Taught*, p. 10.

113. Ibid., p. 7.

114. P. Miller, *Long Division*, pp. 52–53, 372.

115. Flora, *State*, vol. 1, chap. 10.

116. M. Danylewycz, B. Light, and A. Prentice, "The Evolution of the Sexual Division of Labour in Teaching: A Nineteenth-Century Ontario and Quebec Case Study," *Histoire Sociale/Social History* 16, no. 31 (1983): 81–109; M. Danylewycz and A. Prentice, "Teachers, Gender and Bureaucratizing School Systems in Nineteenth Century Montreal and Toronto," *History of Education Quarterly* 24, no. 1 (1984): 75–100.

117. Theobald, *Knowing*; M. R. Theobald, "Women's Teaching Labour, the Family and the State in Nineteenth-Century Victoria," in M. R. Theobald and R. J. W. Selleck, *Family, School and State in Australian History* (Sydney: Allen and Unwin, 1990). In her book on the New South Wales public service, Desley Deacon similarly argues that while by the 1870s head offices of departments in Sydney continued to be exclusively male preserves, no consistent policy emerged toward the employment of women. Many country and suburban post and telegraph offices were run by women employed on equal terms with men; as in the case of schools, many of these offices became family fiefdoms. Desley Deacon, *Managing Gender: The State, the New Middle Class and Women Workers, 1830–1930* (Melbourne: Oxford University Press, 1989).

118. Theobald, "Women's Teaching Labor," p. 27; R. J. W. Selleck, "Mary Helena Stark: The Troubles of a Nineteenth-Century State School Teacher," in Prentice and Theobald, *Women Who Taught*.

119. See Prentice and Theobald, *Women Who Taught*, p. 15.

120. Theobald notes, however, that she found only two references to the breast-feeding of infants by married women teachers in the thousands of documents she read in the files of the Victorian Education Department. Theobald, *Knowing,* p. 177.

121. Theobald, "Women's Teaching Labor," p. 36; Theobald, *Knowing,* p. 141. See also Tyler, "Irene Tuckerman," pp. 52–67.

7. Social Movements, Individual Agency, and the School

1. Quoted in Hurt, *Elementary Schooling,* p. 111.

2. HMI inspector, 1847, quoted in D. Vincent, *Literacy,* p. 73.

3. William Cobbett, *Advice to Young Men,* quoted in R. Johnson, "'Really Useful Knowledge': Radical Education and Working Class Culture, 1790–1848," in J. Clarke et al. (eds.), *Working Class Culture* (London: Hutchinson, 1979), p. 78.

4. Quote from Arthur Symons's essay "Edgware Road: A Study in Living," in Gagnier, *Subjectivities,* p. 122.

5. Inspector Moseley, 1845, quoted in R. Johnson, "Educational Policy," p. 104.

6. *Labour Advocate,* South Australia, 16 March 1878.

7. Michel Foucault, "La pousière et le nuage," in Michelle Perrot (ed.), *L'Impossible prison* (Paris: Éditions du Seuil, 1980), p. 35; my translation.

8. Christian Garvé, 1786, quoted in Melton, *Absolutism,* p. 145.

9. Maynes, *Schooling in Western Europe,* p. 44.

10. Corrigan et al., "Political Space," pp. 21, 24.

11. Curtis, *Building,* p. 110.

12. Ibid., p. 315.

13. Hunter, "Pastoral Bureaucracy"; Hunter, *Rethinking,* pp. 103, 132, 166.

14. Hunter, *Rethinking,* p. 103.

15. P. Willis, *Learning to Labour: How Working Class Kids Get Working Class Jobs* (Westmead: Saxon House, 1978); A. McRobbie, "Working Class Girls and the Culture of Femininity," in Women's Studies Group, Centre for Contemporary Cultural Studies, University of Birmingham, *Women Take Issue* (London: Hutchinson, 1978).

16. David Vincent, *Bread, Knowledge and Freedom: A Study of Nineteenth-Century Working-Class Autobiography* (London: Methuen, 1982); D. Vincent, *Literacy.*

17. Mary Jo Maynes, "The Contours of Childhood: Demography, Strategy, and Mythology of Childhood in French and German Lower-Class Autobiographies," in J. R. Gillis, L. Tilly, and D. Levine (eds.), *The European Experience of Declining Fertility, 1850–1970* (Cambridge, Mass.: Blackwell, 1992), p. 107.

18. Quoted in D. Vincent, *Bread,* p. 6.

19. Ibid., p. 36.

20. Maynes, *Taking the Hard Road,* p. 38.

21. The Penny Post, representing a massive reduction in the cost of postage, was introduced in 1840 for the express purpose of facilitating communication between working people separated by long distances, not least to encourage labor mobility and the sense of nationhood. Letter writing between working-class family members does not seem to have increased for many years, but those working-class activists most keen to use the mail were still on the wrong side of the law. Sending

threatening letters, a capital offense until 1823, was in the 1840s still punishable by transportation for life, and under the Seditious Meetings Act of 1817, it remained illegal for the members or officers of political societies to write to each other. D. Vincent, *Literacy,* pp. 33, 230.

22. D. Vincent, *Bread,* pp. 91, 93. For an interesting discussion of "awakening," see L. Johnson, *The Modern Girl: Girlhood and Growing Up* (Sydney: Allen and Unwin, 1993).

23. D. Vincent, *Literacy,* p. 196.

24. The pursuit of useful knowledge for each one of the working-class biographers, Vincent concludes, "was nothing less than to effect a transformation in his consciousness and in his relationship with the external world." D. Vincent, *Bread,* p. 135.

25. Ibid., p. 136; D. Vincent, *Literacy,* p. 7.

26. D. Vincent, *Bread,* p. 136.

27. Ibid., p. 135.

28. According to a contemporary commentator (1867), "A working man who is moderately well-read, who is capable of expressing himself in proper and appropriate language, of writing a well-phrased letter, or drawing up an address or the heading of a subscription list in suitable terms, is a rarity in the workshop, and is regarded and honoured as such by his fellow-workmen, who speak for him as a great 'scholard,' refer to him to decide disputes for them, or tell them how to write their most particular letters, put their grievances into addresses and petitions, or act as secretary to their meetings and associations, and be their spokesman when occasion shall require." Quoted in D. Vincent, *Literacy,* p. 265.

29. Quoted in P. H. J. H. Gosden (ed.), *How They Were Taught: An Anthology of Contemporary Accounts of Learning and Teaching in England, 1800–1950* (Oxford: Basil Blackwell, 1969), p. 49.

30. Curtis, *Building,* pp. 316, 321.

31. Maynes, *Taking the Hard Road,* pp. 88, 96.

32. Ibid., pp. 90, 92–93, 97.

33. Maynes, "Contours," pp. 101–24.

34. D. Vincent, *Literacy,* pp. 83, 153.

35. Nan Hackett, "A Different Form of 'Self': Narrative Style in British Nineteenth-Century Working-Class Autobiography," *biography* 12, no. 3 (1989): 208–25.

36. Ibid., p. 223.

37. M. J. Maynes, "Gender and Narrative Form in French and German Working-Class Autobiographies," in Personal Narratives Group (ed.), *Interpreting Women's Lives: Feminist Theory and Personal Narratives* (Bloomington: Indiana University Press, 1989), pp. 108, 113.

38. Gagnier, *Subjectivities.*

39. Ibid., pp. 144, 142, 42.

40. William Morris, "The Society of the Future" (1887), quoted in ibid., p. 275.

41. Ibid., pp. 62–93.

42. Ibid., pp. 59–62. The letters Gagnier refers to are published in Margaret Llewelyn Davies (ed.), *Maternity: Letters from Working Women* [1915] (London: Virago, 1978). The editor notes that the cooperative movement was largely composed of better-paid manual workers. The women officeholders of the guild, who wrote the letters, lived in better conditions than the average working woman. About a third of the letters report a history of unproblematic pregnancies and confinements; the rest chronicle a range of serious material and physical hardships. The same letters also form part of the evidence for Seccombe's work on fertility decline.

43. One woman wrote, "I often think women are really worse than beasts. During the time of pregnancy, the male beast keeps entirely from the female: not so with the woman; she is at the prey of a man just the same as though she was not pregnant. . . . As soon as the birth is over, she is tortured again. If the woman does not feel well she must not say so, as a man has such a lot of ways of punishing a woman if she does not give in to him. . . ." Davies, *Maternity,* pp. 48–49. The numbers in parentheses refer to page numbers in the 1978 edition of Davies's book.

44. Ross notes that the mothers' "autostarvation" was partly a struggle for control resembling in some odd way anorexia as it appears today—indeed, anorexia was identified as a syndrome during this period. E. Ross, *Love and Toil: Motherhood in Outcast London, 1870–1918* (New York: Oxford University Press, 1993), pp. 54–55.

45. Similar findings have been reported again and again by social historians. In a fine analysis of marital relations, Ayers and Lambertz, for example, argue that in tacit agreement with their husbands, most wives bore alone the enormous physical and mental strains of managing on inadequate incomes. Their reward was continued "autonomy" in managing the house, the confidence of their husbands, and avoidance of the violence that demands for additional money almost inevitably provoked. Pat Ayers and Jan Lambertz, "Marriage Relations, Money and Domestic Violence in Working-Class Liverpool, 1919–39," in Jane Lewis (ed.), *Labour and Love: Women's Experience of Home and Family, 1850–1940* (Oxford: Basil Blackwell, 1986).

46. Gagnier, *Subjectivities,* pp. 59–62. See also Koven and Mitchel, "Womanly Duties"; Koven and Mitchel, *Mothers;* G. Bock and P. Thane (eds.), *Maternity and Gender Policies: Women and the Rise of the European Welfare States, 1880s–1950s* (London: Routledge, 1991).

47. Ironically, while their daughters *did* have fewer children, most oral histories reveal the younger women's bitterness about mothers not telling them about sex.

48. R. Johnson, "'Really Useful Knowledge'"; Ross, *Love and Toil,* p. 147; Hobsbawm, *Age of Capital,* pp. 226–27; Eley, "Nations," p. 328; Eley, "Edward Thompson," p. 31.

49. E. P. Thompson, *Making,* p. 451.

50. Ibid., p. 458. Rules of the apparently all-male Small-ware Weavers' Society from the 1750s, for example, noted (obviously aware of some scope for improvement), "If we consider this Society, not as a Company of Men met to regale themselves with Ale and Tobacco, and talk indifferently of all Subjects: but rather as a Society sitting to Protect the Rights and Privileges of a Trade by which some

hundreds of People . . . subsist . . . how awkward does it look to see its members jumbled promiscuously one amongst another, talking indifferently on all subjects." Quoted in ibid., p. 457.

51. Quoted in Hunter, *Rethinking*, p. 73.

52. E. P. Thompson, *Making*, pp. 468–69.

53. B. Taylor, *Eve*, pp. 222–23.

54. See in particular R. Johnson, "'Really Useful Knowledge'"; and R. Johnson, "Radical Education and the New Right," in A. Rattansi and D. Reeder, *Rethinking Radical Education: Essays in Honour of Brian Simon* (London: Lawrence and Wishart, 1992).

55. Cobbett, 1833, quoted in R. Johnson, "Radical Education," p. 280.

56. Quoted in T. Laqueur, "Working-Class Demand and the Growth of English Elementary Education, 1750–1850," in L. Stone (ed.), *Schooling and Society: Studies in the History of Education* (Baltimore: Johns Hopkins University Press, 1976), p. 192.

57. R. Johnson, "'Really Useful Knowledge.'"

58. Brian Simon, *The Two Nations and the Educational Structure, 1780–1870* (London: Lawrence and Wishart, 1974), p. 268.

59. Owen, 1838, quoted in R. Johnson, "'Really Useful Knowledge,'" p. 96.

60. R. Johnson, "Radical Education," p. 280.

61. Maynes, *Schooling in Western Europe*, chap. 6, pp. 103, 113–14.

62. R. Johnson, "'Really Useful Knowledge,'" p. 100.

63. Eley, "Edward Thompson," pp. 25–27, quoting Michael Vester.

64. Barkin, "Social Control," pp. 46, 50.

65. Ibid., p. 49.

66. Eley, "Edward Thompson," p. 29.

67. Quoted in ibid., p. 35.

68. Ruth L. Smith and Deborah M. Valenze, "Mutuality and Marginality: Liberal Moral Theory and Working-Class Women in Nineteenth-Century England," *Signs* 13, no. 2 (1988): 287–88.

69. Ibid., pp. 277–78.

70. Rousseau, *Emile*, pp. 332–33, 359.

71. Gagnier, *Subjectivities*, pp. 126, 136.

72. Maynes, *Schooling in Western Europe*, p. 136.

73. *SAPP*, 1896, no. 44, p. 14.

74. Quoted in D. Tyack, *The One Best System* (Cambridge, Mass.: Harvard University Press, 1974), p. 60.

75. Quoted in Finkelstein, *Governing*, p. 123.

8. The Reconstruction of Private Life

1. Letter to a young girl, quoted in Tilly and Scott, *Women*, p. 108.

2. Eight-year-old street trader, quoted in Carolyn Steedman, *Tidy House* (London: Virago Press, 1982), p. 57.

3. Simpson, *Treatise*, p. 125.

4. Tilly and Scott, *Women*, p. 102.

5. Quoted in Rose, *Limited Livelihoods*, p. 135.

6. *New South Wales Parliamentary Debates*, Australia, 17 October, 1895.

7. East Prussian landlord, quoted in P. R. Galloway, E. A. Hammel, and R. D. Lee, "Fertility Decline in Prussia," *Population Studies* 48 (1994): 135.

8. F. Madden MLA, *Victorian Parliamentary Debates*, Australia, 26 November 1895, p. 3496.

9. Levine, *Reproducing*, p. 191; Neville Hicks, *"This Sin and Scandal": Australia's Population Debate, 1891–1911* (Canberra: Australian National University Press, 1978), p. xvi; Mark J. Stern, *Society and Family Strategy: Erie County, New York, 1850–1920* (Albany: SUNY Press, 1987), p. 7.

10. Geraldine Jonçich Clifford, "'Daughters into Teachers': Educational and Demographic Influences on the Transformation of Teaching into 'Women's Work' in America," in Prentice and Theobald, *Women Who Taught*, p. 126.

11. J. C. Caldwell, "Mass Education as a Determinant of the Timing of Fertility Decline," *Population and Development Review* 6, no. 2 (1980): 232.

12. "Starting"—the delaying of first pregnancy after marriage—was also important, although not as statistically important.

13. See John Knodel, "Family Limitation and the Fertility Transition: Evidence from the Age Patterns of Fertility in Europe and Asia," *Population Studies* 31, no. 2 (1977): 219–49.

14. Hicks, *This Sin*.

15. Quoted in ibid., pp. 22–23.

16. Quoted in ibid., pp. 57, 59.

17. Quoted in ibid., p. 65.

18. Quoted in ibid., p. 48.

19. In England, for example, Fabian socialists such as Wells and Shaw advocated forced sterilization to prevent the spread of the "social disease of poverty," while the vicar in the poorest area of East End recommended penal settlements in isolated parts of the country, where the inmates would be well treated under life sentences, "and will not under any circumstances be allowed to propagate their species and so to propagate their type." Gagnier, *Subjectivities*, p. 119.

20. George Alter, "Theories of Fertility Decline: A Nonspecialist's Guide to the Current Debate," in J. R. Gillis, L. A. Tilly, and D. Levine (eds.), *The European Experience of Declining Fertility, 1850–1970: The Quiet Revolution* (Oxford: Blackwell, 1992), pp. 20–21. See also R. I. Woods, "Approaches to the Fertility Transition in Victorian England," *Population Studies* 41, no. 2 (1987): 283–311.

21. For a recent feminist commentary, see Alison MacKinnon, "Were Women Present at the Demographic Transition? Questions from a Feminist Historian to Historical Demographers," *Gender and History* 7, no. 2 (1995): 222–40.

22. J. C. Caldwell, "Toward a Restatement of Demographic Transition Theory," *Population and Development Review* 2, nos. 3–4 (1976): 358.

23. Gillis, Tilly, and Levine, *The European Experience,* p. 5; Alter, "Theories," p. 21.

24. Caldwell, "Mass Education," p. 225.

25. Caldwell, "Toward a Restatement," p. 345.

26. This family form bears many resemblances to the peasant and artisan households described in chapter 1.

27. Caldwell, "Mass Education," pp. 225–26.

28. Ibid., pp. 227–28.

29. Stern, *Society.*

30. Ibid., pp. 109–14.

31. Levine, *Reproducing,* chap. 4.

32. Caldwell himself argues that authoritarian schools cannot modernize mentalities, but believes that late-nineteenth-century elementary schools in the West did have modernizing effects.

33. Levine, *Reproducing,* pp. 175–76, 202, 212.

34. Although Levine argues that the adoption of the male breadwinner norm was closely related to family limitation, he notes that two major occupational groups conformed to a different logic. Miners, among the first to adopt male breadwinner families, were among the last to limit fertility, while textile workers, well known for their dependence on married women's paid work, were among the pioneers of the demographic transition.

35. Nancy Folbre, "Of Patriarchy Born: The Political Economy of Fertility Decisions," *Feminist Studies* 9, no. 2 (1983): 261, 270. See also Nancy Folbre, *Who Pays for the Kids? Gender and the Structures of Constraint* (London: Routledge, 1994).

36. Quoted in Ross, "Fierce Questions," p. 594.

37. Wally Seccombe, "Starting to Stop: Working-Class Fertility Decline in Britain," *Past and Present* 126 (1990): 152. See also "Debate," *Past and Present* 134 (1992): 200–211; and Wally Seccombe, "Men's 'Marital Rights' and Women's 'Wifely Duties': Changing Conjugal Relations in the Fertility Decline," in Gillis, Tilly, and Levine, *The European Experience.*

38. Seccombe, "Starting to Stop," p. 187. In contrast to some feminist commentators, Seccombe does not argue that all working women at the time disliked sex.

39. Ross, *Love and Toil,* p. 107. For some groups of women, nevertheless, the pleasure of sex came first. Maynes notes that in Saxon mining communities in the 1860s, suggestions that the poor should have fewer children always brought an angry response from the women: "This little pleasure is the only one we've got left; we're never gonna let them take it away from us." Quoted in Maynes, "Contours," p. 115.

40. Ross, *Love and Toil,* pp. 98–100. One measure of the desire of women to limit the size of their families was an increasing rate of abortions. See, for example, Seccombe, *Weathering,* pp. 158–59, 193; Patricia Knight, "Women and Abortion in Victorian and Edwardian England," *History Workshop* 4 (1977): 57–68.

41. See, for example, R. I. Wood, "Approaches," pp. 297, 309.

42. See, for example, J. Allen, "Contextualising Late Nineteenth-Century Feminism: Problems and Comparisons," *Journal of the Canadian Historical Association* 1, no. 1 (1990): 35–36.

43. Seccombe, "Starting to Stop," p. 186; Levine, *Reproducing*, chap. 4.

44. Malthus himself, however, was totally opposed to the use of contraception.

45. Szreter, *Fertility*.

46. Ibid., p. 351. Other commentators put greater emphasis on the usefulness of many sons as supplementary breadwinners in mining families. Mining communities combined high fertility with very high infant mortality and very low levels of married women's employment.

47. Szreter, *Fertility*, p. 426; Ross, *Love and Toil*, p. 58.

48. Simon Szreter, *Falling Fertilities and Changing Sexualities in Europe since c. 1850: A Comparative Survey of National Demographic Patterns* (Canberra: Research School of Social Sciences, Australian National University, 1996). By the later decades of the nineteenth century, Ross notes, sex was a mysterious and forbidden arena for working-class girls in London, whose mothers were struggling to keep them sexually ignorant and thus "respectable." Because sexual talk was suppressed in the working-class Victorian and Edwardian cultures of most regions, sex was one arena in which it was nearly impossible for wives to develop a collective sense of where their "rights" or "interests" lay. Ross, *Love and Toil*, pp. 98–100.

49. H. Hartmann's "Capitalism, Patriarchy and Job Segregation by Sex," in Zillah R. Eisenstein (ed.), *Capitalist Patriarchy and the Case for Socialist Feminism* (New York: Monthly Review Press, 1979), is an early, clear, and categorical statement of this thesis; since then, it has become the subject of wide-ranging debates and has inspired much more detailed and finely grained historical work.

50. B. Taylor, *Eve*. A more recent overview of these issues is Rose, *Limited Livelihoods*.

51. B. Taylor, *Eve*, p. 273; Seccombe, *Weathering*, chap. 4, pp. 111–123; Seccombe, "Patriarchy Stabilised."

52. Cynthia Cockburn, "The Gendering of Jobs: Workplace Relations and the Reproduction of Sex Segregation," in Sylvia Walby (ed.), *Gender Segregation at Work* (Milton Keynes: Open University Press, 1988), p. 5.

53. Katrina Honeyman and Jordan Goodman, "Women's Work, Gender Conflict, and Labour Markets in Europe, 1500–1900," *Economic History Review* 44, no. 4 (1991): 623; Marilyn J. Boxer and Jean H. Quataert (eds.), *Connecting Spheres: Women in the Western World, 1500 to the Present* (New York: Oxford University Press, 1987), p. 118.

54. B. Taylor, *Eve*, p. 272.

55. In households where men's wages fell below subsistence level, the opposite tended to be the case. Szreter, for example, refers to a 1908 Birmingham study which shows that in two impoverished wards, more than half of new mothers went to work in order to make family incomes come close to the subsistence minimum.

Even though they could not breastfeed their babies, infant mortality actually decreased, because there was more to eat. Szreter, *Fertility*, p. 244.

56. In British coal mining, for example, men in larger, more mechanized mines where individual wages were paid supported the exclusion of women workers, but those in small pits, used to working as small subcontractors employing family members, strongly opposed it. Jane Mark-Lawson and Anne Witz, "From 'Family Labour' to 'Family Wage'? The Case of Women's Labour in Nineteenth-Century Coalmining," *Social History* 13, no. 2 (1988).

57. Seccombe, *Weathering*, p. 118.

58. E. Jordan, "Female Unemployment in England and Wales, 1851–1911: An Examination of the Census Figures for 15–19 Year Olds," *Social History* 13, no. 2 (1988): 185.

59. Barbara Franzoi, "'. . . With the Wolf Always at the Door . . .': Women's Work in Domestic Industry in Britain and Germany," in Boxer and Quataert, *Connecting Spheres*, p. 153.

60. For a clear exposition of this argument, see Seccombe, "Patriarchy Stabilised."

61. Quoted in B. Taylor, *Eve*, p. 100.

62. E. P. Thompson, *Making*, pp. 376, 384; R. H. Bremmer, *Children and Youth in America: A Documentary History*, vol. 1: *1600–1865* (Cambridge, Mass.: Harvard University Press, 1970), p. 624; Maris A. Vinovskis, "Family and Schooling in Colonial and Nineteenth-Century America," *Journal of Family History* 12, nos. 1–3 (1987): 29; Hopkins, *Childhood*, pp. 219, 200–201. In the English countryside, according to Hurt, the Agricultural Children's Act, which came into force in 1875, was almost universally ignored by local authorities. Hurt, *Elementary Schooling*, p. 199.

63. Per Bolin-Hort, *Work, Family and the State: Child Labour and the Organisation of Production in the British Cotton Industry, 1780–1920* (Lund: Lund University Press, 1989), pp. 308–309.

64. In London alone, there were by 1878 fifty philanthropic societies for children, from orphanages, homes, and emigration societies to organizations for various forms of street trading. The first English Society for the Prevention of Cruelty to Children was set up in Liverpool in 1883; a year later, one was established in London. The National Society (the NSPCC) dates from 1889. The same year, the first Prevention of Cruelty to Children Act was passed, mandating penalties for those having custody of boys under fourteen and girls under sixteen who willfully ill-treated, neglected, abandoned, or exposed their charges. Hopkins, *Childhood*, pp. 200–201.

65. A. T. Allen, "Gardens," p. 440; Grundy, "Free Schooling," p. 173; P. Miller, *Long Division*, p. 35.

66. See, for example, Pollock, *Forgotten Children*, pp. 63–64.

67. Mandler, *Uses of Charity*.

68. Quoted in V. A. Zelizer, *Pricing the Priceless Child: The Changing Social Value of Children* (New York: Basic Books, 1985), p. 69.

69. Maynes, *Taking the Hard Road*, p. 115.

70. Gordon, *Heroes*, pp. 181, 183, 188.

71. In France, where serious enforcement of school attendance came only at a time when families were not so reliant on child labor, the pressure to choose work over school could produce wrenching awareness of the injustices and injuries of poverty. In contrast to Germany, however, the biographers represented their childhoods as "not so bad, despite everything," and overwhelmingly reported close and warm relationships with their mothers and often fathers. Maynes, "Contours," p. 101–102, 116–17, 121; Maynes, *Taking the Hard Road*, pp. 77–84.

72. Ross, *Love and Toil*, p. 161.

73. Bruce Bellingham, "Waifs and Strays: Child Abandonment, Foster Care, and Families in Mid-Nineteenth-Century New York," in Mandler, *Uses of Charity*.

74. Barbara Brenzel, *Daughters of the State: A Social Portrait of the First Reform School for Girls in North America, 1865–1905* (Cambridge, Mass.: MIT Press, 1983).

75. Rooke and Schnell's work on Canadian Protestant orphan homes in the second half of the nineteenth century is an example of a more pessimistic interpretation of similar evidence. Many of the homes, they note, refused to return children to their families when they reached the formal age of demission. In the few cases in which parents contested this power, the courts upheld the home's jurisdiction. P. T. Rooke and R. L. Schnell (eds.), *Studies in Childhood History: A Canadian Perspective* (Calgary, Alberta: Detselig Enterprises, 1982), pp. 166, 175–76.

76. Linda Gordon, "Feminism and Social Control: The Case of Child Abuse and Neglect," in J. Mitchell and A. Oakley (eds.), *What Is Feminism? A Re-examination* (Oxford: Basil Blackwell, 1986), pp. 63–84. See also L. Gordon, *Heroes*.

77. L. Gordon, "Feminism," p. 76.

78. Ibid., p. 82.

79. Ibid., p. 80.

80. C. Nardinelli, "Child Labour and the Factory Acts," *Journal of Economic History* 40, no. 4 (1980): 746.

81. Seccombe, *Weathering*, pp. 35–36.

82. Lee Shai Weissbach, *Child Labor Reform in Nineteenth-Century France: Assuring the Future Harvest* (Baton Rouge: Louisiana State University Press, 1989), p. 19.

83. Claudia Goldin and Kenneth Sokoloff, "Women, Children, and Industrialization in the Early Republic: Evidence from the Manufacturing Censuses," *Journal of Economic History* 42, no. 4 (1982): 747–48, 753. The authors note that "child" was not defined in a uniform way in different enumerations.

84. See, for example, Cunningham, "Employment," p. 147; Hurt, *Elementary Schooling*, pp. 39, 197–98.

85. Hopkins, *Childhood*, p. 219.

86. See, for example, C. Nardinelli, *Child Labor and the Industrial Revolution* (Bloomington: Indiana University Press, 1990).

87. D. J. Hogan, *Class and Reform: School and Society in Chicago, 1880–1930* (Philadelphia: University of Pennsylvania Press, 1985), pp. 55–56.

88. Hurt, *Elementary Schooling,* pp. 39, 197–98. Extending this argument, Musgrove argues that compulsory education was a necessity in England by the 1870s not because children were at work, but because increasingly they were not. Katz and Davey similarly speculate that regional youth unemployment was one of the main motivations behind compulsory schooling. F. Musgrove, "Population Changes and the Status of the Young," in P. Musgrove (ed.), *Sociology, History and Education* (London: Methuen, 1970); M. B. Katz and I. E. Davey, "Youth and Early Industrialization in a Canadian City," in J. Demos and S. S. Boocock, *Turning Points: Historical and Sociological Essays on the Family* (Chicago: University of Chicago Press, 1978).

89. On the enormous variety of such work, see, for example, A. Davin, "Child Labour, the Working-Class Family, and Domestic Ideology in Nineteenth-Century Britain," *Development and Change* 13 (1982): 633–52; J. Bullen, "Hidden Workers: Child Labour and the Family Economy in Late Nineteenth-Century Urban Ontario," *Labour/Le Travail* 18 (1986): 163–87; K. Wimshurst, "Child Labour and School Attendance in South Australia, 1890–1915," *Historical Studies* 19, no. 76 (1981): 388–411.

90. Quoted in Hurt, *Elementary Schooling,* p. 206; Ellen Ross, "Survival Networks: Women's Neighbourhood Sharing in London before World War I," *History Workshop* 15 (1983): 16.

91. Zelizer, *Pricing,* pp. 79, 83.

92. Quoted in Scott, "Woman Worker," p. 425.

93. Victorian Parliamentary Papers, Australia, 1893, *Census of the Colony of Victoria for 1891,* 3–9–192.

94. For a discussion of these issues, see Nancy Folbre "The Unproductive Housewife: Her Evolution in Nineteenth-Century Economic Thought," *Signs* 16, no. 3 (1991): 463–84; D. Deacon, "Political Arithmetic: The Nineteenth-Century Australian Census and the Construction of the Dependent Woman," *Signs* 11, no. 1 (1985): 27–47; Bridget Hill, "Women, Work and the Census: A Problem for Historians of Women," *History Workshop Journal* 35 (1993): 78–94; Humphries, "Most Free," p. 931.

95. Boxer and Quataert, *Connecting Spheres,* p. 218.

96. E. J. Rotella, "Women's Labour Force Participation and the Decline of the Family Economy in the United States," *Explorations in Economic History* 17 (1980): 96.

97. Marjorie G. Cohen, *Women's Work: Markets and Economic Development in Nineteenth-Century Ontario* (Toronto: University of Toronto Press, 1988), p. 119.

98. In 1901, 40 percent of the French female labor force was married; the equivalent figure for the north was 58 percent. Price, *Social History,* p. 214.

99. Quoted in B. Hill, *Women, Work,* p. 89.

100. M. Haines, "Industrial Work and the Family Life Cycle, 1889/90," in Paul Uselding (ed.), *Research in Economic History: A Research Manual,* vol. 4 (Greenwich, Conn.: JAI Press, 1979), analyzes a collection of 8,544 budgets of working-class

families in the United States, Belgium, France, Germany, Switzerland, and Great Britain. The last set of data is analyzed in more detail in L. H. Lees, "Getting and Spending: The Family Budgets of English Industrial Workers in 1890," in John Merriman (ed.), *Consciousness and Class Experience in Nineteenth-Century Europe* (New York: Holmes and Meier, 1979). George Alter, "Work and Income in the Family Economy: Belgium, 1853 and 1891," *Journal of Interdisciplinary History* 15, no. 2 (1984): 255–76, reports similar findings. Hogan, *Class*, uses several collections of budgets in Chicago. C. Goldin, "Family Strategies and the Family Economy in the Late Nineteenth Century: The Role of Secondary Workers," in T. Hershberg, *Philadelphia: Work, Space, Family and Group Experience in the Nineteenth Century* (New York: Oxford University Press, 1981), uses the 1880 manuscript census data for Philadelphia.

101. Levine, *Reproducing,* p. 175; Haines, "Industrial Work," p. 303.

102. Goldin, "Family Strategies," p. 284.

103. Lees, "Getting and Spending," pp. 173–74.

104. Ibid., p. 173; Haines, "Industrial Work," p. 302.

105. P. B. Walters and P. J. O'Connell, "The Family Economy, Work, and Educational Participation in the United States, 1890–1940," *American Journal of Sociology* 93, no. 5 (1988): 1123; Goldin, "Family Strategies," pp. 296–304.

106. Hogan, *Class,* pp. 105–109.

107. Ibid., p. 114.

108. Maynes, *Schooling in Western Europe,* p. 48.

109. For some representative studies, see Rubinstein, *School Attendance;* Mary Jo Maynes, *Schooling for the People: Comparative Local Studies of Schooling History in France and Germany, 1750–1850* (New York: Holmes and Meir, 1985); Walters and O'Connell, "Family Economy," p. 1117; M. B. Katz, *The People of Hamilton, Canada West: Family and Class in a Mid-Nineteenth Century City* (Cambridge, Mass.: Harvard University Press, 1975); M. B. Katz and I. E. Davey, "School Attendance and Early Industrialization in a Canadian City: A Multivariate Analysis," *History of Education Quarterly* 18, no. 3 (1978): 271–93.

110. S. E. Houston and A. Prentice, *Schooling and Scholars in Nineteenth-Century Ontario* (Toronto: University of Toronto Press, 1988), p. 344.

111. Ian Davey, "Growing Up in a Working-Class Community: School and Work in Hindmarsh," in P. Grimshaw et al. (eds.), *Families in Colonial Australia* (Sydney: Allen and Unwin, 1985).

112. Ross, "Fierce Questions," p. 578; Ross, *Love and Toil,* pp. 209–15; Ross, "Survival Networks," p. 10. See also A. I. Griffith and D. E. Smith, "Constructing Cultural Knowledge: Mothering as Discourse," in J. Gaskell and A. McLaren (eds.), *Women and Education: A Canadian Perspective* (Calgary, Alberta: Detseling Enterprises, 1987).

113. Ellen Ross, "Mothers and the State in Britain, 1904–1914," in Gillis, Tilly, and Levine, *The European Experience,* pp. 53–55; Ross, *Love and Toil,* chap. 6, p. 197.

114. Ross, "Mothers," pp. 48–52.

115. Steedman, "Prisonhouses," p. 13.

116. Steinfeld, *Invention*, p. 137; Simpson, *Treatise*, p. 83. Courts did continue to sanction "reasonable" violence against wives and native peoples.

117. Steinfeld, *Invention*, pp. 146, 152, 149.

118. Simpson, *Treatise*, p. 125.

119. Zelizer, *Pricing*, pp. 140–43; Simpson, *Treatise*, p. 126.

120. Zelizer, *Pricing*, chap. 5.

121. Carol Brown, "Mothers, Fathers and Children: From Private to Public Patriarchy," in Lydia Sargent (ed.), *Women and Revolution: A Discussion of the Unhappy Marriage of Marxism and Feminism* (London: Pluto Press, 1981).

122. This is one aspect of what Donzelot (and before him the French historian Jean-Louis Flandrin) called a transformation from the early modern "government of families" to the modern "government through the family." Donzelot, *Policing*, p. 92.

123. Fitz, "The Child," p. 293.

124. Hogan, *Class*, pp. 62–65. Boys were brought before the court mostly for actual crimes, while girls were most often accused of potential moral failings.

125. Other influential critics were concerned with what they saw as the courts' erroneous environmentalist beliefs. Most of poverty and delinquency, professional psychologists argued, was genetically based and could be eliminated only through eugenic measures. S. Schlossman, "End of Innocence: Science and the Transformation of Progressive Juvenile Justice, 1899–1917," *History of Education* 7, no. 3 (1978): 207–18.

126. Harry Hendrick, "The History of Childhood and Youth," *Social History* 9, no. 1 (1984): 87–96.

127. Since women ceased to be juridical persons on marriage, and single women could marry at any moment, neither came under the jurisdiction of laws framed in terms of "persons." J. A. Scutt, "In Pursuit of Equality: Women and Legal Thought, 1788–1984," in J. Goodnow and C. Pateman, *Women, Social Science and Public Policy* (Sydney: Allen and Unwin, 1985), pp. 118–19.

128. John R. Gillis, "Gender and Fertility Decline among the British Middle Classes," in Gillis, Tilly, and Levine, *The European Experience*, p. 31.

129. See, for example, Marilyn Waring, *Counting for Nothing: What Men Value and What Women Are Worth* (Wellington: Allen and Unwin, 1988).

Conclusion

1. R. R. Johnson, "Politics Redefined," *William and Mary Quarterly* 35, no. 4 (1978): 713.

2. Folbre, "Of Patriarchy Born," p. 261.

3. Philip Corrigan, "Feudal Relics or Capitalist Monuments? Notes on the Sociology of Unfree Labour," *Sociology* 11, no. 3 (1977): 435–63.

4. Anthony Giddens, "Nation-States and Violence," in *Social Theory and Modern Sociology* (Cambridge: Polity Press, 1987), pp. 174–75.

5. Foucault himself warned against "a widespread and facile tendency, which one should combat, to designate that which has just occurred as the primary enemy. . . . This simple attitude entails a number of dangerous consequences [such as] an inclination to seek out some cheap form of archaism or some imaginary past forms of happiness that people did not, in fact, have at all. For instance . . . it is very amusing to see how contemporary sexuality is described as something absolutely terrible. To think that it is only possible now to make love after turning off the television! and in mass-produced beds! "Not like that wonderful time when . . . 'Well, what about those wonderful times when people worked eighteen hours a day and there were six people in a bed, if one was lucky enough to have a bed! There is in this hatred of the present a tendency to invoke a completely mythical past." Foucault, "Genealogy," p. 248.

6. Foucault, *History*, p. 130.

7. It was this problematic which led Althusser to describe families as "ideological state apparatuses," inspired Donzelot's animus to housewives, and enticed socialist feminist theoreticians into the swamps of the domestic labor debate—and which still inspires feminist scholarship on the complex links between welfare states, family households, and workplaces.

8. An extensive literature on different welfare state regimes, for example, argues that contemporary western welfare states cluster around three or four types differentiated by people's dependence on the market, the state's intervention in social stratification, and perhaps also their treatment of childbearing and women's unpaid labor. See, for example, Gosta Esping-Andersen, *The Three Worlds of Welfare Capitalism* (Cambridge: Polity Press, 1990), and A. S. Orloff, "Gender and the Social Rights of Citizenship: The Comparative Analysis of State Policies and Gender Relations," *American Sociological Review* 58, no. 3 (1993): 303–28.

9. Raymond Williams, *Marxism and Literature* (Oxford: Oxford University Press, 1977), p. 110.

10. Ibid., p. 112.

11. Levine, "Review."

Selected Bibliography

Abercrombie, N.; S. Hill; and B. S. Turner. *Sovereign Individuals of Capitalism.* London: Allen and Unwin, 1986.

Allen, A. T. "Gardens of Children, Gardens of God: Kindergartens and Day-Care Centres in Nineteenth-Century Germany." *Journal of Social History* 19, no. 3 (1986): 433–50.

———. "Spiritual Motherhood: German Feminists and the Kindergarten Movement, 1848–1911." *History of Education Quarterly* 22, no. 3 (1982): 319–39.

Allen, J. "Contextualising Late Nineteenth-Century Feminism: Problems and Comparisons." *Journal of the Canadian Historical Association* 1, no. 1 (1990): 17–36.

Allen, J. A. *Sex and Secrets: Crimes Involving Australian Women since 1880.* Melbourne: Oxford University Press, 1990.

Alter, G. "Theories of Fertility Decline: A Nonspecialist's Guide to the Current Debate." In J. R. Gillis, L. A. Tilly, and D. Levine (eds.), *The European Experience of Declining Fertility, 1850–1970.* Oxford: Blackwell, 1992.

———. "Work and Income in the Family Economy: Belgium, 1853 and 1891." *Journal of Interdisciplinary History* 15, no. 2 (1984): 255–76.

Amussen, S. D. *An Ordered Society: Gender and Class in Early Modern England.* New York: Blackwell, 1988.

Anderson, B. *Imagined Communities.* London: Verso, 1991.

Anderson, P. *Lineages of the Absolutist State* [1974]. London: Verso, 1989.

Anderson, P., and T. Nairn. "Origins of the Present Crisis." *New Left Review,* no. 23 (1964): 26–53.

Applewhite, H. B., and D. G. Levy (eds.). *Women and Politics in the Age of the Democratic Revolution.* Ann Arbor: University of Michigan Press, 1990.

Archer, M. *The Social Origins of Educational Systems.* London: Sage Publications, 1979.

Ariès, P. *Centuries of Childhood.* Harmondsworth: Penguin, 1973.

Arnaud-Duc, N. "The Law's Contradictions." In G. Fraise and M. Perrot (eds.), *A History of Women in the West.* Vol 4: *Emerging Feminism from Revolution to World War.* Cambridge, Mass.: Belknap Press, 1993.

Ayers, P., and J. Lambertz. "Marriage Relations, Money and Domestic Violence in Working-Class Liverpool, 1919–39." In J. Lewis (ed.), *Labour and Love: Women's Experience of Home and Family, 1850–1940.* Oxford: Basil Blackwell, 1986.

Backhouse, C. "Married Women's Property Law in Nineteenth-Century Canada." *Law and History Review* 6, no. 2 (1988): 211–57.

Baechler, J., et al. (eds.). *Europe and the Rise of Capitalism.* Oxford: Basil Blackwell, 1988.

Barkin, K. "Social Control and the Volksschule in Vormärz Prussia." *Central European History* 16, no. 1 (1983): 31–52.

Bellingham, B. "Waifs and Strays: Child Abandonment, Foster Care, and Families in Mid-Nineteenth-Century New York." In P. Mandler (ed.), *The Uses of Charity: The Poor on Relief in the Nineteenth-Century Metropolis.* Philadelphia: University of Pennsylvania Press, 1990.

Berg, M. "What Difference Did Women's Work Make to the Industrial Revolution?" *History Workshop Journal,* no. 35 (1993): 22–44.

Berg, M., and P. Hudson. "Rehabilitating the Industrial Revolution." *Economic History Review* 45, no. 1 (1992): 45–50.

Bisson, T. N. "The 'Feudal Revolution.'" *Past and Present,* no. 142 (1994).

Blaschke, K. "The Reformation and the Rise of the Territorial State." In J. D. Tracy (ed.), *Luther and the Modern State in Germany.* Ann Arbor, Mich.: Edwards Brothers, 1986.

Bloch, R. H. "The Gendered Meaning of Virtue in Revolutionary America." *Signs* 13, no. 1 (1987): 37–58.

Blum, C. *Rousseau and the Republic of Virtue: The Language of Politics in the French Revolution.* Ithaca: Cornell University Press, 1986.

Bock, G., and P. Thane (eds.). *Maternity and Gender Policies: Women and the Rise of the European Welfare States, 1880s–1950s.* London: Routledge, 1991.

Bolin-Hort, P. *Work, Family and the State: Child Labour and the Organisation of Production in the British Cotton Industry, 1780–1920.* Lund: Lund University Press, 1989.

Bowen, J. *A History of Western Education.* Vol. 3: *The Modern West, Europe and the New World.* London: Methuen, 1986.

Bowles, S., and H. Gintis. *Schooling in Capitalist America.* London: Routledge and Kegan Paul, 1976.

Boxer, M. J., and J. H. Quataert (eds.). *Connecting Spheres: Women in the Western World, 1500 to the Present.* New York: Oxford University Press, 1987.

Brady, T. A. "Luther and the State: The Reformer's Teaching in Its Social Setting." In J. D. Tracy (ed.), *Luther and the Modern State in Germany.* Ann Arbor, Mich.: Edwards Brothers, 1986.

Bremmer, R. H. *Children and Youth in America: A Documentary History.* Vol. 1: *1600–1865.* Cambridge, Mass.: Harvard University Press, 1970.

Brenzel, B. *Daughters of the State: A Social Portrait of the First Reform School for Girls in North America, 1865–1905.* Cambridge, Mass.: MIT Press, 1983.

Brewer, J. *The Sinews of Power: War, Money and the English State, 1688–1783.* London: Unwin Hyman, 1989.

Brown, C. "Mothers, Fathers and Children: From Private to Public Patriarchy." In Lydia Sargent (ed.), *Women and Revolution: A Discussion of the Unhappy Marriage of Marxism and Feminism.* London: Pluto Press, 1981.

Brundage, J. A. *Law, Sex and Christian Society in Medieval Europe.* Chicago: University of Chicago Press, 1987.

Bullen, J. "Hidden Workers: Child Labour and the Family Economy in Late Nineteenth-Century Urban Ontario." *Labour/Le Travail,* no. 18 (1986): 163–87.

Burke, P., and R. Porter. *Language, Self and Society: A Social History of Language.* Cambridge: Polity Press, 1991.

Burnett, J. (ed.). *Destiny Obscure: Autobiographies of Childhood, Education and Family from the 1820s to the 1920s.* London: Allen Lane, 1982.

Burstyn, J. "Women's Education in England during the Nineteenth Century: A Review of the Literature." *History of Education* 6, no. 1 (1977): 11–19.

Caldwell, J. C. "Mass Education as a Determinant of the Timing of Fertility Decline." *Population and Development Review* 6, no. 2 (1980): 225–55.

———. "Toward a Restatement of Demographic Transition Theory." *Population and Development Review* 2, nos. 3–4 (1976): 321–66.

Calhoun, C. "Nationalism and Ethnicity." *Annual Review of Sociology* 19 (1993): 211–39.

Calhoun, C. (ed.). *Habermas and the Public Sphere.* Cambridge, Mass.: MIT Press, 1992.

Cameron, V. "Political Exposures: Sexuality and Caricature in the French Revolution." In L. Hunt (ed.), *Eroticism and the Body Politic.* Baltimore: Johns Hopkins University Press, 1991.

Cannadine, D. "The Past and the Present in the English Industrial Revolution, 1880–1980." *Past and Present,* no. 103 (1984): 149–58.

Cava, A. "French Feminism and Maternity: Theories and Policies, 1890–1918." In G. Bock and P. Thane (eds.), *Maternity and Gender Policies: Women and the Rise of the European Welfare States, 1880s–1950s.* London: Routledge, 1991.

Chalmers, T. *The Christian and Civic Economy of Large Towns.* Vol. 1. Glasgow: Chalmers and Collins, 1821.

Clark, A. "The Rhetoric of Chartist Domesticity: Gender, Language, and Class in the 1830s and 1840s." *Journal of British Studies* 31, no. 1 (1992): 62–88.

Clark, A. *Women's Silence, Men's Violence: Sexual Assault in England, 1770–1845.* London: Pandora, 1987.

Clark, L. L. *Schooling the Daughters of Marianne: Textbooks and the Socialization of Girls in Modern French Primary Schools.* Albany: State University of New York Press, 1984.

Clawson, M. A. *Constructing Brotherhood: Class, Gender and Fraternalism.* Princeton: Princeton University Press, 1989.

———. "Early Modern Fraternalism and the Patriarchal Family." *Feminist Studies* 6, no. 2 (1980): 368–91.

Clifford, G. J. "'Daughters into Teachers': Educational and Demographic Influences on the Transformation of Teaching into 'Women's Work' in America." In A. Prentice and M. Theobald (eds.), *Women Who Taught: Perspectives on the History of Women and Teaching.* Toronto: University of Toronto Press, 1991.

Cockburn, C. *Brothers: Male Dominance and Technological Change.* London: Pluto Press, 1983.

———. "The Gendering of Jobs: Workplace Relations and the Reproduction of Sex

Segregation." In S. Walby (ed.), *Gender Segregation at Work.* Milton Keynes: Open University Press, 1988.

Cohen, M. G. *Women's Work: Markets and Economic Development in Nineteenth-Century Ontario.* Toronto: University of Toronto Press, 1988.

Cohn, J. *Romance and the Erotics of Property: Mass-Market Fiction for Women.* Durham, N.C.: Duke University Press, 1988.

Coleman, W. *Death Is a Social Disease: Public Health and Political Economy in Early Industrial France.* Madison: University of Wisconsin Press, 1982.

Colley, L. "Whose Nation? Class and National Consciousness in Britain, 1750–1830." *Past and Present,* no. 113 (1986): 97–117.

Collins, R. "Functional and Conflict Theories of Educational Stratification." *American Sociological Review* 36, no. 6 (1971): 1002–1019.

Condon, B. (ed.). *The Confidential Letterbook of the South Australian Inspector General of Schools, 1880–1914.* Adelaide: Murray Park CAE, 1976.

Conley, C. A. "No Pedestals: Women and Violence in Late Nineteenth-Century Ireland." *Journal of Social History* 28, no. 4 (1995): 801–18.

Coontz, S. *The Social Origins of Private Life: A History of American Families, 1600–1900.* London: Verso, 1988.

Corrigan, P. "Feudal Relics or Capitalist Monuments? Notes on the Sociology of Unfree Labour." *Sociology* 11, no. 3 (1977): 435–63.

Corrigan, P. (ed.). *Capitalism, State Formation and Marxist Theory.* London: Quartet Books, 1980.

Corrigan, P.; B. Curtis; and R. Lanning. "The Political Space of Schooling." In T. Wotherspoon (ed.), *The Political Economy of Canadian Schooling.* Toronto: Methuen, 1987.

Corrigan, P., and D. Sayer. *The Great Arch: English State Formation as Cultural Revolution.* Oxford: Basil Blackwell, 1985.

Countryman, E. *The American Revolution.* London: Penguin Books, 1991.

Cunningham, H. "The Employment and Unemployment of Children in England c. 1680–1851." *Past and Present,* no. 126 (1990).

Curtis, B. *Building the Educational State: Canada West, 1836–1871.* London: Falmer Press, 1988.

———. "The Canada *Blue Books* and the Administrative Capacity of the Canadian State, 1822–1867." *Canadian Historical Review* 74, no. 4 (1993): 535–65.

———. "Gender in the Regime of Statistical Knowledge/Power." ANZHES Conference, Melbourne, 1993, typescript.

———. "Preconditions of the Canadian State: Educational Reform and the Construction of a Public in Upper Canada, 1837–1846." *Studies in Political Economy,* no. 10 (1983).

———. "Representation and State Formation in the Canadas, 1790–1850." *Studies in Political Economy,* no. 28 (1989): 59–87.

———. "Révolution gouvernementale et savoir politique au Canada-Uni." *Sociologie et sociétés* 24 (1992): 169–79.

———. *True Government by Choice Men: Inspection, Education and State Formation in Canada West.* Toronto: University of Toronto Press, 1992.

Dandeker, C. *Surveillance, Power and Modernity: Bureaucracy and Discipline from 1700 to the Present Day.* Cambridge: Polity Press, 1990.

Danylewycz, M.; B. Light; and A. Prentice. "The Evolution of the Sexual Division of Labour in Teaching: A Nineteenth-Century Ontario and Quebec Case Study." *Histoire Sociale/Social History* 16, no. 31 (1983): 81–109.

Danylewycz, M., and A. Prentice. "Teachers, Gender and Bureaucratizing School Systems in Nineteenth-Century Montreal and Toronto." *History of Education Quarterly* 24, no. 1 (1984): 75–100.

Davey, I. "Capitalism, Patriarchy and the Origins of Mass Schooling: The Radical Debate." In A. Rattansi and D. Reeder, *Rethinking Radical Education: Essays in Honour of Brian Simon.* London: Lawrence and Wishart, 1992.

———. "Growing Up in a Working-Class Community: School and Work in Hindmarsh." In P. Grimshaw et al. (eds.), *Families in Colonial Australia.* Sydney: Allen and Unwin, 1985.

Davidoff, L. *The Best Circles.* London: Hutchinson, 1986.

———. "Class and Gender in Victorian England." In J. L. Newton, M. P. Ryan, and J. R. Walkowitz (eds.), *Sex and Class in Women's History.* London: Routledge and Kegan Paul, 1983.

———. "Mastered for Life: Servant and Wife in Victorian and Edwardian Britain." *Journal of Social History* 7, no. 4 (1974): 406–28.

Davidoff, L., and C. Hall. *Family Fortunes: Men and Women of the English Middle Class, 1780–1850.* London: Hutchinson, 1987.

Davies, M. L. *Maternity: Letters from Working Women.* London: Virago, 1978.

Davin, A. "Child Labour, the Working Class Family, and Domestic Ideology in Nineteenth-Century Britain." *Development and Change* 13 (1982): 633–52.

———. "'Mind You Do As You Are Told': Reading Books for Board School Girls, 1870–1902." *Feminist Review*, no. 3 (1979): 89–98.

Deacon, D. *Managing Gender: The State, the New Middle Class and Women Workers, 1830–1930.* Melbourne: Oxford University Press, 1989.

———. "Political Arithmetic: The Nineteenth-Century Australian Census and the Construction of the Dependant Woman." *Signs* 11, no. 1 (1985): 27–47.

Dean, M. *The Constitution of Poverty: Toward a Genealogy of Liberal Governance.* London: Routledge, 1991.

de Vries, J. *European Urbanization, 1500–1800.* Cambridge, Mass.: Harvard University Press, 1984.

Dickens, A. G., and J. M. Tonkin. *The Reformation in Historical Thought.* Cambridge, Mass.: Harvard University Press, 1985.

Dolan, F. E. *Dangerous Familiars: Representations of Domestic Crime in England, 1550–1700.* Ithaca: Cornell University Press, 1994.

Donzelot, J. *L'Invention du social: Essay sur le déclin des passions politiques.* Paris: Fayard, 1984.

——. *The Policing of Families*. New York: Pantheon Books, 1979.

Dowling, L. "Esthetes and Effeminati." *Raritan* 12, no. 3 (1993): 52–68.

Dyhouse, C. "Social Darwinistic Ideas and the Development of Women's Education in England, 1880–1920." *History of Education* 5, no. 1 (1976): 41–58.

——. "Towards a 'Feminine' Curriculum for English Schoolgirls: The Demands of Ideology, 1870–1963." *Women's Studies International Quarterly* 1, no. 4 (1978): 297–311.

Ehrenreich, B., and D. English. *For Her Own Good: 150 Years of the Experts' Advice to Women*. London: Pluto Press, 1979.

Eldridge, C. C. (ed.). *British Imperialism in the Nineteenth Century*. London: Macmillan, 1984.

Eley, G. "Edward Thompson, Social History and Political Culture: The Making of a Working-Class Public, 1780–1850." In H. J. Kaye and K. McClelland (eds.), *E. P. Thompson: Critical Perspectives*. Cambridge: Polity Press, 1990.

——. "Nationalism and Social History." *Social History* 6, no. 1 (1981): 83–107.

——. "Nations, Publics and Political Cultures." In C. Calhoun (ed.), *Habermas and the Public Sphere*. Cambridge, Mass.: MIT Press, 1992.

Elias, N. *The Civilising Process: The History of Manners*. Oxford: Basil Blackwell, 1978.

——. *The Civilising Process: State Formation and Civilisation*. Oxford: Basil Blackwell, 1982.

Engels, F. *The Condition of the Working Class in England* [1892]. London: Panther Books, 1969.

Esping-Andersen, G. *The Three Worlds of Welfare Capitalism*. Cambridge: Polity Press, 1990.

Farge, A., and M. Foucault. *Le désordre des familles: Lettres de cachet des Archives de la Bastille*. Paris: Gallimard, 1982.

Finkelstein, B. *Governing the Young: Teacher Behavior in Popular Primary Schools in Nineteenth-Century United States*. New York: Falmer Press, 1989.

Fitz, J. "The Child as a Legal Subject." In R. Dale et al. (eds.), *Politics, Patriarchy and Practice*. London: Falmer Press, 1981.

Fletcher, A., and J. Stevenson (eds.). *Order and Disorder in Early Modern England*. Cambridge: Cambridge University Press, 1985.

Fliegelman, J. *Prodigals and Pilgrims: The American Revolution against Patriarchal Authority, 1750–1800*. New York: Cambridge University Press, 1982.

Flora, P. *State, Economy and Society in Western Europe, 1815–1975: A Data Handbook in Two Volumes*. Frankfurt: Campus Verlag, 1983.

Floud, R.; A. Gregory; and K. Wachter. *Height, Health and History: Nutritional Status in the United Kingdom, 1750–1980*. Cambridge: Cambridge University Press, 1989.

Folbre, N. "Of Patriarchy Born: The Political Economy of Fertility Decisions." *Feminist Studies* 9, no. 2 (1983): 261–84.

———. "The Unproductive Housewife: Her Evolution in Nineteenth-Century Economic Thought." *Signs* 16, no. 3 (1991): 463–84.

———. *Who Pays for the Kids? Gender and the Structures of Constraint.* London: Routledge, 1994.

Foucault, M. *Discipline and Punish: The Birth of the Prison.* London: Penguin, 1979.

———. "Governmentality." In G. Burchell, C. Gordon, and P. Miller (eds.), *The Foucault Effect: Studies in Governmentality.* London: Harvester/Wheatsheaf, 1991.

———. *The History of Sexuality.* Vol. 1: *An Introduction.* Harmondsworth: Penguin, 1981.

———. "La pousière et le nuage." In M. Perrot (ed.), *L'Impossible prison.* Paris: Éditions du Seuil, 1980.

———. "On the Genealogy of Ethics: An Overview of Work in Progress." In P. Rabinow (ed.), *The Foucault Reader.* Harmondsworth: Penguin Books, 1986.

Fox-Genovese, E. "Property and Patriarchy in Classical Political Theory." *Radical History Review,* nos. 2–3 (1977): 36–59.

Fraise, G. "A Philosophical History of Sexual Difference." In G. Fraise and M. Perrot (eds.), *A History of Women in the West.* Vol. 4: *Emerging Feminism from Revolution to World War.* Cambridge, Mass.: Belknap Press, 1993.

Frith, S. "Socialization and Rational Schooling: Elementary Education in Leeds before 1870." In P. McCann (ed.), *Popular Education and Socialization in the Nineteenth Century.* London: Methuen, 1977.

Fuchs, R. G. "Preserving the Future of France: Aid to the Poor and Pregnant in Nineteenth-Century Paris." In P. Mandler (ed.), *The Uses of Charity: The Poor on Relief in the Nineteenth-Century Metropolis.* Philadelphia: University of Pennsylvania Press, 1990.

Furet, F., and J. Ozouf. *Reading and Writing: Literacy in France from Calvin to Jules Ferry.* Cambridge: Cambridge University Press, 1982.

Gagnier, R. *Subjectivities: A History of Self-Representation in Britain.* New York: Oxford University Press, 1991.

Gamble, A. *An Introduction to Modern Social and Political Thought.* London: Macmillan, 1981.

Gardner, P. *The Lost Elementary Schools of Victorian England.* London: Croom Helm, 1984.

Gawthrop, R., and G. Strauss. "Protestantism and Literacy in Early Modern Germany." *Past and Present,* no. 104 (1984): 31–55.

Gemie, S. "What Is a School? Defining and Controlling Primary Schooling in Early Nineteenth-Century France." *History of Education* 21, no. 2 (1992): 129–47.

George, R. M. "Homes in the Empire, Empires in the Home." *Cultural Critique,* no. 26 (1993–94): 95–127.

Gerth, H. H., and C. Wright Mills (eds.). *From Max Weber: Essays in Sociology.* London: Routledge and Kegan Paul, 1952.

Giddens, Anthony. "Nation-States and Violence." In *Social Theory and Modern Sociology.* Cambridge: Polity Press, 1987.

Gidney, R. D., and D. A. Lawr. "Bureaucracy vs Community? The Origins of Bureaucratic Procedure in the Upper Canadian School System." *Journal of Social History* 13, no. 3 (1980): 438–57.

Gillis, J. R. *For Better, for Worse: British Marriages, 1660 to the Present.* New York: Oxford University Press, 1985.

———. "Gender and Fertility Decline among the British Middle Classes." In J. R. Gillis, L. A. Tilly, and D. Levine (eds.), *The European Experience of Declining Fertility, 1850–1970: The Quiet Revolution.* Cambridge: Blackwell, 1992.

———. "Peasant, Plebeian and Proletarian Marriage in Britain, 1600–1900." In D. Levine (ed.), *Proletarianization and Family History.* New York: Academic Press, 1984.

———. *Youth and History: Transition and Change in European Age Relations, 1770 to the Present.* New York: Academic Press, 1981.

Gillis, J. R.; L. Tilly; and D. Levine (eds.). *The European Experience of Declining Fertility, 1850–1970: The Quiet Revolution.* Cambridge: Blackwell, 1992.

Goldin, C. "Family Strategies and the Family Economy in the Late Nineteenth Century: The Role of Secondary Workers." In T. Hershberg, *Philadelphia: Work, Space, Family and Group Experience in the Nineteenth Century.* New York: Oxford University Press, 1981.

Goldin, C., and K. Sokoloff. "Women, Children, and Industrialization in the Early Republic: Evidence from the Manufacturing Censuses." *Journal of Economic History* 42, no. 4 (1982): 741–74.

Goldstone, J. A. "Reinterpreting the French Revolution." *Theory and Society* 13 (1984): 697–713.

Gordon, C. "Governmental Rationality: An Introduction." In G. Burchell, C. Gordon, and P. Miller (eds.), *The Foucault Effect: Studies in Governmentality.* London: Harvester/Wheatsheaf, 1991.

Gordon, L. "Feminism and Social Control: The Case of Child Abuse and Neglect." In J. Mitchell and A. Oakley (eds.), *What Is Feminism: A Re-Examination.* Oxford: Basil Blackwell, 1986.

———. *Heroes of Their Own Lives: The Politics and History of Family Violence.* London: Virago, 1989.

Gorsline, D. *What People Wore: A Visual History of Dress from Ancient Times to the Twentieth Century.* London: Orbis Publishing, 1978.

Gosden, P. H. J. H. (ed.). *How They Were Taught: An Anthology of Contemporary Accounts of Learning and Teaching in England, 1800–1950.* Oxford: Blackwell, 1969.

Graff, H. S. *The Labyrinths of Literacy: Reflections on Literacy Past and Present.* London: Falmer Press, 1987.

Green, A. *Education and State Formation: The Rise of Education Systems in England, France and the USA.* London: Macmillan, 1990.

Green, L. "The Education of Women in the Reformation." *History of Education Quarterly* 19, no. 1 (1979): 93–116.

Green, N. "Female Education and School Competition: 1820–1850." *History of Education Quarterly* 18, no. 2 (1978): 129–43.

Grew, R., and P. J. Harrigan. *School, State and Society: The Growth of Elementary Schooling in Nineteenth-Century France—A Quantitative Analysis.* Ann Arbor: University of Michigan Press, 1991.

Grieco, S. F. M. "The Body, Appearance and Sexuality." In N. Z. Davis and A. Farge (eds.), *A History of Women in the West.* Vol. 3: *Renaissance and Enlightenment Paradoxes.* Cambridge, Mass.: Belknap Press, 1993.

Griffith, A. I., and D. E. Smith. "Constructing Cultural Knowledge: Mothering as Discourse." In J. Gaskell and A. McLaren (eds.), *Women and Education: A Canadian Perspective.* Calgary: Detseling Enterprises, 1987.

Grimshaw, P.; M. Lake; A. McGrath; and M. Quartly. *Creating a Nation.* Melbourne: McPhee Gribble, 1994.

Grumet, M. *Bitter Milk: Women and Teaching.* Amherst: University of Massachusetts Press, 1988.

——. "Pedagogy for Patriarchy: The Feminization of Teaching." *Interchange* 12, nos. 2–3 (1981): 165–84.

Grundy, D. "The Formation of a Disordered Teaching Service in Victoria, 1851–1871." *History of Education Review* 18, no. 2 (1989): 1–20.

——. "Free Schooling and the State in South Australia, 1875–1898." In I. Palmer (ed.), *Melbourne Studies in Education 1983.* Melbourne: Melbourne University Press, 1983.

Gundersen, J. R. "Independence, Citizenship, and the American Revolution." *Signs* 13, no. 1 (1987): 37–58.

Habermas, J. "The Public Sphere." *New German Critique* 3 (1974).

——. *The Structural Transformation of the Public Sphere.* Cambridge: Polity Press, 1989.

Hacker, B. "Women and Military Institutions in Early Modern Europe: A Reconnaissance." *Signs* 6, no. 4 (1981): 643–71.

Hackett, N. "A Different Form of 'Self': Narrative Style in British Nineteenth-Century Working-Class Autobiography." *biography* 12, no. 3 (1989): 208–25.

Hahn, S., and J. Prude (eds.). *The Countryside in the Age of Capitalist Transformation: Essays in the History of Rural America.* Chapel Hill: University of North Carolina Press, 1985.

Haines, M. "Industrial Work and the Family Life Cycle, 1889/90." In Paul Uselding (ed.), *Research in Economic History: A Research Manual,* vol. 4. Greenwich, Conn.: JAI Press, 1979.

Hall, C. "Competing Masculinities: Thomas Carlyle, John Stuart Mill and the Case of Governor Eyre." In *White, Male and Middle Class: Explorations in Feminism and History.* Cambridge: Polity Press, 1992.

———. "The Home Turned Upside Down? The Working-Class Family in Cotton Textiles, 1780–1850." In E. Whitelegg et al. (eds.), *The Changing Experience of Women.* Oxford: Martin Robertson, 1982.

———. "Missionary Stories: Gender and Ethnicity in England in the 1830s and 1840s." In *White, Male and Middle Class: Explorations in Feminism and History.* Cambridge: Polity Press, 1992.

———. "The Tale of Samuel and Jemima: Gender and Working-Class Culture in Nineteenth-Century England." In H. J. Kaye and K. McClelland (eds.), *E. P. Thompson: Critical Perspectives.* Cambridge: Polity Press, 1990.

Hall, L. A. "Forbidden by God, Despised by Men: Masturbation, Medical Warnings, Moral Panic and Manhood in Great Britain, 1850–1950." In J. C. Fout (ed.), *Forbidden History: The State, Society and the Regulation of Sexuality in Modern Europe.* Chicago: University of Chicago Press, 1992.

Hamilton, D. *Learning about Education: An Unfinished Curriculum.* Milton Keynes: Open University Press, 1990.

———. *Towards a Theory of Schooling.* London: Falmer Press, 1989.

Hammerton, J. *Cruelty and Companionship: Conflict in Nineteeenth-Century Married Life.* London: Routledge, 1992.

Hanley, S. "Engendering the State: Family Formation and State Building in Early Modern France." *French Historical Studies* 16, no. 1 (1989): 4–27.

———. "Family and State in Early Modern France: The Marriage Pact." In M. Boxer and J. Quataert (eds.), *Connecting Spheres: Women in the Western World, 1500 to the Present.* New York: Oxford University Press, 1987.

———. *The Lit de Justice of the Kings of France.* Princeton: Princeton University Press, 1983.

Hanmer, J. "Violence and Social Control of Women." In G. Littlejohn et al., *Power and the State.* London: Croom Helm, 1978.

Harrison, R., and F. Mort. "Patriarchal Aspects of Nineteenth-Century Class Formation: Property Relations, Marriage and Divorce, and Sexuality." In P. Corrigan (ed.), *Capitalism, State Formation and Marxist Theory.* London: Quartet Books, 1980.

Hartmann, H. "Capitalism, Patriarchy and Job Segregation by Sex." In Z. R. Eisenstein (ed.), *Capitalist Patriarchy and the Case for Socialist Feminism.* New York: Monthly Review Press, 1979.

Haskell, T. L. "Capitalism and the Origins of Humanitarian Sensibility." Pts. 1 and 2. *American Historical Review* 90, no. 2 (1985): 339–61; 90, no. 3 (1985): 547–66.

Hausen, K. "Family and Role-Division: The Polarisation of Sexual Stereotypes in the Nineteenth Century—An Aspect of the Dissociation of Work and Family Life." In R. J. Evans and W. R. Lee, *The German Family: Essays on the Social History of the Family in Nineteenth- and Twentieth-Century Germany.* London: Croom Helm, 1981.

Hay, D. "Property, Authority and the Criminal Law." In D. Hay et al., *Albion's Fatal Tree: Crime and Society in Eighteenth-Century England*. London: Allen Lane, 1975.

Hendrick, H. "The History of Childhood and Youth." *Social History* 9, no. 1 (1984): 87–96.

Henriques, J., et al. *Changing the Subject: Psychology, Social Regulation and Subjectivity*. London: Methuen, 1984.

Hicks, N. *"This Sin and Scandal": Australia's Population Debate, 1891–1911*. Canberra: Australian National University Press, 1978.

Higonnet, P. "The Politics of Linguistic Terrorism and Grammatical Hegemony during the French Revolution." *Social History* 5, no. 1 (1980): 41–69.

Hill, B. "Women, Work and the Census: A Problem for Historians of Women." *History Workshop Journal*, no. 35 (1993): 78–94.

Hill, C. *Society and Puritanism in Pre-Revolutionary England*. London: Secker and Warburg, 1964.

Hirschman, A. O. *The Passions and the Interests: Political Arguments for Capitalism before Its Triumph*. Princeton: Princeton University Press, 1977.

Hobsbawm, E. J. *The Age of Capital, 1848–1875*. London: Abacus, Sphere Books, 1985.

——. *The Age of Empire, 1875–1914*. New York: Vintage Books, 1989.

——. *The Age of Revolution*. London: Abacus, Sphere Books, 1977.

——. *Nations and Nationalism since 1780*. Cambridge: Cambridge University Press, 1990.

Hobsbawm, E., and T. Ranger (eds.). *The Invention of Tradition*. Cambridge: Cambridge University Press, 1983.

Hodgkin, K. "Thomas Whythorne and the Problems of Mastery." *History Workshop*, no. 29 (1990): 20–41.

Hogan, D. "The Market Revolution and Disciplinary Power: Joseph Lancaster and the Psychology of the Early Classroom System." *History of Education Quarterly* 29, no. 3 (1989): 381–417.

Hogan, D. J. *Class and Reform: School and Society in Chicago, 1880–1930*. Philadelphia: University of Pennsylvania Press, 1985.

Holcombe, L. "Victorian Wives and Property: Reform of the Married Women's Property Law, 1857–1882." In M. Vicinus (ed.), *A Widening Sphere: Changing Roles of Victorian Women*. Bloomington: Indiana University Press, 1980.

——. *Wives and Property: Reform of the Married Women's Property Law in Nineteenth-Century England*. Toronto: University of Toronto Press, 1983.

Honeyman, K., and J. Goodman. "Women's Work, Gender Conflict, and Labour Markets in Europe, 1500–1900." *Economic History Review* 44, no. 4 (1991): 608–28.

Hopkins, E. *Childhood Transformed: Working-Class Children in Nineteenth-Century England*. Manchester: Manchester University Press, 1994.

Houston, R. A. *Literacy in Early Modern Europe: Culture and Education, 1500–1800*. London: Longman, 1988.

Houston, S. E., and A. Prentice. *Schooling and Scholars in Nineteenth-Century Ontario.* Toronto: University of Toronto Press, 1988.

Hsia, R. Po-Chia. *Social Discipline in the Reformation: Central Europe, 1550–1750.* London: Routledge, 1989.

Humphries, J. "'The Most Free from Objection . . . ': The Sexual Division of Labour and Women's Work in Nineteenth-Century England." *Journal of Economic History* 47, no. 4 (1987): 929–49.

Hunt, L. *The Family Romance of the French Revolution.* Berkeley: University of California Press, 1992.

———. "Pornography and the French Revolution." In L. Hunt (ed.), *The Invention of Pornography: Obscenity and the Origins of Modernity, 1500–1800.* New York: Zone Books, 1993.

———. "The Unstable Boundaries of the French Revolution." In M. Perrot (ed.), *A History of Private Life.* Vol. 4: *From the Fires of Revolution to the Great War.* Cambridge, Mass.: Belknap Press, 1990.

Hunter, I. "The Pastoral Bureaucracy: Towards a Less Principled Understanding of State Schooling." In D. Meredyth and D. Tyler (eds.), *Child and Citizen: Genealogies of Schooling and Subjectivity.* Brisbane: ICPS, Griffith University, 1993.

———. *Rethinking the School: Subjectivity, Bureaucracy, Criticism.* Sydney: Allen and Unwin, 1994.

Hurt, J. *Elementary Schooling and the Working Classes, 1860–1918.* London: Routledge and Kegan Paul, 1979.

Hyams, B. K. "The Teacher in South Australia in the Second Half of the Nineteenth Century." *Australian Journal of Education* 15, no. 3 (1971): 278–94.

Ignatieff, M. "State, Civil Society and Total Institutions: A Critique of Recent Social Histories of Punishment." In S. Cohen and A. Scull (eds.), *Social Control and the State.* Oxford: Basil Blackwell, 1985.

Ingram, M. *Church Courts, Sex and Marriage in England, 1570–1640.* Cambridge: Cambridge University Press, 1987.

Johansson, E. "The History of Literacy in Sweden." In H. J. Graff (ed.), *Literacy and Social Development in the West.* Cambridge: Cambridge University Press, 1981.

———. "Literacy Campaigns in Sweden." In R. J. Arnove and H. Graff (eds.), *National Literacy Campaigns: Historical and Comparative Perspectives.* New York: Plenum Press, 1987.

Johansson, S. R. "Centuries of Childhood/Centuries of Parenting: Philippe Ariès and the Modernization of Privileged Infancy." *Journal of Family History* 12, no. 4 (1987): 343–65.

Johnson, L. *The Modern Girl: Girlhood and Growing Up.* Sydney: Allen and Unwin, 1993.

Johnson, R. "Educational Policy and Social Control in Early Victorian England." *Past and Present*, no. 49 (1970): 96–119.

———. "Notes on the Schooling of the English Working Class, 1780–1850." In R.

Dale et al. (eds.), *Schooling and Capitalism*. London: Routledge and Kegan Paul, 1976.

———. "Radical Education and the New Right." In A. Rattansi and D. Reeder, *Rethinking Radical Education: Essays in Honour of Brian Simon*. London: Lawrence and Wishart, 1992.

———. "'Really Useful Knowledge': Radical Education and Working Class Culture, 1790–1848." In J. Clarke et al. (eds.), *Working Class Culture*. London: Hutchinson, 1979.

Johnson, R. R. "Politics Redefined." *William and Mary Quarterly* 35, no. 4 (1978): 691–32.

Jones, K., and K. Williamson. "The Birth of the Schoolroom: A Study of the Transformation in the Discursive Conditions of English Popular Education in the First Half of the Nineteenth Century." *Ideology and Consciousness*, no. 6 (1979): 59–110.

Jordan, C. *Renaissance Feminism: Literary Texts and Political Models*. Ithaca: Cornell University Press, 1990.

Jordan, E. "Female Unemployment in England and Wales, 1851–1911: An Examination of the Census Figures for 15–19 Year Olds." *Social History* 13, no. 2 (1988): 175–90.

Joyce, P. "The People's English: Language and Class in England c. 1840–1920." In P. Burke and R. Porter, *Language, Self and Society: A Social History of Language*. Cambridge: Polity Press, 1991.

Kaestle, C. F. "'Between the Scylla of Brutal Ignorance and the Charybdis of a Literary Education': Elite Attitudes toward Mass Schooling in Early Industrial England and America." In L. Stone (ed.), *Schooling and Society*. Baltimore: Johns Hopkins University Press, 1976.

Kaestle C. F. (ed.). *Joseph Lancaster and the Monitorial School Movement: A Documentary History*. New York: Teachers College Press, Columbia University, 1973.

Kaestle, C. F., and M. A. Vinovskis. "From Apron Strings to ABCs: Parents, Children and Schooling in Nineteenth-Century Massachusetts." In J. Demos and S. S. Boocock (eds.), *Turning Points: Historical and Sociological Essays on the Family*. Chicago: University of Chicago Press, 1978.

Kaiser, D. *Politics and War: European Conflict from Philip II to Hitler*. Cambridge, Mass.: Harvard University Press, 1990.

Karant-Nunn, S. C. "The Reality of Early Lutheran Education: The Electoral District of Saxony—A Case Study." In *Responsibility for the World: Luther's Intentions and Their Effects. Lutherjahrbuch*. Göttingen: Vandenhoeck and Ruprecht, 1990.

Katz, M. B. *The Irony of Early School Reform: Educational Innovation in Early Nineteenth-Century Massachusetts*. Cambridge, Mass.: Harvard University Press, 1968.

———. *The People of Hamilton, Canada West: Family and Class in a Mid-Nineteenth-Century City*. Cambridge, Mass.: Harvard University Press, 1975.

Katz, M. B., and I. E. Davey. "School Attendance and Early Industrialization in a Canadian City: A Multivariate Analysis." *History of Education Quarterly* 18, no. 3 (1978): 271–93.

———. "Youth and Early Industrialization in a Canadian City." In J. Demos and S. S. Boocock, *Turning Points: Historical and Sociological Essays on the Family.* Chicago: University of Chicago Press, 1978.

Kelly, J. "Early Feminist Theory and the Querelle des Femmes, 1400–1789." In *Women, History and Theory.* Chicago: University of Chicago Press, 1984.

Kerber, L. K. "'I Have Don . . . Much to Carrey on the Warr': Women and the Shaping of Republican Ideology after the American Revolution." In H. B. Applewhite and D. G. Levy (eds.), *Women and Politics in the Age of the Democratic Revolution.* Ann Arbor: University of Michigan Press, 1990.

Kett, J. F. "Curing the Disease of Precocity." In J. Demos and S. S. Boocock, *Turning Points: Historical and Sociological Essays on the Family.* Chicago: University of Chicago Press, 1978.

Kiernan, V. "Languages and Conquerors." In P. Burke and R. Porter, *Language, Self and Society: A Social History of Language.* Cambridge: Polity Press, 1991.

Klein, L. "The Third Earl of Shaftesbury and the Progress of Politeness." *Eighteenth-Century Studies* 18, no. 2 (1984–85): 186–214.

Knight, P. "Women and Abortion in Victorian and Edwardian England." *History Workshop,* no. 4 (1977): 57–68.

Knodel, J. "Family Limitation and the Fertility Transition: Evidence from the Age Patterns of Fertility in Europe and Asia." *Population Studies* 31, no. 2 (1977): 219–49.

Kocka, J. "Problems of Working-Class Formation in Germany: The Early Years, 1800–1875." In I. Katznelson and A. Zolberg (eds.), *Working-Class Formation.* Princeton: Princeton University Press, 1986.

Koven, S., and S. Mitchel. *Mothers of a New World: Maternalist Politics and the Origins of Welfare States.* New York: Routledge, 1994.

———. "Womanly Duties: Maternalist Politics and the Origins of Welfare States in France, Germany, Great Britain, and the United States, 1880–1920." *American Historical Review* 95, no. 4 (1990): 1076–1108.

Kriedte, P. *Peasants, Landlords and Merchant Capitalists: Europe and the World Economy, 1500–1800.* Cambridge: Cambridge University Press, 1983.

Kriedte, P.; H. Medick; and J. Schlumbohm. *Industrialization before Industrialization: Rural Industry in the Genesis of Capitalism.* Cambridge: Cambridge University Press, 1981.

———. "Proto-industrialisation Revisited: Demography, Social Structure, and Modern Domestic Industry." *Continuity and Change* 8, no. 2 (1993): 217–52.

Lamberti, M. *State, Society and the Elementary School in Imperial Germany.* New York: Oxford University Press, 1989.

Landes, J. B. *Women and the Public Sphere in the Age of the French Revolution.* Ithaca: Cornell University Press, 1988.

Langins, J. "Words and Institutions during the French Revolution." In P. Burke and R. Porter (eds.), *The Social History of Language*. Cambridge: Cambridge University Press, 1987.

Laqueur, T. "Orgasm, Generation, and the Politics of Reproductive Biology." In C. Gallagher and T. Laqueur (eds.), *The Making of the Modern Body: Sexuality and Society in the Nineteenth Century*. Berkeley: University of California Press, 1987.

Laqueur, T. W. *Making Sex: Body and Gender from the Greeks to Freud*. Cambridge, Mass.: Harvard University Press, 1990.

——. "Working-Class Demand and the Growth of English Elementary Education, 1750–1850." In L. Stone (ed.), *Schooling and Society: Studies in the History of Education*. Baltimore: Johns Hopkins University Press, 1976.

Laslett, P.; K. Oosterveen; and R. M. Smith (eds.). *Bastardy and Its Comparative History*. Cambridge, Mass.: Harvard University Press, 1980.

Lazonick, W. "Industrial Relations and Technical Change: The Case of the Self-Acting Mule." *Cambridge Journal of Economics* 3, no. 3 (1979): 231–62.

Lees, L. H. "Getting and Spending: The Family Budgets of English Industrial Workers in 1890." In J. Merriman (ed.), *Consciousness and Class Experience in Nineteenth-Century Europe*. New York: Holmes & Meier, 1979.

——. "The Survival of the Unfit: Welfare Policies and Family Maintenance in Nineteenth-Century London." In P. Mandler (ed.), *The Uses of Charity: The Poor on Relief in the Nineteenth-Century Metropolis*. Philadelphia: University of Pennsylvania Press, 1990.

Levine, D. "Industrialisation and the Proletarian Family in England." *Past and Present*, no. 107 (1985): 168–203.

——. "Production, Reproduction and the Proletarian Family in England, 1500–1851." In D. Levine (ed.), *Proletarianization and Family History*. New York: Academic Press, 1984.

——. "Punctuated Equilibrium: The Modernisation of the Proletarian Family in the Age of Nascent Capitalism." *International Labour and Working Class History*, no. 39 (1991): 3–20.

——. *Reproducing Families: The Political Economy of English Population History*. Cambridge: Cambridge University Press, 1987.

——. "Review of Bruce Curtis, *Building the Educational State*, and Chad Gaffield, *Language, Schooling and Cultural Conflict*." Typescript, 1989.

Lis, C., and H. Soly. "Policing the Early Modern Proletariat, 1450–1850." In D. Levine (ed.), *Proletarianization and Family History*. New York: Academic Press, 1984.

——. *Poverty and Capitalism in Pre-Industrial Europe*. Brighton: Harvester Press, 1982.

Livi-Bacci, M. *A Concise History of World Population*. Cambridge, Mass.: Blackwell, 1992.

Locke, J. *Second Treatise on Civil Government: An Essay Concerning the True, Origi-

nal Extent and End of Civil Government [1690]. In *Social Contract: Essays by Locke, Hume and Rousseau.* London: Oxford University Press, 1966.

——. *Some Thoughts Concerning Education.* Edited by J. W. and J. S. Yolton. Oxford: Clarendon Press, 1989.

Lown, J. "Not So Much a Factory, More a Form of Patriarchy: Gender and Class during Industrialisation." In E. Gamarnikov et al. (eds.), *Gender, Class and Work.* London: Heineman, 1983.

——. "The Subjection of Labor to Capital: The Rise of the Capitalist System." *Review of Radical Political Economics* 10, no. 1 (1978) 1–31.

——. *Women and Industrialization: Gender and Work in Nineteenth-Century England.* Cambridge: Polity Press, 1990.

Ludtke, A. "The Role of State Violence in the Period of Transition to Industrial Capitalism: The Example of Prussia." *Social History* 4, no. 2 (1979): 175–221.

Lukes, S. "Conclusion." In M. Carrithers, S. Collins, and S. Lukes (eds.), *The Category of the Person: Anthropology, Philosophy, History.* Cambridge: Cambridge University Press, 1985.

MacKinnon, A. "Were Women Present at the Demographic Transition? Questions from a Feminist Historian to Historical Demographers." *Gender and History* 7, no. 2 (1995): 222–40.

Macpherson, C. B. *The Political Theory of Possessive Individualism: Hobbes to Locke.* London: Oxford University Press, 1962.

Malthus, T. R. *An Essay on the Principle of Population* [1803]. Cambridge: Cambridge University Press, 1992.

Mandel, E. *Marxist Economic Theory.* London: Merlin Press, 1968.

Mandler, P. (ed.). *The Uses of Charity: The Poor on Relief in the Nineteenth-Century Metropolis.* Philadelphia: University of Pennsylvania Press, 1990.

Mangan, J. A., and J. Walvin (eds.). *Manliness and Morality: Middle-Class Masculinity in Britain and America, 1800–1940.* Manchester: Manchester University Press, 1987.

Mann, M. "European Development: Approaching a Historical Explanation." In J. Baechler et al. (eds.), *Europe and the Rise of Capitalism.* Oxford: Basil Blackwell, 1989.

Mark-Lawson, J., and A. Witz. "From 'Family Labour' to 'Family Wage'? The Case of Women's Labour in Nineteenth-Century Coalmining." *Social History* 13, no. 2 (1988): 151–74.

Marx K. *Capital.* Vol. 1 [1867]. New York: International Publishers, 1967.

Maynes, M. J. "The Contours of Childhood: Demography, Strategy, and Mythology of Childhood in French and German Lower-Class Autobiographies." In J. R. Gillis, L. A. Tilly, and D. Levine (eds.), *The European Experience of Declining Fertility, 1850–1970.* Oxford: Blackwell, 1992.

——. "Gender and Narrative Form in French and German Working-Class Autobiographies." In Personal Narratives Group (ed.), *Interpreting Women's Lives:*

Feminist Theory and Personal Narratives. Bloomington: Indiana University Press, 1989.

——. *Schooling for the People: Comparative Local Studies of Schooling History in France and Germany, 1750–1850.* New York: Holmes and Meier.

——. *Schooling in Western Europe: A Social History.* Albany: State University of New York Press, 1985.

——. *Taking the Hard Road: Life Course in French and German Workers' Autobiographies in the Era of Industrialization.* Chapel Hill: University of North Carolina Press, 1995.

Maynes, M. J., and T. Taylor. "Germany." In J. M. Hawes and N. R. Hiner, *Children in Historical and Comparative Perspective: An International Handbook.* New York: Greenwood Press, 1991.

Maza, S. "Politics, Culture and the Origins of the French Revolution." *Journal of Modern History* 61, no. 4 (1989): 704–23.

McCann, P. "The Indian Origins of Bell's Monitorial System." In *International Currents in Educational Ideas and Practices.* Proceedings of the 1987 Annual Conference of the History of Education Society of Great Britain, University of Hull, Evington, Leicester, 1987.

McCulloch, J. *Colonial Psychiatry and "the African Mind."* Cambridge: Cambridge University Press, 1995.

McEvedy, C., and R. Jones. *Atlas of World Population History.* Harmondsworth: Penguin Books, 1978.

McNeill, W. H. *The Pursuit of Power: Technology, Armed Force and Society since AD 1000.* Oxford: Basil Blackwell, 1983.

McRobbie, A. "Working Class Girls and the Culture of Femininity." In Women's Studies Group, Centre for Contemporary Cultural Studies, University of Birmingham, *Women Take Issue.* London: Hutchinson, 1978.

Medick, H. "The Proto-industrial Family Economy." In P. Kriedte, H. Medick, and J. Schlumbohm, *Industrialization before Industrialization.* Cambridge: Cambridge University Press, 1981.

Melton, J. Van Horn. *Absolutism and the Eighteenth-Century Origins of Compulsory Schooling in Prussia and Austria.* Cambridge: Cambridge University Press, 1988.

Mendels, F. "Proto-industrialisation: The First Phase of Industrialisation." *Journal of Economic History* 32, no. 1 (1972): 241–61.

Miller, P. *Long Division: State Schooling in South Australian Society.* Adelaide: Wakefield Press, 1986.

Miller, P., and I. Davey. "Family, Schooling and the Patriarchal State." In M. R. Theobald and R. J. W. Selleck, *Family, School and State in Australian History.* Sydney: Allen and Unwin, 1990.

Miller, P. J. "Factories, Monitorial Schools and Jeremy Bentham: The Origins of the 'Management Syndrome' in Popular Education." *Journal of Educational Administration and History* 5, no. 2 (1973): 10–20.

Minge-Kalman, W. "The Industrial Revolution and the European Family: The Institutionalization of 'Childhood' as a Market for Family Labour." *Comparative Studies in Society and History* 20, no. 3 (1978): 454–68.

Minor, I. "Working-Class Women and the Matrimonial Law Reform, 1890–1914." In D. E. Martin and D. Rubinstein (eds.), *Ideology and the Labour Movement*. London: Croom Helm, 1979.

Mitterauer, M. *A History of Youth*. Oxford: Blackwell, 1993.

———. "Servants and Youth." *Continuity and Change* 5, no. 1 (1990): 11–38.

Monter, W. "Protestant Wives, Catholic Saints, and the Devil's Handmaid: Women in the Age of Reformations." In R. Bridenthal et al. (eds.), *Becoming Visible: Women in European History*. 2nd ed. Boston: Houghton Mifflin, 1987.

Morgan, J. *Godly Learning: Puritan Attitudes towards Reason, Learning and Education, 1560–1640*. Cambridge: Cambridge University Press, 1986.

Musgrove, F. "Population Changes and the Status of the Young." In P. Musgrove (ed.), *Sociology, History and Education*. London: Methuen, 1970.

Nardinelli, C. "Child Labour and the Factory Acts." *Journal of Economic History* 40, no. 4 (1980): 739–55.

———. *Child Labour and the Industrial Revolution*. Bloomington: Indiana University Press, 1990.

Obelkevich, J. (ed.). *Religion and the People, 800–1700*. Chapel Hill: University of North Carolina Press, 1979.

Obelkevich, J.; L. Roper; and R. Samuel. *Disciplines of Faith: Studies in Religion, Politics and Patriarchy*. London: Routledge and Kegan Paul, 1987.

Oestreich, G. *Neostoicism and the Early Modern State*. Cambridge: Cambridge University Press, 1982.

Offen, K. "The New Sexual Politics of French Revolutionary Historiography." *French Historical Studies* 16, no. 4 (1990): 909–22.

Ogilvie, S. C. "Coming of Age in a Corporate Society: Capitalism, Pietism and Family Authority in Rural Württemberg, 1590–1740." *Continuity and Change* 1, no. 3 (1986): 279–331.

———. "Proto-industrialization in Europe." *Continuity and Change* 8, no. 2 (1993): 159–79.

Orloff, A. S. "Gender and the Social Rights of Citizenship: The Comparative Analysis of State Policies and Gender Relations." *American Sociological Review* 58, no. 3 (1993): 303–28.

———. *The Politics of Pensions: A Comparative Analysis of Britain, Canada and the United States, 1880–1940*. Madison: University of Wisconsin Press, 1993.

Orren, K. *Belated Feudalism: Labor, the Law, and Liberal Development in the United States*. Cambridge: Cambridge University Press, 1991.

Outram, D. *The Body and the French Revolution: Sex, Class and Political Culture*. New Haven: Yale University Press, 1989.

———. "Le langage mâle de la vertu: Women and the Discourse of the French Revolution." In P. Burke and R. Porter, *The Social History of Language*. Cambridge: Cambridge University Press, 1987.

——. "Revolution and Repression." *Comparative Studies in Society and History* 34, no. 1 (1992): 58–67.

Parker, G. *The Military Revolution: Military Innovation and the Rise of the West, 1500–1800.* Cambridge: Cambridge University Press, 1988.

——. "Success and Failure during the First Century of the Reformation." *Past and Present,* no. 136 (1992): 43–82.

Pateman, C. "The Fraternal Social Contract: Some Observations on Patriarchal Civil Society." In J. Keane (ed.), *Civil Society and the State: New European Perspectives.* London: Verso, 1988.

——. *The Sexual Contract.* Cambridge: Polity Press, 1988.

Perrot, M. "On the Formation of the French Working Class." In I. Katznelson and A. R. Zolberg (eds.), *Working-Class Formation: Nineteenth-Century Patterns in Western Europe and the United States.* Princeton: Princeton University Press, 1986.

——. "The Three Ages of Industrial Discipline in Nineteenth-Century France." In J. M. Merriman, *Consciousness and Class Experience in Nineteenth-Century Europe.* New York: Holmes and Meir, 1979.

Philips, D. "Good Men to Associate and Bad Men to Conspire: Associations for the Prosecution of Felons in England, 1760–1860." In D. Day and F. Snyder, *Policing and Prosecution in Britain, 1750–1850.* Oxford: Clarendon Press, 1989.

Pinchbeck, I. *Women Workers and the Industrial Revolution, 1750–1850* [1930]. London: Virago, 1981.

Pollard, S. *Britain's Prime and Britain's Decline: The British Economy, 1870–1914.* London: Edward Arnold, 1989.

——. *European Economic Integration, 1815–1970.* London: Thames and Hudson, 1974.

——. *Peaceful Conquest: The Industrialisation of Europe, 1760–1970.* Oxford: Oxford University Press, 1986.

Pollock, L. A. *Forgotten Children: Parent-Child Relations from 1500 to 1900.* Cambridge: Cambridge University Press, 1983.

Prentice, A. "The Feminization of Teaching." In S. M. Trofimenkoff and A. Prentice, *The Neglected Majority: Essays in Canadian Women's History.* Toronto: McClelland and Stewart, 1977.

Prentice, A., and M. Theobald (eds.). *Women Who Taught: Perspectives on the History of Women and Teaching.* Toronto: University of Toronto Press, 1991.

Price, R. *A Social History of Nineteenth-Century France.* London: Hutchinson, 1987.

Pringle, R. *Secretaries Talk: Sexuality, Power and Work.* Sydney: Allen and Unwin, 1988.

Purvis, J. *A History of Women's Education in England.* Milton Keynes: Open University Press, 1991.

——. "Working-Class Women and Adult Education in Nineteenth-Century Britain." *History of Education* 9, no. 3 (1980): 183–212.

Quataert, J. E. "The Shaping of Women's Work in Manufacturing: Guilds, Households, and the State in Central Europe, 1648–1870." *American Historical
Review* 90, no. 5 (1985): 1122–48.

Quataert, J. H. "Teamwork in Saxon Homeweaving Families in the Nineteenth
Century." In R. B. Joeres and M. J. Maynes (eds.), *German Women in the
Eighteenth and Nineteenth Centuries*. Bloomington: Indiana University Press,
1986.

Rabinow, P. (ed.). *The Foucault Reader.* London: Penguin, 1986.

Ramirez, F. O., and J. Boli. "The Political Construction of Mass Schooling: European Origins and Worldwide Institutionalization." *Sociology of Education* 60,
no. 1 (1987): 2–17.

Rebel, H. *Peasant Classes: The Bureaucratization of Property and Family Relations
under Early Habsburg Absolutism, 1511–1636*. Princeton: Princeton University Press, 1983.

Rendall, J. "Virtue and Commerce." In E. Kennedy and S. Mendus (eds.), *Women in
Western Political Philosophy: Kant to Nietzsche*. Brighton, Sussex: Wheatsheaf Books, 1987.

Richardson, J. G. "Historical Sequences and the Origins of Common Schooling in
the American States." In J. G. Richardson (ed.), *Handbook of Theory and Research in the Sociology of Education*. New York: Greenwood, 1986.

———. "Settlement Patterns and the Governing Structures of Nineteenth-Century
School Systems." *American Journal of Education* 92, no. 2 (1984): 178–206.

———. "Variation in the Date of Enactment of Compulsory School Attendance Laws:
An Empirical Enquiry." *Sociology of Education* 53, no. 3 (1980): 153–63.

Roberts, M. L. *Civilization without Sexes: Reconstructing Gender Relations in Postwar France, 1917–1927*. Chicago: University of Chicago Press, 1994.

Robisheaux, T. "Peasants and Pastors: Rural Youth Control and the Reformation in
Hohenloe, 1540–1680." *Social History* 6, no. 3 (1981): 281–300.

———. *Rural Society and the Search for Order in Early Modern Germany*. Cambridge:
Cambridge University Press, 1989.

Rooke, P. T., and R. L. Schnell (eds.). *Studies in Childhood History: A Canadian
Perspective*. Calgary, Alberta: Detselig Enterprises, 1982.

Roper, L. "The Common Man, the Common Good, Common Women: Gender and
Meaning in the German Reformation Commune." *Social History* 12, no. 1
(1987): 1–22.

———. *The Holy Household: Women and Morals in Reformation Augsburg*. Oxford:
Clarendon Press, 1989.

———. *Oedipus and the Devil: Witchcraft, Sexuality and Religion in Early Modern
Europe*. London: Routledge, 1994.

Rose, S. O. "Gender and Labour History: The Nineteenth-Century Legacy." *International Review of Social History* 38 (1993), Supplement, pp. 145–62.

———. *Limited Livelihoods: Gender and Class in Nineteenth-Century England*. Berkeley: University of California Press, 1992.

Ross, E. "'Fierce Questions and Taunts': Married Life in Working-Class London, 1870–1914." *Feminist Studies* 8, no. 3 (1982): 575–602.

——. *Love and Toil: Motherhood in Outcast London, 1870–1918.* New York: Oxford University Press, 1993.

——. "Mothers and the State in Britain, 1904–1914." In J. R. Gillis, L. A. Tilly, and D. Levine (eds.), *The European Experience of Declining Fertility, 1850–1970.* Oxford: Blackwell, 1992.

——. "Survival Networks: Women's Neighbourhood Sharing in London before World War I." *History Workshop*, no. 15 (1983): 4–27.

Rotella, E. J. "Women's Labour Force Participation and the Decline of the Family Economy in the United States." *Explorations in Economic History* 17 (1980): 95–117.

Rousseau, J. J. *Emile* [1762]. London: Everyman's Library, Dent, 1963.

——. *The Social Contract* [1762]. In *Social Contract: Essays by Locke, Hume and Rousseau.* London: Oxford University Press, 1966.

Rowbotham, S. "The Trouble with Patriarchy." In R. Samuel (ed.), *People's History and Socialist Theory.* London: Routledge and Kegan Paul, 1981.

Rubinstein, D. *School Attendance in London, 1870–1904: A Social History.* New York: A. M. Kelly Publishers, 1969.

Rudolph, R. L. "The European Family and Economy: Central Themes and Issues." *Journal of Family History* 17, no. 2 (1992): 119–38.

Rury, J. R. "Vocationalism for Home and Work: Women's Education in the United States, 1880–1930." *History of Education Quarterly* 24, no. 1 (1984): 21–44.

Ryan, M. P. *Cradle of the Middle Class: The Family in Oneida County, New York, 1790–1865.* Cambridge: Cambridge University Press, 1981.

Sabean, D. *Power in the Blood: Popular Culture and Village Discourse in Early Modern Germany.* Cambridge: Cambridge University Press, 1984.

——. *Property, Production, and Family in Neckerhausen, 1700–1870.* Cambridge: Cambridge University Press, 1990.

Samuel, R. "Workshop of the World: Steam Power and Hand Technology in Mid-Victorian Britain." *History Workshop*, no. 3 (1977): 6–72.

Sandin, B. "Education, Popular Culture and the Surveillance of the Population in Stockholm between 1600 and the 1840s." *Continuity and Change* 3, no. 3 (1988): 357–90.

Schiebinger, L. "Skeletons in the Closet: The First Illustrations of the Female Skeleton in Eighteenth-Century Anatomy." In C. Gallagher and T. Laqueur, *The Making of the Modern Body: Sexuality and Society in the Nineteenth Century.* Berkeley: University of California Press, 1987.

Schilling, H. "The Reformation and the Rise of the Early Modern State." In J. D. Tracy (ed.), *Luther and the Modern State in Germany.* Ann Arbor, Mich.: Edwards Brothers, 1986.

Schlossman, S. "End of Innocence: Science and the Transformation of Progressive Juvenile Justice, 1899–1917." *History of Education* 7, no. 3 (1978): 207–18.

Schochet, G. J. *Patriarchalism in Political Thought.* Oxford: Blackwell, 1975.

——. "Patriarchalism, Politics and Mass Attitudes in Stuart England." *Historical Journal* 12, no. 3 (1969): 413–41.

Schwarzkopf, J. *Women in the Chartist Movement.* London: Macmillan, 1991.

Scott A. J., and M. Storper (eds.). *Production, Work, Territory: The Geographical Anatomy of Industrial Capitalism.* Boston: Unwin Hyman, 1986.

Scott, J. W. "French Feminists and the Rights of 'Man': Olympe de Gouge's Declarations." *History Workshop,* no. 28 (1989): 1–21.

——. "On Language, Gender and Working-Class History." In *Gender and the Politics of History.* New York: Columbia University Press, 1988.

——. "The Woman Worker." In G. Fraise and M. Perrot (eds.), *A History of Women in the West.* Vol. 4: *Emerging Feminism from Revolution to World War.* Cambridge, Mass.: Belknap Press, 1993.

Scribner, R. W. "The Reformation, Popular Magic, and the 'Disenchantment of the World.'" *Journal of Interdisciplinary History* 23, no. 3 (1993): 475–94.

Scutt, J. A. "In Pursuit of Equality: Women and Legal Thought, 1788–1984." In J. Goodnow and C. Pateman, *Women, Social Science and Public Policy.* Sydney: Allen and Unwin, 1985.

Seccombe, W. "Men's 'Marital Rights' and Women's 'Wifely Duties': Changing Conjugal Relations in the Fertility Decline." In J. R. Gillis, L. A. Tilly, and D. Levine (eds.), *The European Experience of Declining Fertility, 1850–1970: The Quiet Revolution.* Cambridge: Blackwell, 1992.

——. *A Millennium of Family Change: Feudalism to Capitalism in Northwestern Europe.* London: Verso 1992.

——. "Patriarchy Stabilised: The Construction of the Male Breadwinner Wage Norm in Nineteenth-Century Britain." *Social History* 11, no. 1 (1986): 53–76.

——. "Starting to Stop: Working-Class Fertility Decline in Britain." *Past and Present,* no. 126 (1990): 151–86.

——. *Weathering the Storm: Working-Class Families from the Industrial Revolution to the Fertility Decline.* London: Verso, 1993.

——. "The Western European Pattern in Historical Perspective: A Response to David Levine." *Journal of Historical Sociology* 3, no. 1 (1990): 50–74.

Selleck, R. J. W. "Mary Helena Stark: The Troubles of a Nineteenth-Century State School Teacher." In A. Prentice and M. Theobald (eds.), *Women Who Taught: Perspectives on the History of Women and Teaching.* Toronto: University of Toronto Press, 1991.

Shanley, M. L. "Marriage Contract and Social Contract in Seventeenth-Century English Political Thought." *Western Political Quarterly* 32 (1979): 79–91.

Shanley, M. L., and C. Pateman (eds.). *Feminist Interpretations and Political Theory.* University Park: Pennsylvania State University Press, 1991.

Simon, B. *The Two Nations and the Educational Structure, 1780–1870.* London: Lawrence and Wishart, 1974.

Simpson, A. H. *A Treatise on the Law and Practice Relating to Infants*. 3rd ed. London: Stevens and Haynes, 1909.

Smith, A. *Wealth of Nations*. London: J. M. Dent, 1937.

Smith, R. L., and D. M. Valenze. "Mutuality and Marginality: Liberal Moral Theory and Working-Class Women in Nineteenth-Century England." *Signs* 13, no. 2 (1988): 277–98.

Smith-Rosenberg, C. "The Female World of Love and Ritual: Relations between Women in Nineteenth-Century America." *Signs* 1, no. 1 (1975): 1–29.

Soysal, Y., and D. Strang. "Construction of the First Mass Education Systems in Nineteenth-Century Europe." *Sociology of Education* 62, no. 4 (1989): 277–88.

Spender, D. *Man Made Language*. London: Routledge and Kegan Paul, 1980.

Stanley, A. "Conjugal Bonds and Wage Labor: Rights of Contract in the Age of Emancipation." *Journal of American History* 75 (1988): 471–500.

Stansell, C. *City of Women: Sex and Class in New York, 1789–1860*. Urbana: University of Illinois Press, 1987.

Staves, S. *Married Women's Separate Property in England, 1660–1833*. Cambridge, Mass.: Harvard University Press, 1990.

Steedman, C. "'Listen How the Caged Bird Sings': Amarjit's Song." In C. Steedman, C. Urwin, and V. Walkerdine (eds.), *Language, Gender and Childhood*. London: Routledge and Kegan Paul, 1985.

———. "'The Mother Made Conscious': The Historical Development of Primary School Pedagogy." *History Workshop*, no. 20 (1985): 149–63.

———. "Prisonhouses." *Feminist Review*, no. 20 (1985): 7–21.

———. *Tidy House*. London: Virago Press, 1982.

Steinfeld, R. J. *The Invention of Free Labor: The Employment Relation in English and American Law and Culture, 1350–1870*. Chapel Hill: University of North Carolina Press, 1991.

Stern, M. J. *Society and Family Strategy: Erie County, New York, 1850–1920*. Albany: SUNY Press, 1987.

Stoler, A. L. *Race and the Education of Desire: Foucault's History of Sexuality and the Colonial Order of Things*. Durham, N.C.: Duke University Press, 1995.

Stone, L. *The Family, Sex and Marriage in England 1500–1800*. London: Weidenfeld and Nicolson, 1977.

Strauss, G. "Lutheranism and Literacy: A Reassessment." In K. von Greyerz, *Religion and Society in Early Modern Europe*. London: Allen and Unwin, 1984.

———. *Luther's House of Learning: Indoctrination of the Young in the German Reformation*. Baltimore: Johns Hopkins University Press, 1978.

———. "The Social Function of Schools in the Lutheran Reformation in Germany." *History of Education Quarterly* 28, no. 2 (1988): 191–206.

Summers, A. *Damned Whores and God's Police*. Ringwood: Penguin, 1975.

Szreter, S. *Falling Fertilities and Changing Sexualities in Europe since c. 1850: A Comparative Survey of National Demographic Patterns*. Canberra: Research School of Social Sciences, Australian National University, 1996.

———. *Fertility, Class and Gender in Britain, 1860–1940.* Cambridge: Cambridge University Press, 1996.

Taylor, B. *Eve and the New Jerusalem: Socialism and Feminism in the Nineteenth Century.* London: Virago Press, 1983.

Taylor, C. *Sources of the Self: The Making of the Modern Identity.* Cambridge: Cambridge University Press, 1992.

Thane, P. "Women and the Poor Law in Victorian and Edwardian England." *History Workshop,* no. 6 (1978): 29–51.

Theobald, M. "The Accomplished Woman and the Propriety of Intellect: A New Look at Women's Education in Britain and Australia, 1800–1850." *History of Education* 17, no. 1 (1988): 21–35.

———. *Knowing Women: Origins of Women's Education in Nineteenth-Century Australia.* Cambridge: Cambridge University Press, 1996.

———. "Women's Teaching Labour, the Family and the State in Nineteenth-Century Victoria." In M. R. Theobald and R. J. W. Selleck, *Family, School and State in Australian History.* Sydney: Allen and Unwin, 1990.

Thomas, K. "Women and the Civil War Sects." *Past and Present,* no. 13 (1958): 42–62.

Thompson, D. "Women and Nineteenth-Century Radical Politics: A Lost Dimension." In J. Mitchell and A. Oakley, *The Rights and Wrongs of Women.* Harmondsworth: Penguin, 1976.

Thompson, E. P. "Eighteenth-Century English Society: Class Struggle without Class?" *Social History* 3, no. 2 (1978): 133–65.

———. *The Making of the English Working Class.* Harmondsworth: Penguin, 1968.

———. "Patrician Society, Plebeian Culture." *Journal of Social History* 7, no. 4 (1974): 382–405.

———. "The Peculiarities of the English." In E. P. Thompson, *The Poverty of Theory and Other Essays.* London: Merlin Press, 1978.

———. "Rough Music: Le charivari anglais." *Annales, Economies, Societies, Civilisations* 27, no. 2 (1972): 285–312.

———. "Time, Work-Discipline, and Industrial Capitalism." *Past and Present,* no. 38 (1967): 56–97.

Tilly, C. "Cities and States in Europe, 1000–1800." *Theory and Society* 18, no. 4 (1989): 563–84.

———. *Coercion, Capital and European States, 990–1992.* Oxford: Blackwell, 1992.

———. "Demographic Origins of the European Proletariat." In D. Levine (ed.), *Proletarianization and Family History.* New York: Academic Press, 1984.

Tilly, L. A., and J. W. Scott. *Women, Work and Family.* New York: Holt, Rinehart and Winston, 1978.

Tomes, N. "'A Torrent of Abuse': Crimes of Violence between Working-Class Men and Women in London, 1840–1875." *Journal of Social History* 11, no. 3 (1978): 328–45.

Tomlins, C. *Law, Labor and Ideology in the Early American Republic.* Cambridge: Cambridge University Press, 1993.

——. "Subordination, Authority, Law: Subjects in Labor History." *International Labor and Working-Class History*, no. 47 (1995): 56–90.

Tracy, J. D. (ed.). *Luther and the Modern State in Germany.* Ann Arbor, Mich.: Edwards Brothers, 1986.

Tyack, D. *The One Best System.* Cambridge, Mass.: Harvard University Press, 1974.

Tyack, D., and E. Hansot. *Learning Together: A History of Co-education in American Public Schools.* New Haven: Yale University Press, 1990.

Tyler, D. "The Case of Irene Tuckerman: Understanding Sexual Violence and the Protection of Women and Girls, Victoria 1890—1925." *History of Education Review* 15, no. 2 (1986): 52–67.

Underdown, D. E. "The Taming of the Scold: The Enforcement of Patriarchal Authority in Early Modern England." In A. Fletcher and J. Stevenson (eds.), *Order and Disorder in Early Modern England.* Cambridge: Cambridge University Press, 1985.

Vincent, A. *Theories of the State.* Oxford: Blackwell, 1987.

Vincent, D. *Bread, Knowledge and Freedom: A Study of Nineteenth-Century Working Class Autobiography.* London: Methuen, 1982.

——. *Literacy and Popular Culture: England, 1750–1914.* Cambridge: Cambridge University Press, 1993.

Vinovskis, M. A. "Family and Schooling in Colonial and Nineteenth-Century America." *Journal of Family History* 12, nos. 1–3 (1987): 19–37.

Walters, P. B., and P. J. O'Connell. "The Family Economy, Work, and Educational Participation in the United States, 1890–1940." *American Journal of Sociology* 93, no. 5 (1988): 1116–52.

Waring, M. *Counting for Nothing: What Men Value and What Women Are Worth.* Wellington: Allen and Unwin, 1988.

Weber, M. *Economy and Society.* Berkeley: University of California Press, 1978.

——. *The Protestant Ethic and the Spirit of Capitalism.* London: Unwin, 1930.

——. "The Social Psychology of the World Religions." In H. H. Gerth and C. Wright Mills (eds.), *From Max Weber: Esssays in Sociology.* London: Routledge and Kegan Paul, 1970.

Weissbach, L. S. *Child Labor Reform in Nineteenth-Century France: Assuring the Future Harvest.* Baton Rouge: Louisiana State University Press, 1989.

Wiesner, M. E. "Guilds, Male Bonding and Women's Work in Early Modern Germany." *Gender and History* 1, no. 2 (1989): 125–37.

——. "Spinning Out Capital: Women's Work in the Early Modern Economy." In R. Bridenthal et al. (eds.), *Becoming Visible: Women in European History.* 2nd ed. Boston: Houghton Mifflin, 1987.

——. "Wandervogels and Women: Journeymen's Concepts of Masculinity in Early Modern Germany." *Journal of Social History* 24, no. 4 (1991): 767–82.

——. *Women and Gender in Early Modern Europe.* Cambridge: Cambridge University Press, 1993.

——. "Women's Response to the Reformation." In R. Po-chia Hsia, (ed.), *The German People and the Reformation.* Ithaca: Cornell University Press, 1988.

Williams, R. *The Long Revolution*. Harmondsworth: Penguin, 1965.

——. *Marxism and Literature*. Oxford: Oxford University Press, 1977.

Willis, P. *Learning to Labour: How Working Class Kids Get Working Class Jobs*. Westmead: Saxon House, 1978.

Wilson, S. "The Myth of Motherhood a Myth: The Historical View of European Child-Rearing." *Social History* 9, no. 2 (1984): 191–98.

Wimshurst, K. "Child Labour and School Attendance in South Australia, 1890–1915." *Historical Studies* 19, no. 76 (1981): 388–411.

Wood, E. M. *The Pristine Culture of Capitalism*. London: Verso, 1991.

Wood, G. S. *The Radicalism of the American Revolution*. New York: Vintage Books, 1991.

Woodiwiss, A. *Rights v. Conspiracy: A Sociological Essay on the History of Labour Law in the United States*. New York: Berg, 1990.

Woods, R. I. "Approaches to the Fertility Transition in Victorian England." *Population Studies* 41, no. 2 (1987): 283–311.

Young, A. F. "The Women of Boston: 'Persons of Consequence' in the Making of the American Revolution." In H. B. Applewhite and D. G. Levy (eds.), *Women and Politics in the Age of the Democratic Revolution*. Ann Arbor: University of Michigan Press, 1990.

Zelizer, V. A. *Pricing the Priceless Child: The Changing Social Value of Children*. New York: Basic Books, 1985.

Index

PAVLA MILLER is a senior lecturer in the School of Social Science and Planning at Royal Melbourne Institute of Technology in Australia, and author of *Long Division: State Schooling in South Australian Society*.